Full Moon O Sagashite

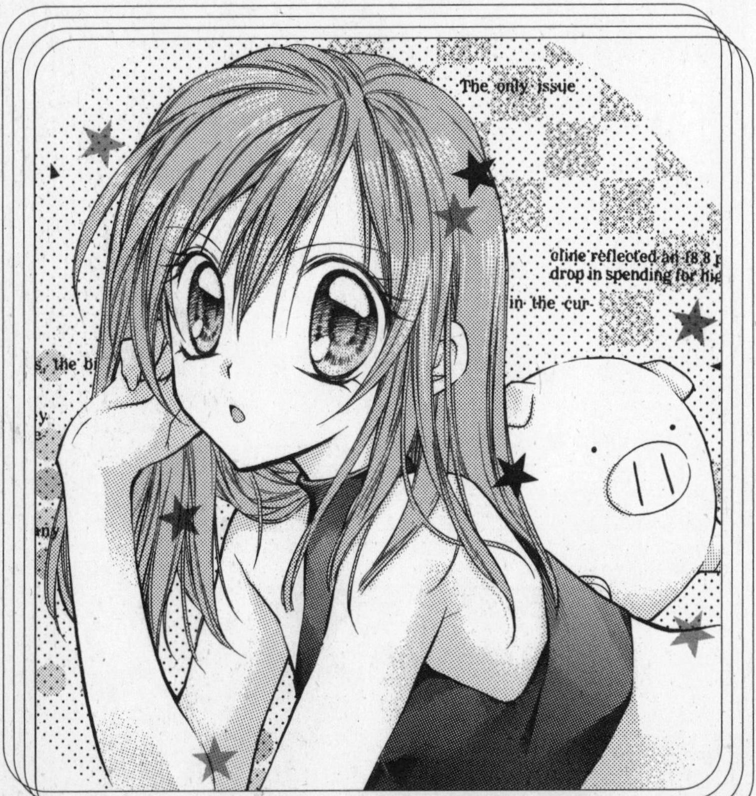
The only issue

6

Story & Art by Arina Tanemura

Table of Contents

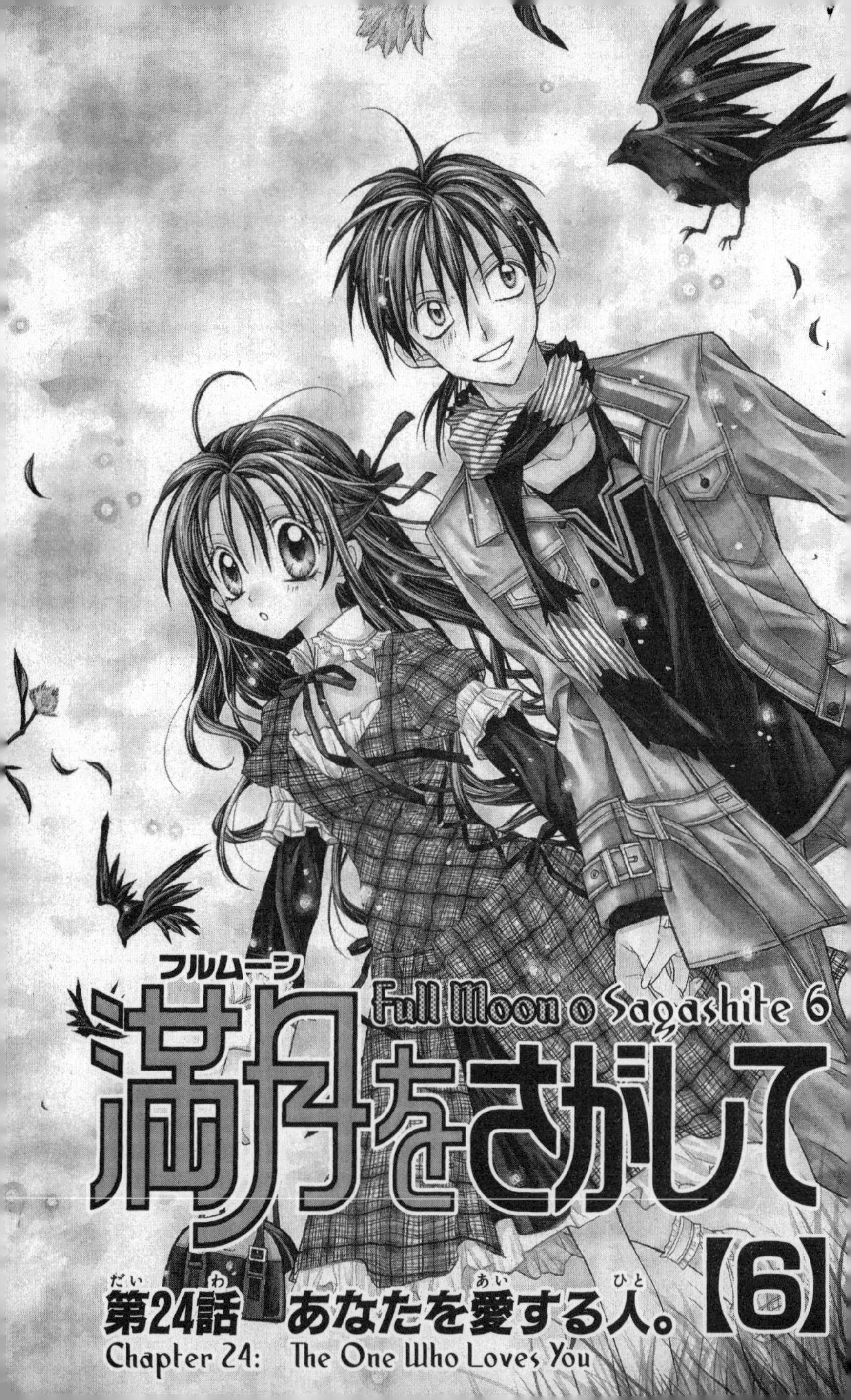
フルムーン
満月をさがして
Full Moon o Sagashite 6
[6]

第24話 あなたを愛する人。

Chapter 24: The One Who Loves You

CHARACTER INTRODUCTIONS

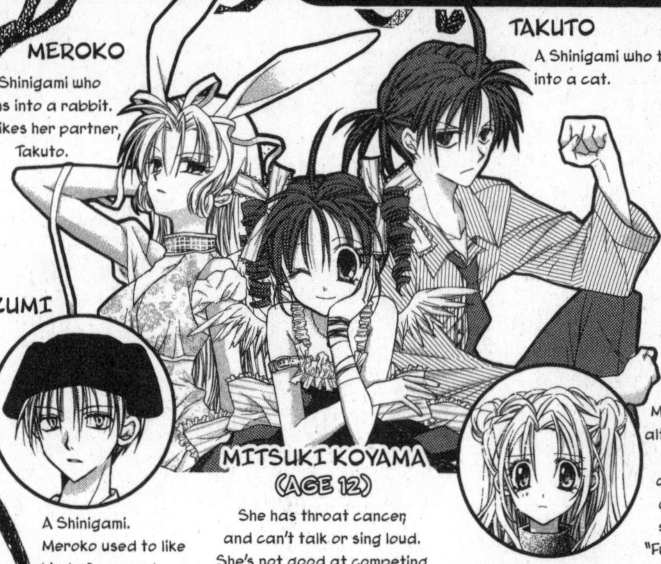

TAKUTO
A Shinigami who turns into a cat.

MEROKO
A Shinigami who turns into a rabbit. She likes her partner, Takuto.

IZUMI
A Shinigami. Meroko used to like him before, and now he likes her.

MITSUKI KOYAMA (AGE 12)
She has throat cancer, and can't talk or sing loud. She's not good at competing or quarreling.

MITSUKI KOYAMA (AGE 16)
Mitsuki's alter ego, who debuts as the singer "Fullmoon."

Full Moon o Sagashite

Mitsuki is 12. She loves Eichi, who's studying in the U.S., and she dreams of fulfilling her promise to him by becoming a singer. But Mitsuki has sarcoma, a form of cancer in her throat. Dr. Wakaoji wants her to have an operation, but Mitsuki refuses because it would destroy her singing voice. One day, two Shinigami appear, Takuto and Meroko, and transform her into a healthy sixteen-year-old. Because of the transformation, Mitsuki is able to make her debut as "Fullmoon."

As Takuto watches over Mitsuki during her successful singing career, he begins to fall in love with her. Meroko, who is in love with Takuto, asks her former partner, Izumi, to prevent the two from getting any closer. However, when Meroko and Izumi come in contact with Mitsuki's pure heart, they change their attitude towards her, and now they watch over Mitsuki too.

The Shinigamiiz discover that Eichi died in an airplane crash and that Mitsuki had known all along. When Mitsuki learns that the Shinigamiiz know the truth about Eichi, she disappears. Takuto finds Mitsuki and tells her that he loves her, but Mitsuki still loves Eichi. The only thing left for her is to keep singing.

Mitsuki's new song is a hit, and she's doing very well when someone stalks her and hurts the people around her. Mitsuki loses confidence in continuing her career but Takuto cheers her on. She decides to continue singing. However, the stalking incident was actually a trap laid by the Shinigami Jonathan, who is in a hurry to retrieve Mitsuki's soul...

STORY THUS FAR

Chapter 24: The One Who Loves You [Cover Copy]
(spoilers follow)

This chapter started moving towards the end of the series.
The incident with Hikari leads to what will be happening to
Takuto. He was wearing winter clothes to hide that.
(I will mention this a little in Chapter 26.)
I tried to make Hikari a model-type character, but...I'm far from being stylish
so I couldn't draw Hikari's charms well. ⌣ I'm sorry. ～ ·.·

It's hard for us to live in this world,
because we hurt so easily.
Let's go on a voyage to find the earth.
You'll hold the treasure in your right hand,
And I'll hold you in my right hand.

⌐ I've been writing the
cover copies recently.

(my Japanese is funny)⌐

Natural Madonna '03 DEEP PURPLE
(spoilers follow)

(Because of space constraints,
I'll put my comments here.
Sorry for suddenly doing this.)

I really like this side story. If you abbreviate the title, it becomes "Nachimado"
(Nachi ⌣ Madoka). ～ ·.· Oh no, love-love!! Oh dear, I'm like an over-indulgent parent.
I think Nachi-kun is a really cool guy! ⊙)⌣ Oh, I think Gutchan is a cool guy too. ⌣
Nachi is the heir to an inn in Kyoto, so things must have been really difficult when he said he
was going to become a musician. I wanted to write Nachi speaking in Kyoto dialect. It's good,
those two being in love-love. ⌣

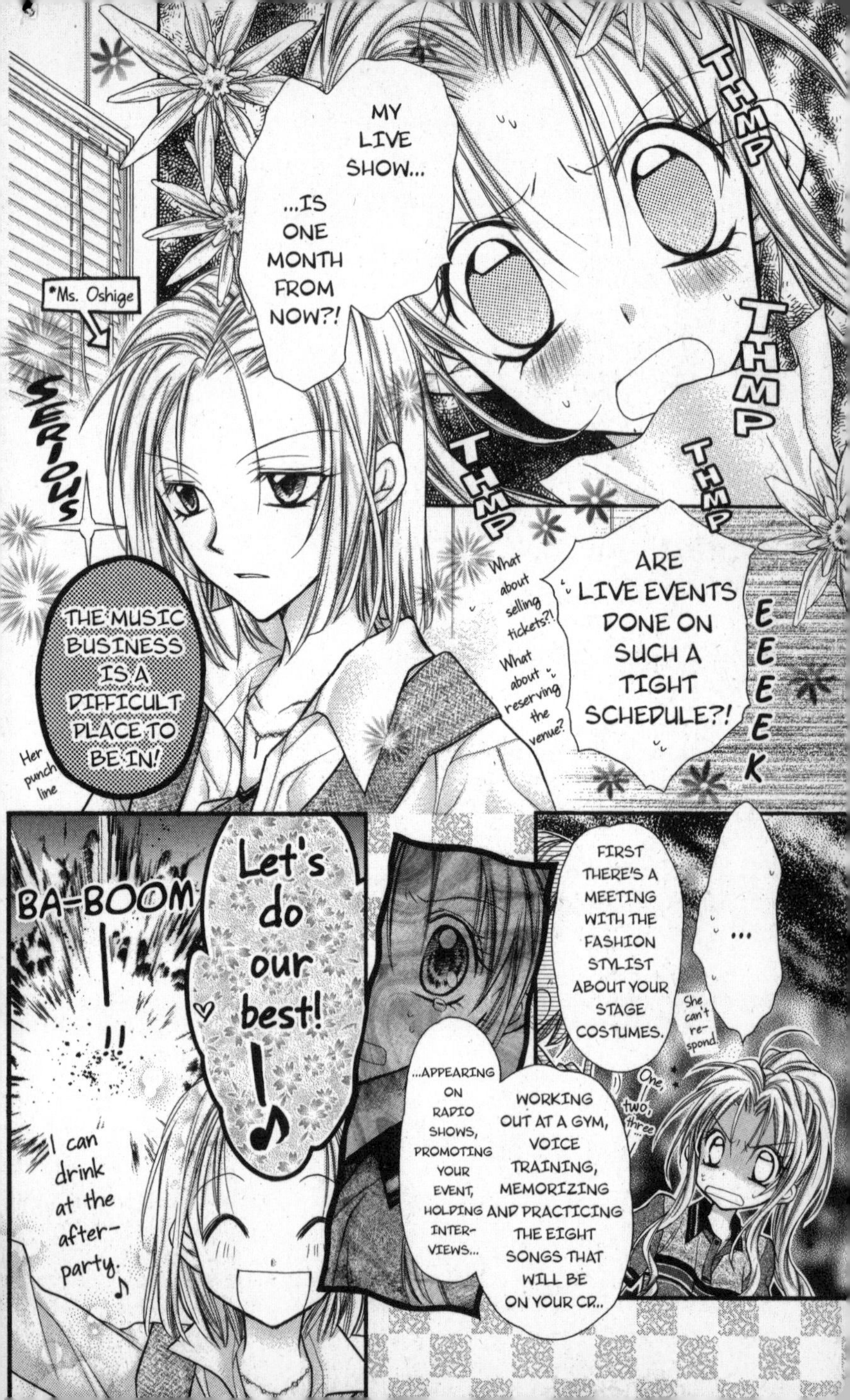
MY LIVE SHOW...
...IS ONE MONTH FROM NOW?!
THMP THMP THMP THMP
ARE LIVE EVENTS DONE ON SUCH A TIGHT SCHEDULE?!
What about selling tickets?! What about reserving the venue?
EEEEEK
*Ms. Oshige
SERIOUS
THE MUSIC BUSINESS IS A DIFFICULT PLACE TO BE IN!
Her punch line
...
She can't respond.
FIRST THERE'S A MEETING WITH THE FASHION STYLIST ABOUT YOUR STAGE COSTUMES.
WORKING OUT AT A GYM, VOICE TRAINING, MEMORIZING AND PRACTICING THE EIGHT SONGS THAT WILL BE ON YOUR CD...
...APPEARING ON RADIO SHOWS, PROMOTING YOUR EVENT, HOLDING INTERVIEWS...
One, two, three...
Let's do our best!
BA-BOOM
!!
I can drink at the after-party.

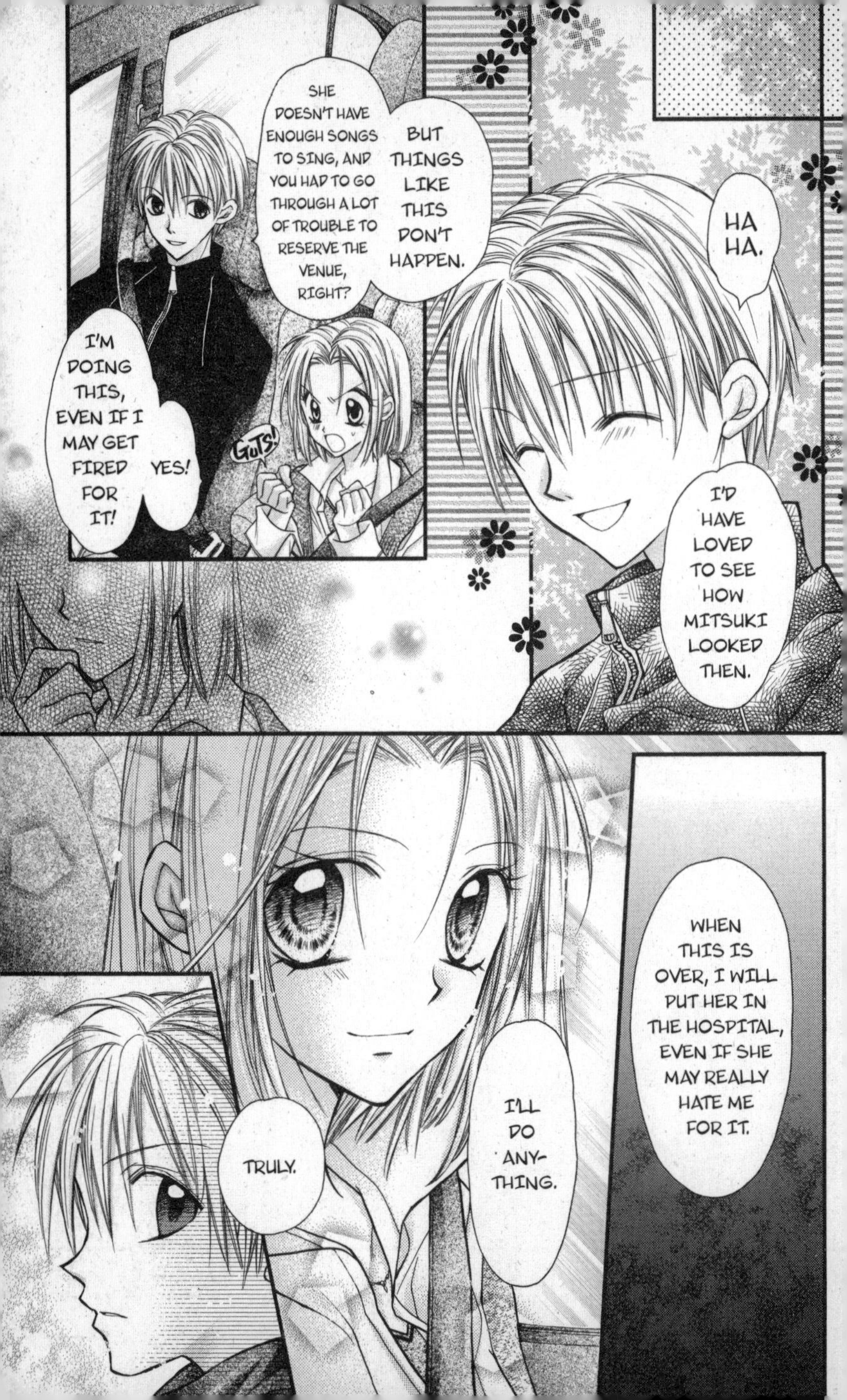
HA HA.
I'D HAVE LOVED TO SEE HOW MITSUKI LOOKED THEN.
BUT THINGS LIKE THIS DON'T HAPPEN.
SHE DOESN'T HAVE ENOUGH SONGS TO SING, AND YOU HAD TO GO THROUGH A LOT OF TROUBLE TO RESERVE THE VENUE, RIGHT?
YES!
GUTS!
I'M DOING THIS, EVEN IF I MAY GET FIRED FOR IT!
WHEN THIS IS OVER, I WILL PUT HER IN THE HOSPITAL, EVEN IF SHE MAY REALLY HATE ME FOR IT.
I'LL DO ANYTHING.
TRULY.

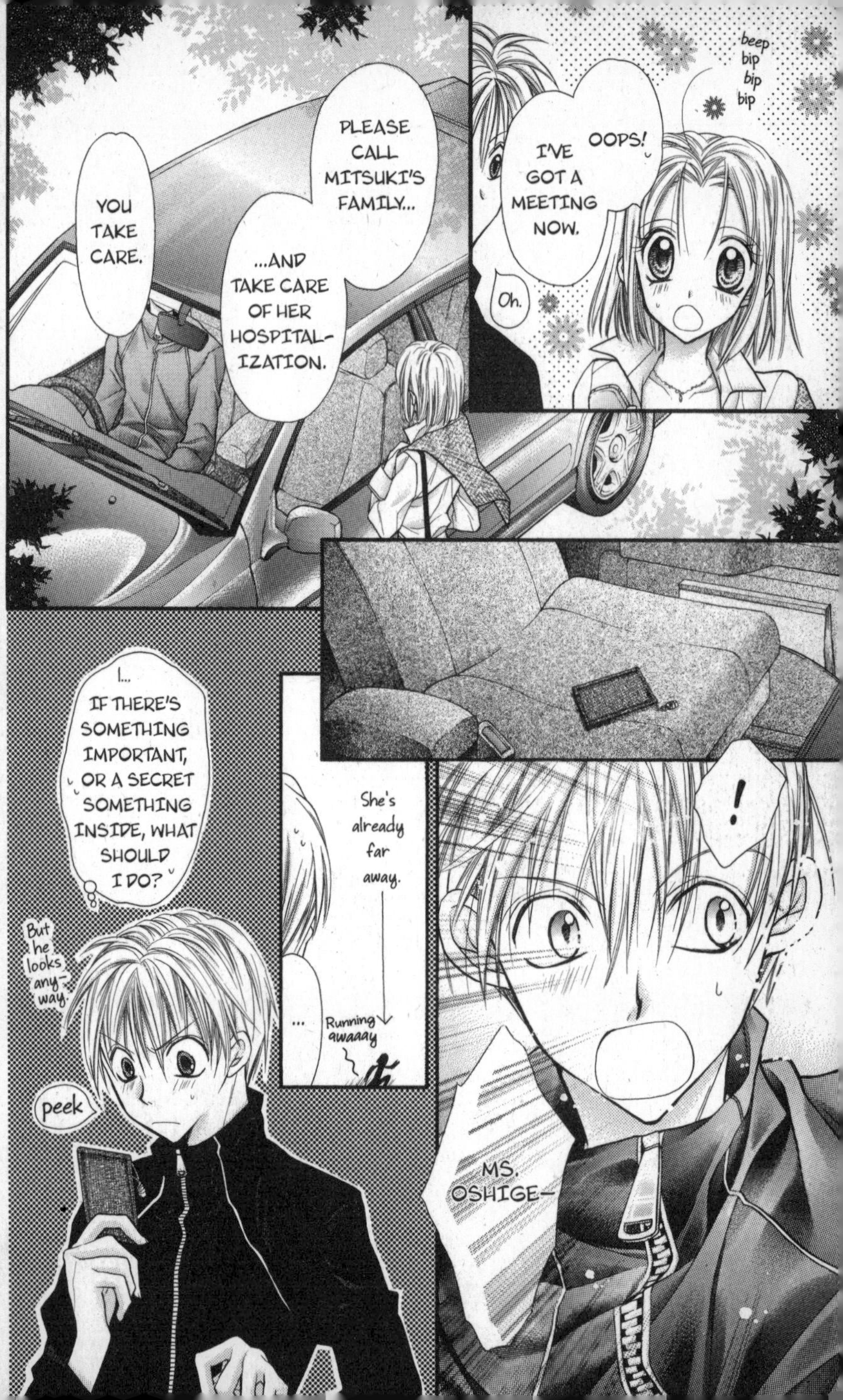
beep bip bip bip
OOPS!
I'VE GOT A MEETING NOW.
Oh.
PLEASE CALL MITSUKI'S FAMILY...
...AND TAKE CARE OF HER HOSPITALIZATION.
YOU TAKE CARE.
!
MS. OSHIGE—
She's already far away.
Running awaaay
...
I... IF THERE'S SOMETHING IMPORTANT, OR A SECRET SOMETHING INSIDE, WHAT SHOULD I DO?
But he looks anyway.
peek

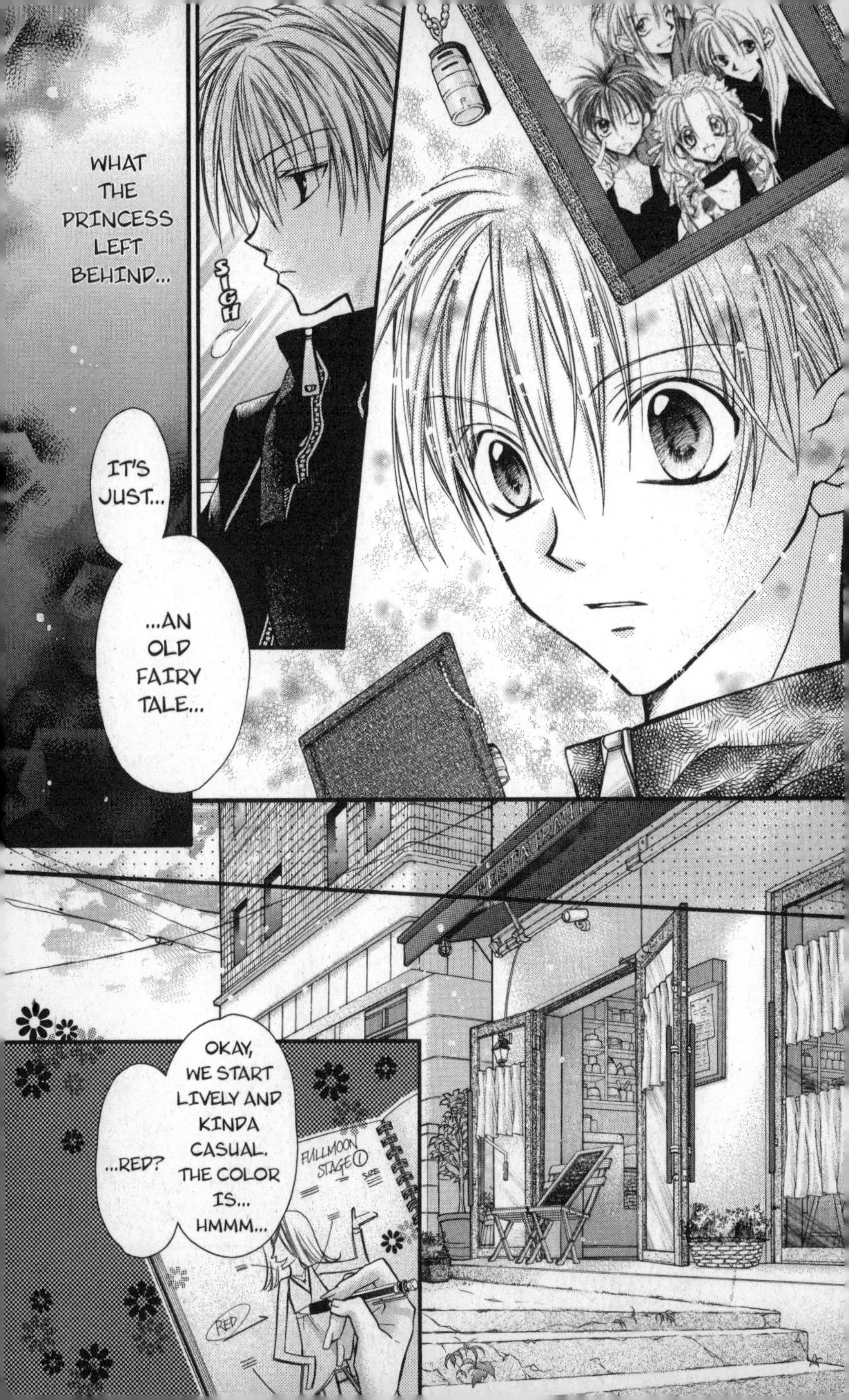
SIGH
WHAT THE PRINCESS LEFT BEHIND...
IT'S JUST...
...AN OLD FAIRY TALE...
RESTAURANT
OKAY, WE START LIVELY AND KINDA CASUAL. THE COLOR IS... HMMM...
...RED?
FULLMOON STAGE 1
SIZE
RED

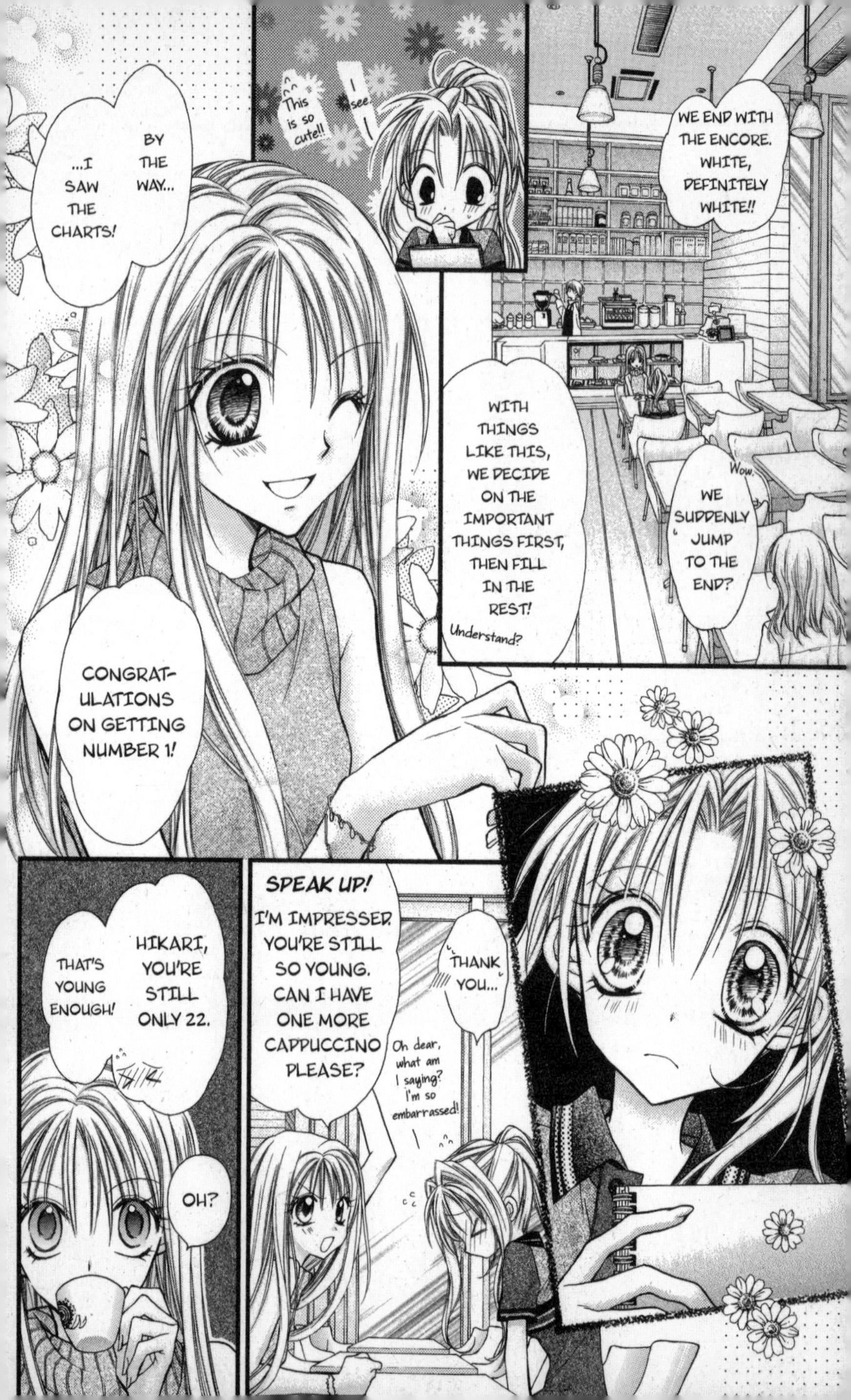
WE END WITH THE ENCORE. WHITE, DEFINITELY WHITE!!
WITH THINGS LIKE THIS, WE DECIDE ON THE IMPORTANT THINGS FIRST, THEN FILL IN THE REST!
Understand?
Wow.
WE SUDDENLY JUMP TO THE END?
I see.
This is so cute!!
BY THE WAY...
...I SAW THE CHARTS!
CONGRAT-ULATIONS ON GETTING NUMBER 1!
THANK YOU...
SPEAK UP!
I'M IMPRESSED. YOU'RE STILL SO YOUNG. CAN I HAVE ONE MORE CAPPUCCINO PLEASE?
Oh dear, what am I saying? I'm so embarrassed!
HIKARI, YOU'RE STILL ONLY 22.
THAT'S YOUNG ENOUGH!
OH?

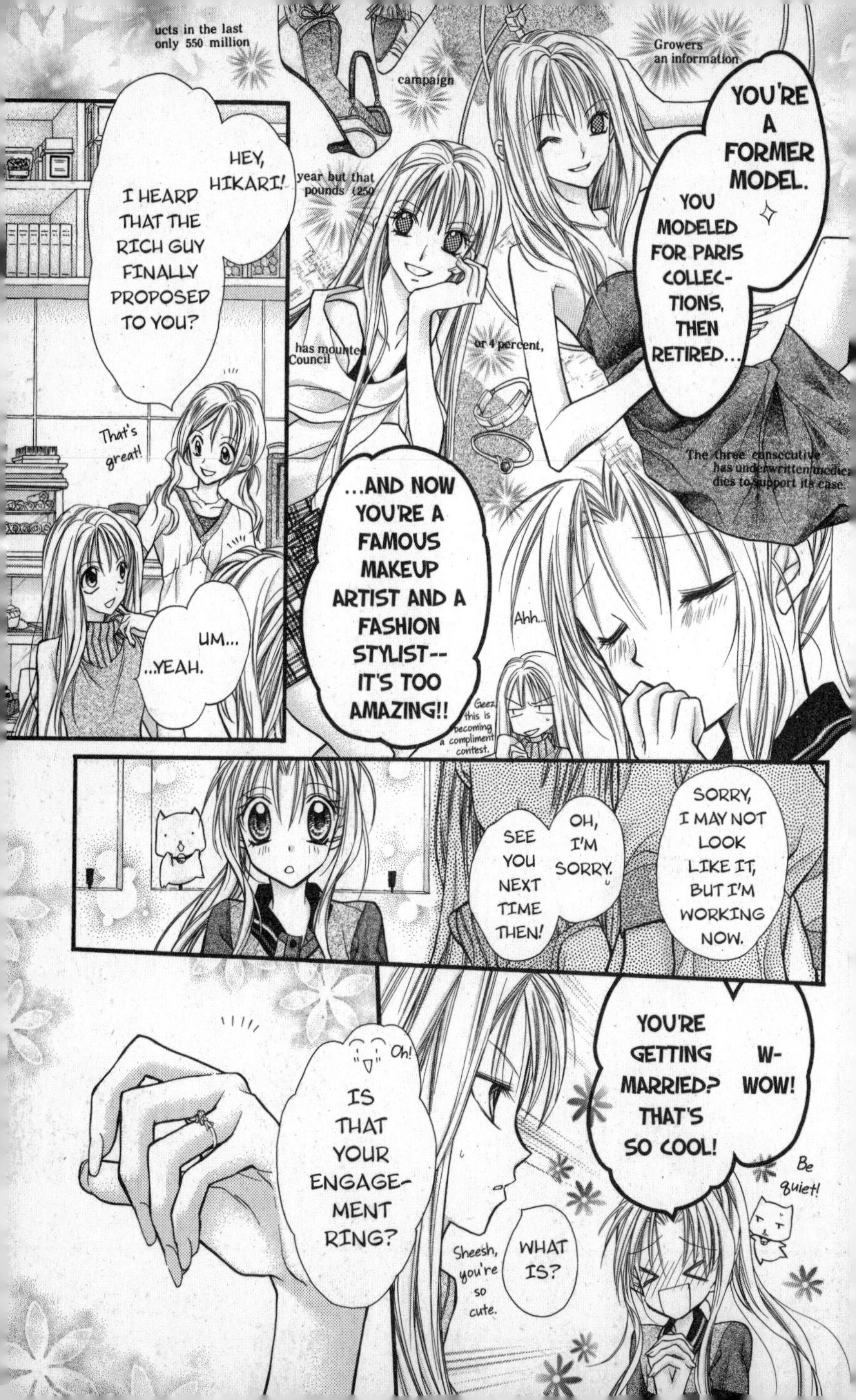
ucts in the last
only 550 million
campaign
Growers
an information
year but that
pounds (250
has mounted
Council
or 4 percent,
The three consecutive
has underwritten medie
dies to support its case
YOU'RE A FORMER MODEL.
YOU MODELED FOR PARIS COLLECTIONS, THEN RETIRED...
...AND NOW YOU'RE A FAMOUS MAKEUP ARTIST AND A FASHION STYLIST-- IT'S TOO AMAZING!!
Ahh...
Geez this is becoming a compliment contest.
HEY, HIKARI!
I HEARD THAT THE RICH GUY FINALLY PROPOSED TO YOU?
That's great!
UM... ...YEAH.
SORRY, I MAY NOT LOOK LIKE IT, BUT I'M WORKING NOW.
OH, I'M SORRY.
SEE YOU NEXT TIME THEN!
W-WOW!
YOU'RE GETTING MARRIED? THAT'S SO COOL!
Be quiet!
Oh!
IS THAT YOUR ENGAGEMENT RING?
WHAT IS?
Sheesh, you're so cute.

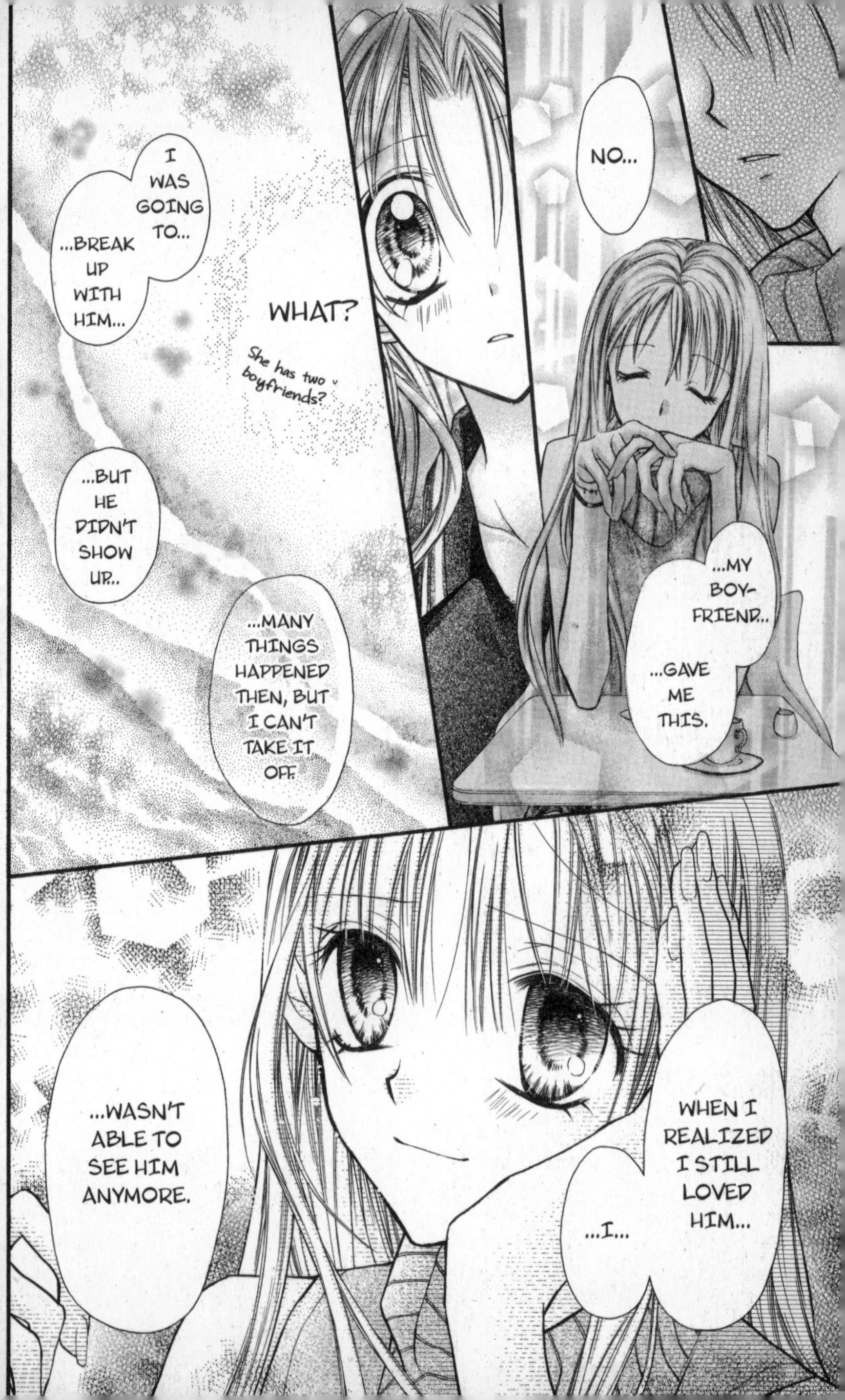
NO...
...MY BOY-FRIEND...
...GAVE ME THIS.
WHAT?
She has two boyfriends?
I WAS GOING TO...
...BREAK UP WITH HIM...
...BUT HE DIDN'T SHOW UP...
...MANY THINGS HAPPENED THEN, BUT I CAN'T TAKE IT OFF.
WHEN I REALIZED I STILL LOVED HIM...
...I...
...WASN'T ABLE TO SEE HIM ANYMORE.

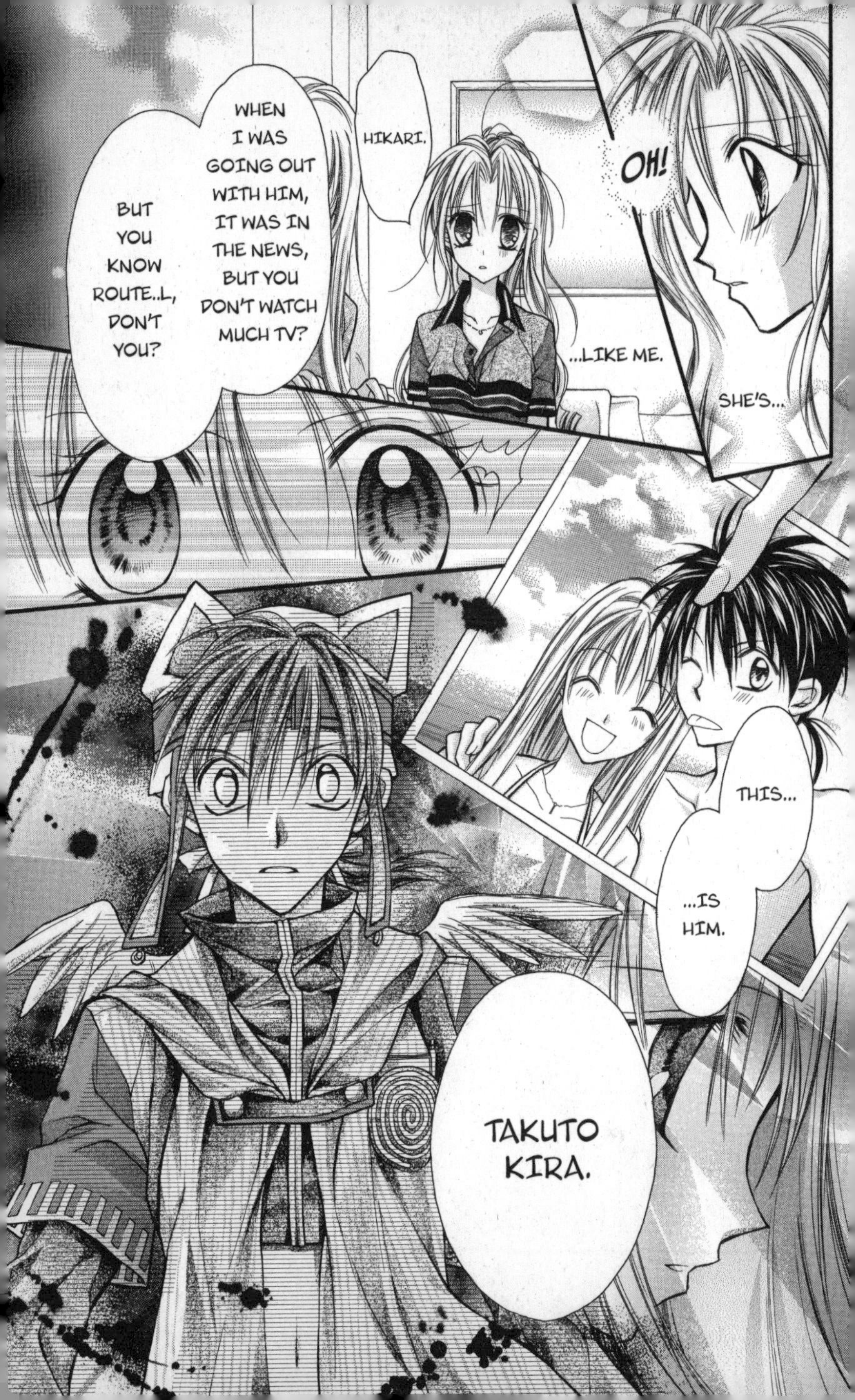
OH!
SHE'S...
...LIKE ME.
HIKARI.
WHEN I WAS GOING OUT WITH HIM, IT WAS IN THE NEWS, BUT YOU DON'T WATCH MUCH TV?
BUT YOU KNOW ROUTE..L, DON'T YOU?
THIS...
...IS HIM.
TAKUTO KIRA.

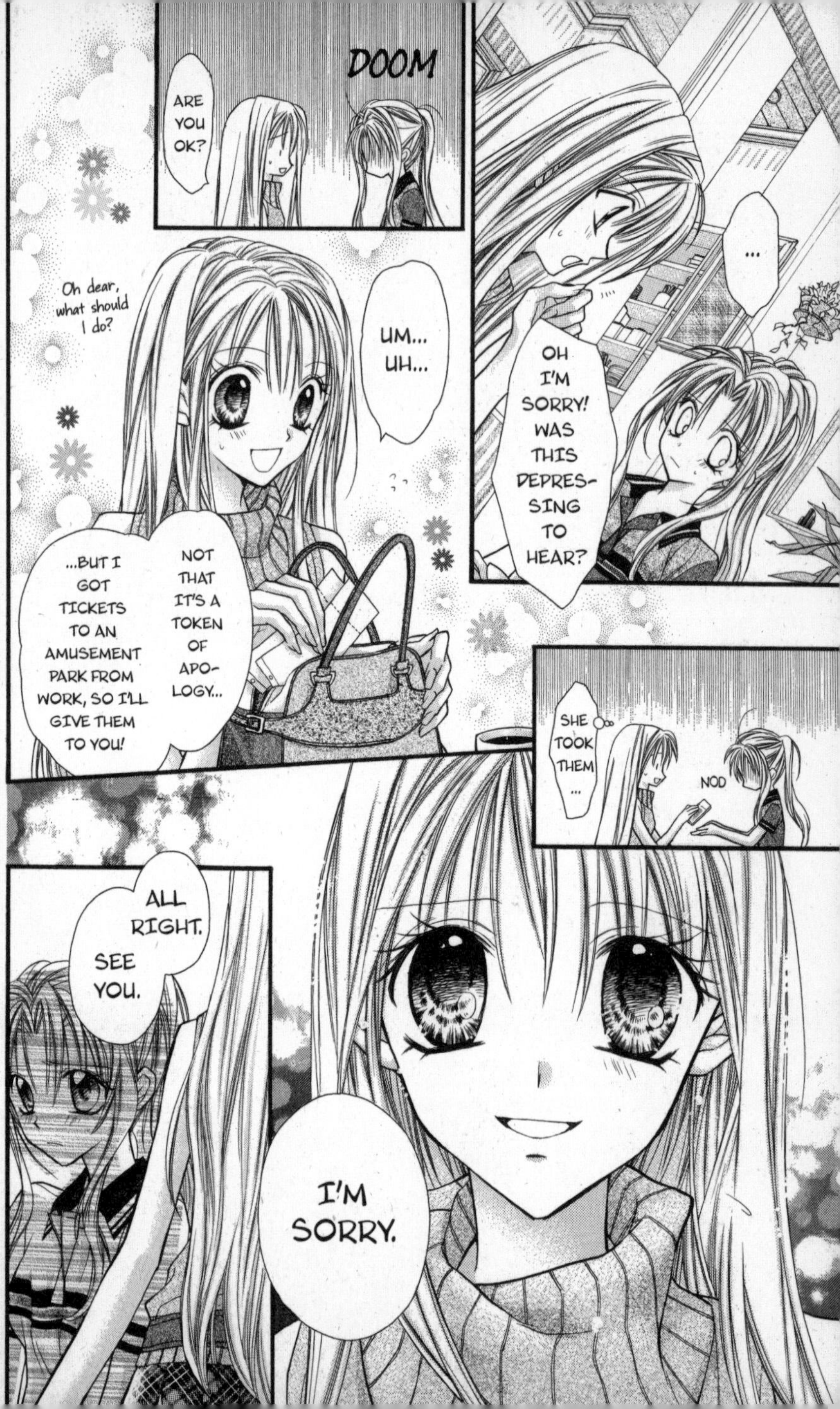
...
OH I'M SORRY! WAS THIS DEPRES-SING TO HEAR?
DOOM
ARE YOU OK?
UM... UH...
Oh dear, what should I do?
NOT THAT IT'S A TOKEN OF APO-LOGY...
...BUT I GOT TICKETS TO AN AMUSEMENT PARK FROM WORK, SO I'LL GIVE THEM TO YOU!
SHE TOOK THEM...
NOD
I'M SORRY.
ALL RIGHT. SEE YOU.

Hello!

**It's Arinacchi.
How's everyone?!**

All right, this is volume 6 of *Full Moon o Sagashite*. (I'm kinda giddy—I haven't been this way in a while.)

In *Ribon* it's the final chapter already, and I'm already half taken in by my new series, but I would like to talk about things so that I have no regrets! (Um...but what I really want to say is that I already drew the manga, but many people said it was hard to understand! So I'll talk about it!)

Oh! Thank you so much for buying my second illustration collection. Apparently, it's selling well. I think there were people who couldn't buy it, so I'm really sorry. They are printing more copies, so I think you can get them at bookstores now. Really, thank you! I will write more about this later!!

Um...it's a bit early, but last year's calendar (which was sold at bookstores) was apparently pretty popular, so there'll be a calendar for next year too!! I'm so happy. This is because everyone bought them!! It's really amazing!!! ////

I will do my best to draw new illustrations for it!!

I'm really eager to do it!!

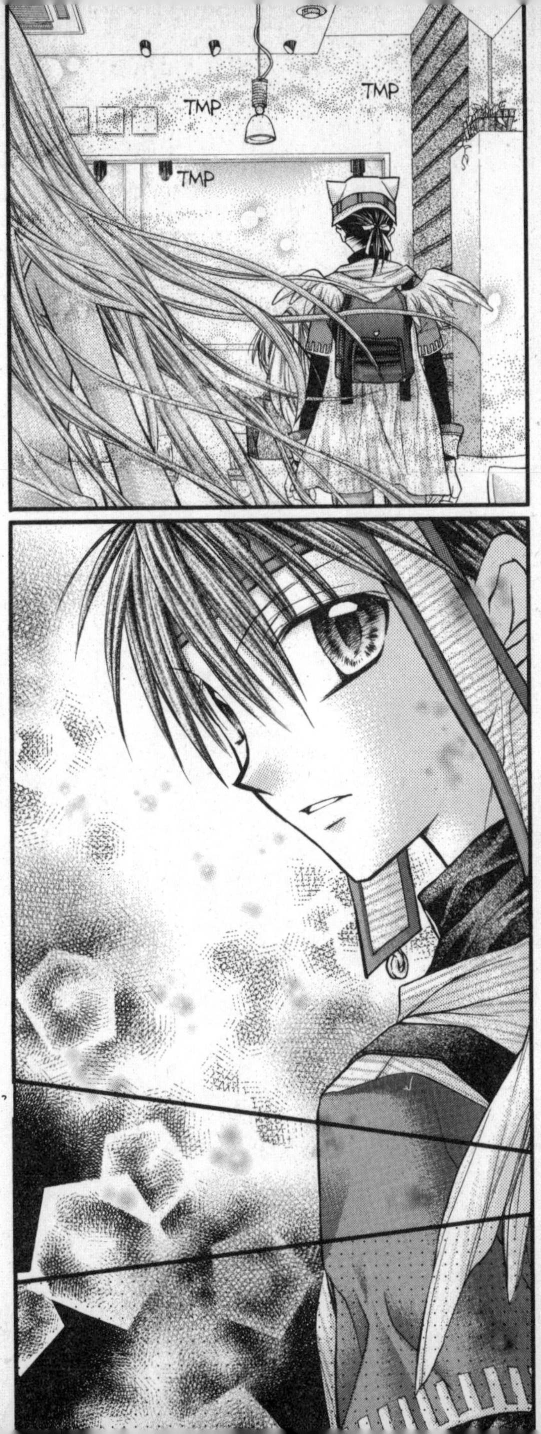
TMP
TMP
TMP

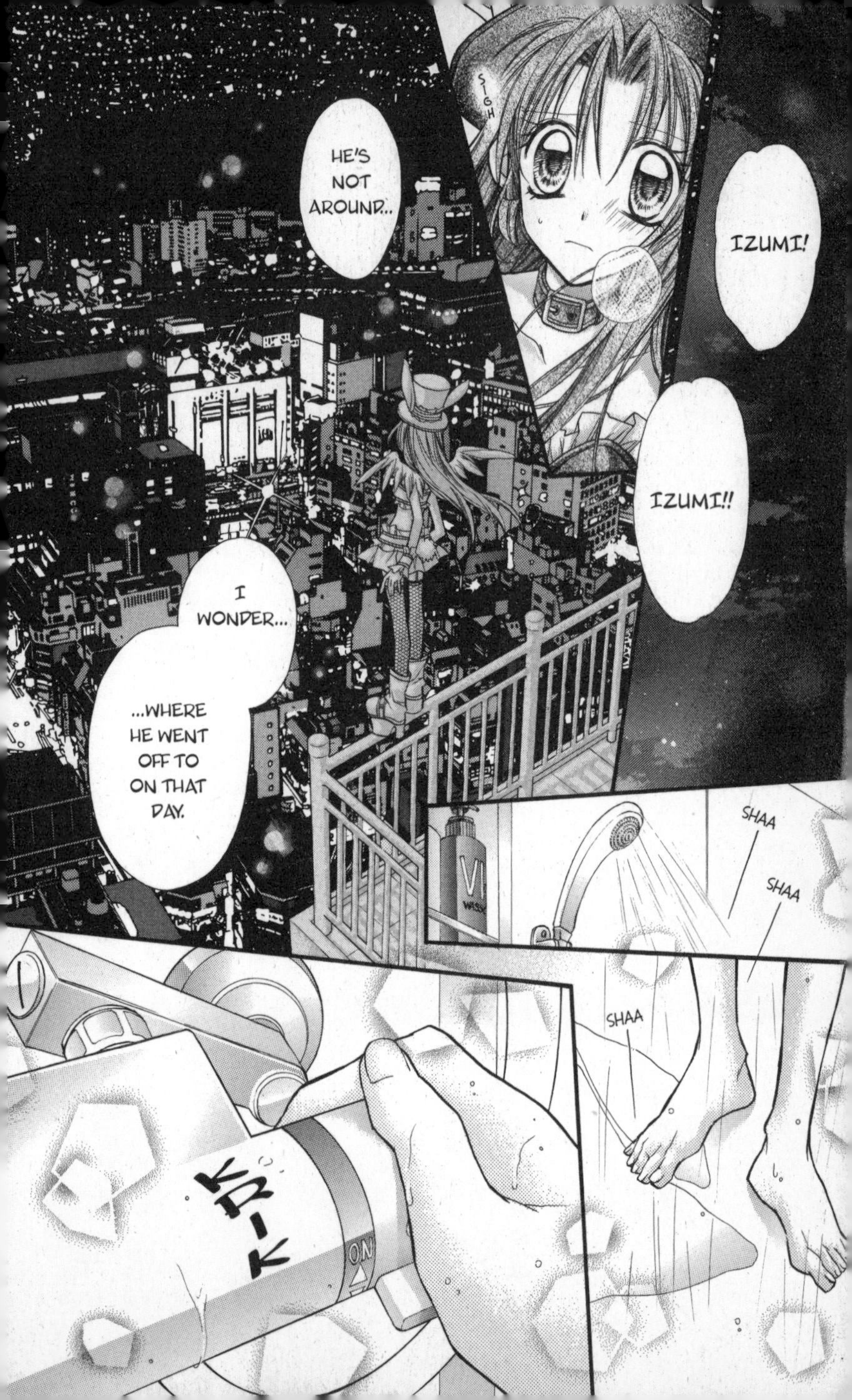
IZUMI!
IZUMI!!
SIGH
HE'S NOT AROUND...
I WONDER...
...WHERE HE WENT OFF TO ON THAT DAY.
SHAA
SHAA
SHAA
KRI-K

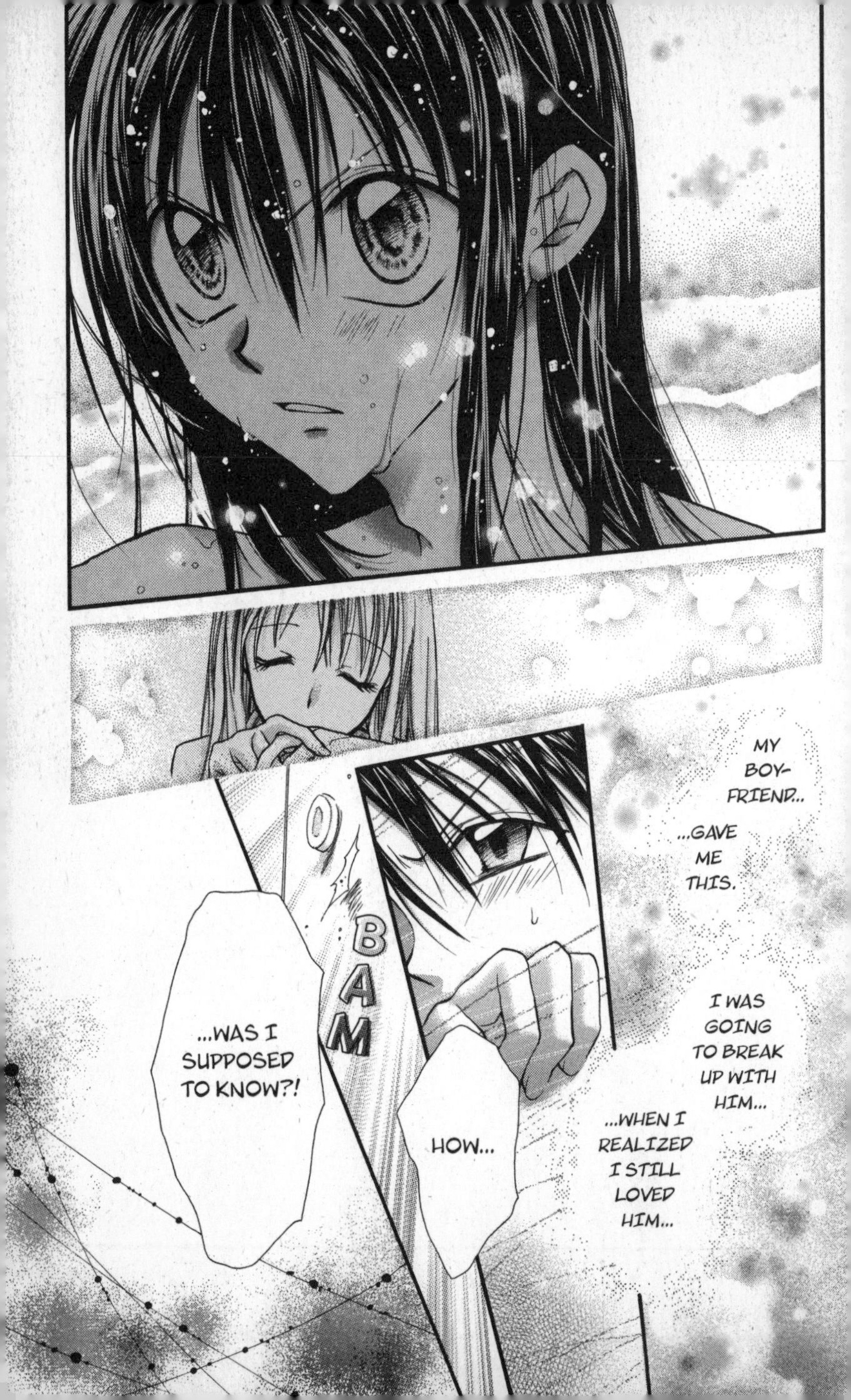
MY BOY-FRIEND...
...GAVE ME THIS.
I WAS GOING TO BREAK UP WITH HIM...
...WHEN I REALIZED I STILL LOVED HIM...
BAM
HOW...
...WAS I SUPPOSED TO KNOW?!

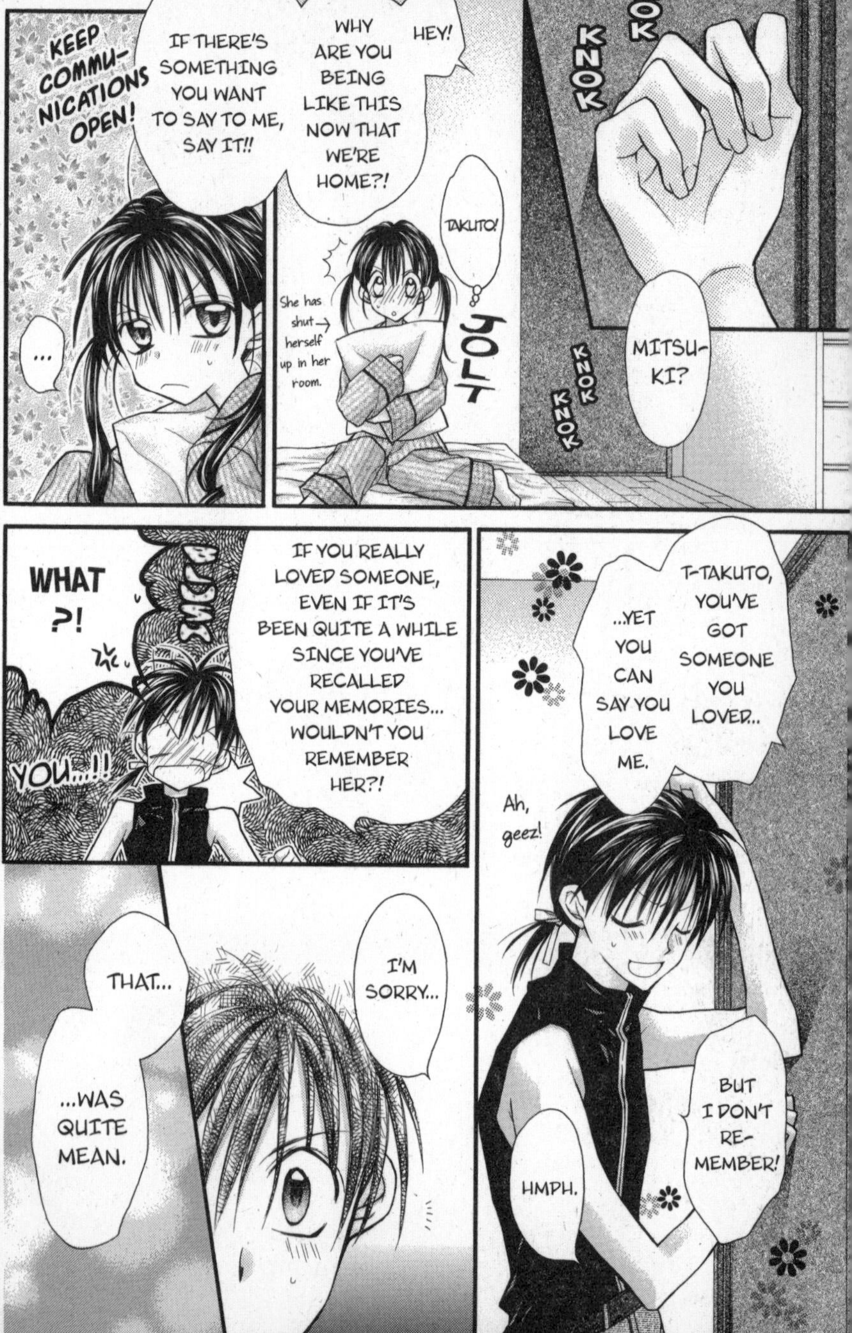
KNOK KNOK
KNOK KNOK
MITSU-KI?
HEY!
WHY ARE YOU BEING LIKE THIS NOW THAT WE'RE HOME?!
TAKUTO!
JOLT
She has shut herself up in her room.
KEEP COMMU-NICATIONS OPEN!
IF THERE'S SOMETHING YOU WANT TO SAY TO ME, SAY IT!!
...
T-TAKUTO, YOU'VE GOT SOMEONE YOU LOVED...
...YET YOU CAN SAY YOU LOVE ME.
Ah, geez!
BUT I DON'T RE-MEMBER!
HMPH.
IF YOU REALLY LOVED SOMEONE, EVEN IF IT'S BEEN QUITE A WHILE SINCE YOU'VE RECALLED YOUR MEMORIES... WOULDN'T YOU REMEMBER HER?!
WHAT?!
YOU...!!
I'M SORRY...
THAT...
...WAS QUITE MEAN.

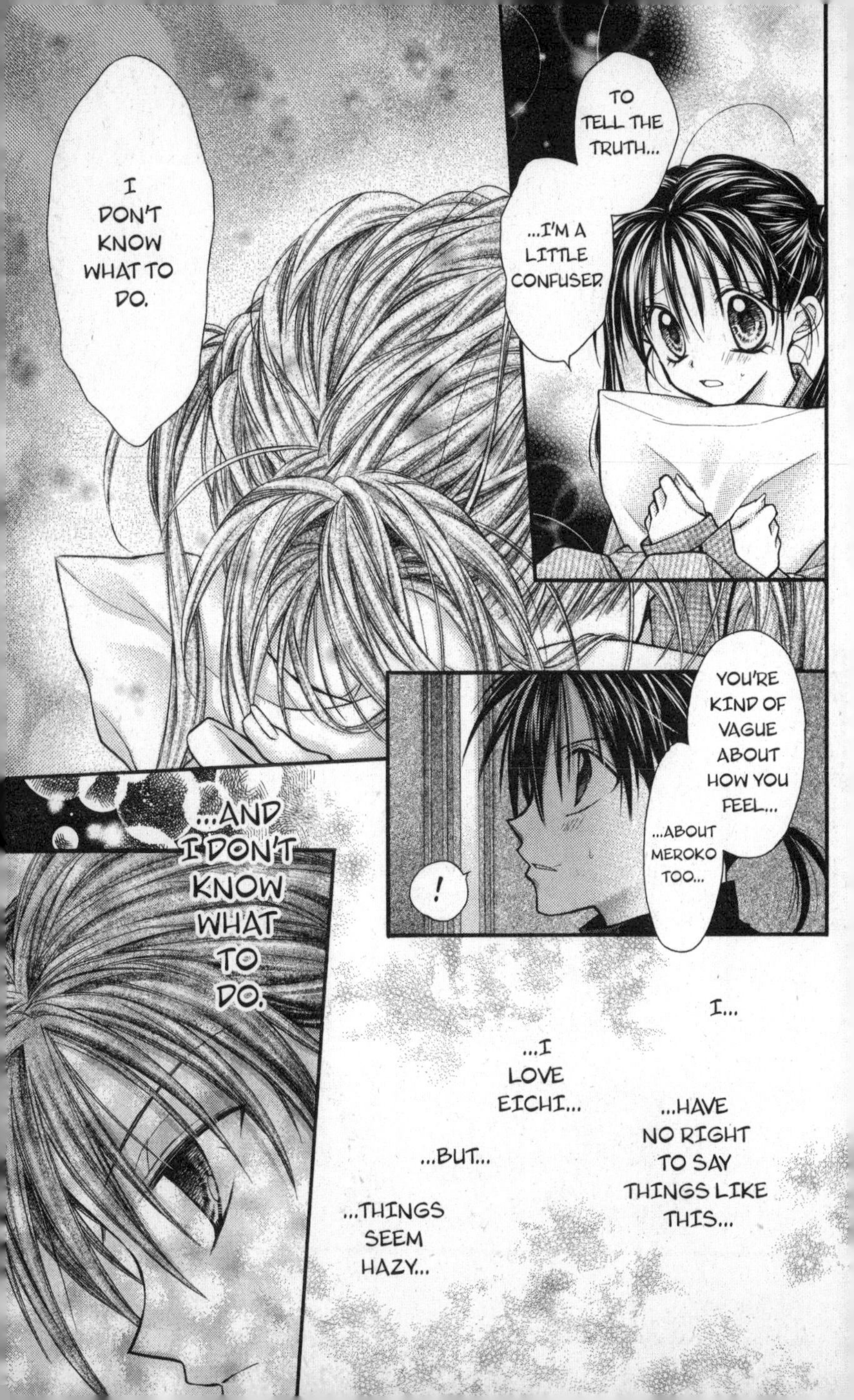
TO TELL THE TRUTH...
...I'M A LITTLE CONFUSED.
I DON'T KNOW WHAT TO DO.
YOU'RE KIND OF VAGUE ABOUT HOW YOU FEEL...
...ABOUT MEROKO TOO...
!
I...
...HAVE NO RIGHT TO SAY THINGS LIKE THIS...
...I LOVE EICHI...
...BUT...
...THINGS SEEM HAZY...
...AND I DON'T KNOW WHAT TO DO.

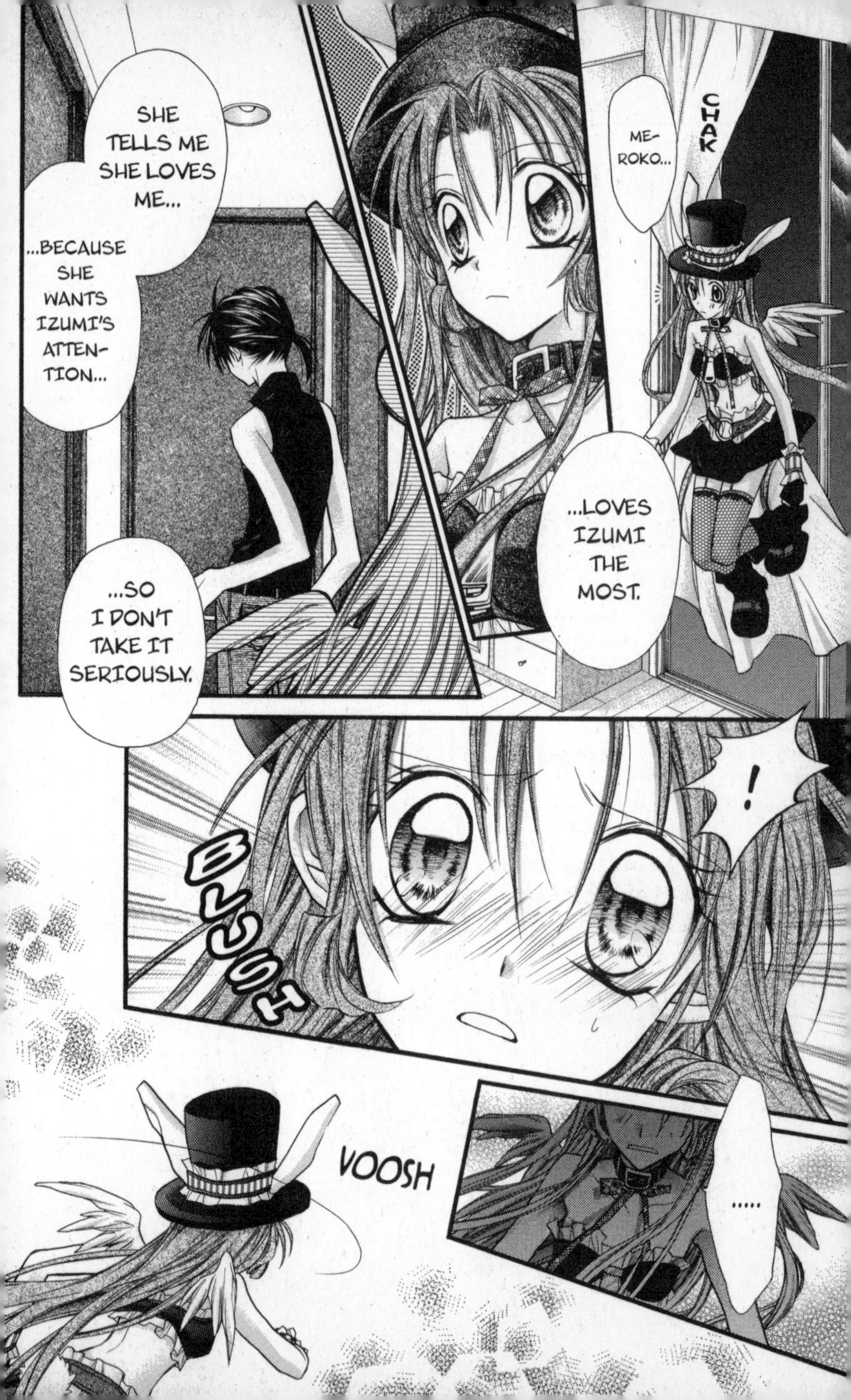
CHAK
ME-ROKO...
...LOVES IZUMI THE MOST.
SHE TELLS ME SHE LOVES ME...
...BECAUSE SHE WANTS IZUMI'S ATTEN-TION...
...SO I DON'T TAKE IT SERIOUSLY.
!
BLUSH
.....
VOOSH

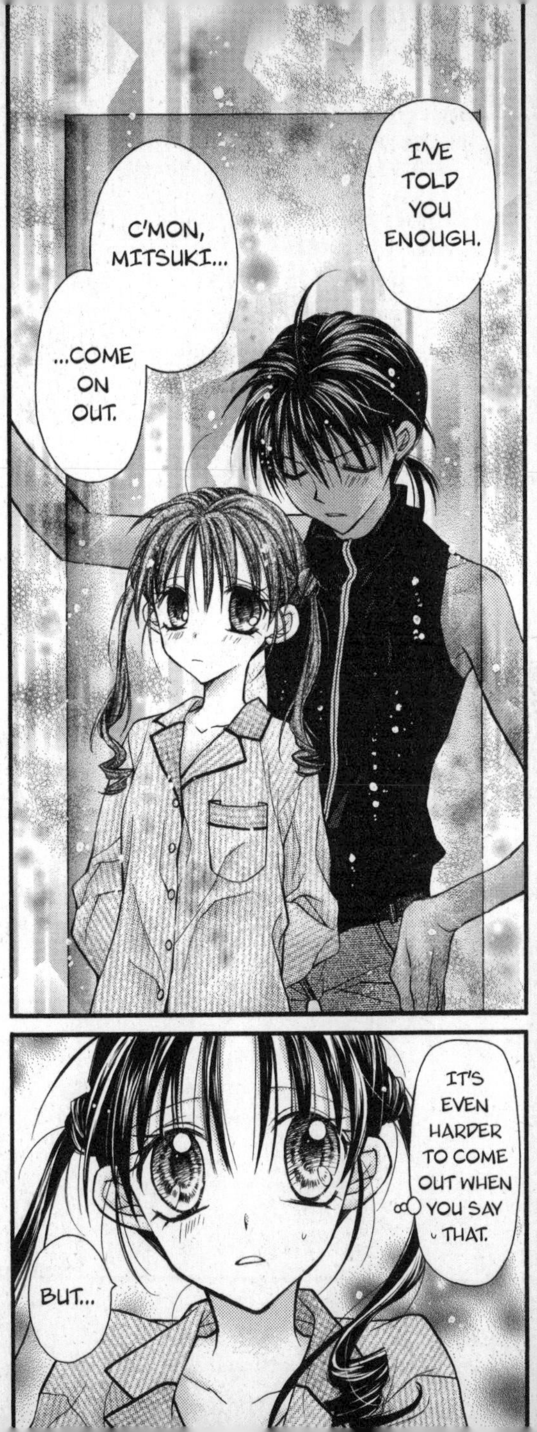
I'VE TOLD YOU ENOUGH.
C'MON, MITSUKI... ...COME ON OUT.
IT'S EVEN HARDER TO COME OUT WHEN YOU SAY THAT.
BUT...

Full Moon o Sagashite Illustration Collection

Arina Tanemura Collection

Since last December I worked on these in between working on the manga.

I had a little time off for New Year's, so I was thinking about how to place the illustrations at Rie-chan's (Minase-san) place in Hiroshima. I started by figuring out what kind of illustrations there were, and fitted them to each page, like a jigsaw puzzle.

Hmmm...
64 pages...
Hmmm...

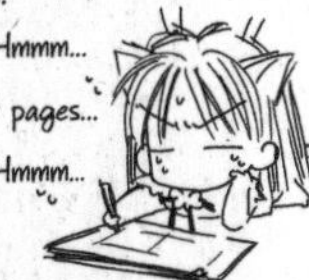

I guess everybody wants that picture included, but...

* I actually did this properly at my desk (smile).

I had a designer do the layouts, then I made some requests (like please put gingham checks in the backgrounds ♪). Then the designer looked at it once more, and I drew the cover illustration. Then we repeated the process.

To tell the truth, illustration collections of shojo manga don't sell very well, so they're prepared to lose money on it (this is what I've heard). It costs almost 2,000 yen... If you don't get much of an allowance, it's hard to buy one... When I was in junior high school, my allowance was 2,500 yen a month.

So the fact that I had one out, when I'm not even an illustrator, is...a miracle?! I was able to have one because the one for Jeanne sold. So it's really due to my fans!!

So that there can be a third one, I will draw from the beginning once again!!

Always in analog.

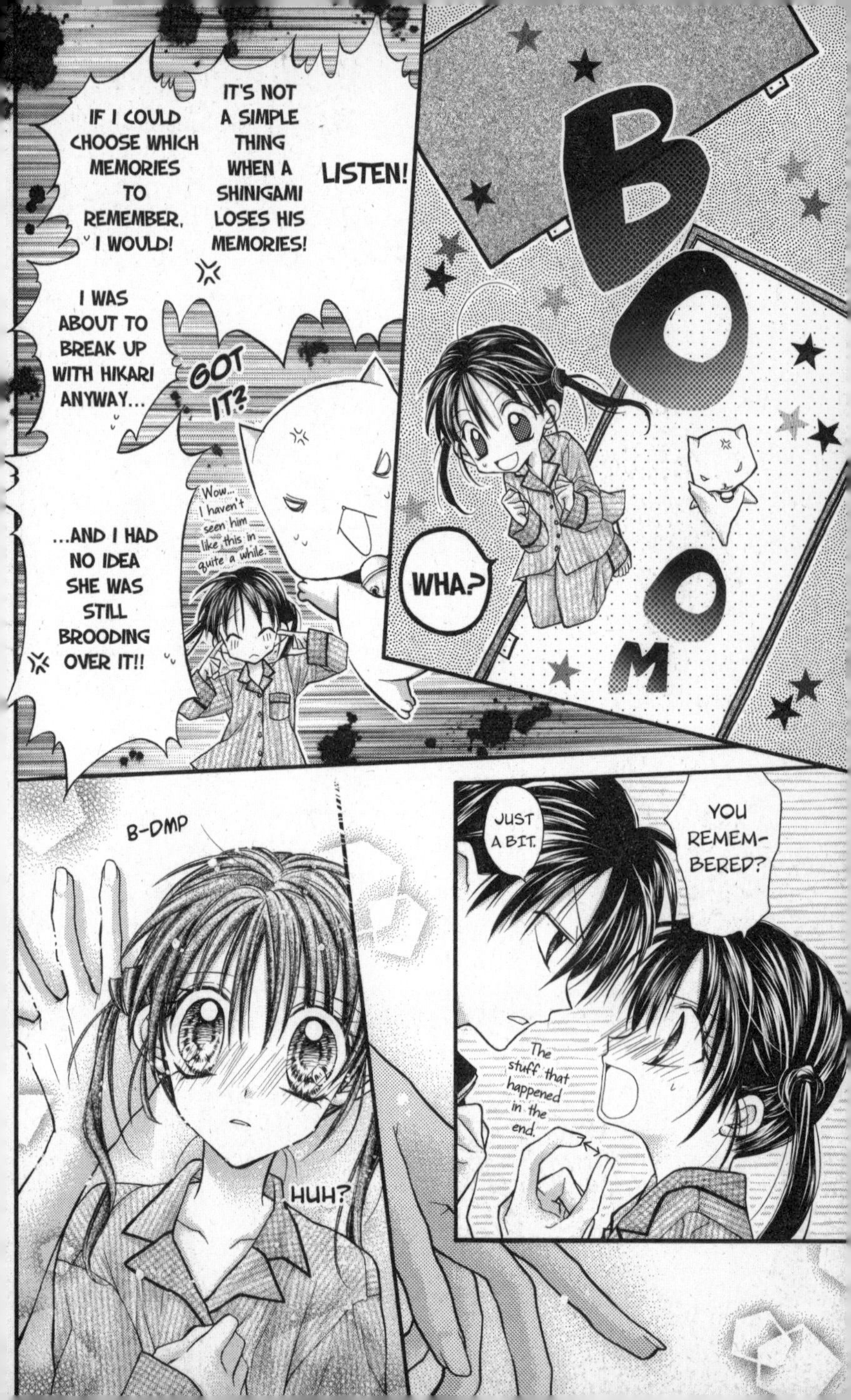
BOOM
WHA?
LISTEN!
IT'S NOT A SIMPLE THING WHEN A SHINIGAMI LOSES HIS MEMORIES!
IF I COULD CHOOSE WHICH MEMORIES TO REMEMBER, I WOULD!
GOT IT?
I WAS ABOUT TO BREAK UP WITH HIKARI ANYWAY...
Wow... I haven't seen him like this in quite a while.
...AND I HAD NO IDEA SHE WAS STILL BROODING OVER IT!!
YOU REMEM-BERED?
JUST A BIT.
The stuff that happened in the end.
B-DMP
HUH?

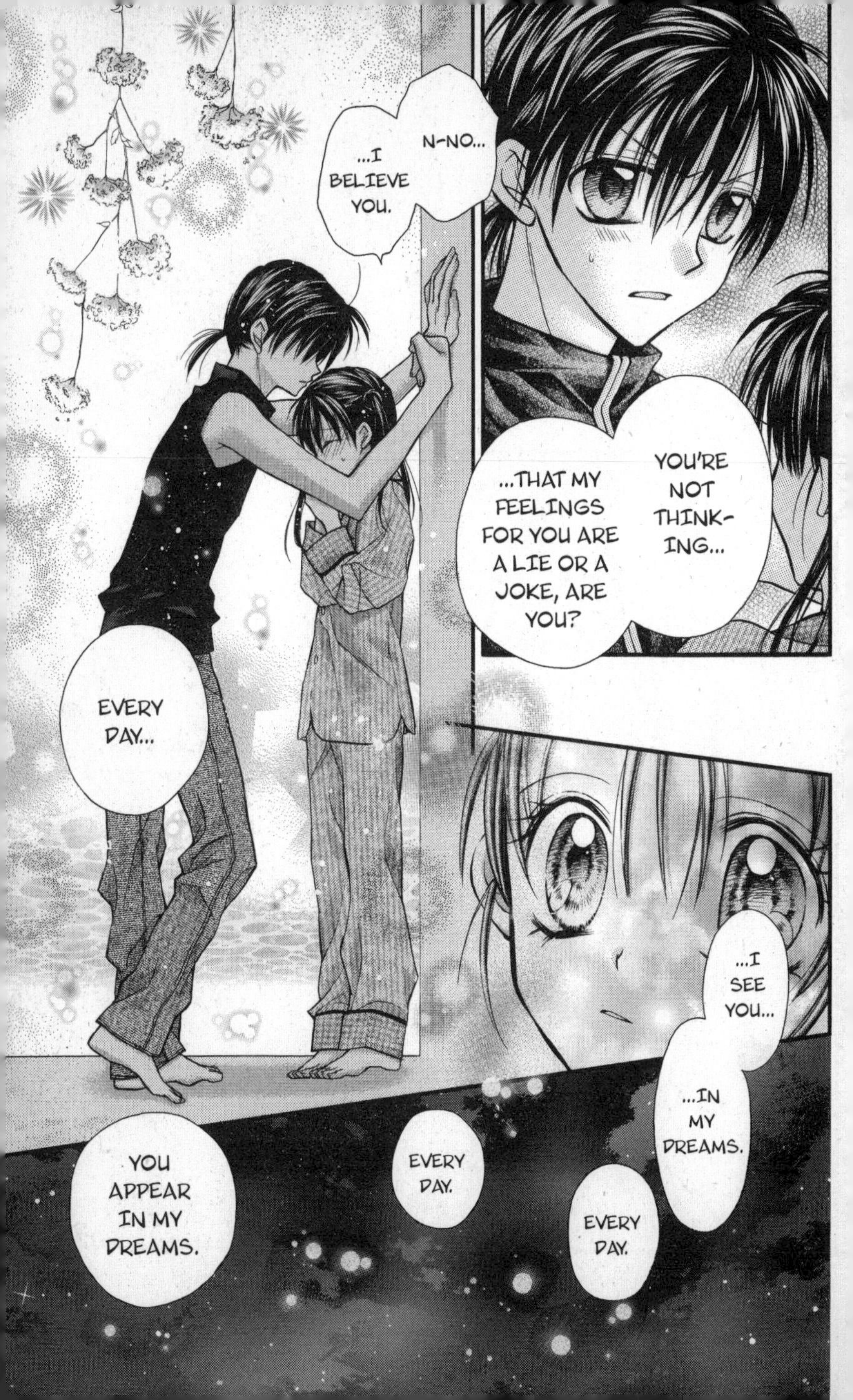
YOU'RE NOT THINKING...
...THAT MY FEELINGS FOR YOU ARE A LIE OR A JOKE, ARE YOU?
N-NO...
...I BELIEVE YOU.
EVERY DAY...
...I SEE YOU...
...IN MY DREAMS.
EVERY DAY.
EVERY DAY.
YOU APPEAR IN MY DREAMS.

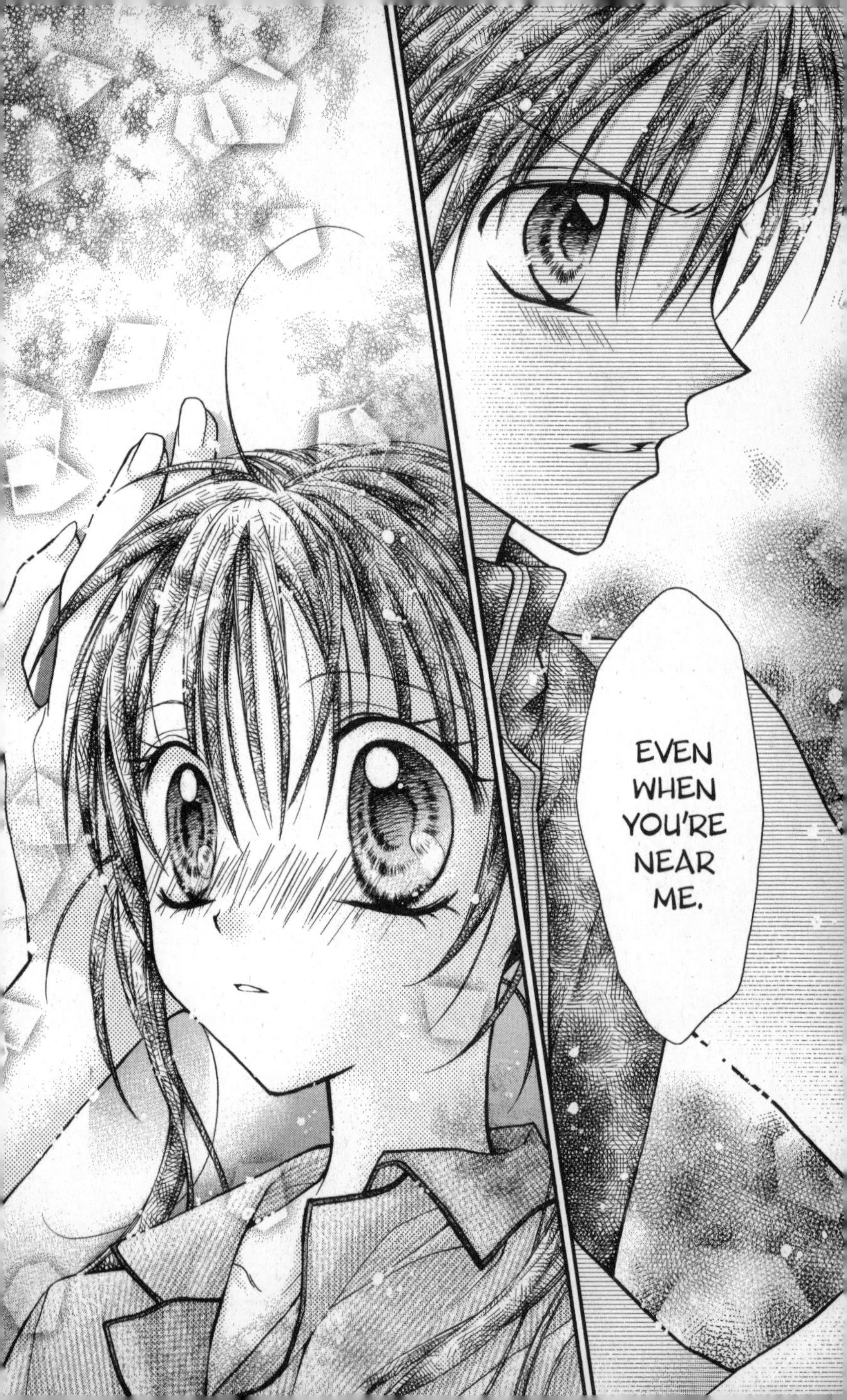
EVEN WHEN YOU'RE NEAR ME.

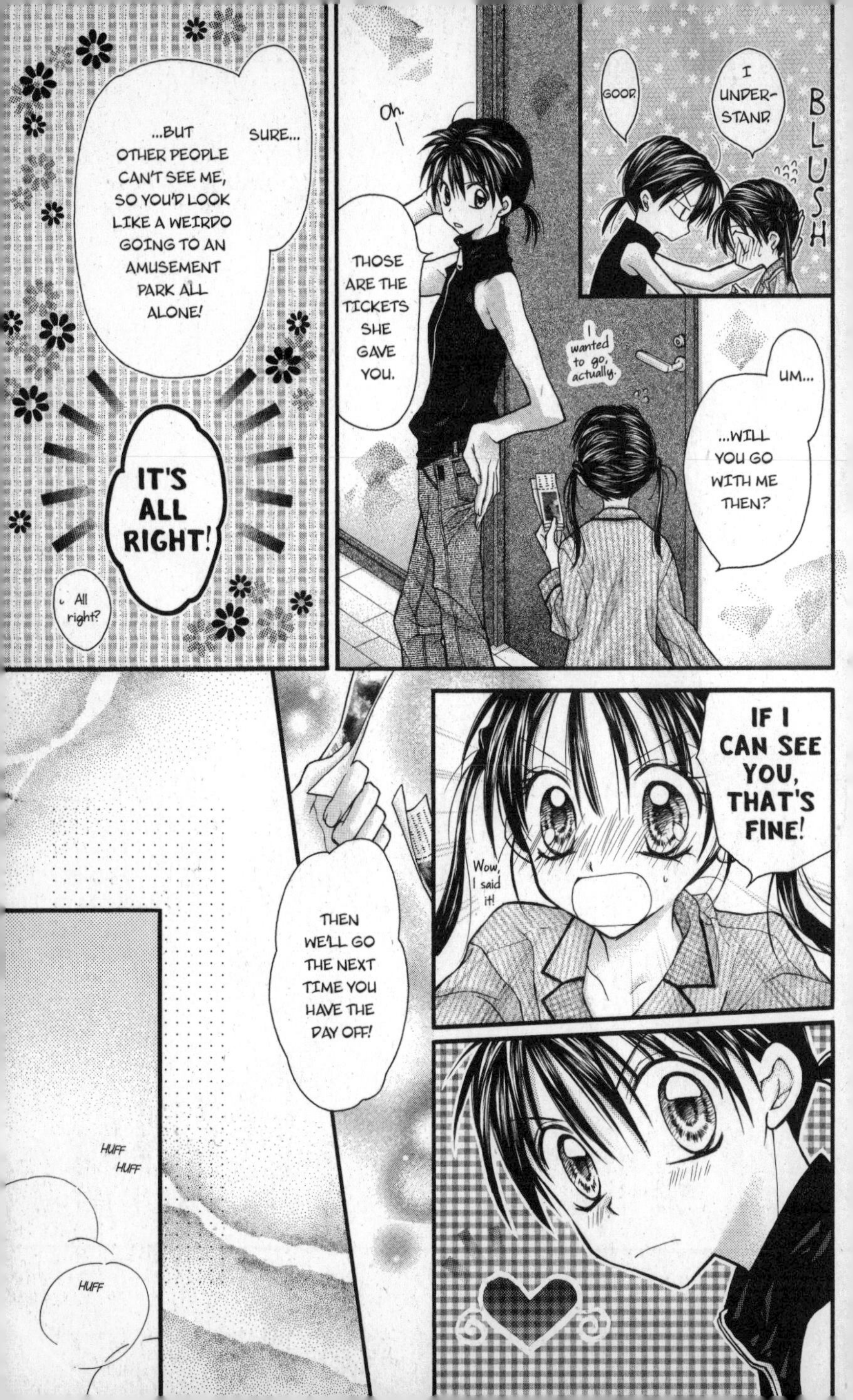
I UNDER-STAND.
GOOD.
BLUSH
UM...
...WILL YOU GO WITH ME THEN?
I wanted to go, actually.
Oh.
THOSE ARE THE TICKETS SHE GAVE YOU.
SURE...
...BUT OTHER PEOPLE CAN'T SEE ME, SO YOU'D LOOK LIKE A WEIRDO GOING TO AN AMUSEMENT PARK ALL ALONE!
IT'S ALL RIGHT!
All right?
IF I CAN SEE YOU, THAT'S FINE!
Wow, I said it!
THEN WE'LL GO THE NEXT TIME YOU HAVE THE DAY OFF!
HUFF
HUFF
HUFF

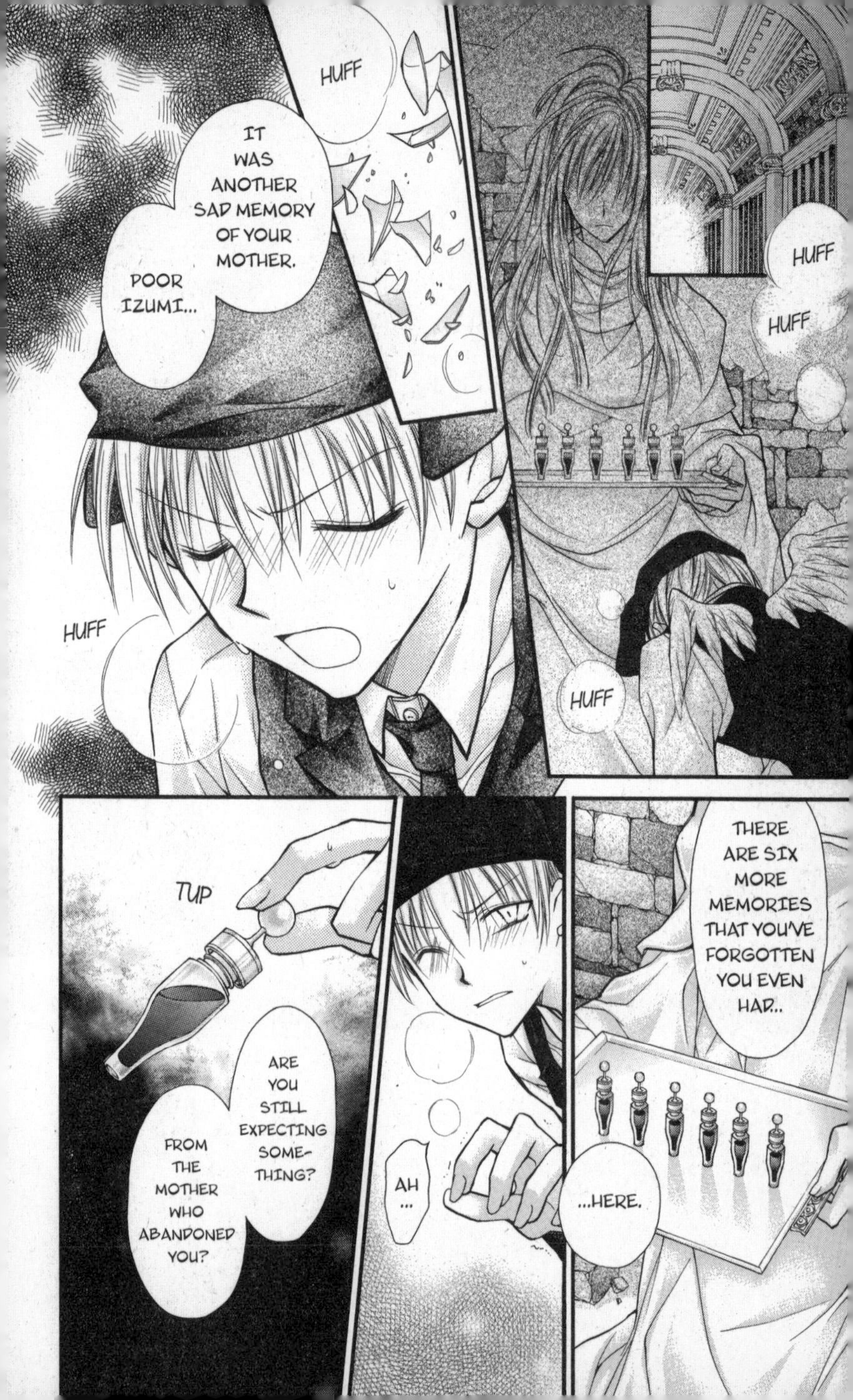
HUFF
HUFF
HUFF
HUFF
IT WAS ANOTHER SAD MEMORY OF YOUR MOTHER.
POOR IZUMI...
HUFF
THERE ARE SIX MORE MEMORIES THAT YOU'VE FORGOTTEN YOU EVEN HAD..
...HERE.
AH ...
TUP
ARE YOU STILL EXPECTING SOME-THING?
FROM THE MOTHER WHO ABANDONED YOU?

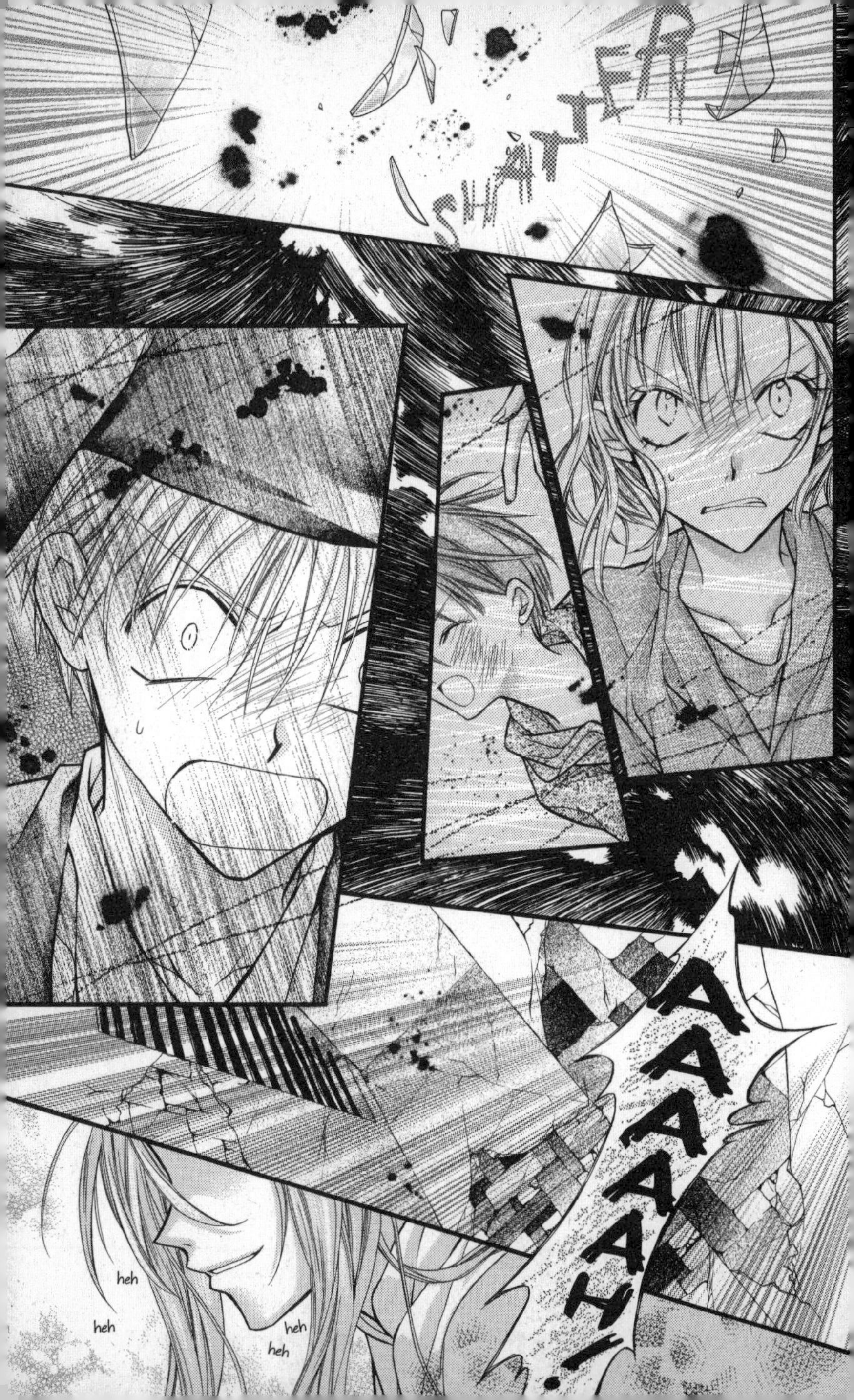
SHATTER
AAAAAAH!
heh
heh
heh
heh

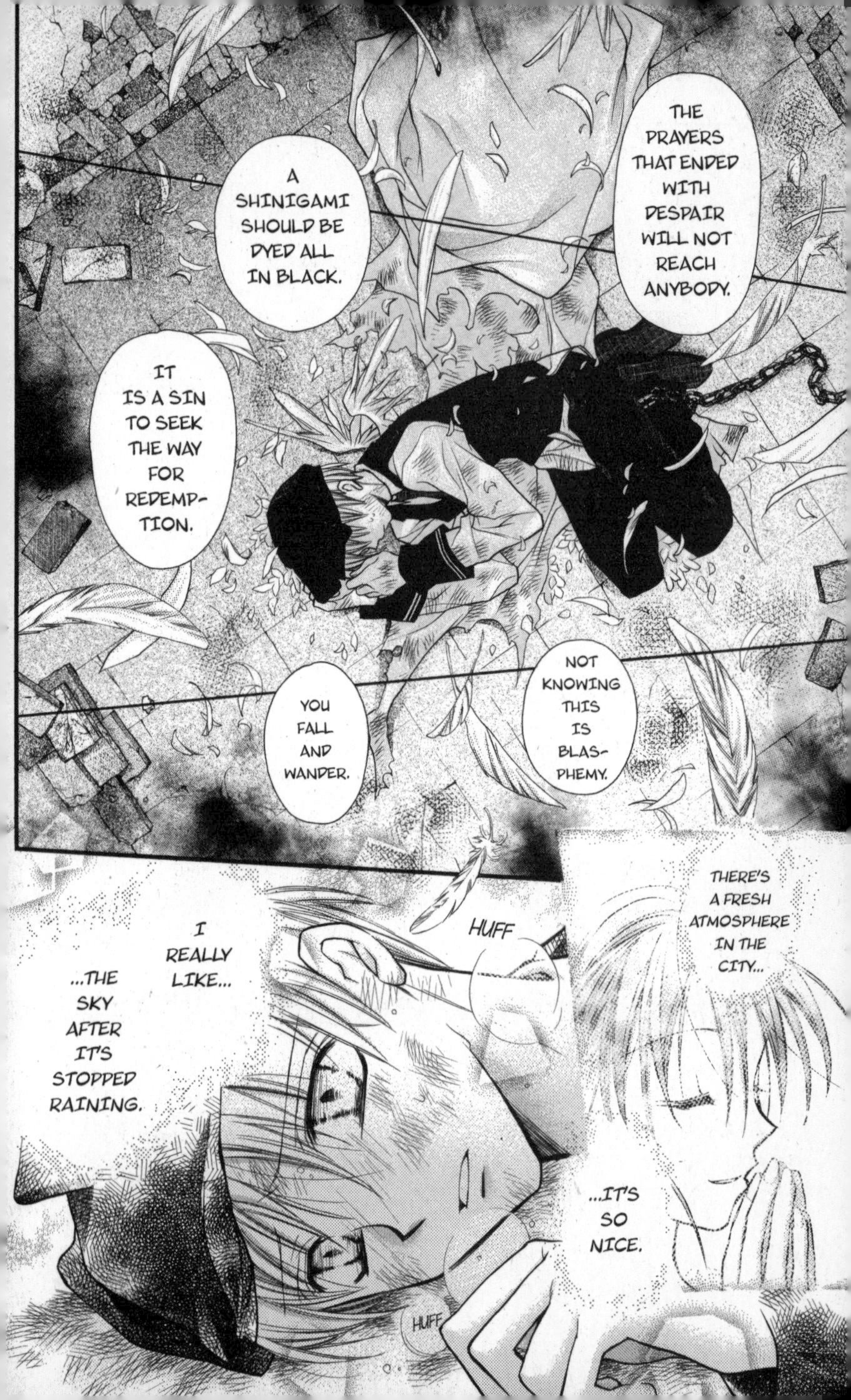
THE PRAYERS THAT ENDED WITH DESPAIR WILL NOT REACH ANYBODY.
A SHINIGAMI SHOULD BE DYED ALL IN BLACK.
IT IS A SIN TO SEEK THE WAY FOR REDEMP-TION.
NOT KNOWING THIS IS BLAS-PHEMY.
YOU FALL AND WANDER.
THERE'S A FRESH ATMOSPHERE IN THE CITY...
HUFF
I REALLY LIKE...
...THE SKY AFTER IT'S STOPPED RAINING.
...IT'S SO NICE.
HUFF

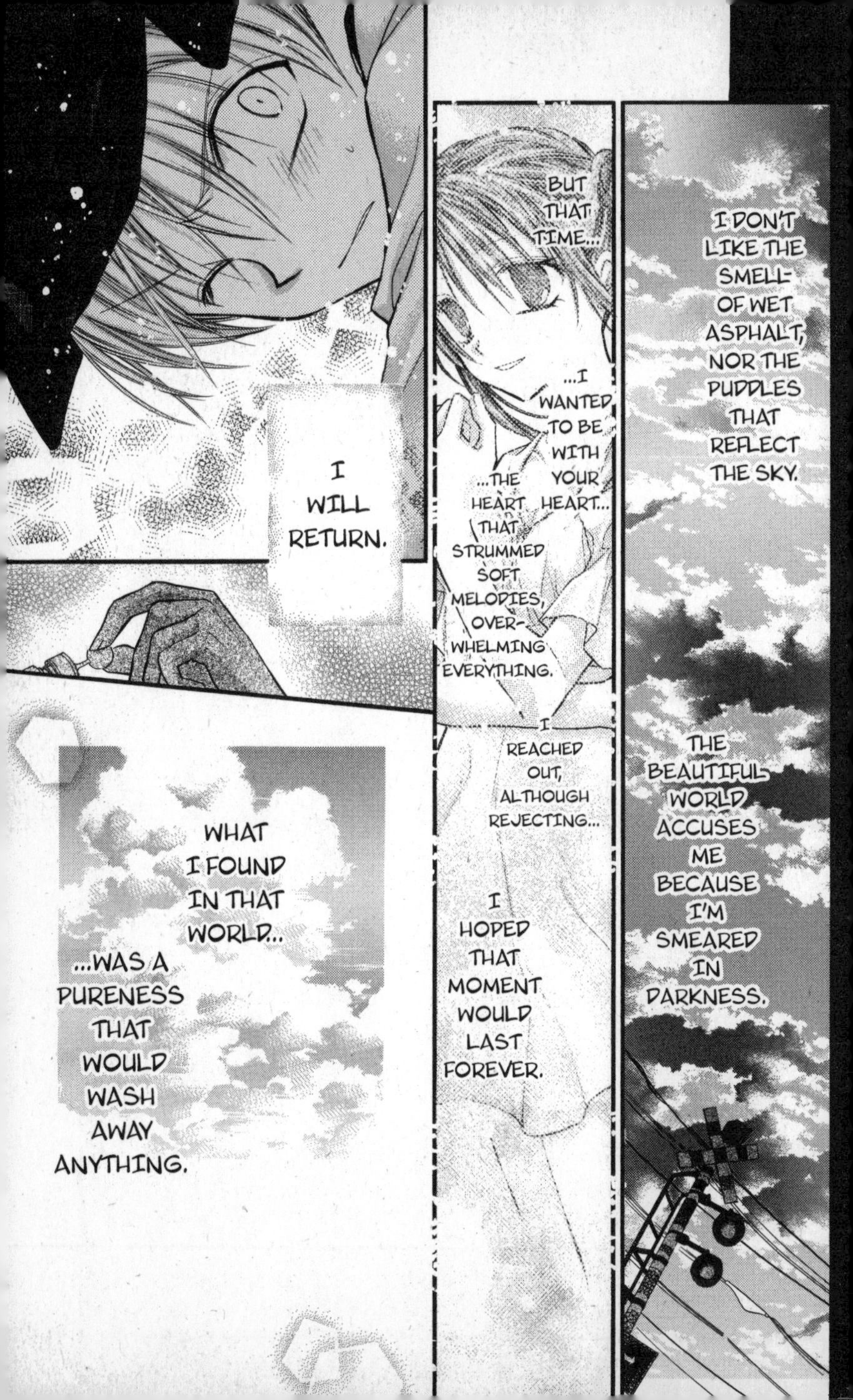
I DON'T LIKE THE SMELL OF WET ASPHALT, NOR THE PUDDLES THAT REFLECT THE SKY.
THE BEAUTIFUL WORLD ACCUSES ME BECAUSE I'M SMEARED IN DARKNESS.
BUT THAT TIME...
...I WANTED TO BE WITH YOUR HEART...
...THE HEART THAT STRUMMED SOFT MELODIES, OVER-WHELMING EVERYTHING.
I REACHED OUT, ALTHOUGH REJECTING...
I HOPED THAT MOMENT WOULD LAST FOREVER.
I WILL RETURN.
WHAT I FOUND IN THAT WORLD...
...WAS A PURENESS THAT WOULD WASH AWAY ANYTHING.

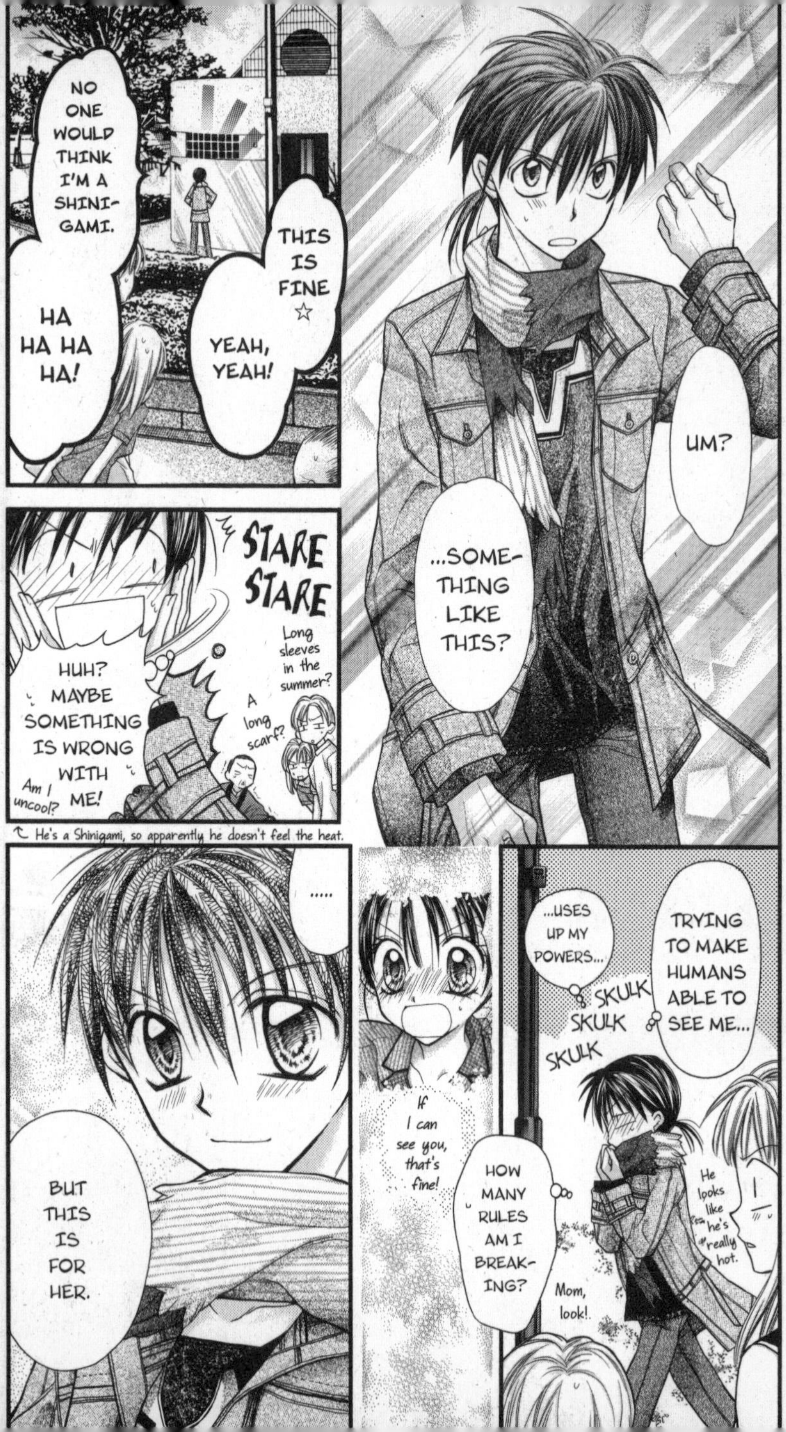
UM?
...SOMETHING LIKE THIS?
THIS IS FINE ☆
NO ONE WOULD THINK I'M A SHINIGAMI.
YEAH, YEAH!
HA HA HA HA!
STARE STARE
Long sleeves in the summer?
A long scarf?
HUH? MAYBE SOMETHING IS WRONG WITH ME!
Am I uncool?
He's a Shinigami, so apparently he doesn't feel the heat.
TRYING TO MAKE HUMANS ABLE TO SEE ME...
...USES UP MY POWERS...
SKULK SKULK SKULK
He looks like he's really hot.
HOW MANY RULES AM I BREAKING?
Mom, look!
If I can see you, that's fine!
.....
BUT THIS IS FOR HER.

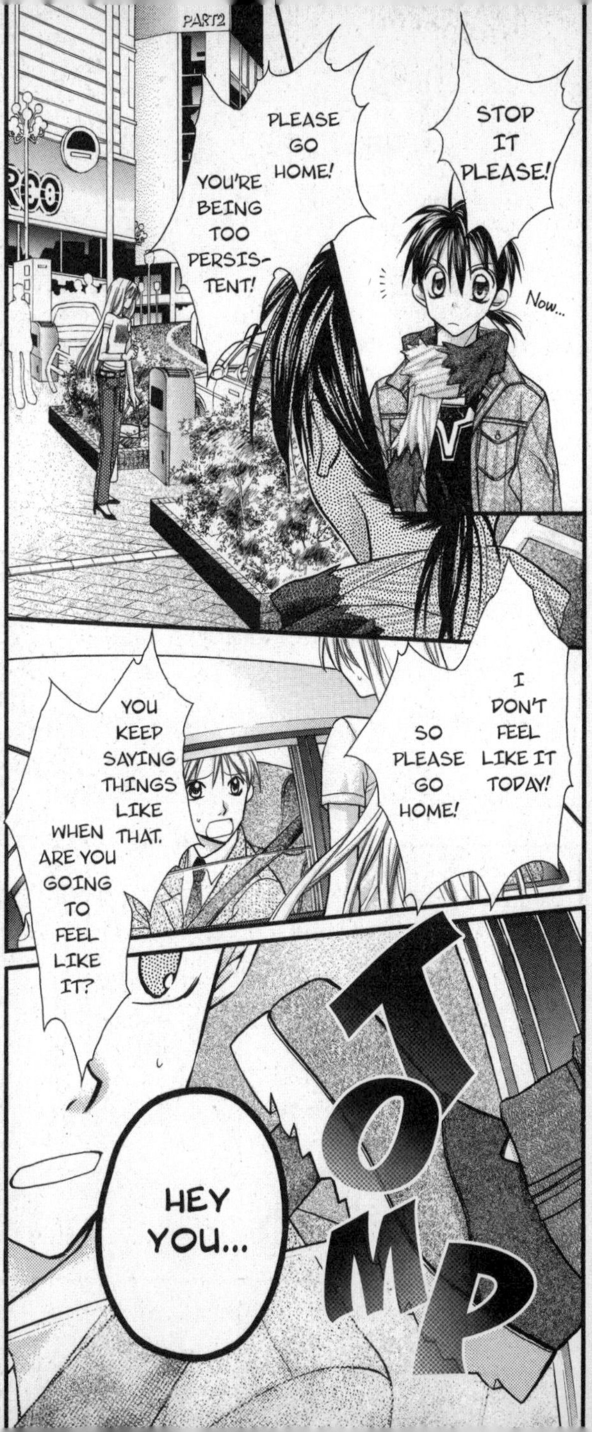
PART2
STOP IT PLEASE!
Now...
PLEASE GO HOME!
YOU'RE BEING TOO PERSIS-TENT!
I DON'T FEEL LIKE IT TODAY!
SO PLEASE GO HOME!
YOU KEEP SAYING THINGS LIKE THAT.
WHEN ARE YOU GOING TO FEEL LIKE IT?
TOMP
HEY YOU...

Penchi de Shakin ☆

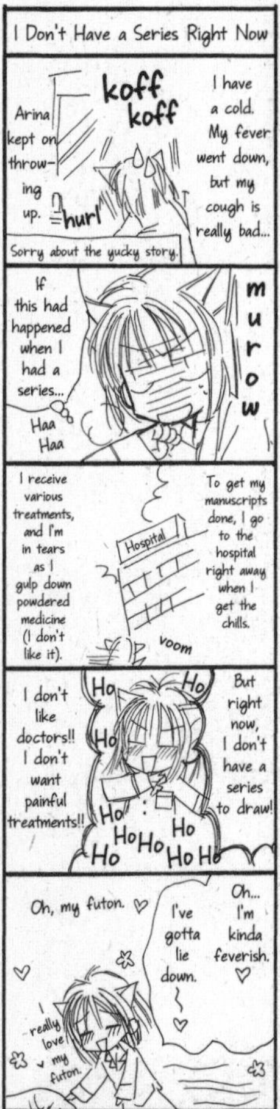
I Don't Have a Series Right Now
I have a cold. My fever went down, but my cough is really bad...
koff koff
Arina kept on throw-ing up.
hurl
Sorry about the yucky story.
murow
If this had happened when I had a series...
Haa Haa
To get my manuscripts done, I go to the hospital right away when I get the chills.
Hospital
I receive various treatments, and I'm in tears as I gulp down powdered medicine (I don't like it).
voom
But right now, I don't have a series to draw!
I don't like doctors!! I don't want painful treatments!!
Ho Ho Ho Ho Ho Ho Ho Ho Ho Ho
Oh... I'm kinda feverish.
I've gotta lie down.
Oh, my futon.
I really love my futon.
koff
koff
gag
murow
※ I'm a fool.
It's okay.. Cheers to fools.

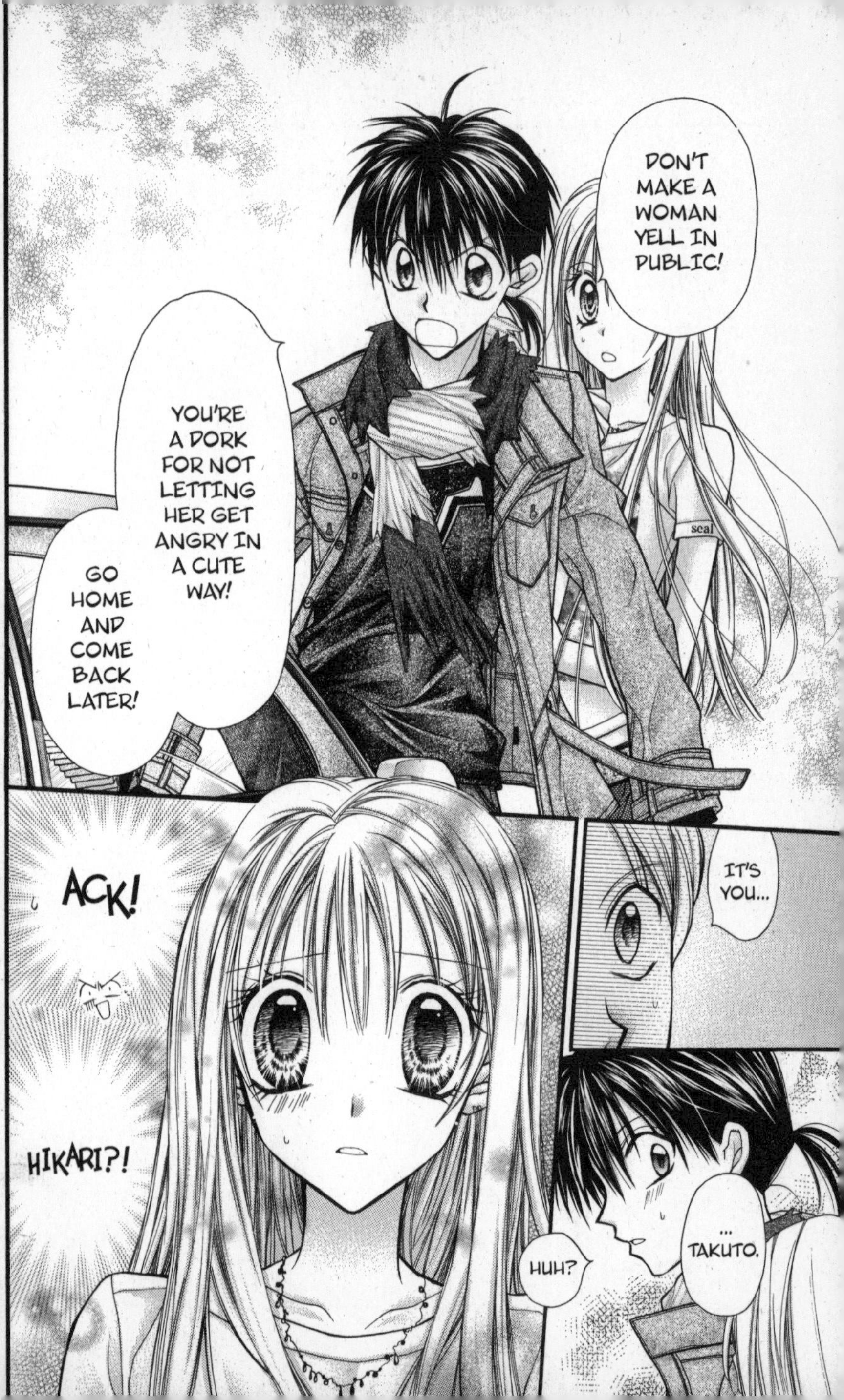
DON'T MAKE A WOMAN YELL IN PUBLIC!
YOU'RE A DORK FOR NOT LETTING HER GET ANGRY IN A CUTE WAY!
GO HOME AND COME BACK LATER!
IT'S YOU...
... TAKUTO.
HUH?
ACK!
HIKARI?!

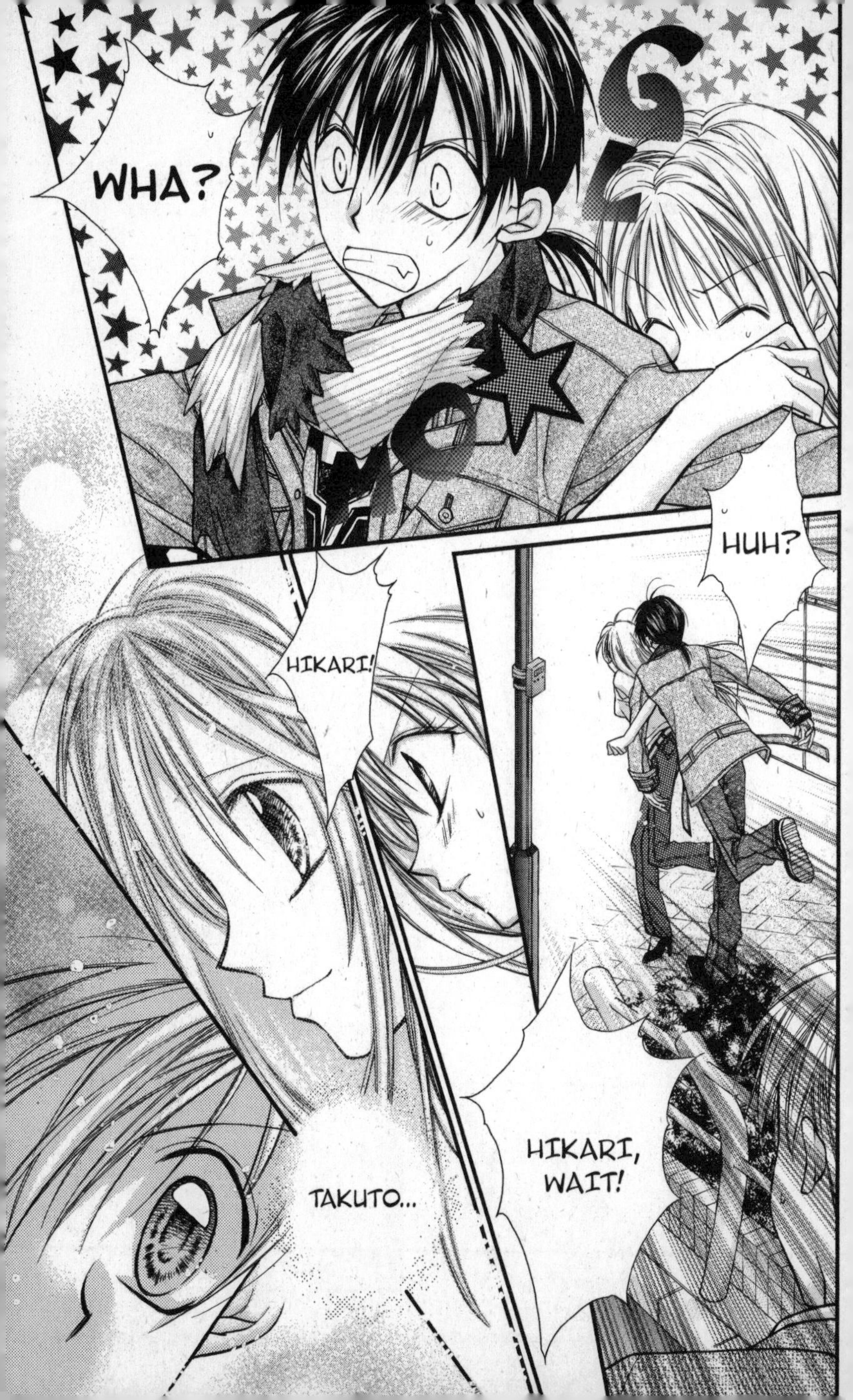
WHA?
HUH?
HIKARI!
HIKARI, WAIT!
TAKUTO...

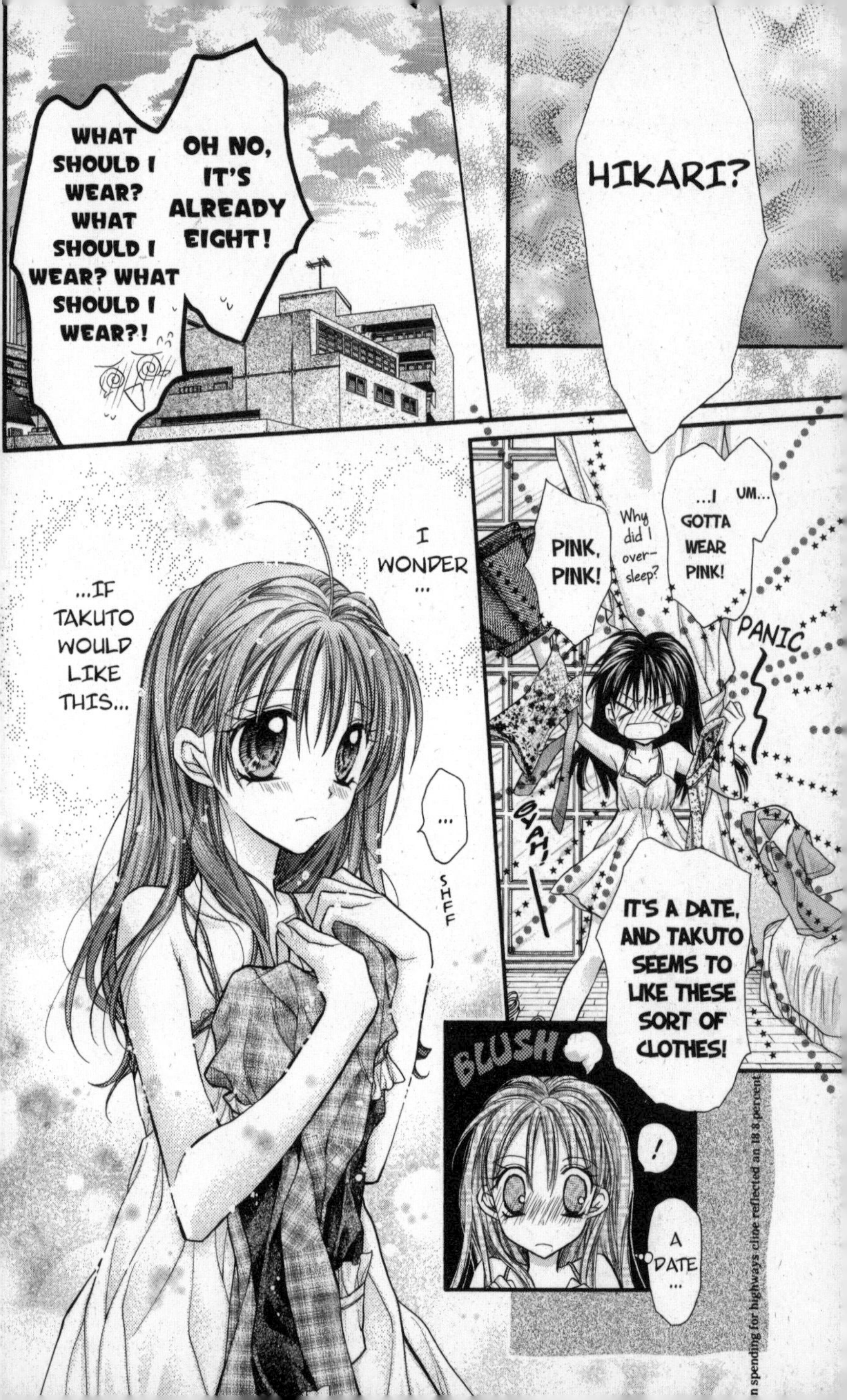
HIKARI?
OH NO, IT'S ALREADY EIGHT!
WHAT SHOULD I WEAR? WHAT SHOULD I WEAR? WHAT SHOULD I WEAR?!
UM...
...I GOTTA WEAR PINK!
Why did I over-sleep?
PINK, PINK!
PANIC
GYAH!
IT'S A DATE, AND TAKUTO SEEMS TO LIKE THESE SORT OF CLOTHES!
BLUSH
!
A DATE...
I WONDER...
...IF TAKUTO WOULD LIKE THIS...
...
SHFF

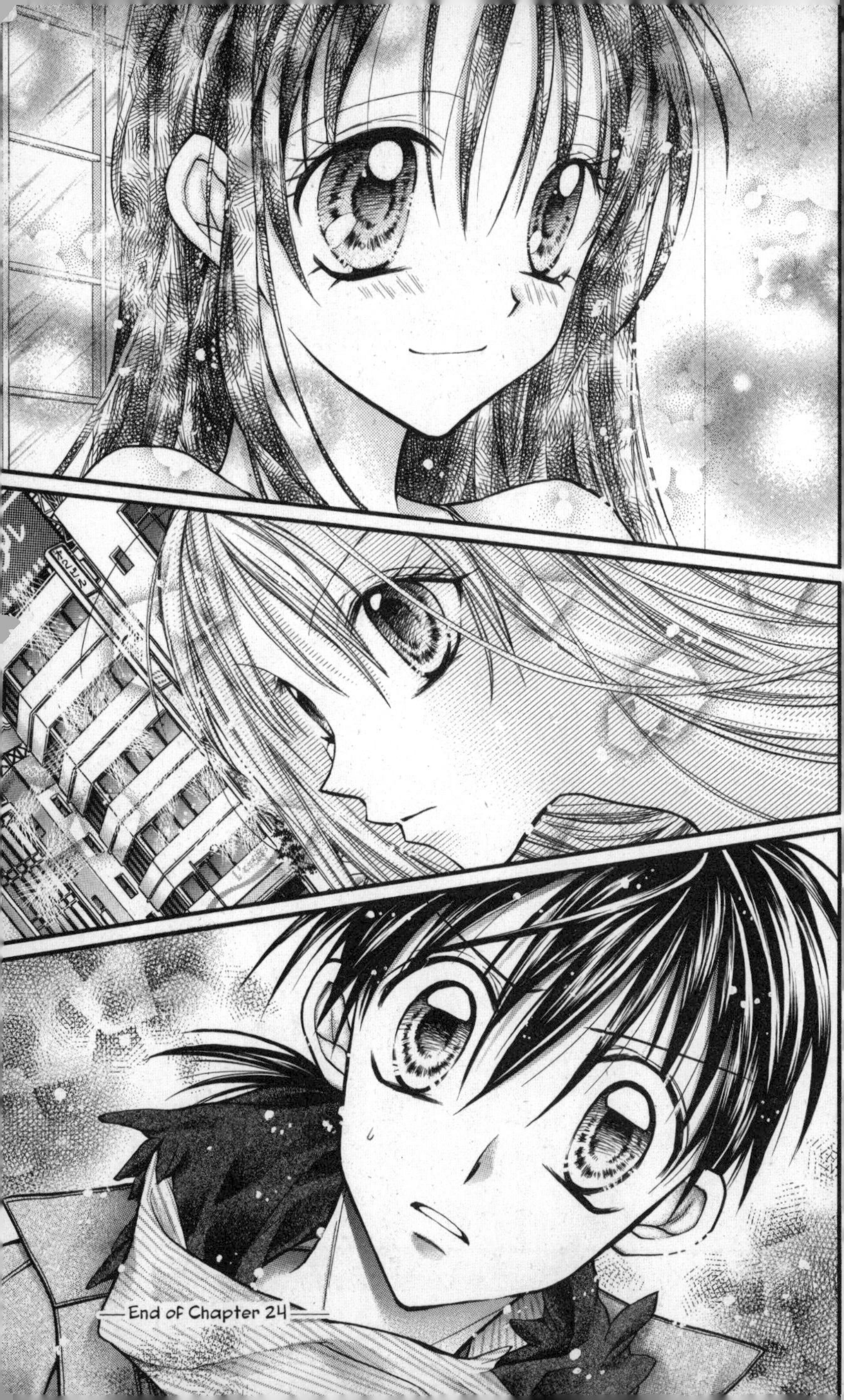
End of Chapter 24

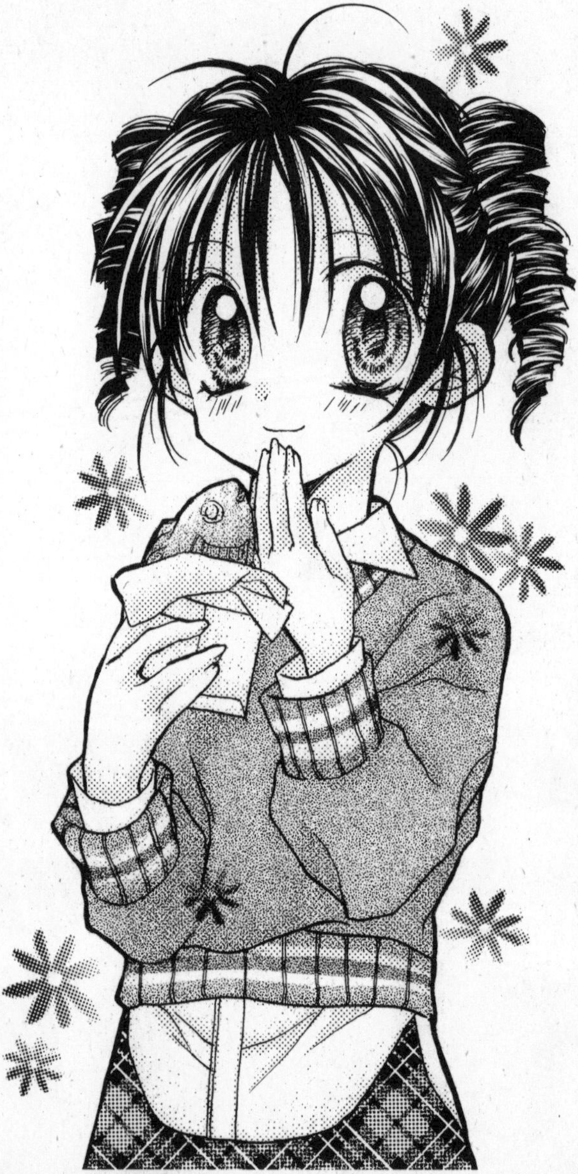

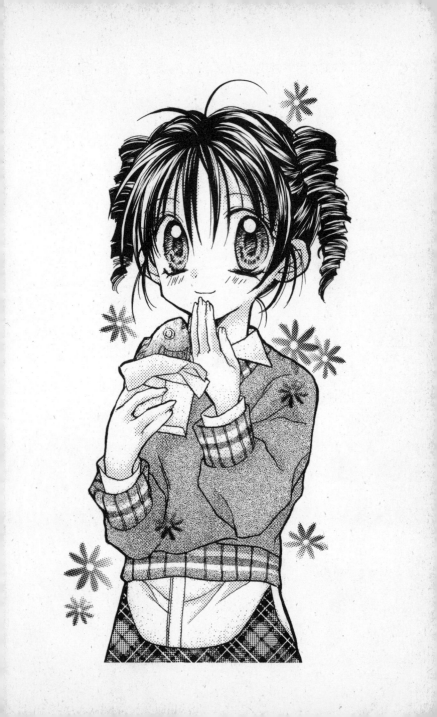

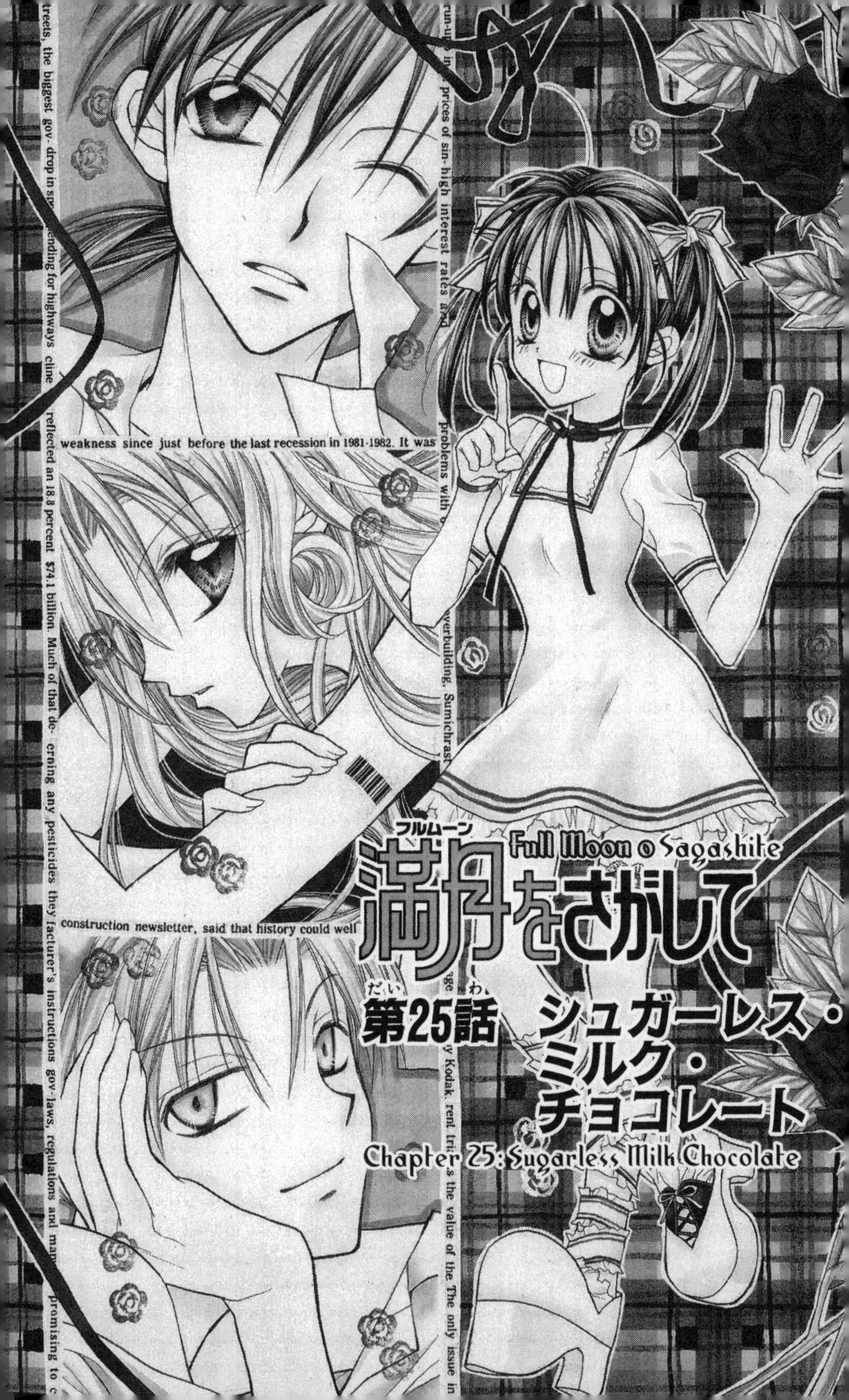

満月をさがして
Full Moon o Sagashite
第25話 シュガーレス・ミルク・チョコレート
Chapter 25: Sugarless Milk Chocolate
weakness since just before the last recession in 1981-1982. It was
construction newsletter, said that history could well

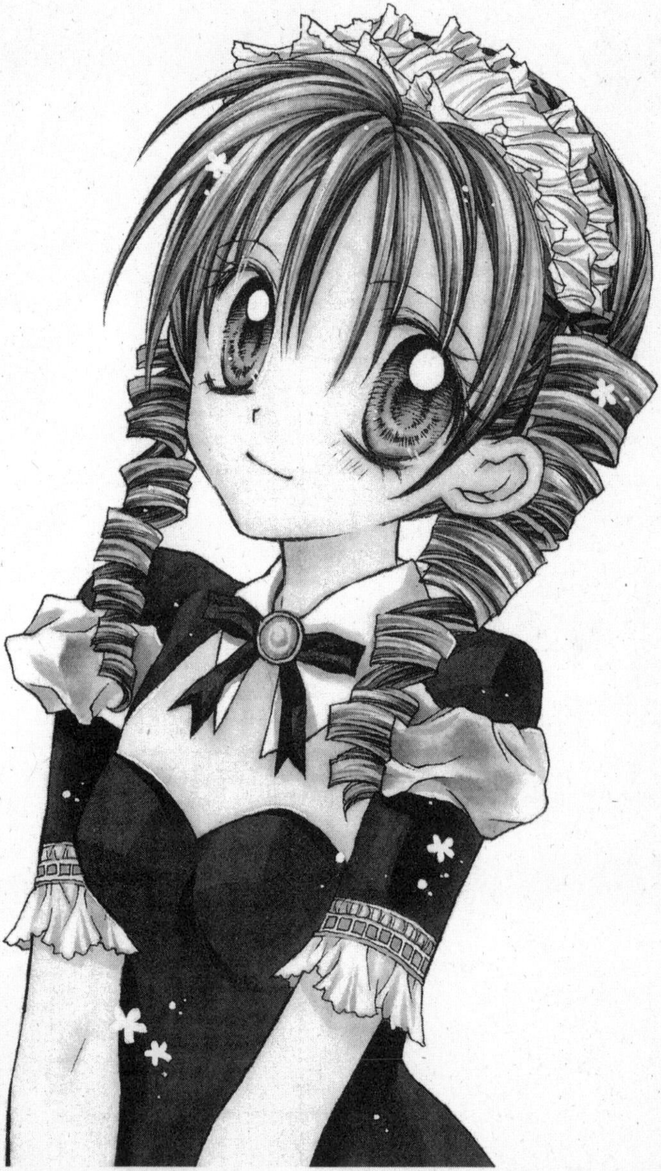

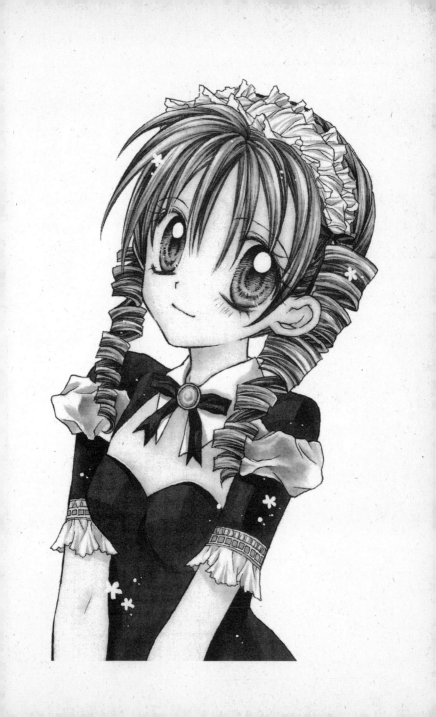

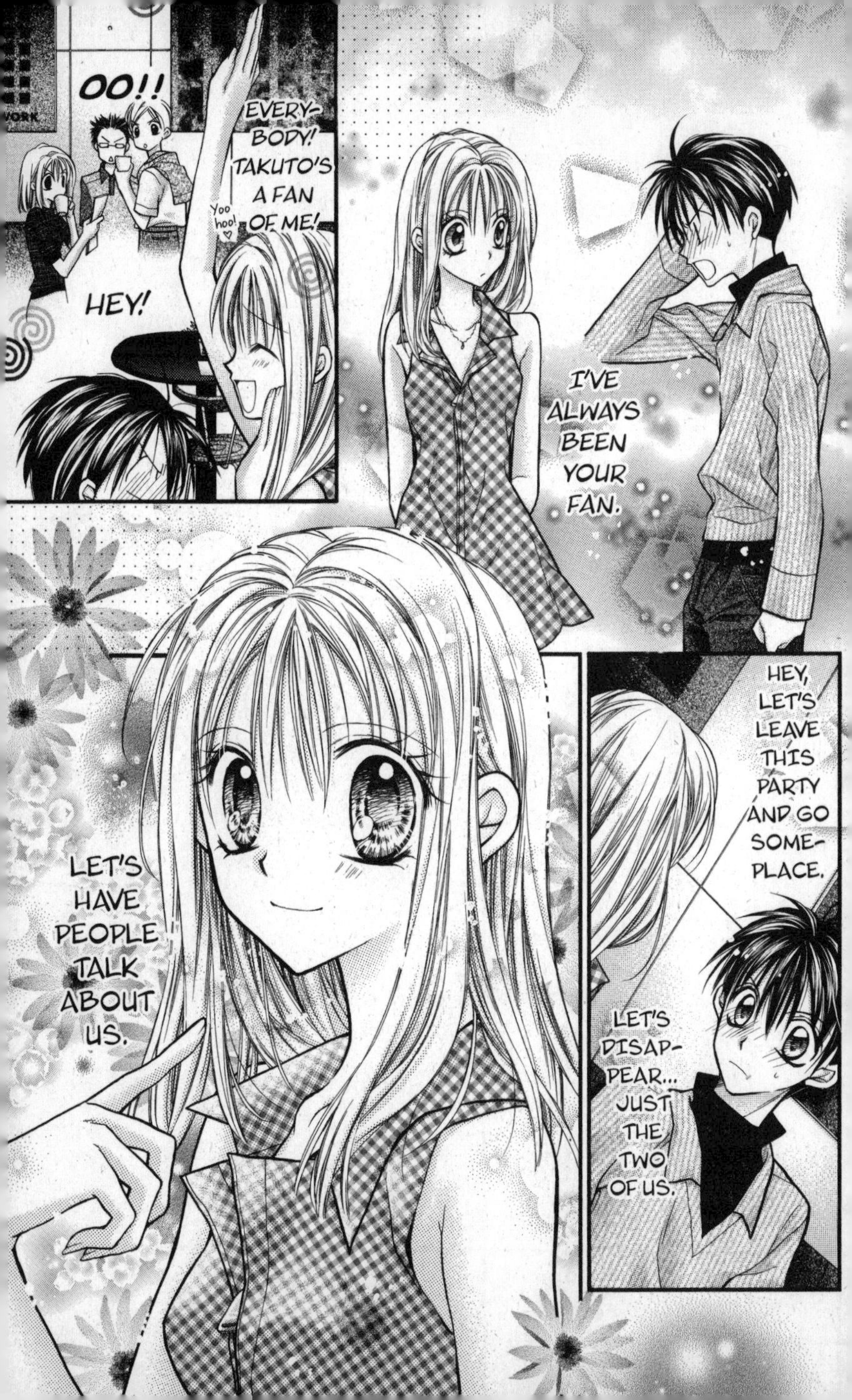
I'VE ALWAYS BEEN YOUR FAN.
EVERY-BODY! TAKUTO'S A FAN OF ME!
OO!!
Yoo hoo!
HEY!
HEY, LET'S LEAVE THIS PARTY AND GO SOME-PLACE.
LET'S DISAP-PEAR... JUST THE TWO OF US.
LET'S HAVE PEOPLE TALK ABOUT US.

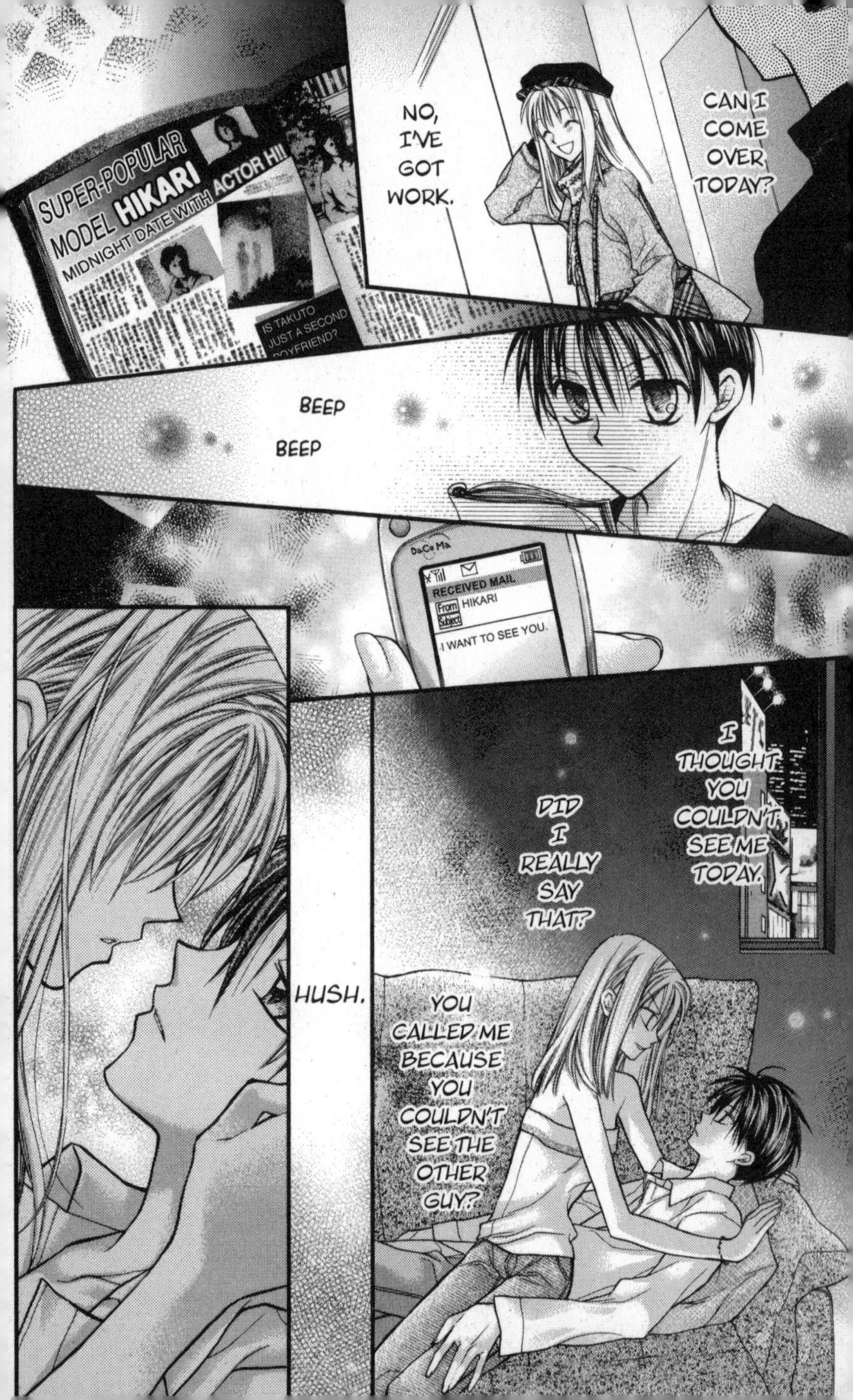
CAN I COME OVER TODAY?
NO, I'VE GOT WORK.
SUPER-POPULAR MODEL HIKARI
MIDNIGHT DATE WITH ACTOR H!!
IS TAKUTO JUST A SECOND BOYFRIEND?
BEEP
BEEP
RECEIVED MAIL
From HIKARI
Subject
I WANT TO SEE YOU.
I THOUGHT YOU COULDN'T SEE ME TODAY.
DID I REALLY SAY THAT?
YOU CALLED ME BECAUSE YOU COULDN'T SEE THE OTHER GUY?
HUSH.

Chapter 25: Sugarless Milk Chocolate

(spoilers follow)

I wrote this title because the love story is the focus. Takkun's love story made my heart flutter....///// Meroko doesn't seem to be able to forget about Izumi-kun, the guy who has no luck with women.

The Cinderella story of Wakaoji-sensei and Oshige-san is like me--how to say...um...I love shojo manga.～～.٤. Both of them work really hard, so it was good. 戸戸 Aww...

I drew the scenes for Ms. Oshige's affair softly, because I thought everybody wouldn't like it... Hmm, people didn't feel strongly either way.

The second half is this: What are you doing Takkun?! Yo!
What is that hand on her waist, you?!!
Well, I drew it but... (smile)

Oh, the scene I like (I stopped choosing pictures when there aren't any) is where Suzu-chan and Oshige-san are talking. It's good to have rivals being friendly.

Cover Copy

Sometimes, it's love that's not sweet with you... ♡

(There was a typo when this was first printed in *Ribon*. I'm sorry.)

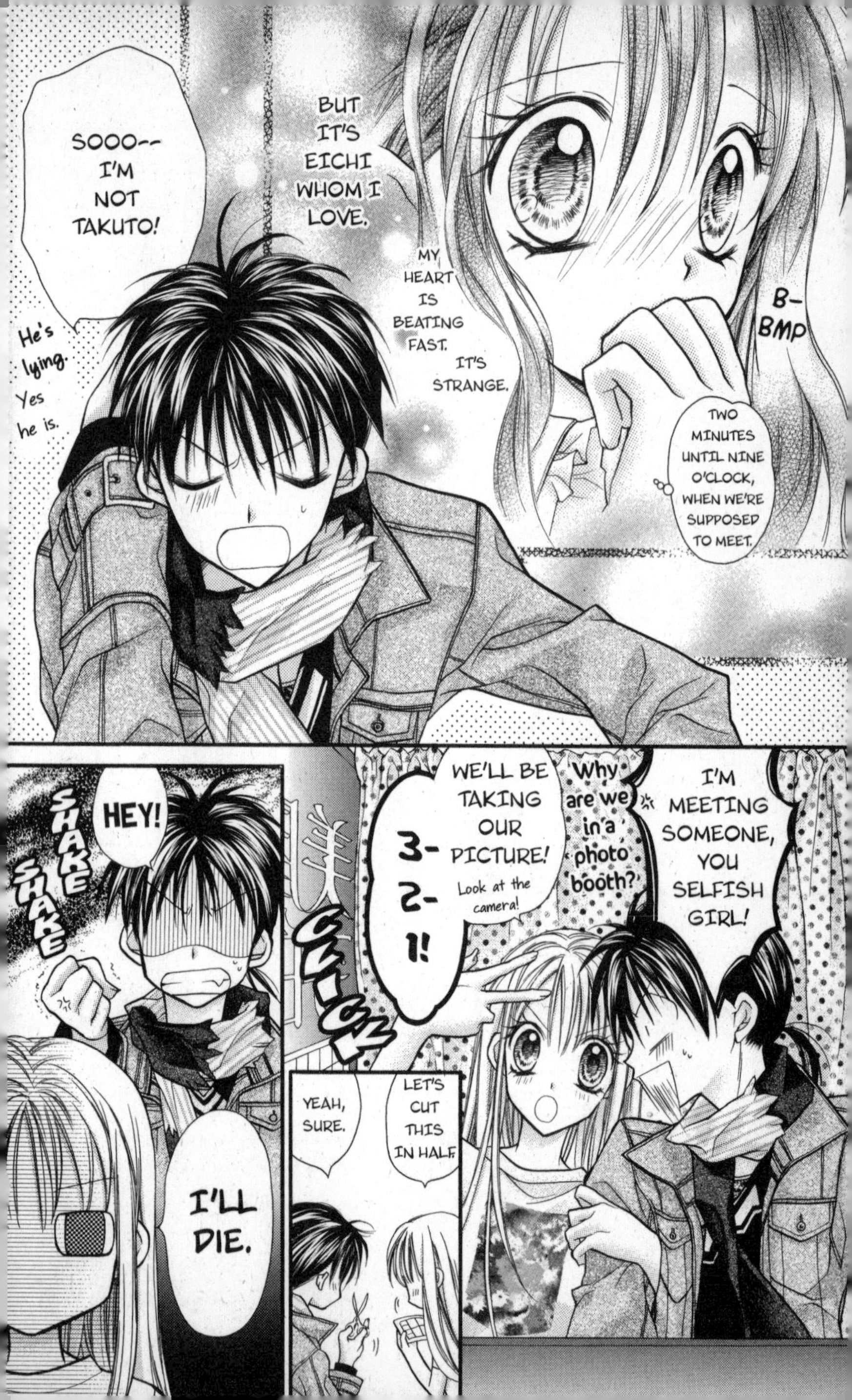
B-BMP
BUT IT'S EICHI WHOM I LOVE.
MY HEART IS BEATING FAST. IT'S STRANGE.
TWO MINUTES UNTIL NINE O'CLOCK, WHEN WE'RE SUPPOSED TO MEET.
SOOO-- I'M NOT TAKUTO!
He's lying. Yes he is.
I'M MEETING SOMEONE, YOU SELFISH GIRL!
Why are we in a photo booth?
WE'LL BE TAKING OUR PICTURE!
Look at the camera!
3- 2- 1!
CLICK
LET'S CUT THIS IN HALF.
YEAH, SURE.
HEY!
SHAKE SHAKE
I'LL DIE.

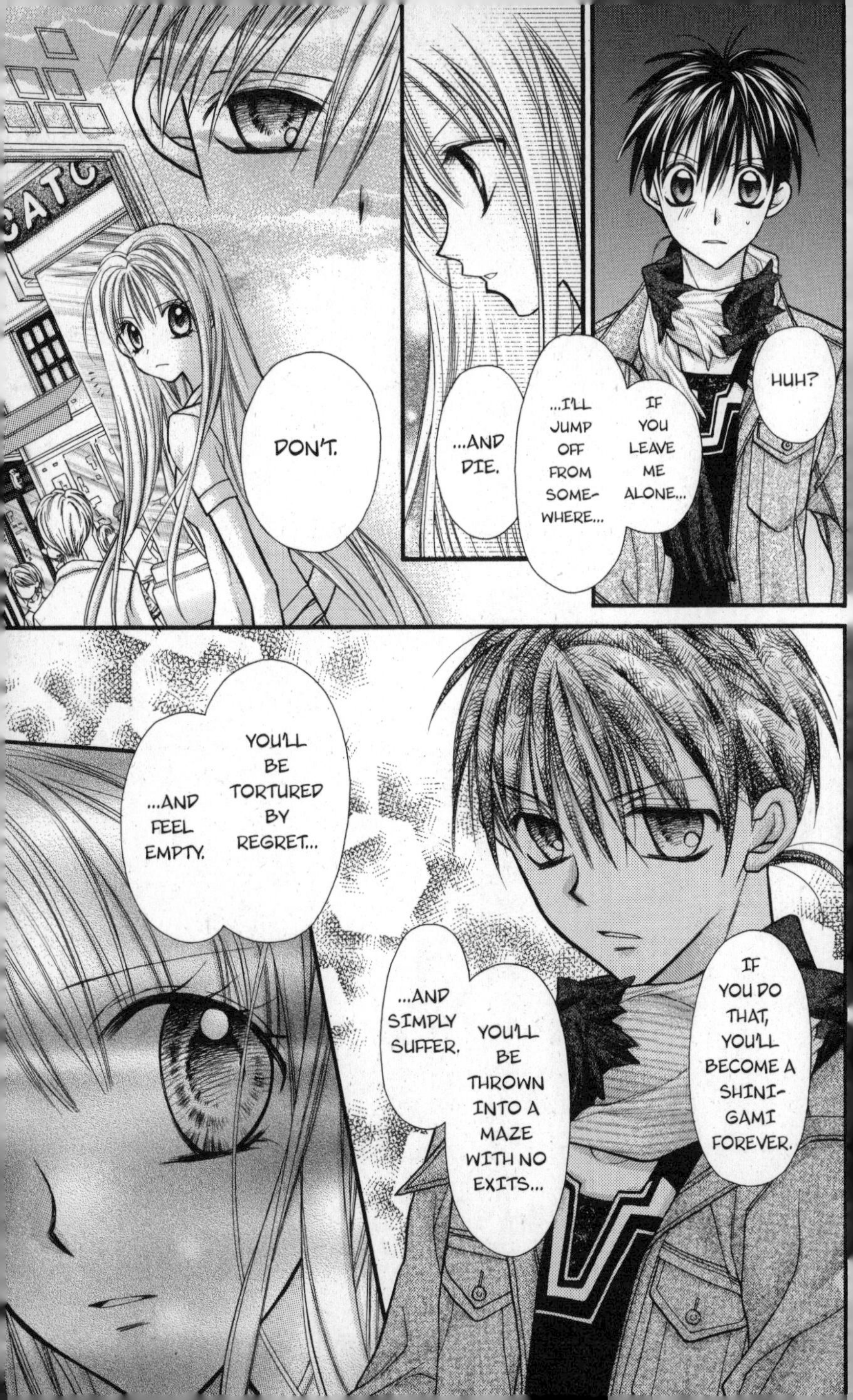
HUH?
IF YOU LEAVE ME ALONE...
...I'LL JUMP OFF FROM SOME-WHERE...
...AND DIE.
DON'T.
IF YOU DO THAT, YOU'LL BECOME A SHINI-GAMI FOREVER.
YOU'LL BE THROWN INTO A MAZE WITH NO EXITS...
...AND SIMPLY SUFFER.
YOU'LL BE TORTURED BY REGRET...
...AND FEEL EMPTY.

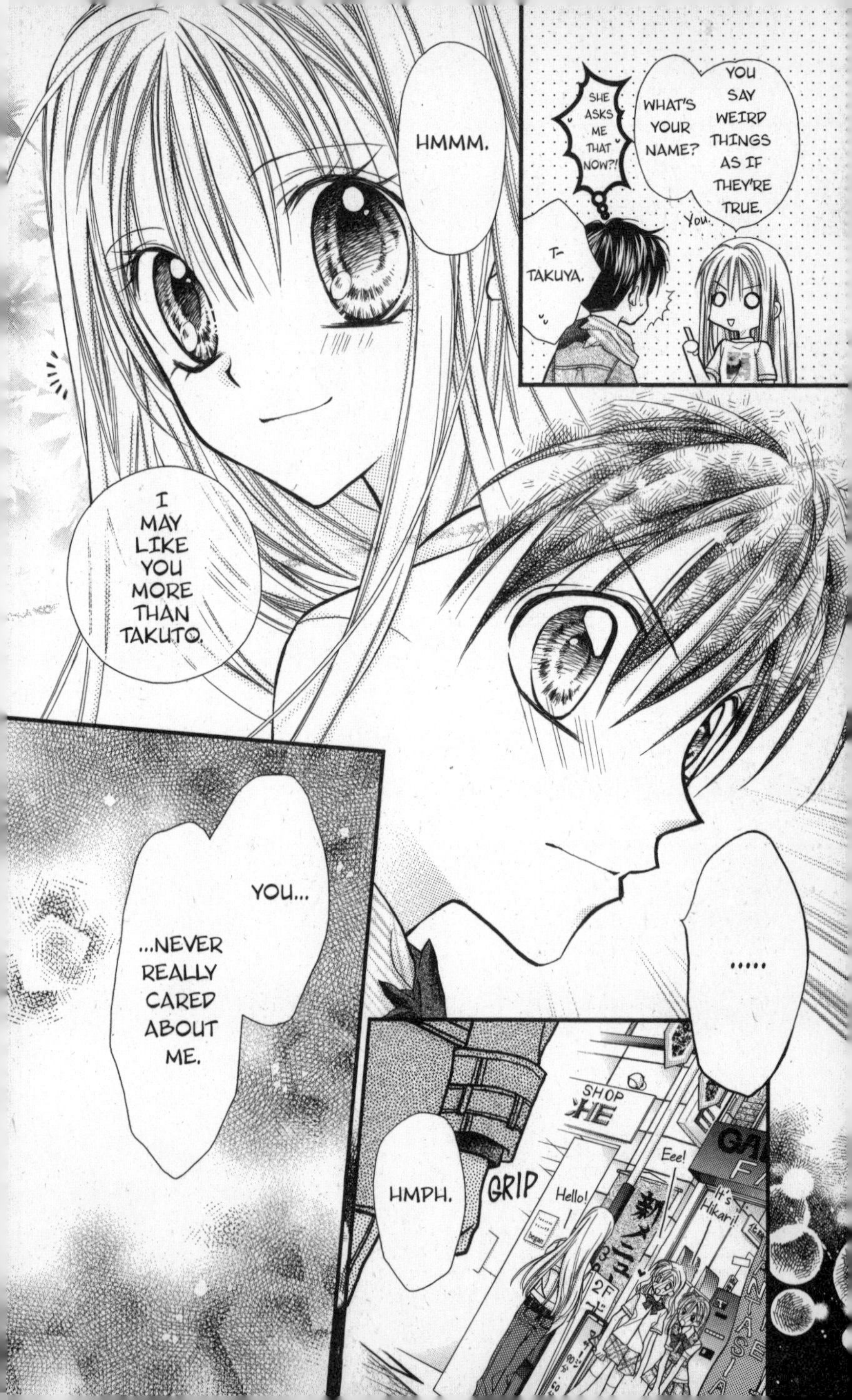
YOU SAY WEIRD THINGS AS IF THEY'RE TRUE.
You.
WHAT'S YOUR NAME?
SHE ASKS ME THAT NOW?!
T-TAKUYA.
HMMM.
I MAY LIKE YOU MORE THAN TAKUTO.
.....
It's Hikari!
Eee!
Hello!
SHOP
GRIP
HMPH.
YOU...
...NEVER REALLY CARED ABOUT ME.

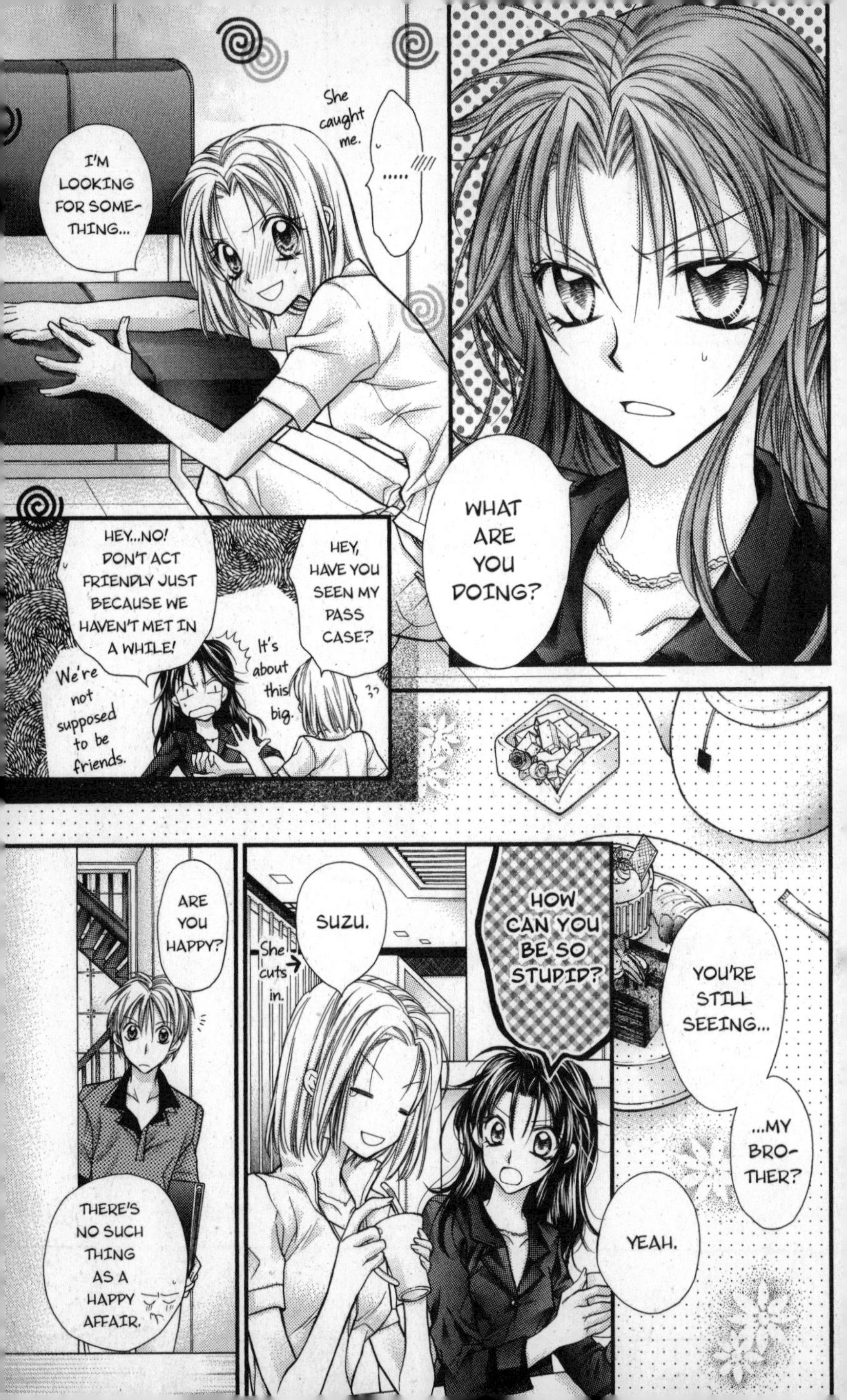
WHAT ARE YOU DOING?
She caught me.
.....
I'M LOOKING FOR SOME-THING...
HEY, HAVE YOU SEEN MY PASS CASE?
It's about this big.
HEY...NO! DON'T ACT FRIENDLY JUST BECAUSE WE HAVEN'T MET IN A WHILE!
We're not supposed to be friends.
YOU'RE STILL SEEING...
...MY BRO-THER?
YEAH.
HOW CAN YOU BE SO STUPID?
SUZU.
She cuts in.
ARE YOU HAPPY?
THERE'S NO SUCH THING AS A HAPPY AFFAIR.

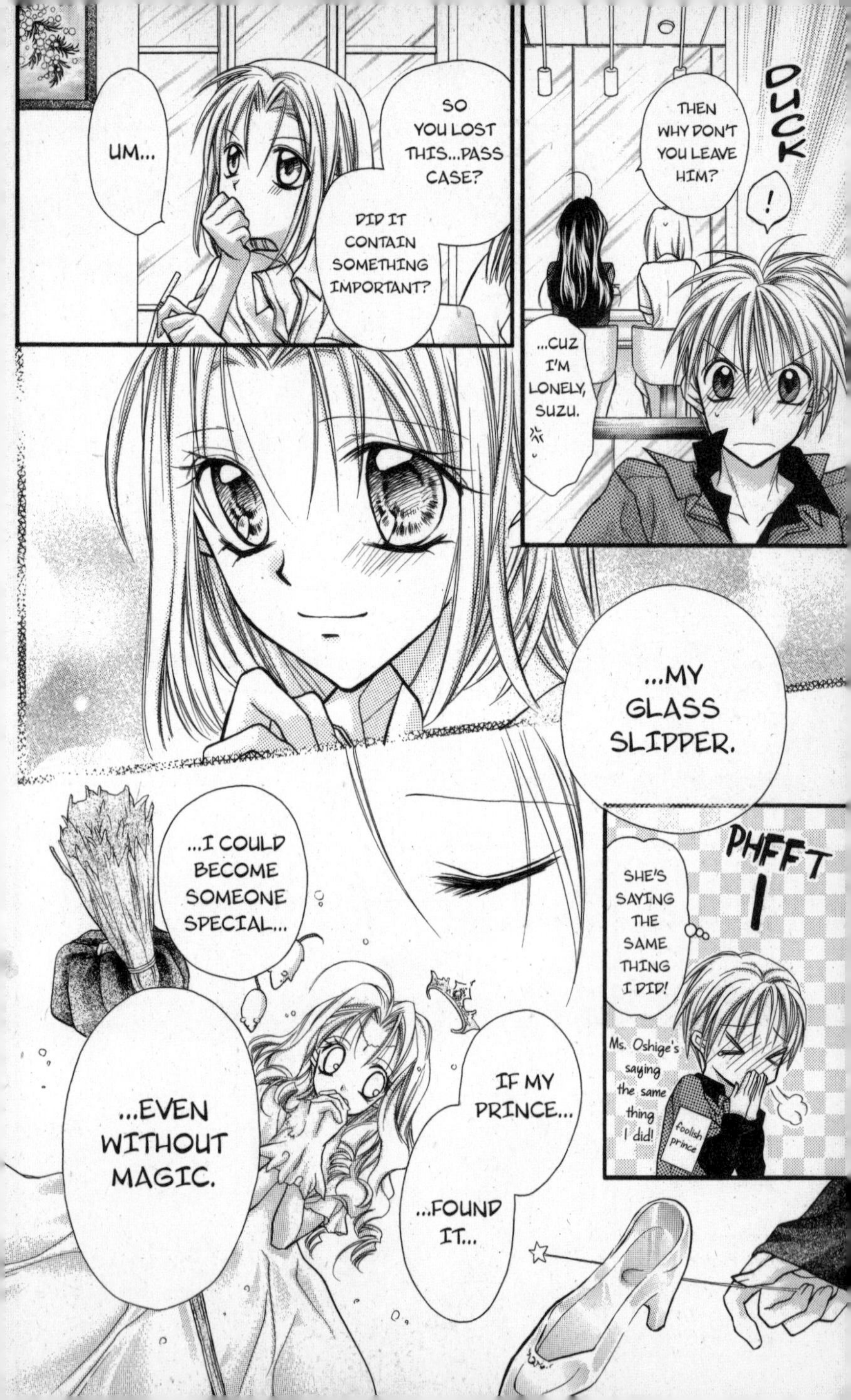
DUCK
THEN WHY DON'T YOU LEAVE HIM?
!
...CUZ I'M LONELY, SUZU.
SO YOU LOST THIS...PASS CASE?
DID IT CONTAIN SOMETHING IMPORTANT?
UM...
...MY GLASS SLIPPER.
PHFFT !
SHE'S SAYING THE SAME THING I DID!
Ms. Oshige's saying the same thing I did!
foolish prince
IF MY PRINCE...
...FOUND IT...
...I COULD BECOME SOMEONE SPECIAL...
...EVEN WITHOUT MAGIC.

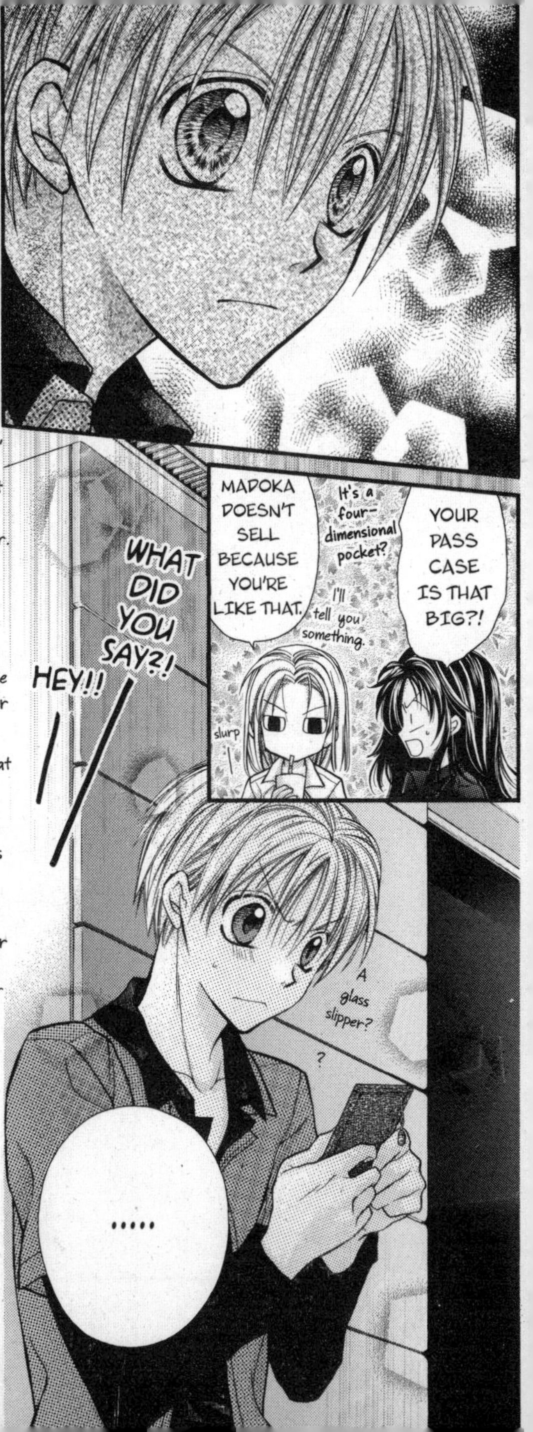
YOUR PASS CASE IS THAT BIG?!
It's a four-dimensional pocket?
I'll tell you something.
MADOKA DOESN'T SELL BECAUSE YOU'RE LIKE THAT.
slurp
WHAT DID YOU SAY?!
HEY!!
A glass slipper?
?
.....

About the Letters I Receive

Thank you always for the letters and the emails from the website!

Well, the last chapter is approaching, and I'd like to put some letters here with my comments. (Because of space constraints, I can't print entire letters. Sorry!)

← I didn't write it in full.

♪I'm Y's father. I'm writing this email for my daughter. As I'm typing this in, my daughter, who's sitting beside me and looking at the display, is asking me to put in one more thing: "Whatdo I have to do so that I can draw well like Tanemura-sensei? Please tell me." Please tell her. From the father and daughter in Sakihama.

(Ari) This is heartwarming. About the question. This is the most frequently asked question since I've become a mangaka. (I think other mangakas get asked this a lot too.)

I answer differently every time. That is because there are many answers. My answers are

- Draw every day. Draw many types of things--everything that you can see.
- Read maps. (This is to develop your space-recognition abilities.)
  ← For example, find where you are now, or decide where you want to go, and walk.
- Go to a school that teaches you how to sketch. (I haven't gone to one, by the way.)
- Go see good paintings and good movies. Get good stimulation.

That's about it.

Since when I was little, I wasn't good at drawing while looking at something. To copy and become good is easy and fast, but you tend to lose your originality.

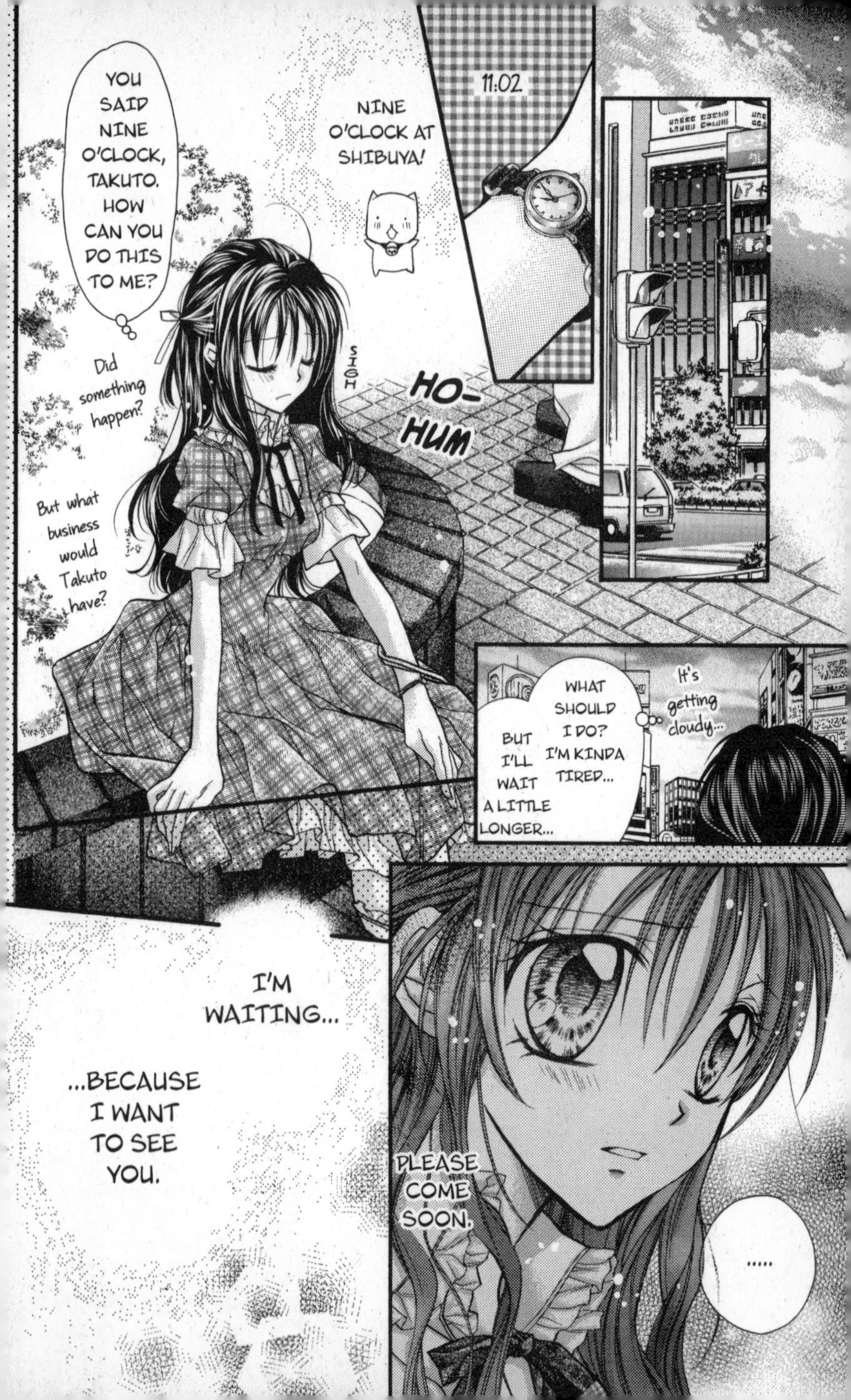
11:02
It's getting cloudy...
WHAT SHOULD I DO? I'M KINDA TIRED...
BUT I'LL WAIT A LITTLE LONGER...
NINE O'CLOCK AT SHIBUYA!
YOU SAID NINE O'CLOCK, TAKUTO. HOW CAN YOU DO THIS TO ME?
SIGH
HO-HUM
Did something happen?
But what business would Takuto have?
.....
PLEASE COME SOON.
I'M WAITING...
...BECAUSE I WANT TO SEE YOU.

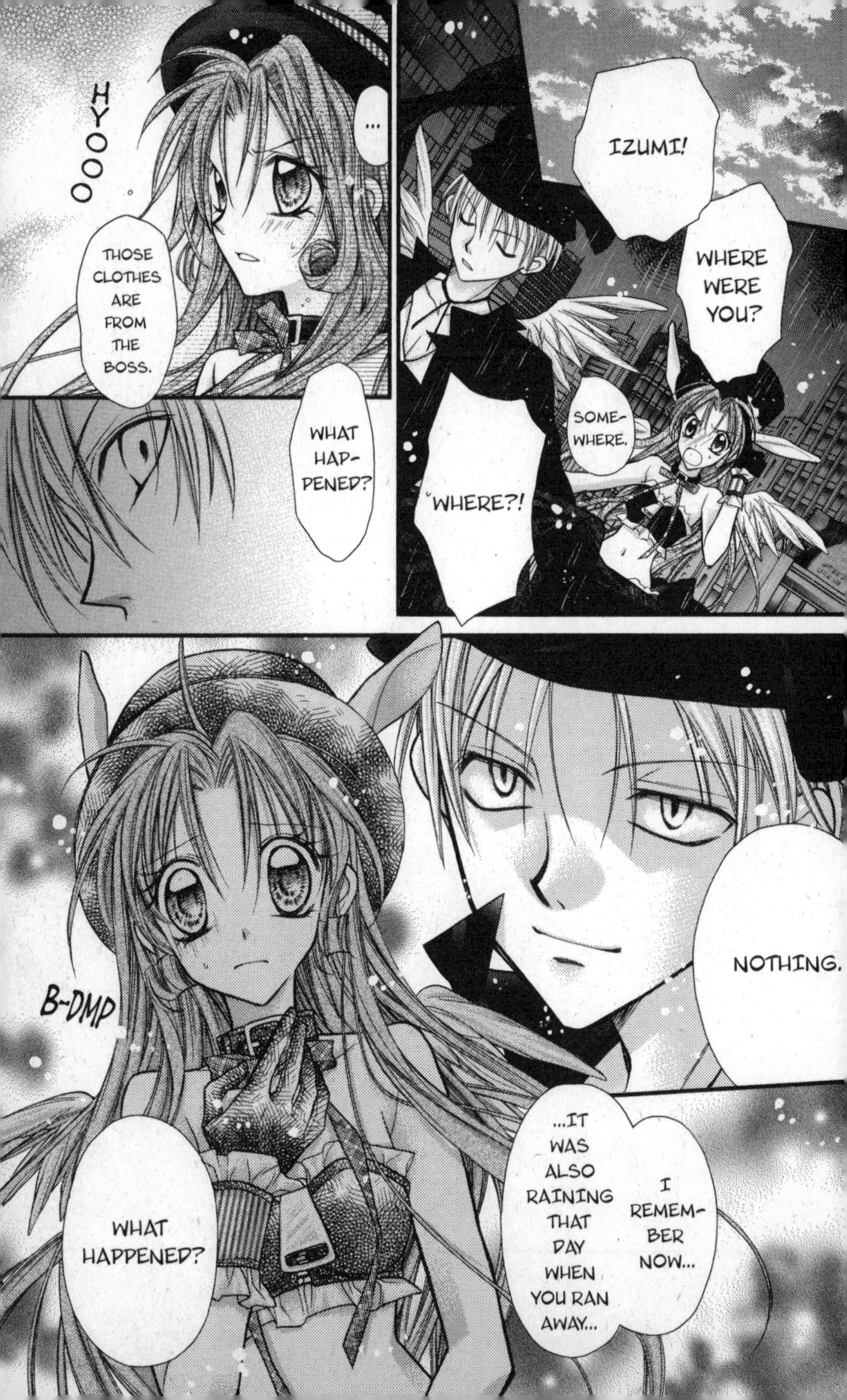
IZUMI!
WHERE WERE YOU?
SOME-WHERE.
WHERE?!
HYOOOO
...
THOSE CLOTHES ARE FROM THE BOSS.
WHAT HAP-PENED?
NOTHING.
B-DMP
I REMEM-BER NOW...
...IT WAS ALSO RAINING THAT DAY WHEN YOU RAN AWAY...
WHAT HAPPENED?

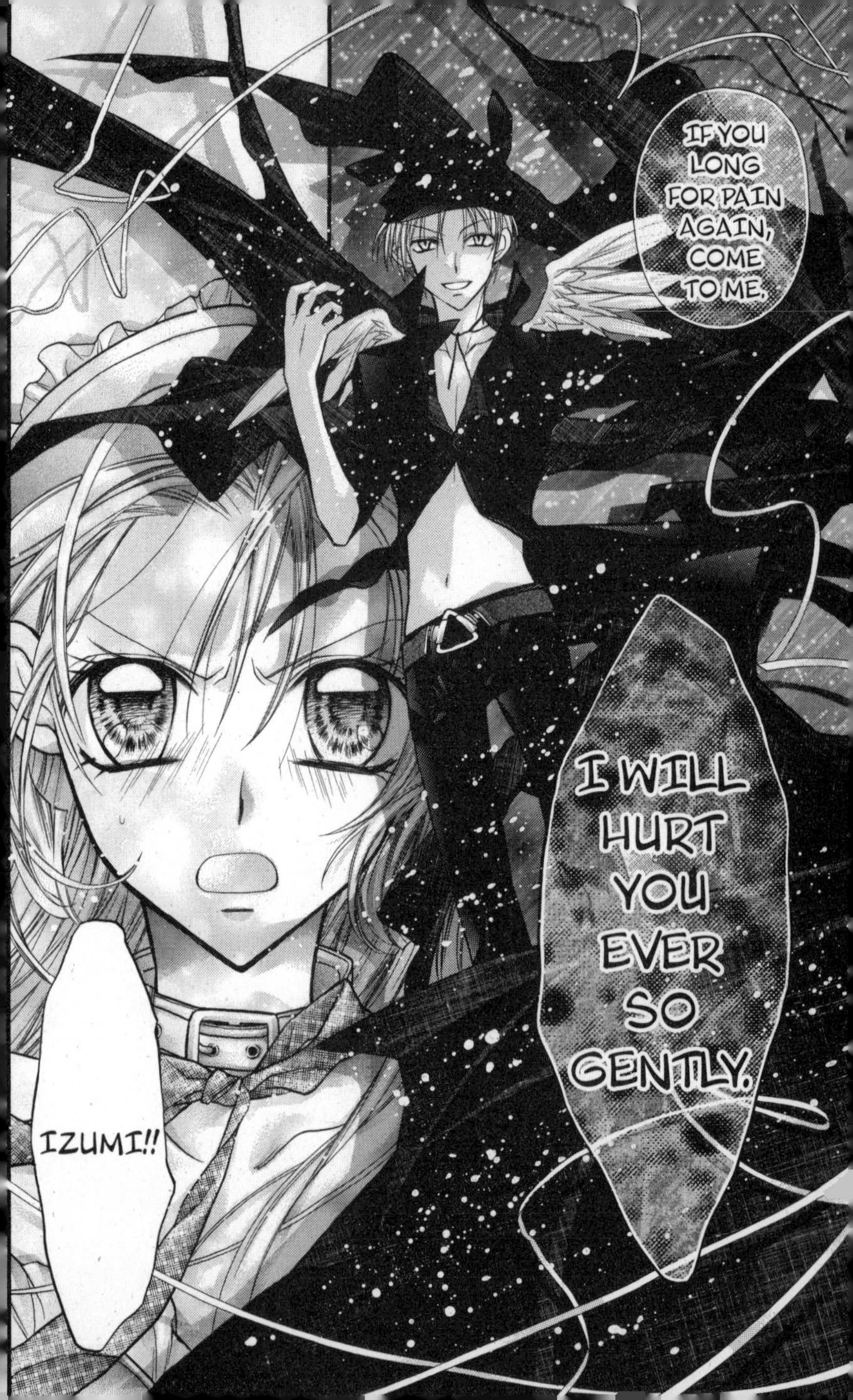
IF YOU LONG FOR PAIN AGAIN, COME TO ME.
I WILL HURT YOU EVER SO GENTLY.
IZUMI!!

About the Letters I Receive 2

♪Hello. I'm writing this email because there's something I'd like to say to Tanemura-san. The other day I read Kyoko and was like, ?Huh?!!? I read the sidebar you wrote about FF10. How you take the ending of 10 depends on the person, and I think there are different opinions. I like Tanemura-san and 10, so Tanemura-san's comment criticizing 10 was a shock to me.

[Ari] The second half (I didn't put that here) was emotional, so I let it slide. Um, this is an email from a 15-year-old who is a third-year in junior high.

I played it last week too!!
What? I like 10?!! An appeal!!

I didn't criticize it?!!
(Somehow these kinds of words, everyone uses them too often without actually understanding the true meaning. I have to be careful too.⌒)
It's all right! I love it!!
I love 10 and 9 both!!

(There are RPGs that I played but didn't quite like. I don't write about them. Not that I dislike them.)
There are things I like in them.

Just because I wasn't convinced by the ending doesn't mean that I didn't like it. No, no.
But I'm sorry if my comments hurt you. I hadn't thought about that.⌒
(And regarding this incident, I just wanted to correct the misunderstanding. I'm not angry at you at all. I'm more open-minded than people think I am.)⌒
So, that's that. Oh I hope the sender is reading this.

!

TMP

IT'S
NOTHING.

Really.

OH...

...
SORRY.

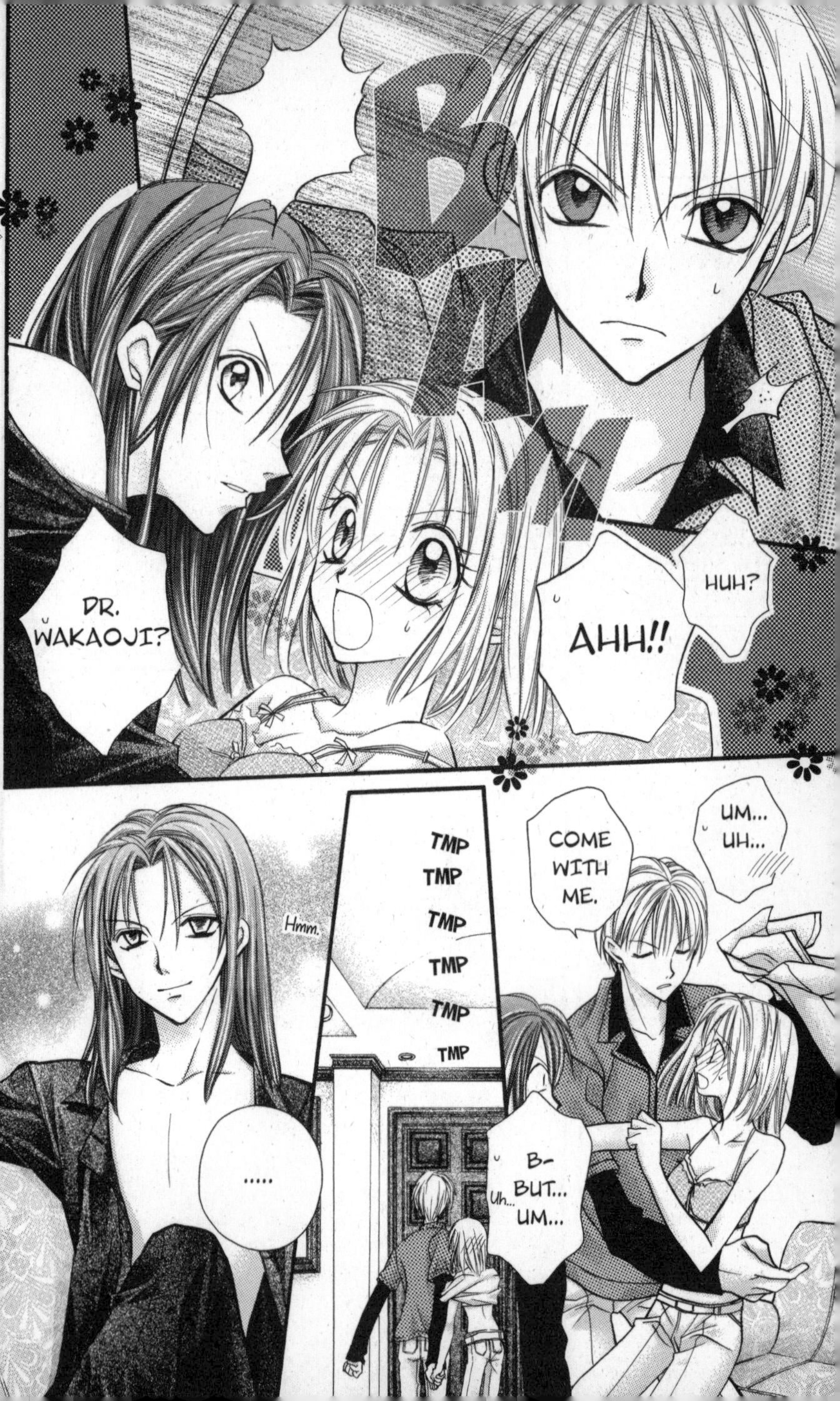
BAM
HUH?
AHH!!
DR. WAKAOJI?
UM... UH...
COME WITH ME.
B- BUT... UM...
Uh...
TMP TMP TMP TMP TMP TMP
Hmm.
.....

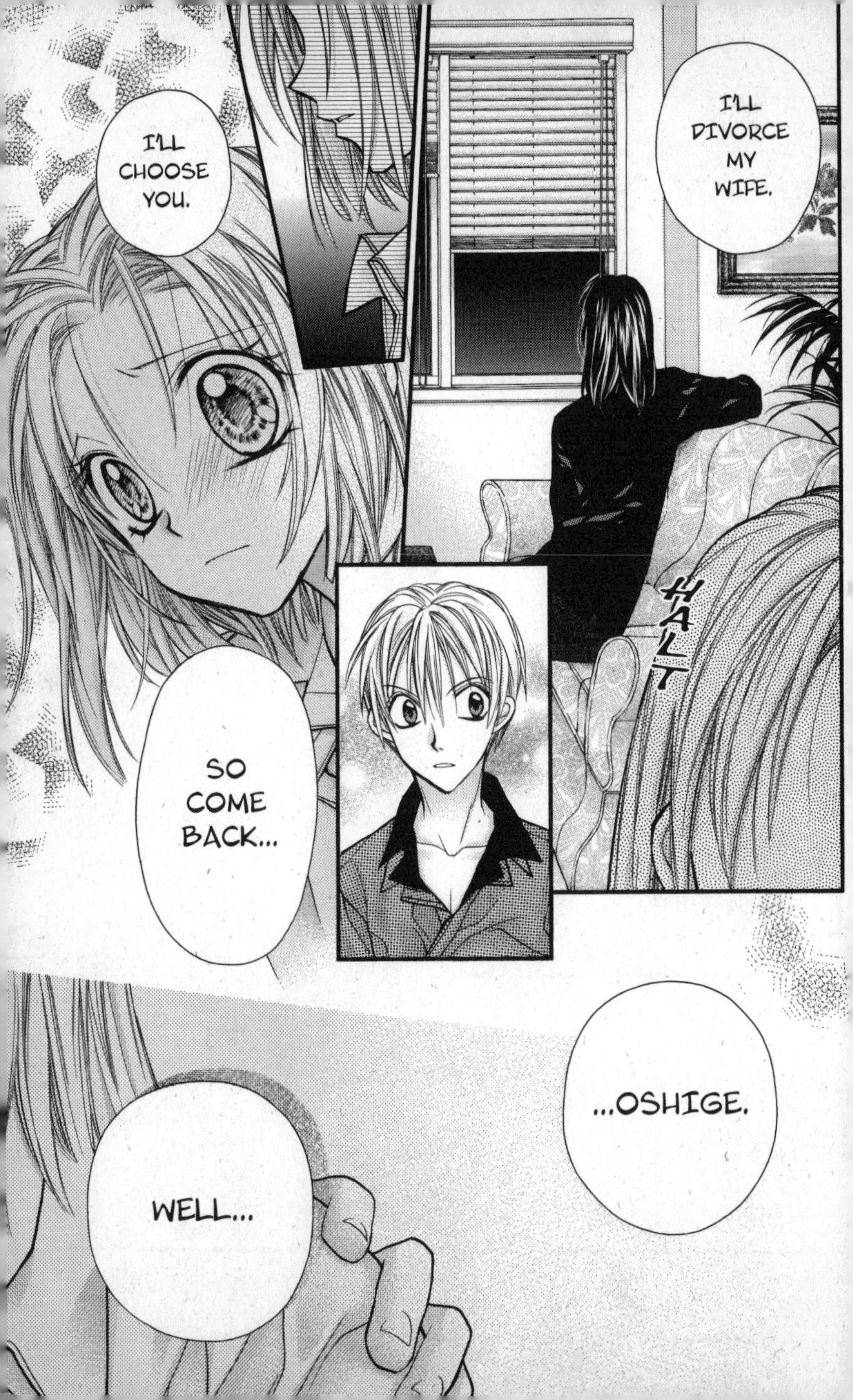
I'LL DIVORCE MY WIFE.
HALT
I'LL CHOOSE YOU.
SO COME BACK...
...OSHIGE.
WELL...

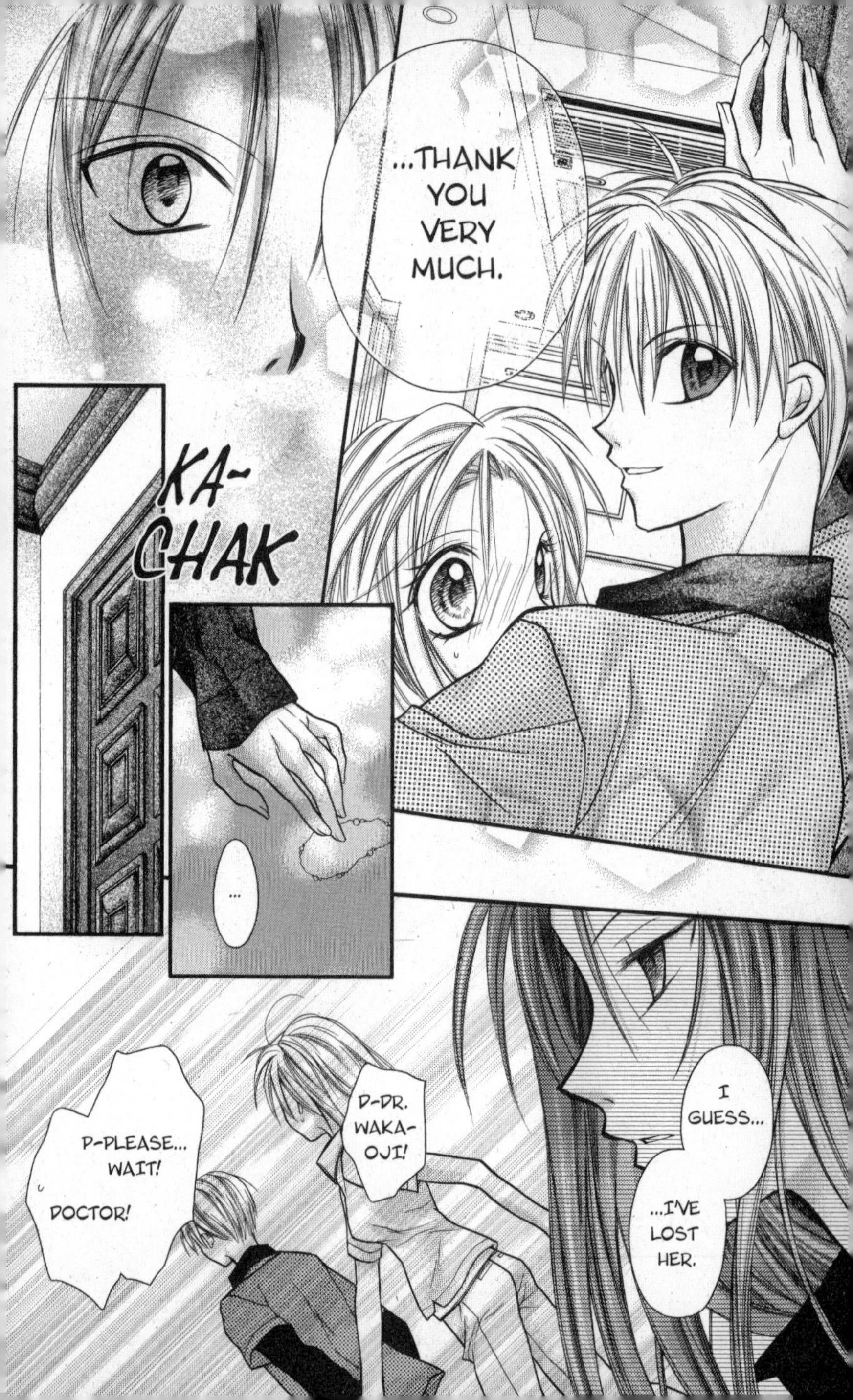
...THANK YOU VERY MUCH.
...
KA-CHAK
I GUESS...
...I'VE LOST HER.
D-DR. WAKAOJI!
P-PLEASE... WAIT!
DOCTOR!

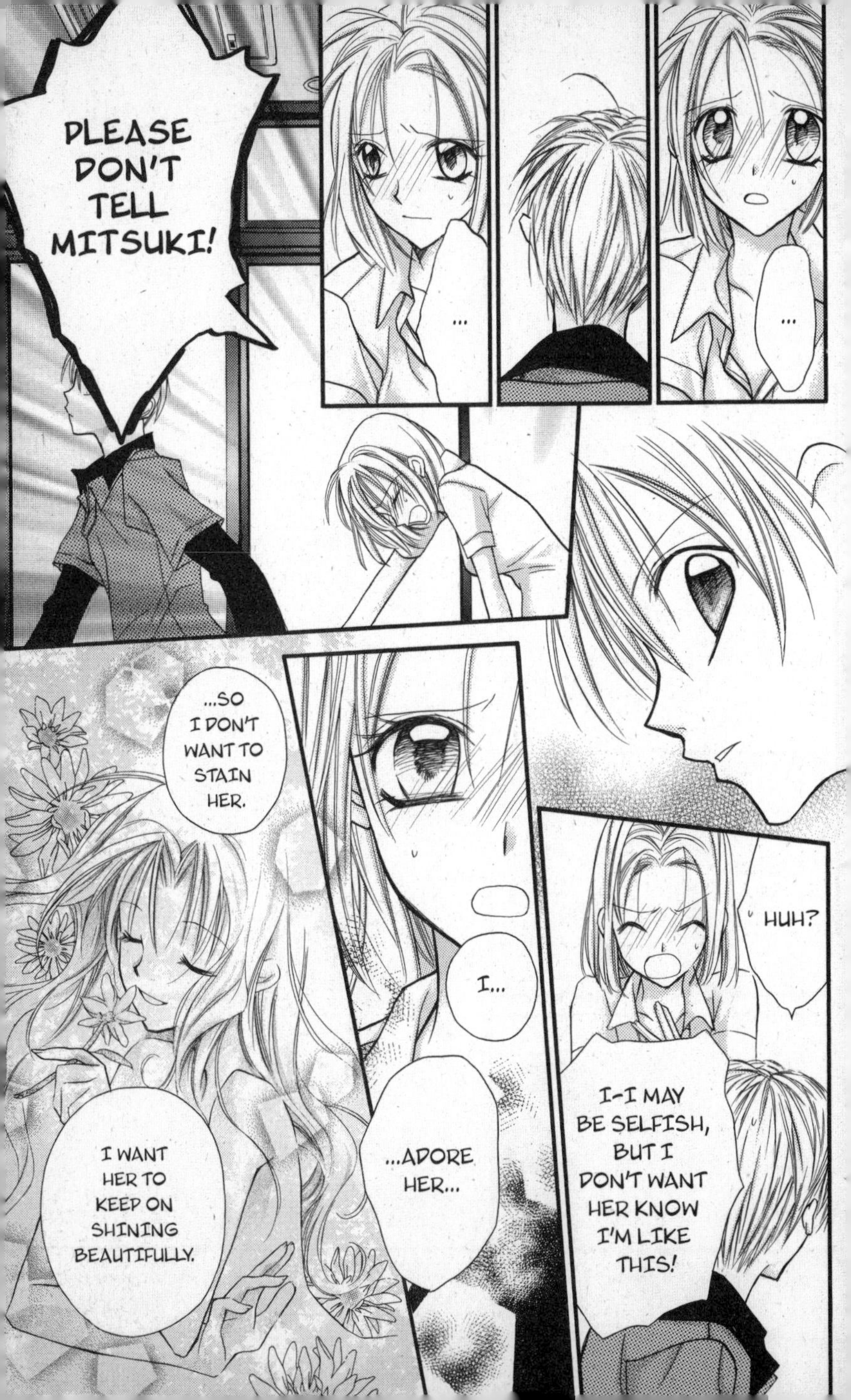
...
...
PLEASE DON'T TELL MITSUKI!
HUH?
I-I MAY BE SELFISH, BUT I DON'T WANT HER KNOW I'M LIKE THIS!
I...
...ADORE HER...
...SO I DON'T WANT TO STAIN HER.
I WANT HER TO KEEP ON SHINING BEAUTIFULLY.

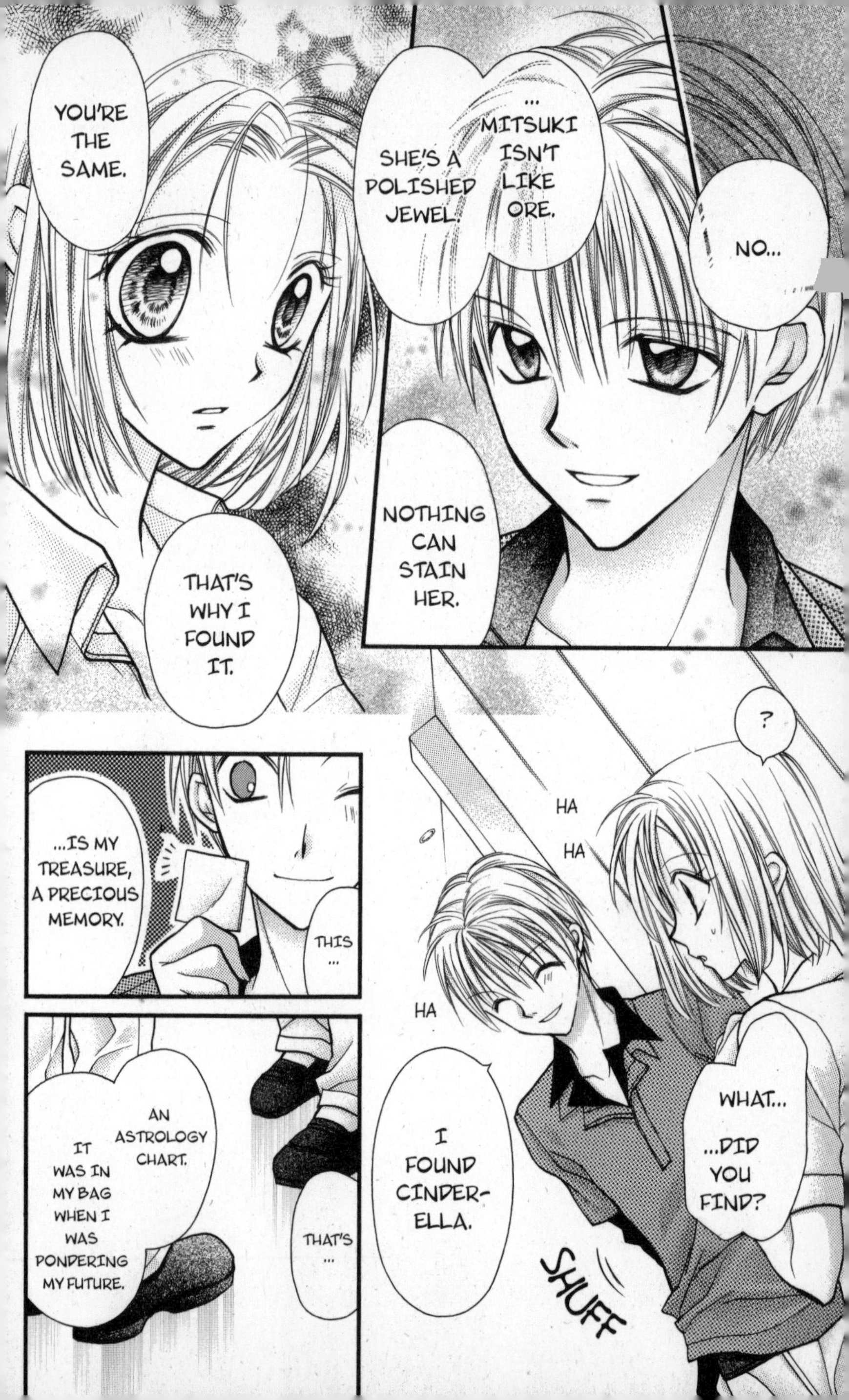
NO...
... MITSUKI ISN'T LIKE ORE.
SHE'S A POLISHED JEWEL.
NOTHING CAN STAIN HER.
YOU'RE THE SAME.
THAT'S WHY I FOUND IT.
?
HA HA
HA
WHAT...
...DID YOU FIND?
I FOUND CINDER-ELLA.
SHUFF
THIS ...
...IS MY TREASURE, A PRECIOUS MEMORY.
THAT'S ...
AN ASTROLOGY CHART.
IT WAS IN MY BAG WHEN I WAS PONDERING MY FUTURE.

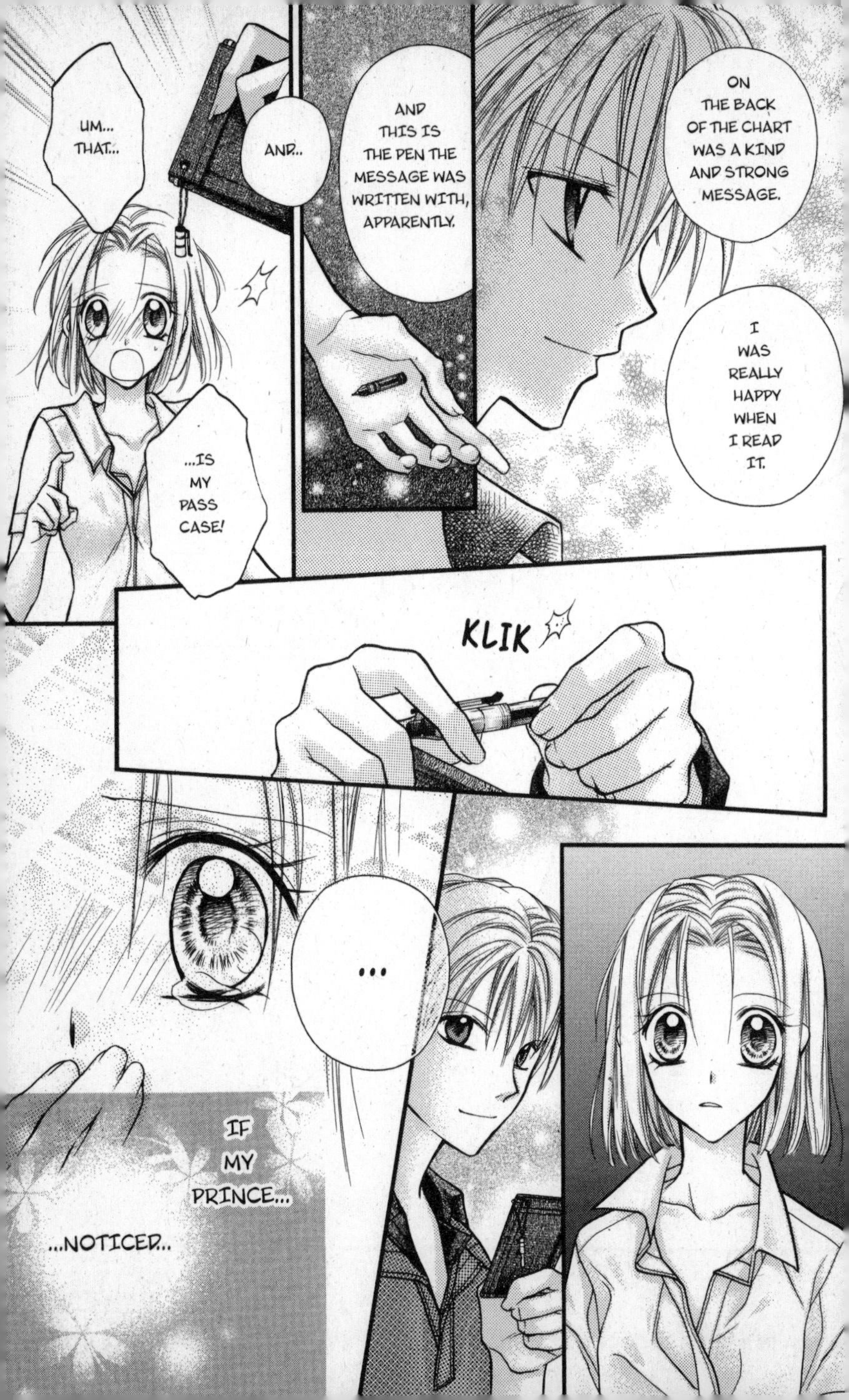
ON THE BACK OF THE CHART WAS A KIND AND STRONG MESSAGE.
I WAS REALLY HAPPY WHEN I READ IT.
AND THIS IS THE PEN THE MESSAGE WAS WRITTEN WITH, APPARENTLY.
AND...
UM... THAT...
...IS MY PASS CASE!
KLIK
...
IF MY PRINCE...
...NOTICED...

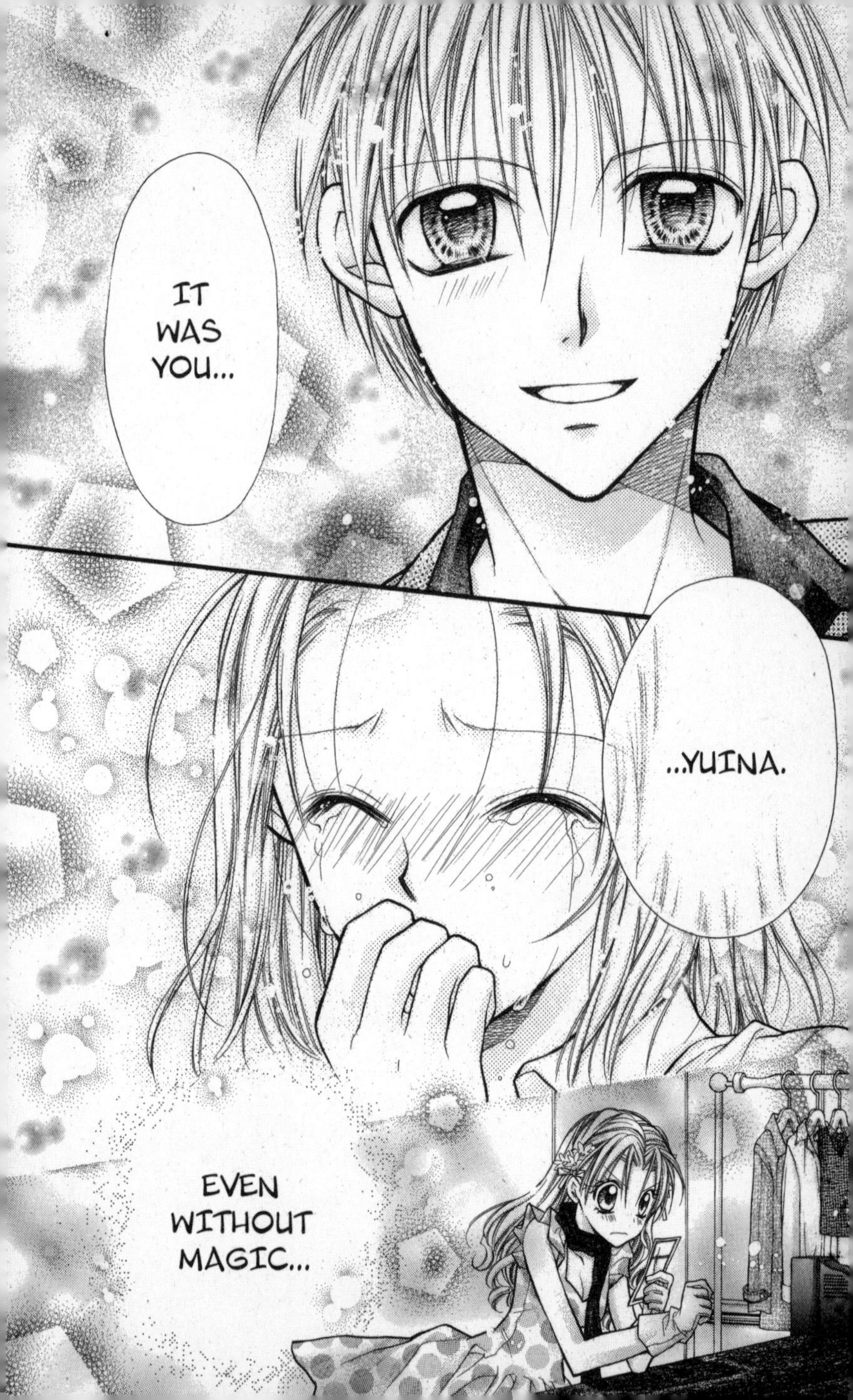
IT WAS YOU...
...YUINA.
EVEN WITHOUT MAGIC...

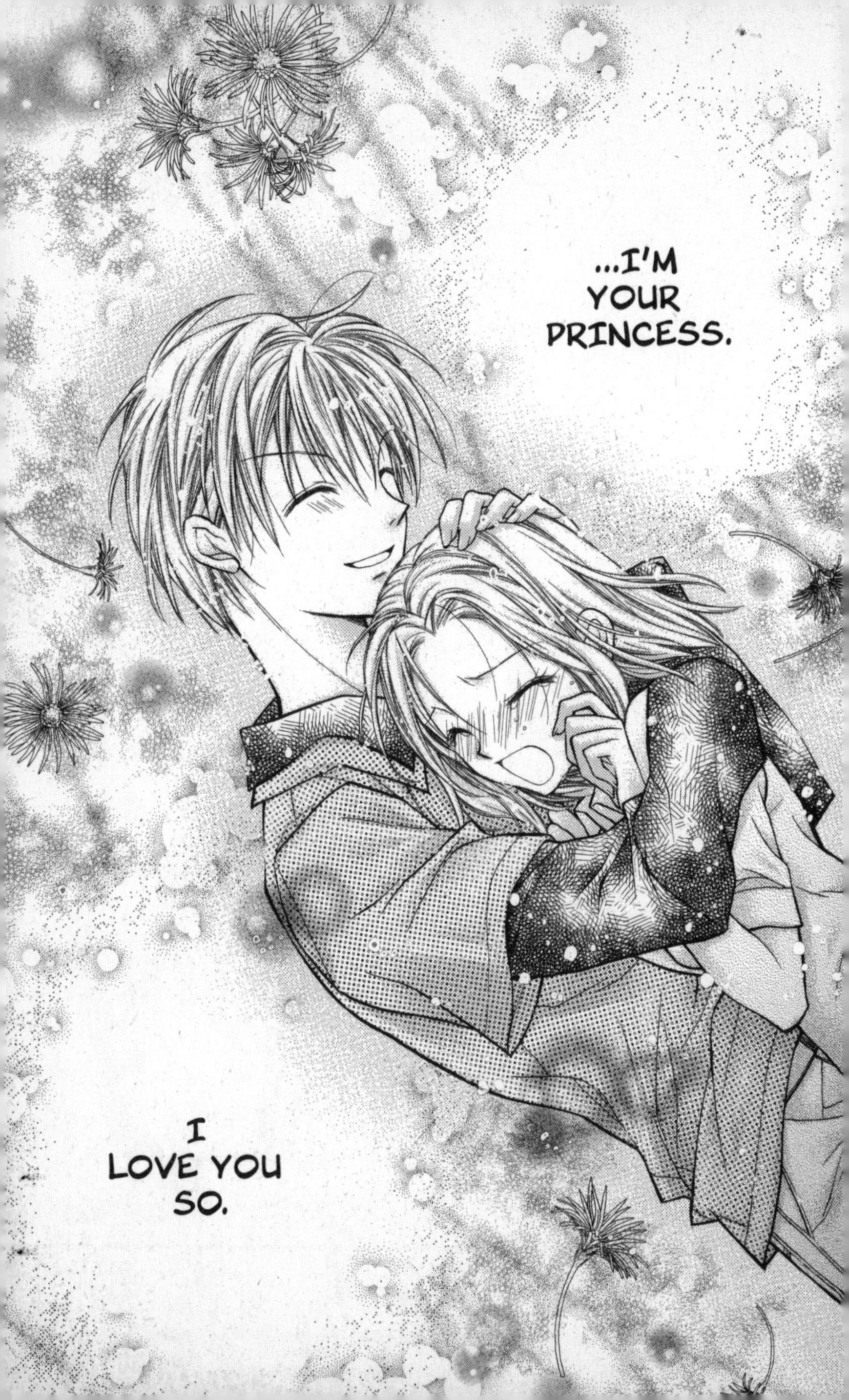
...I'M YOUR PRINCESS.
I LOVE YOU SO.

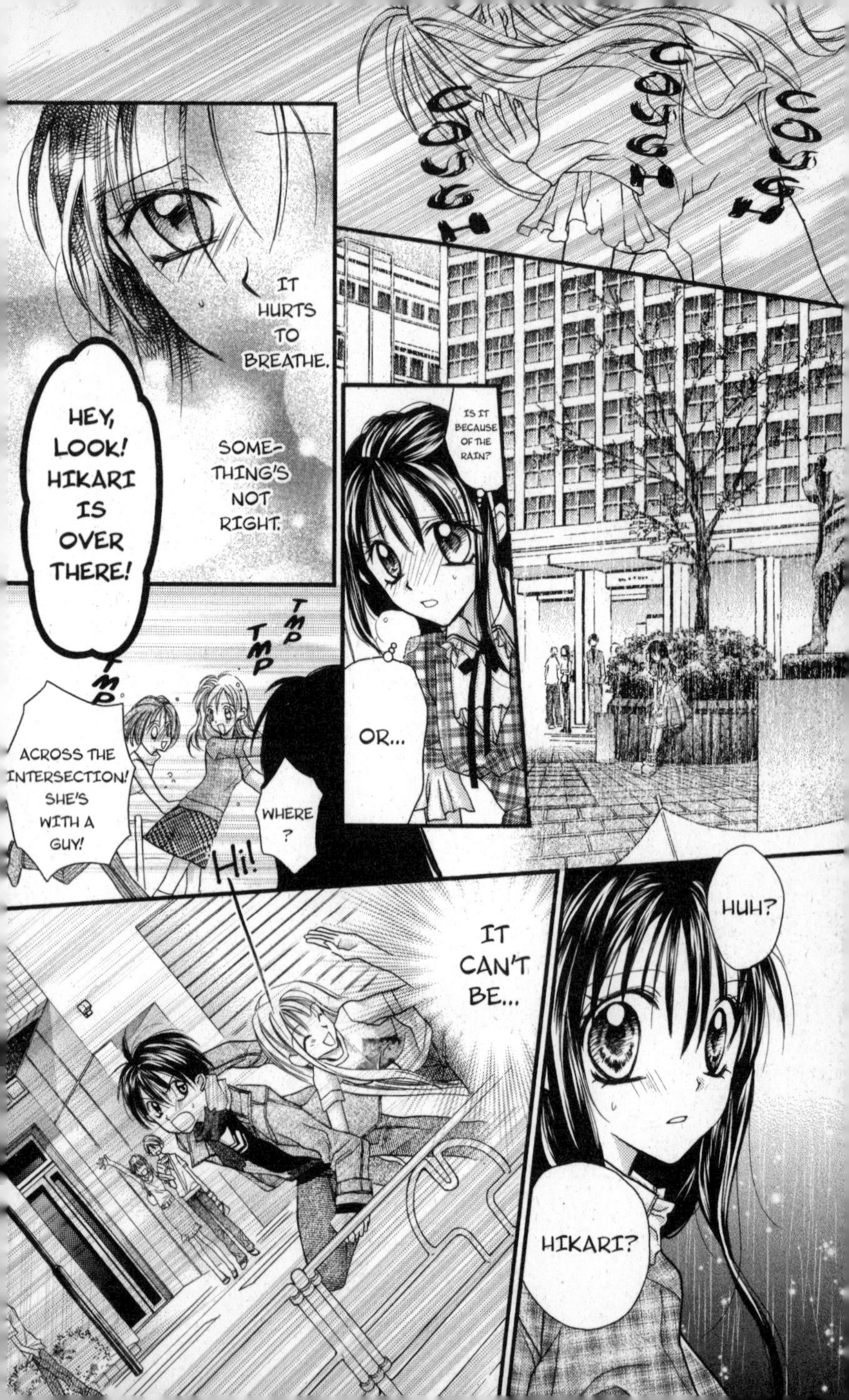
COUGH
COUGH
COUGH
IT HURTS TO BREATHE.
SOME-THING'S NOT RIGHT.
IS IT BECAUSE OF THE RAIN?
OR...
HEY, LOOK! HIKARI IS OVER THERE!
TMP
TMP
TMP
WHERE?
ACROSS THE INTERSECTION! SHE'S WITH A GUY!
HUH?
HIKARI?
IT CAN'T BE...
Hi!

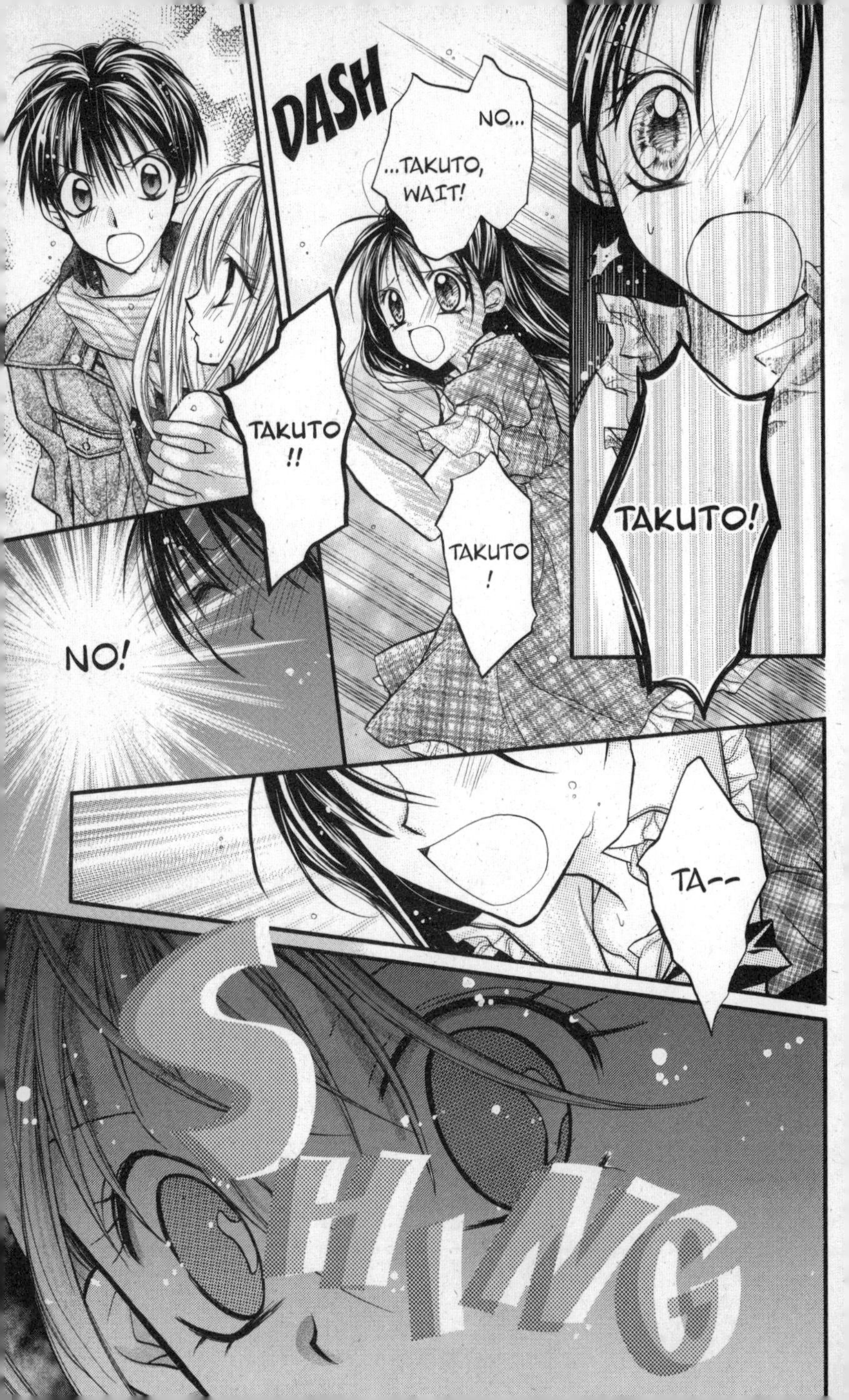
TAKUTO!
DASH
NO...
...TAKUTO, WAIT!
TAKUTO !
TAKUTO !!
NO!
TA--

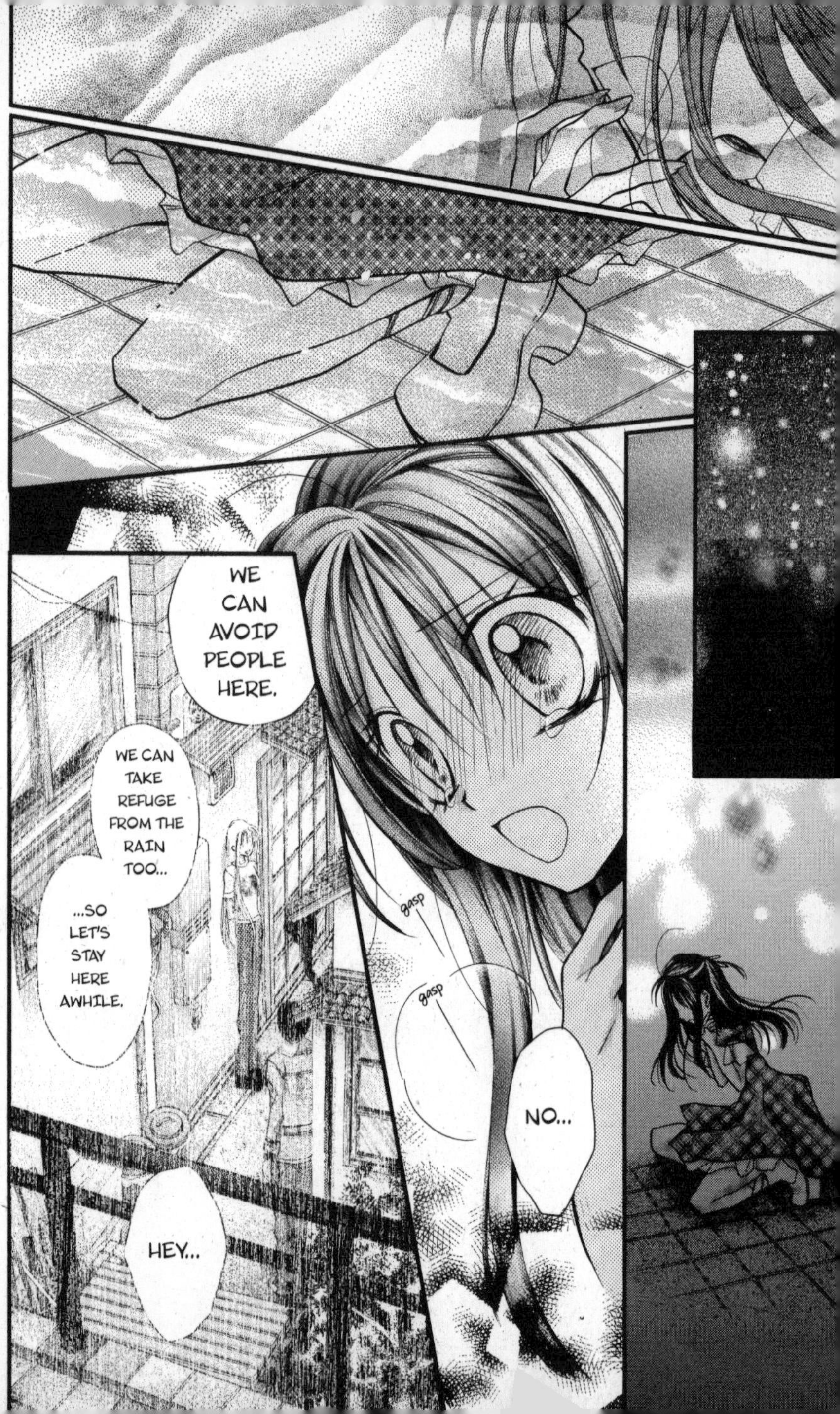
gasp
gasp
NO...
WE CAN AVOID PEOPLE HERE.
WE CAN TAKE REFUGE FROM THE RAIN TOO...
...SO LET'S STAY HERE AWHILE.
HEY...

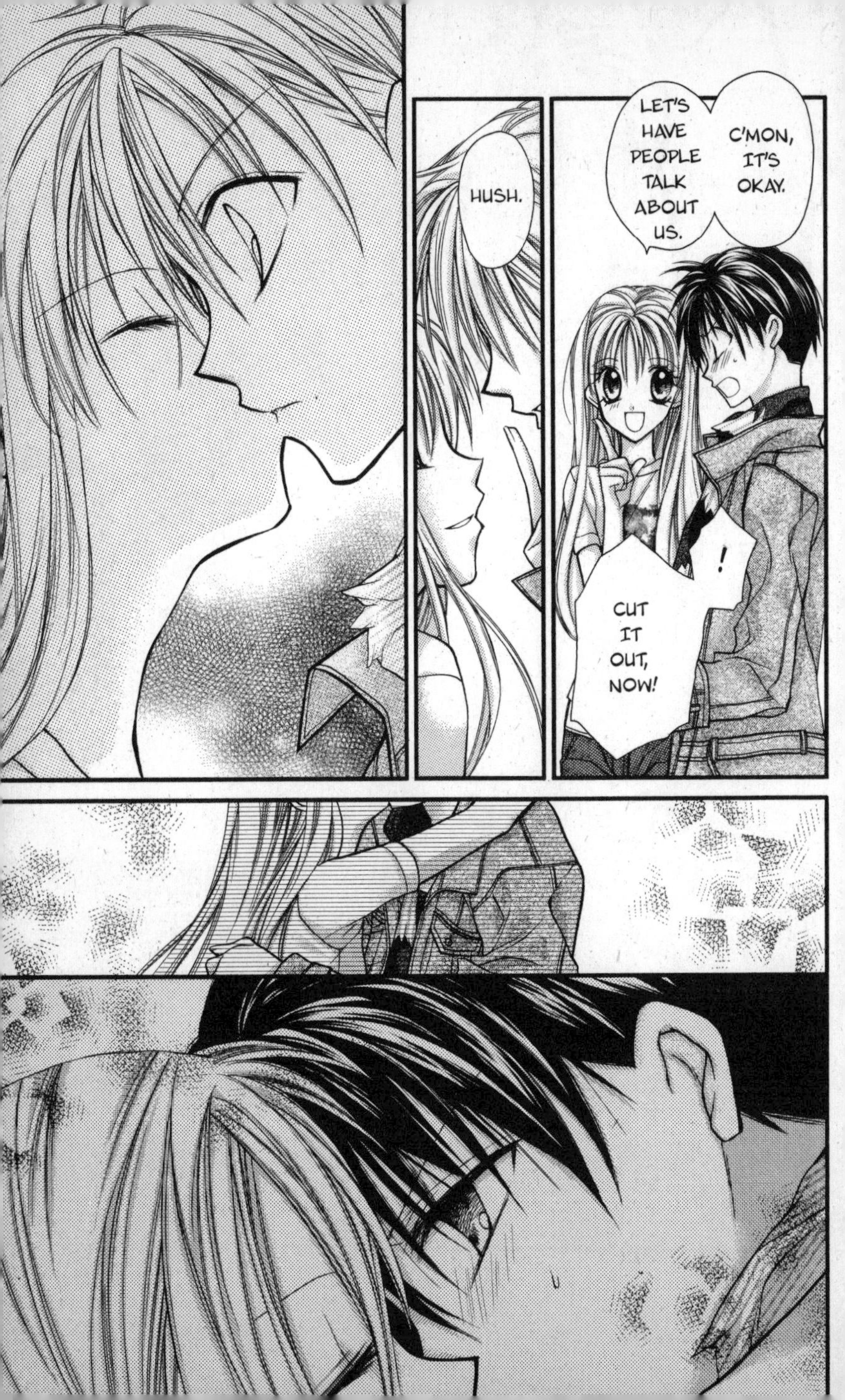
C'MON, IT'S OKAY.
LET'S HAVE PEOPLE TALK ABOUT US.
!
CUT IT OUT, NOW!
HUSH.

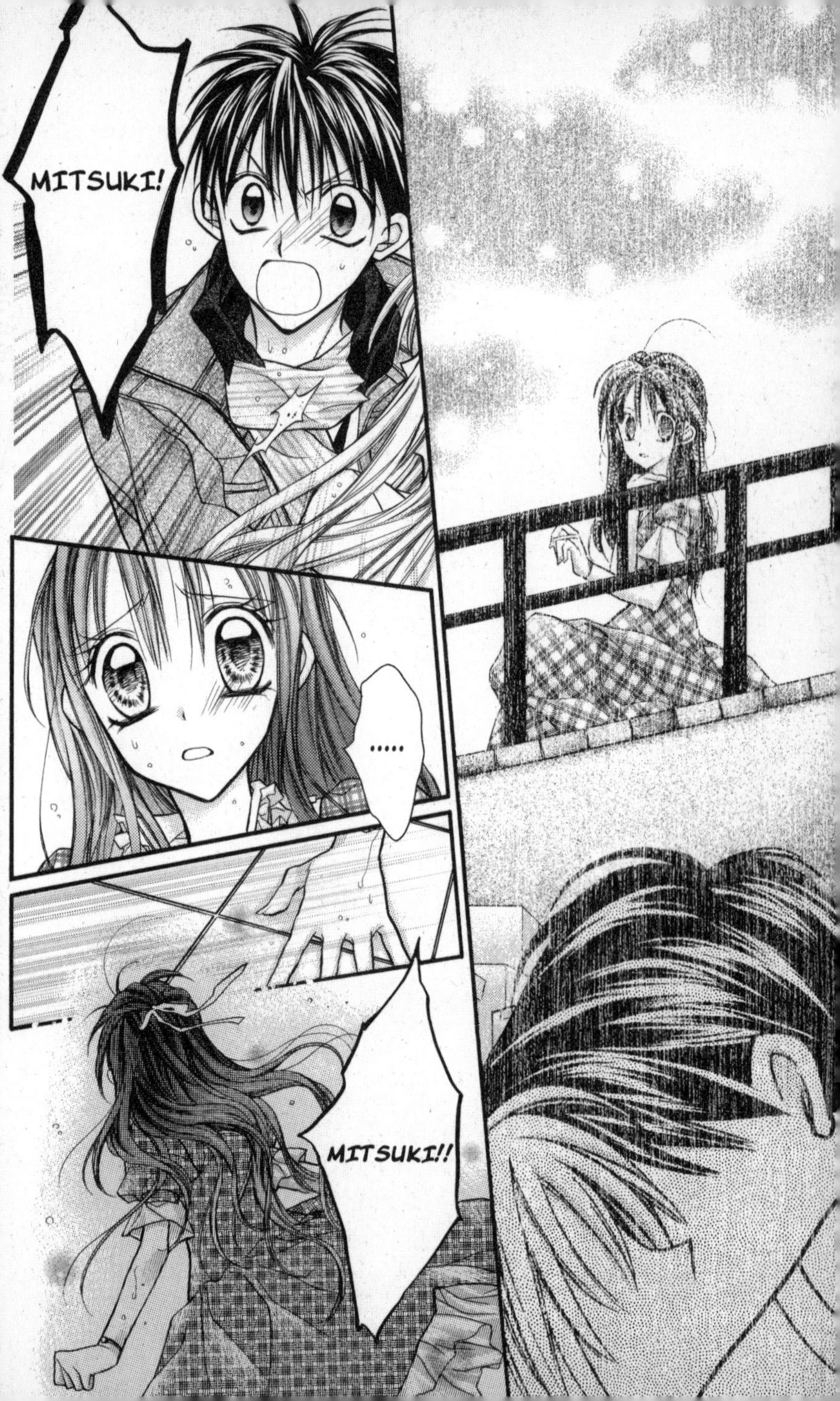
MITSUKI!
.....
MITSUKI!!

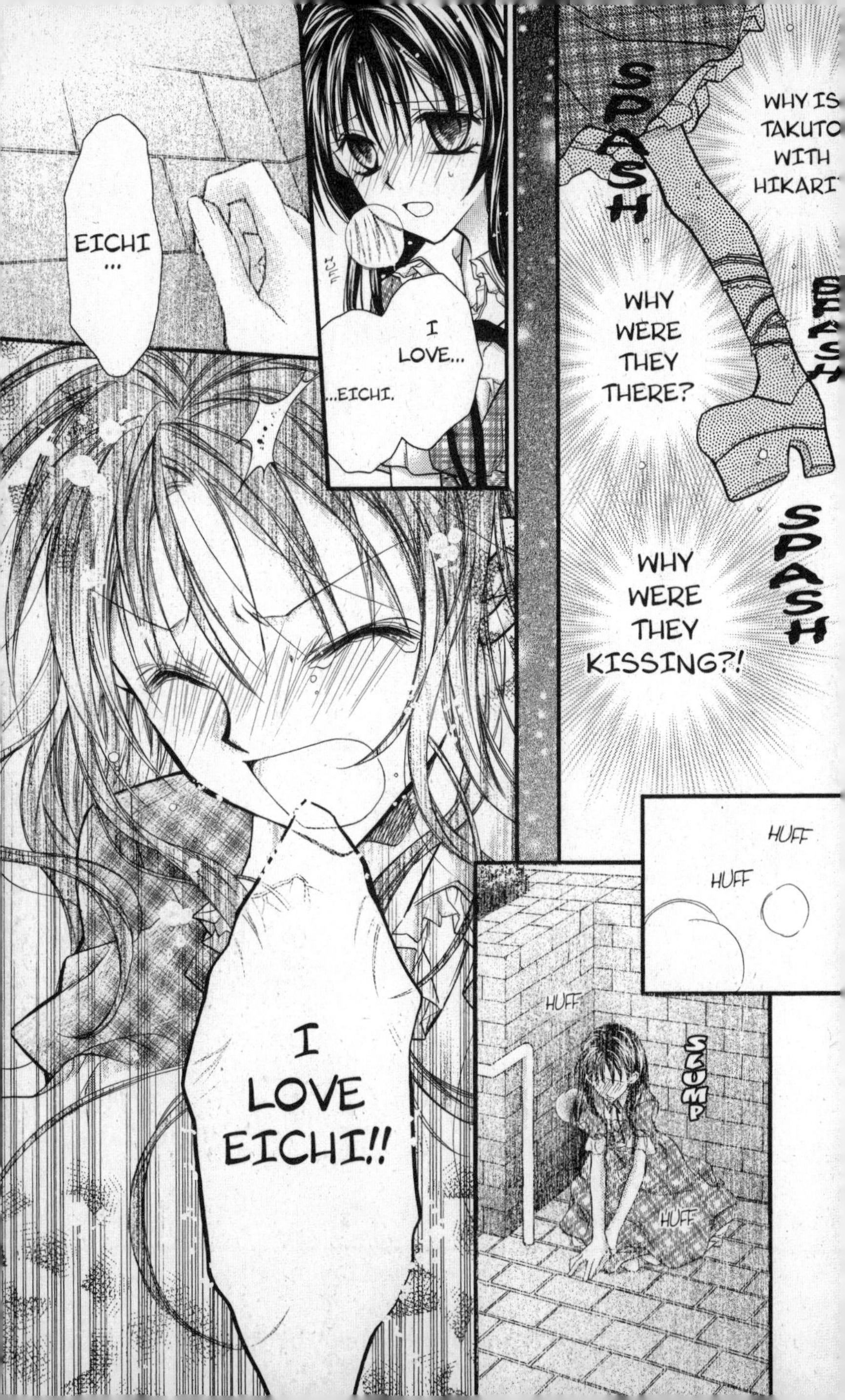

SPASH
WHY IS TAKUTO WITH HIKARI?
WHY WERE THEY THERE?
SPASH
WHY WERE THEY KISSING?!
HUFF
HUFF
HUFF
SLUMP
HUFF
HUFF
I LOVE...
...EICHI.
EICHI...
I LOVE EICHI!!

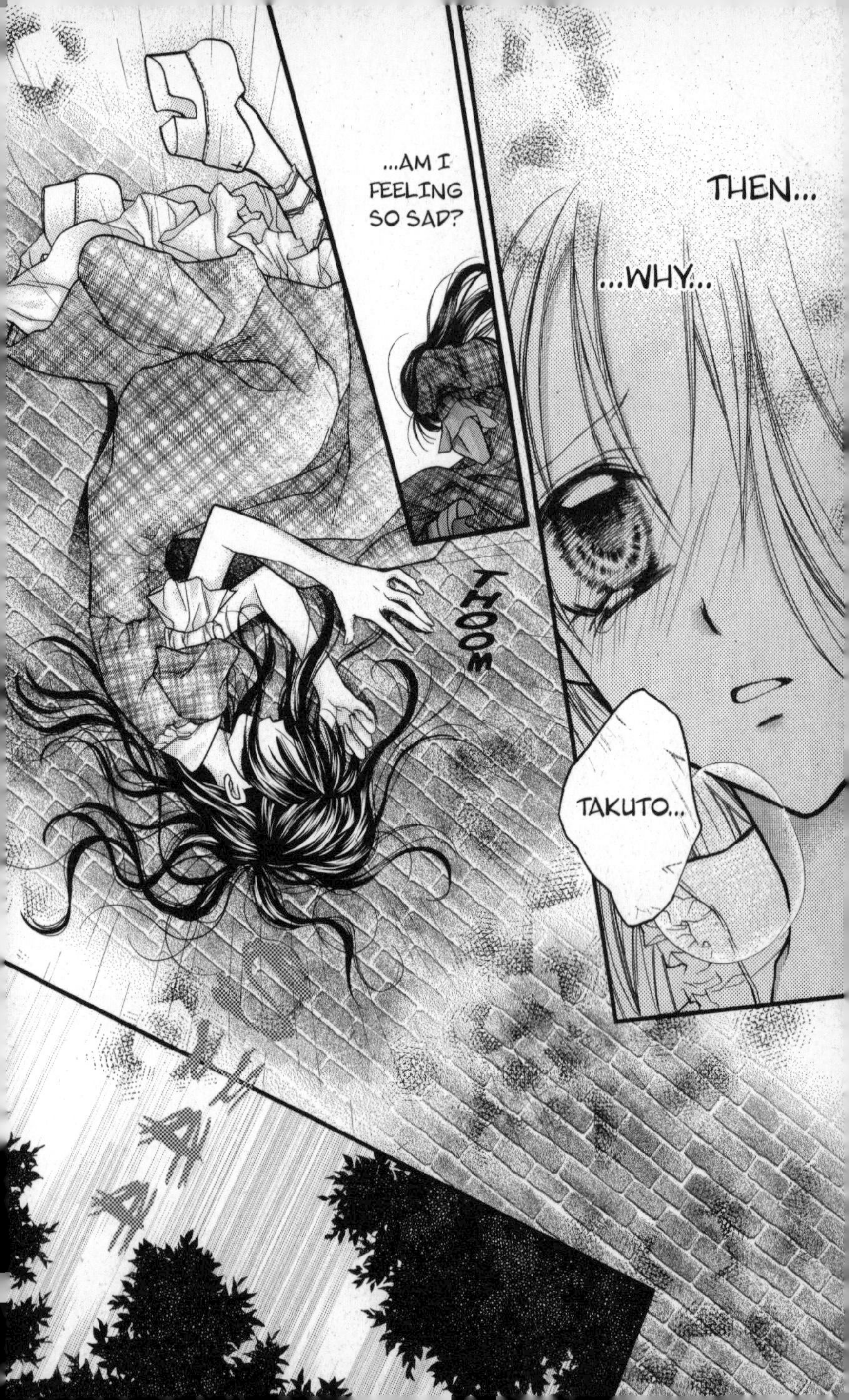
THEN...
...WHY...
TAKUTO...
...AM I FEELING SO SAD?
THOOM

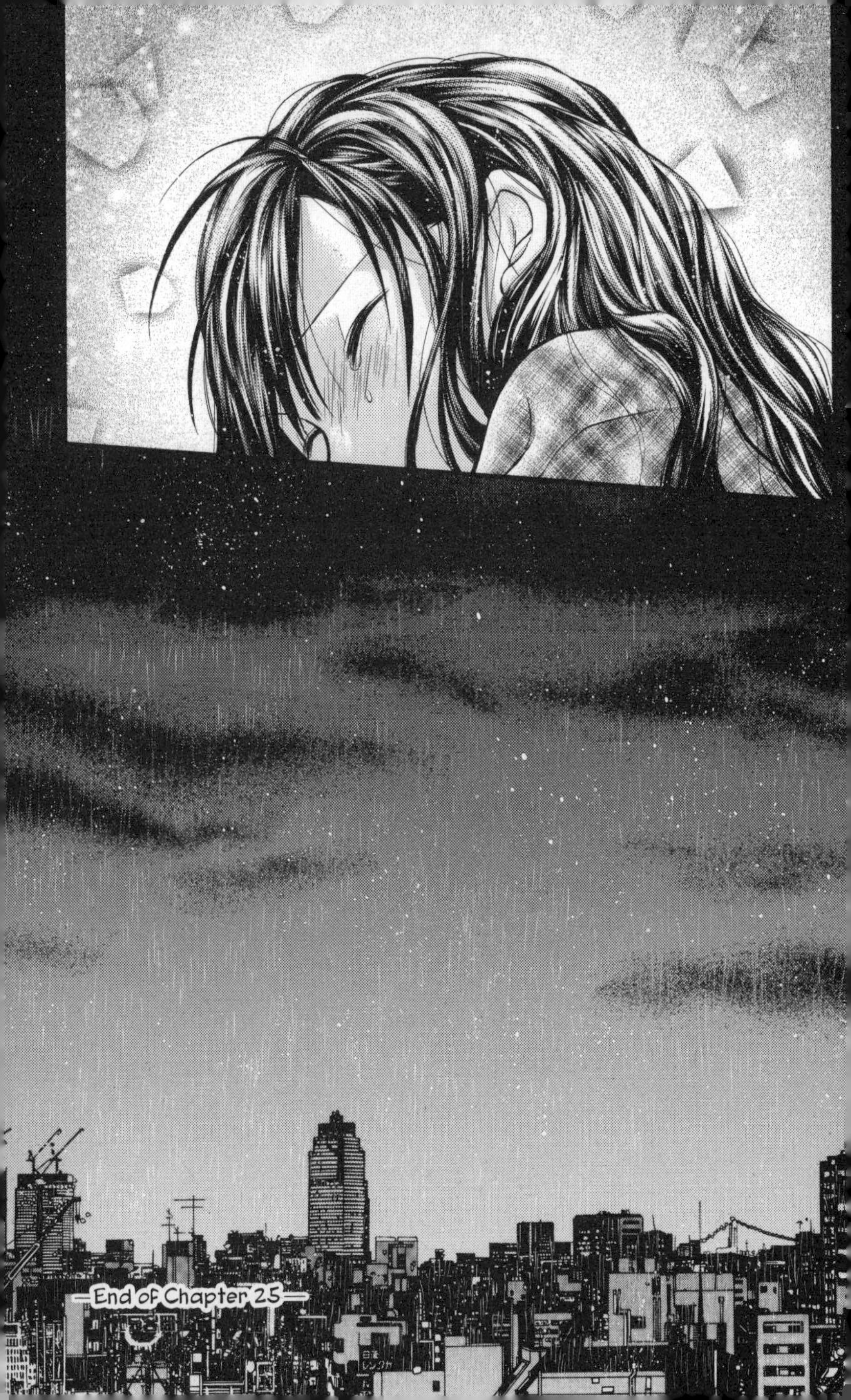
—End of Chapter 25—

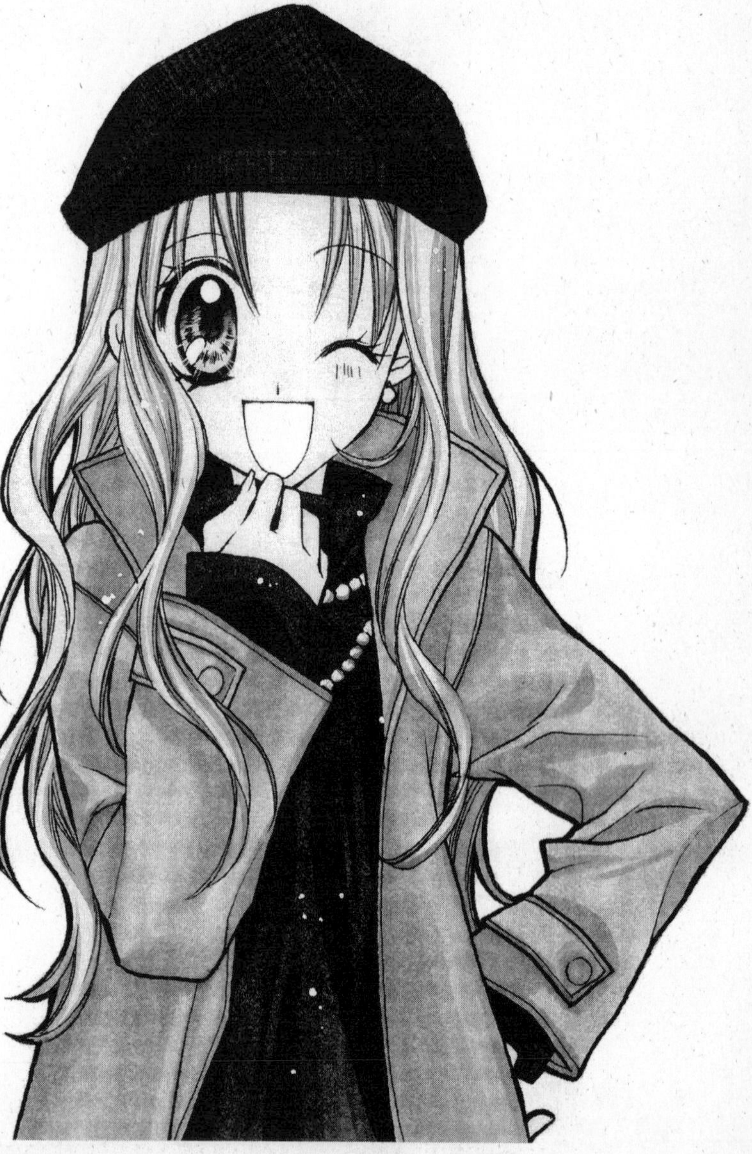

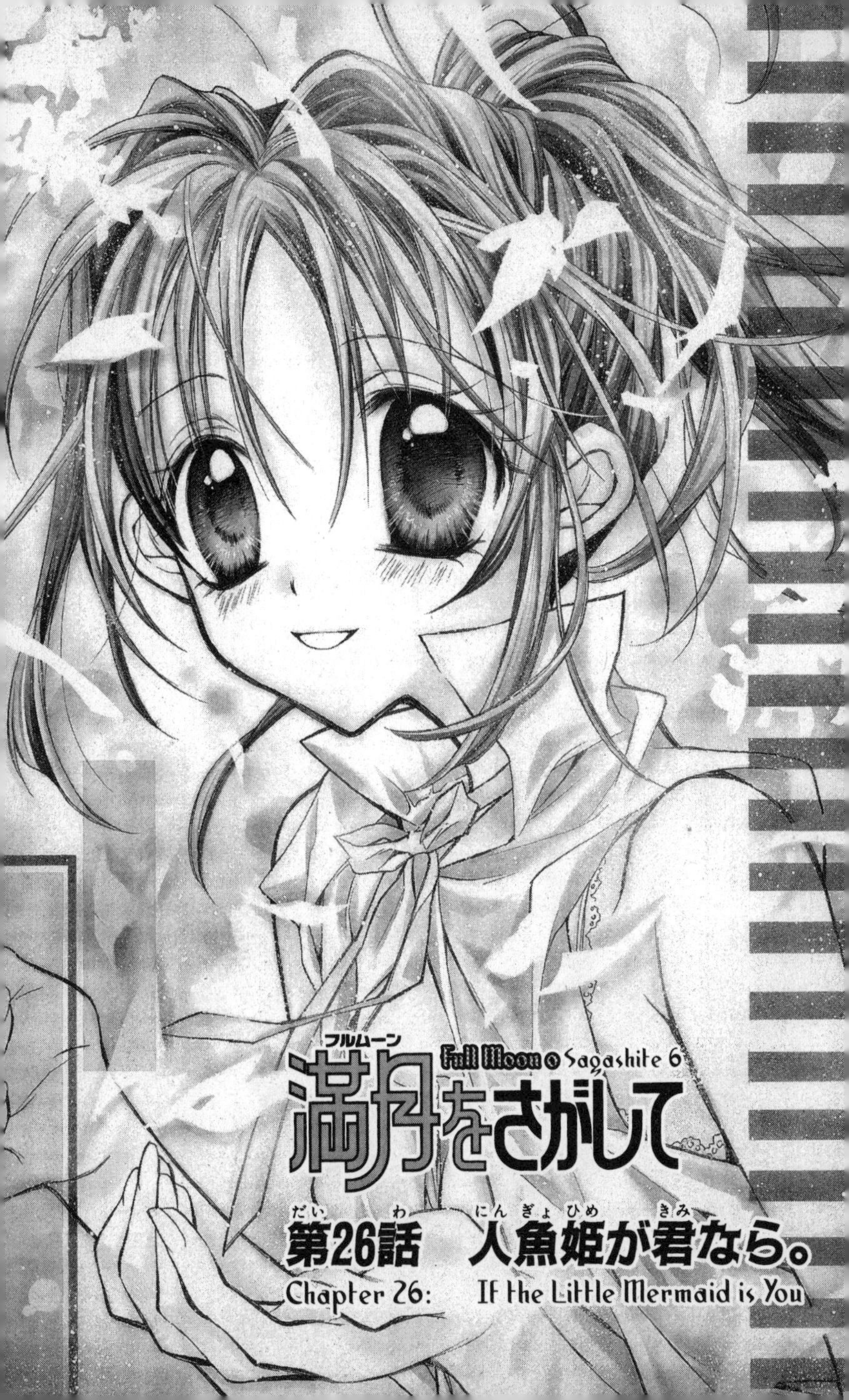
フルムーン
Full Moon o Sagashite 6
満月をさがして
だい わ にんぎょひめ きみ
第26話 人魚姫が君なら。
Chapter 26: If the Little Mermaid is You

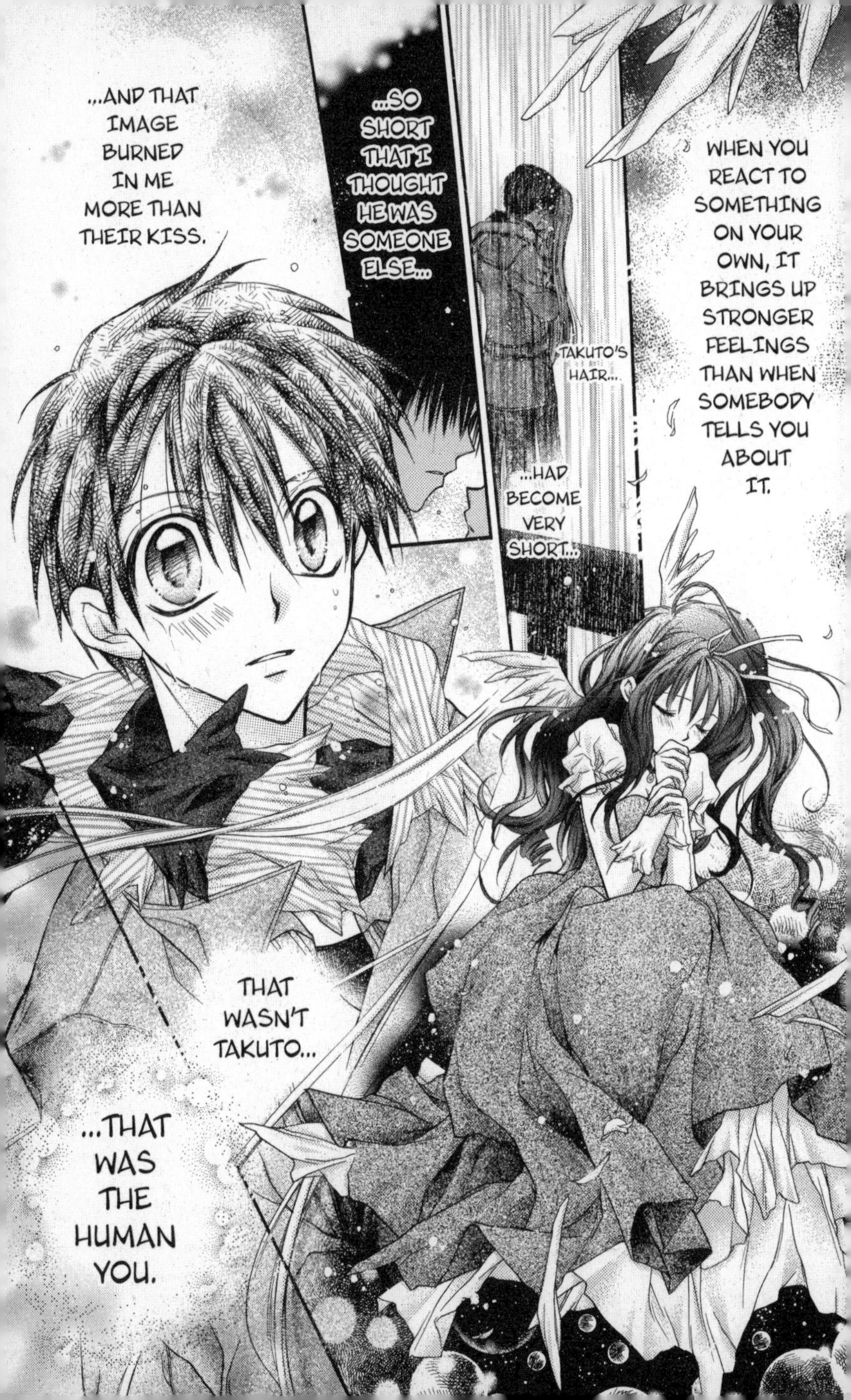

WHEN YOU REACT TO SOMETHING ON YOUR OWN, IT BRINGS UP STRONGER FEELINGS THAN WHEN SOMEBODY TELLS YOU ABOUT IT.
TAKUTO'S HAIR...
...HAD BECOME VERY SHORT...
...SO SHORT THAT I THOUGHT HE WAS SOMEONE ELSE...
...AND THAT IMAGE BURNED IN ME MORE THAN THEIR KISS.
THAT WASN'T TAKUTO...
...THAT WAS THE HUMAN YOU.

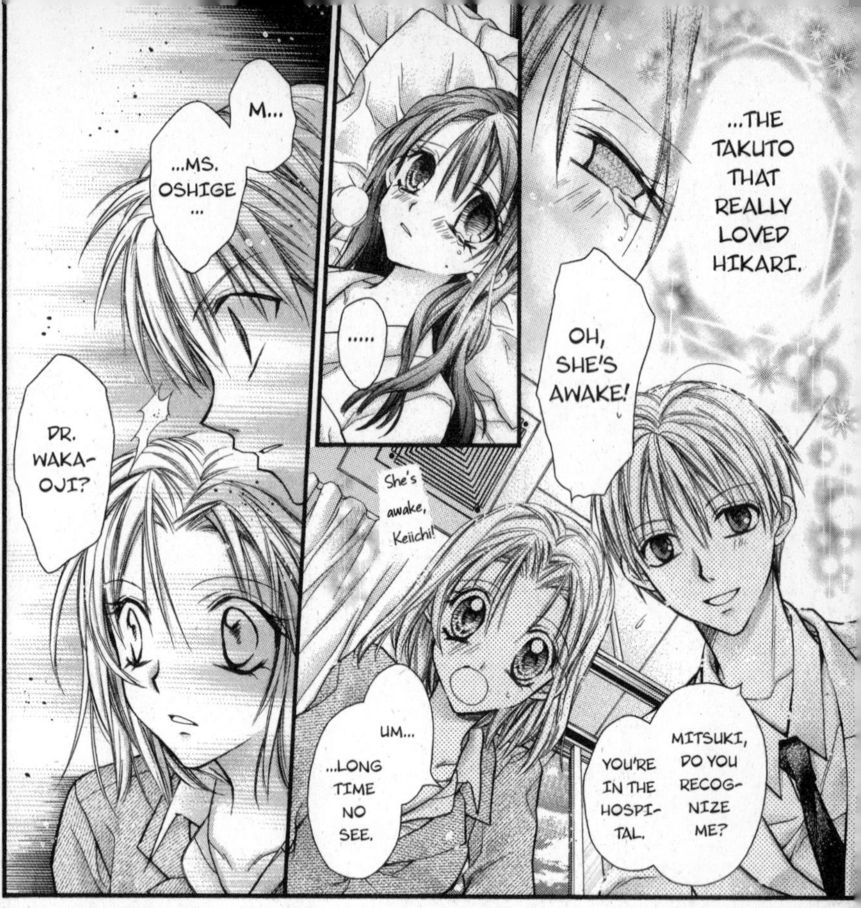
...THE TAKUTO THAT REALLY LOVED HIKARI.
.....
OH, SHE'S AWAKE!
She's awake, Keiichi!
MITSUKI, DO YOU RECOG-NIZE ME?
YOU'RE IN THE HOSPI-TAL.
UM...
...LONG TIME NO SEE.
M...
...MS. OSHIGE ...
DR. WAKA-OJI?

Chapter 26
If the Little Mermaid is You

Cover Copy: Listen to me, I'm always singing, thinking of you...

(spoilers follow)

I kinda like the atmosphere of this chapter. It's good to draw Mitsuki-chan interacting with the adults. Minase-san and Kayorun, my assistants, were saying "the Grandma in this panel is good" and "this Grandma is the best." They really had their attention on Grandma, and I found that interesting.

This type of interaction between the characters is something I hadn't done, so it was a new experience. When I started living on my own, the thing that took me the most courage to do was to buy a TV. Because! It's expensive!! You want something like a 30-inch one in the living room!! Well, Mitsuki-chan probably could only buy a small one, but I think the feelings are the same.

The necklace that Takuto gave Mitsuki-chan was made into a zen-in.

I wanted them to make Eichi's pendant too.

It's good that you can get things that appear in manga. I used to have the Blue Water. (from Nadia)

I got the Flying Stone I wanted too. (Laputa's)

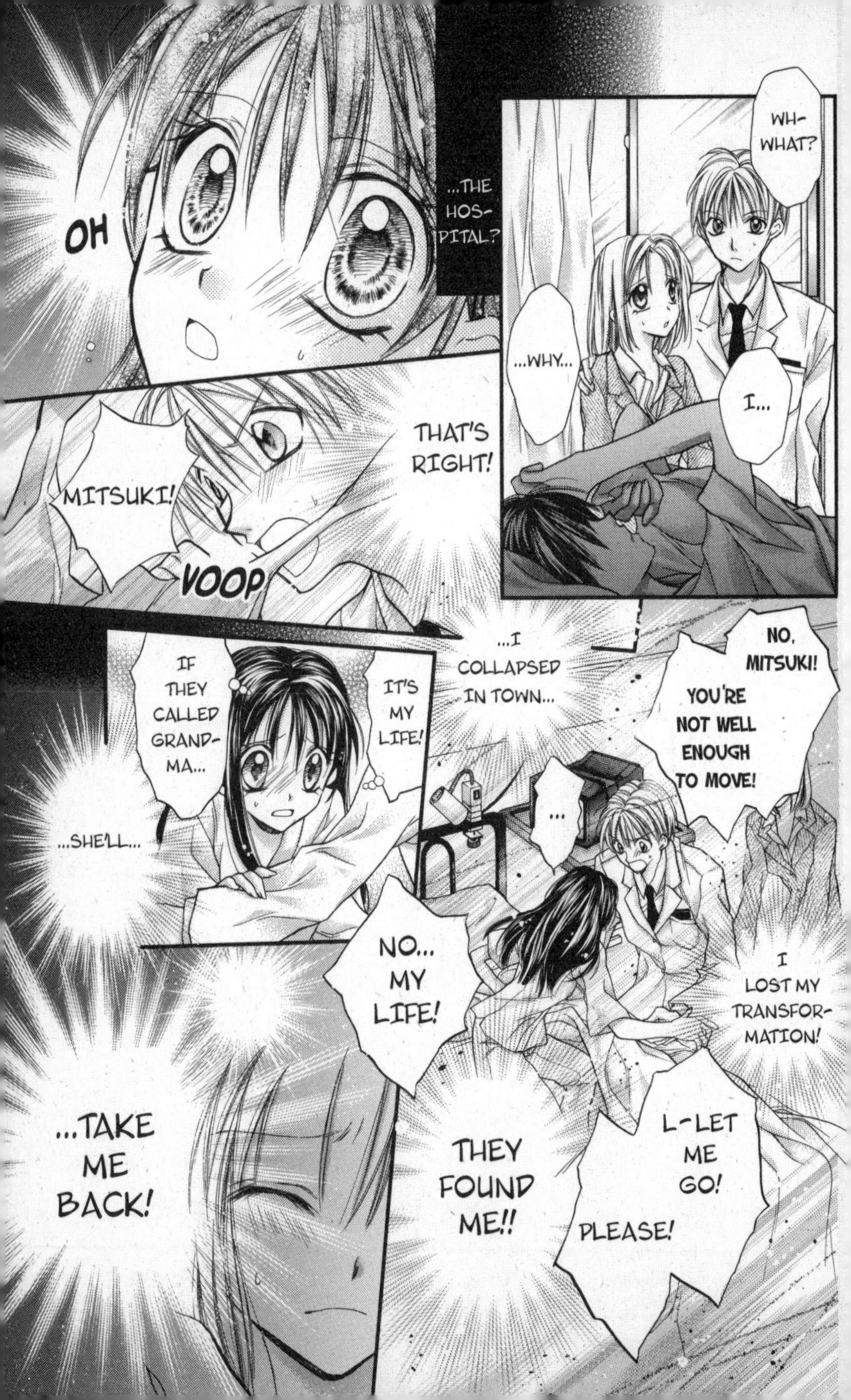
WH-
WHAT?
...WHY...
I...
...THE HOS-PITAL?
OH
THAT'S RIGHT!
MITSUKI!
VOOP
NO, MITSUKI!
YOU'RE NOT WELL ENOUGH TO MOVE!
...I COLLAPSED IN TOWN...
...
IT'S MY LIFE!
IF THEY CALLED GRAND-MA...
...SHE'LL...
I LOST MY TRANSFOR-MATION!
NO... MY LIFE!
L-LET ME GO!
PLEASE!
THEY FOUND ME!!
...TAKE ME BACK!

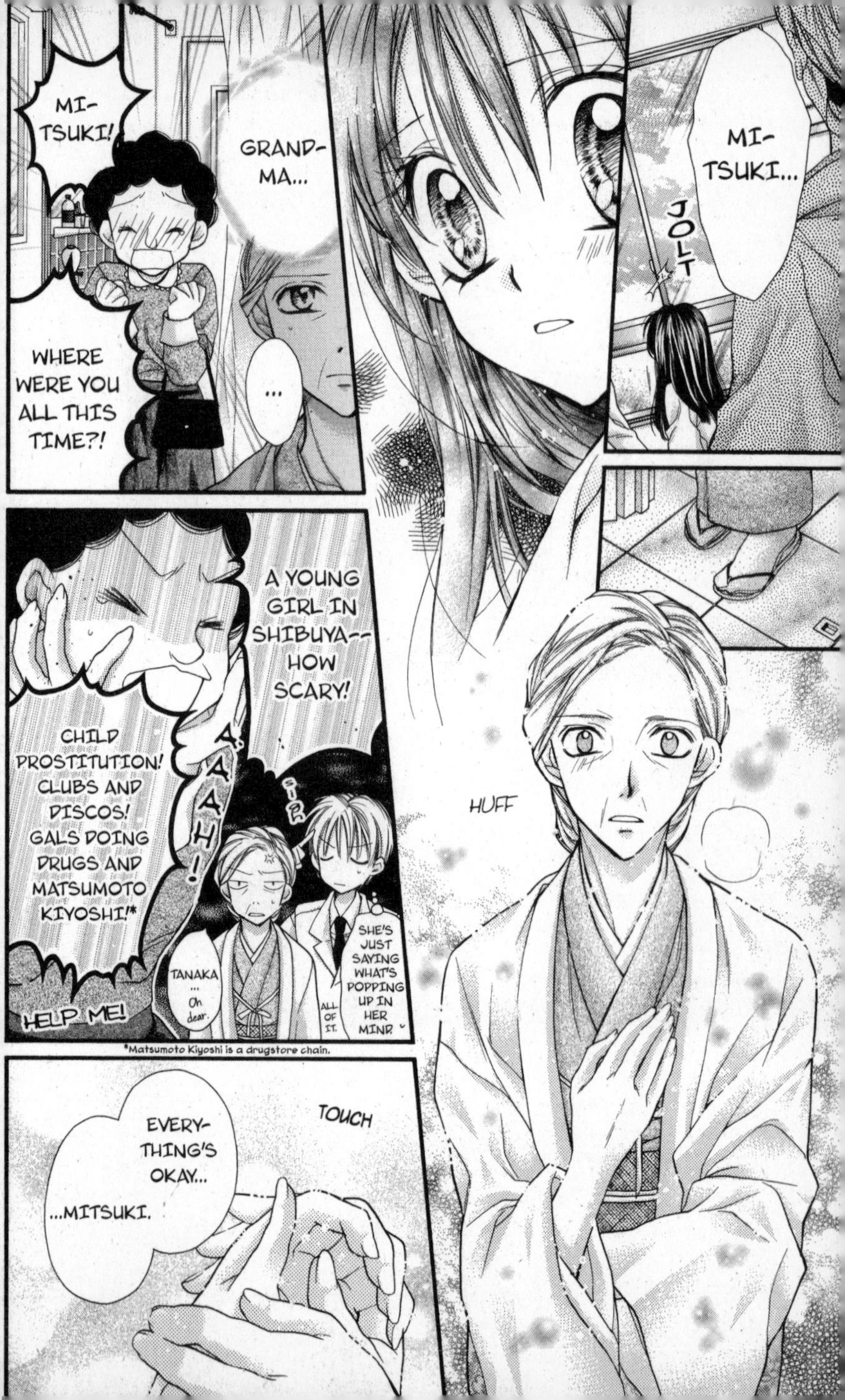
MI-TSUKI...
JOLT
GRAND-MA...
MI-TSUKI!
WHERE WERE YOU ALL THIS TIME?!
...
HUFF
A YOUNG GIRL IN SHIBUYA--HOW SCARY!
CHILD PROSTITUTION! CLUBS AND DISCOS! GALS DOING DRUGS AND MATSUMOTO KIYOSHI!*
AAAH!
HELP ME!
SIR
SHE'S JUST SAYING WHAT'S POPPING UP IN HER MIND.
ALL OF IT.
TANAKA... Oh dear.
TOUCH
EVERY-THING'S OKAY...
...MITSUKI.

*Matsumoto Kiyoshi is a drugstore chain.

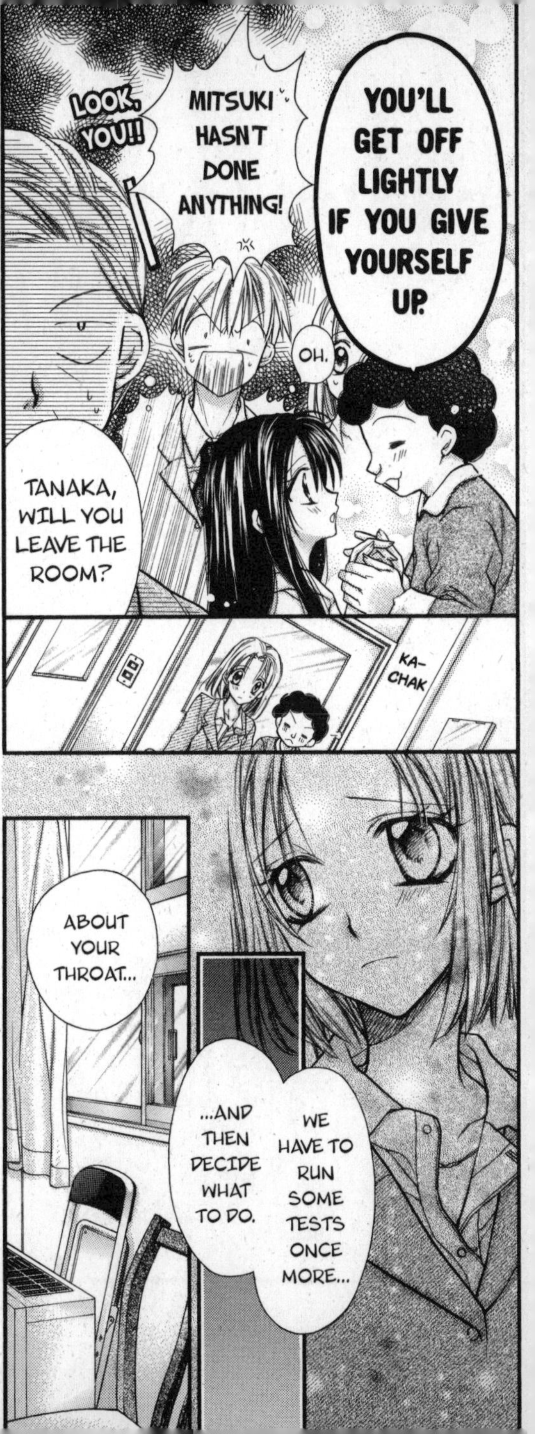
YOU'LL GET OFF LIGHTLY IF YOU GIVE YOURSELF UP.
MITSUKI HASN'T DONE ANYTHING!
LOOK, YOU!!
OH.
TANAKA, WILL YOU LEAVE THE ROOM?
KA-CHAK
ABOUT YOUR THROAT...
WE HAVE TO RUN SOME TESTS ONCE MORE...
...AND THEN DECIDE WHAT TO DO.

About the Letters I Receive 3

♪ You better stop with your cat ears. It's annoying... → What! (smile)

Ari This person seems like a girl in her second year of junior high school. This is a good opportunity for me to say this. That is not me trying to be cute—it's a symbol to make a distinction from my ordinary character. So forgive me!

And if my self-portrait is too cute, who cares? Don't dwell on it!

If I forcibly draw it ugly, it would be exaggerating, and I don't like people who are overly humble. What I should I do...really.

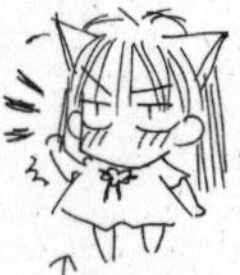

So I will go with it! I will! (Declaration)

You don't have to worry about my looks...Only I need to worry about them...

Anyway, what's cute about this??

♪ Hello! I'm T.M.! My mother and I are reading *Full Moon*. The stories we both love are Chapters 20 and 28. (Ari Chapter 28 will be included in Volume 7.) My mother wants to adopt kids from orphanages after we've all grown up, and I'd like to support her too.

Izumi's story is very deep, and we don't understand all of Izumi's mother's feelings, but there are many mothers who fell like Izumi's mother, and many children with hearts like Izumi's. So, I'd like to make a family for children who are in such environments alone.

Continued →

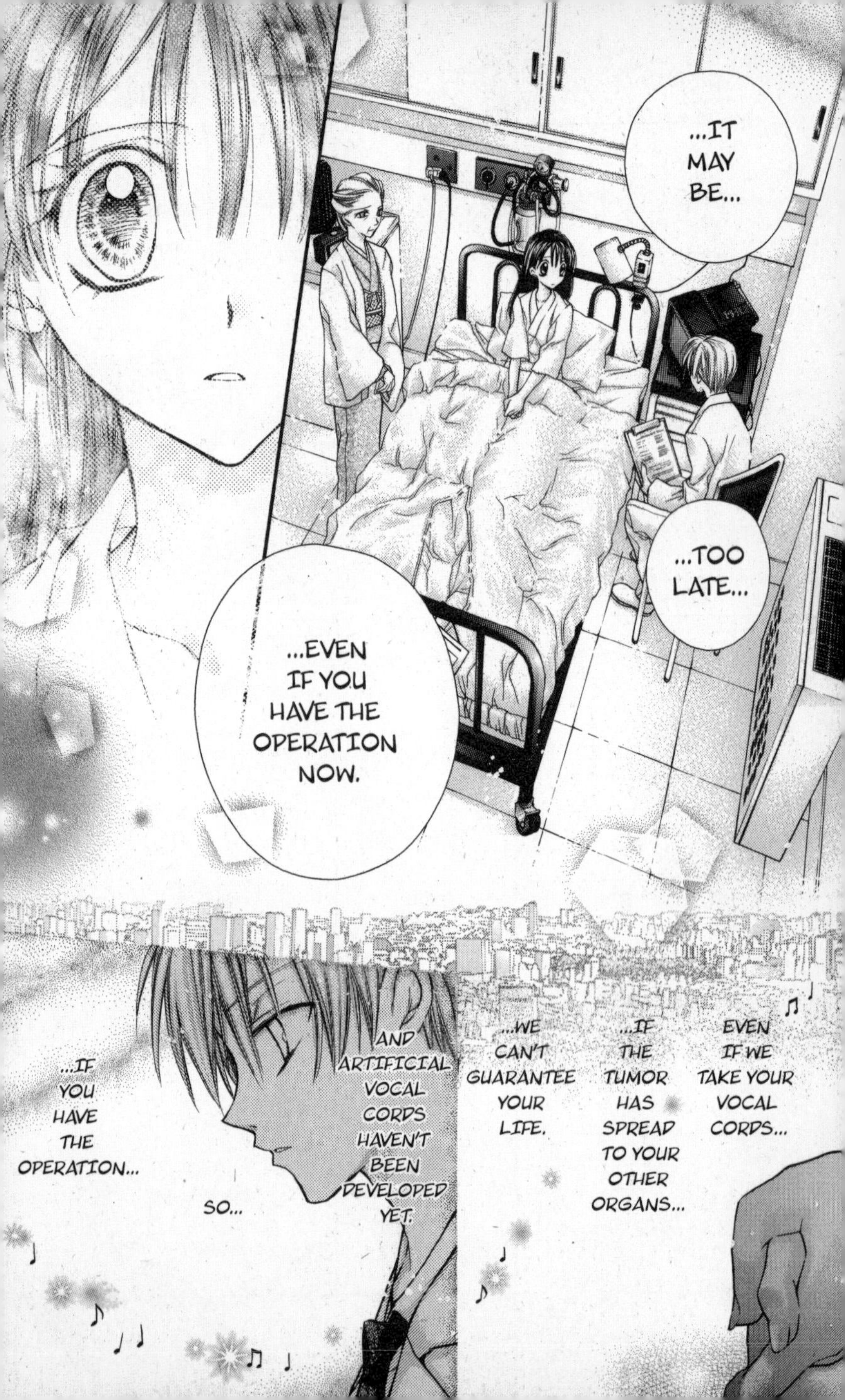
...IT MAY BE...
...TOO LATE...
...EVEN IF YOU HAVE THE OPERATION NOW.
EVEN IF WE TAKE YOUR VOCAL CORDS...
...IF THE TUMOR HAS SPREAD TO YOUR OTHER ORGANS...
...WE CAN'T GUARANTEE YOUR LIFE.
AND ARTIFICIAL VOCAL CORDS HAVEN'T BEEN DEVELOPED YET.
SO...
...IF YOU HAVE THE OPERATION...

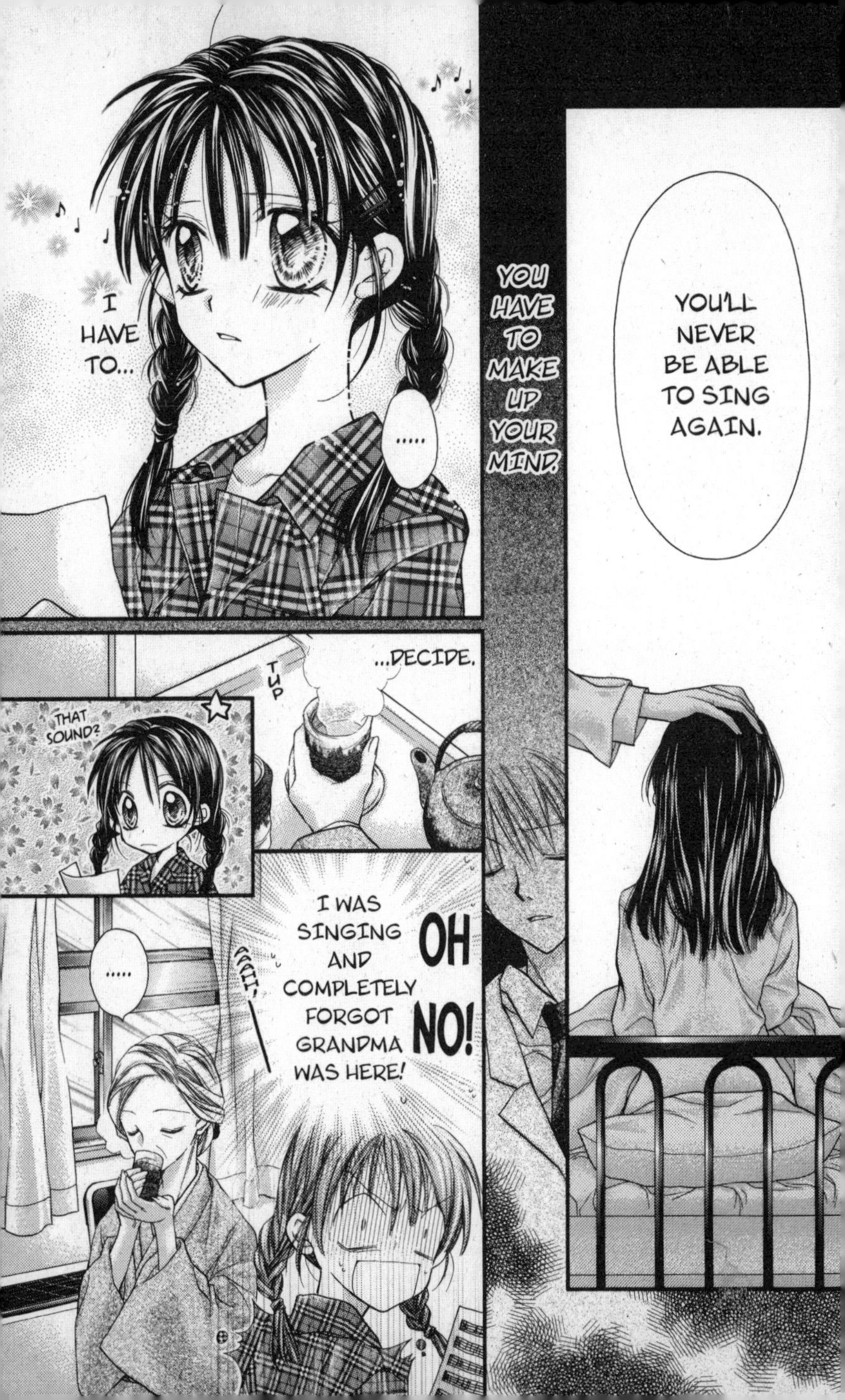
YOU'LL NEVER BE ABLE TO SING AGAIN.
YOU HAVE TO MAKE UP YOUR MIND.
.....
I HAVE TO...
...DECIDE.
TUP
THAT SOUND?
OH NO!
I WAS SINGING AND COMPLETELY FORGOT GRANDMA WAS HERE!
.....

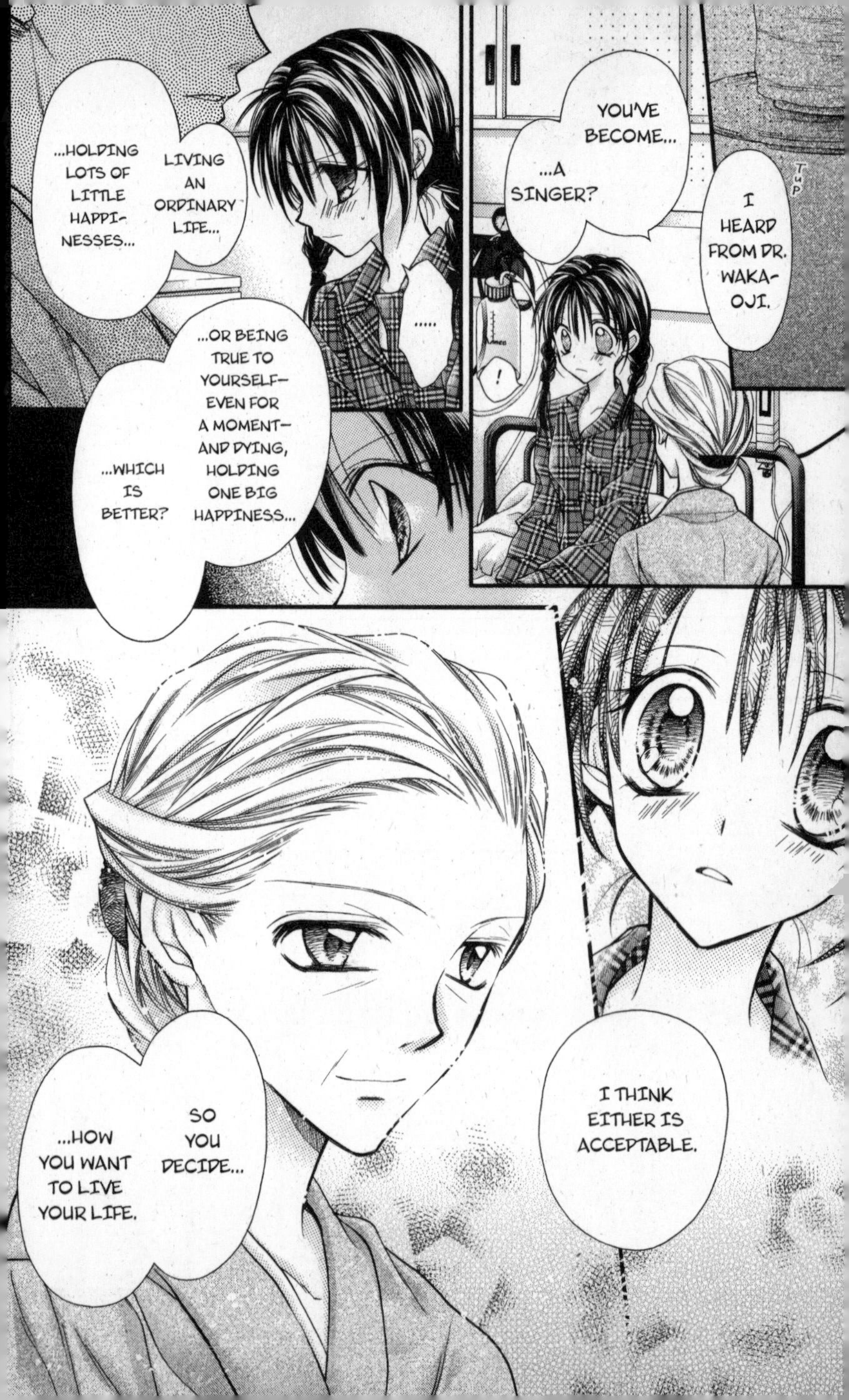
TUP
I HEARD FROM DR. WAKA-OJI.
YOU'VE BECOME...
...A SINGER?
!
LIVING AN ORDINARY LIFE...
...HOLDING LOTS OF LITTLE HAPPI-NESSES...
.....
...OR BEING TRUE TO YOURSELF— EVEN FOR A MOMENT— AND DYING, HOLDING ONE BIG HAPPINESS...
...WHICH IS BETTER?
I THINK EITHER IS ACCEPTABLE.
SO YOU DECIDE...
...HOW YOU WANT TO LIVE YOUR LIFE.

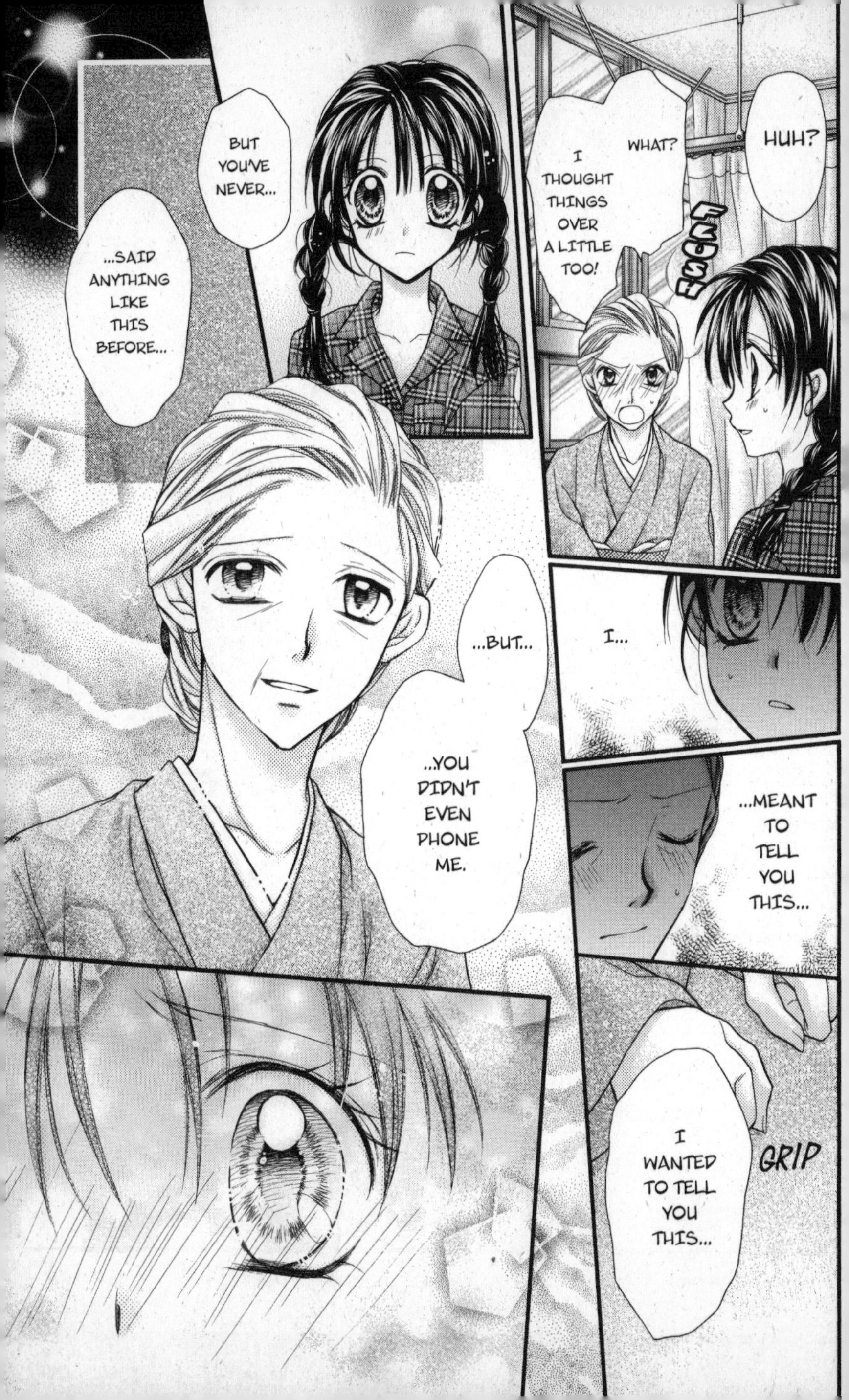
HUH?
WHAT?
I THOUGHT THINGS OVER A LITTLE TOO!
FLUSH
BUT YOU'VE NEVER...
...SAID ANYTHING LIKE THIS BEFORE...
I...
...MEANT TO TELL YOU THIS...
...BUT...
...YOU DIDN'T EVEN PHONE ME.
I WANTED TO TELL YOU THIS...
GRIP

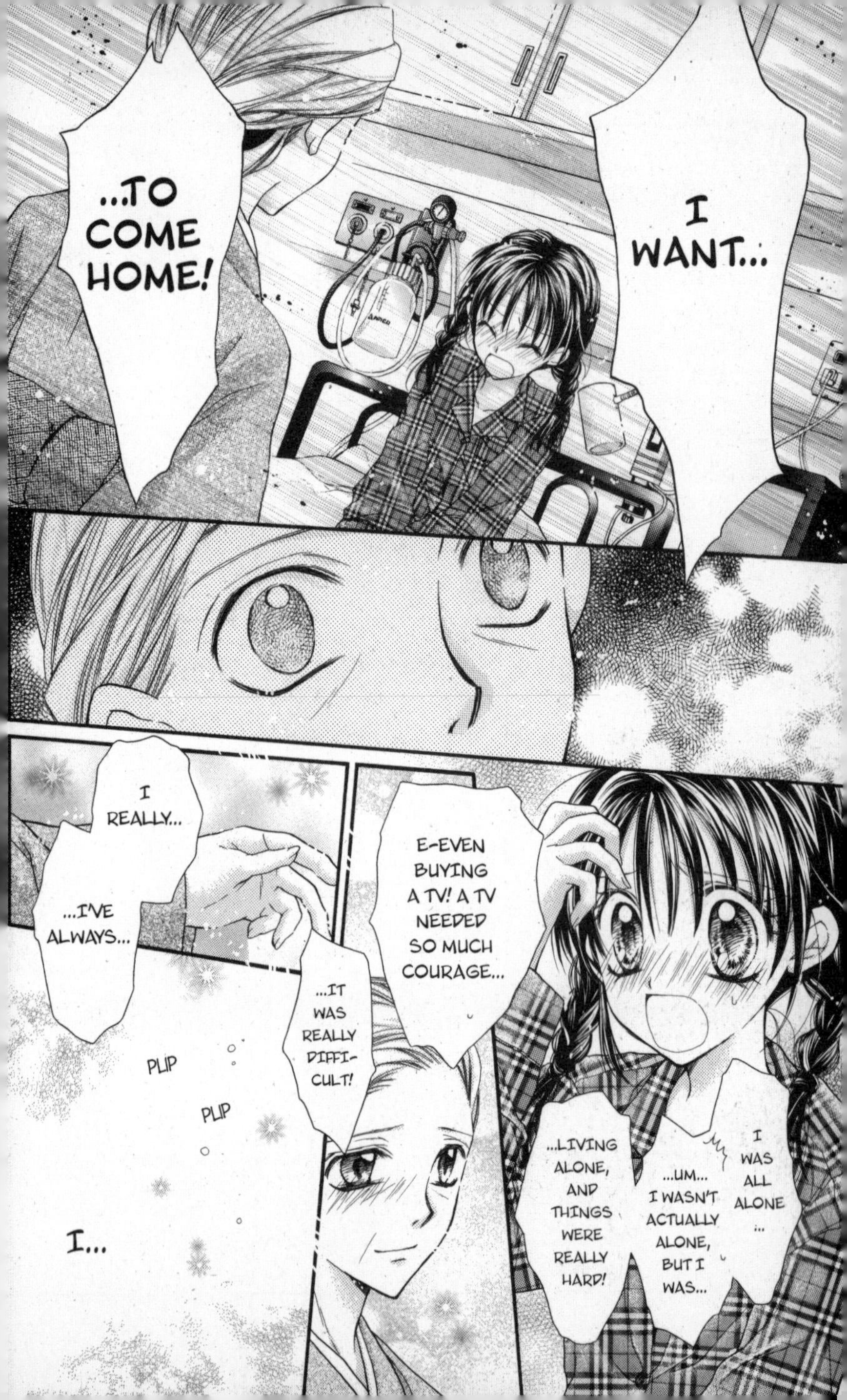
I WANT...
...TO COME HOME!
E-EVEN BUYING A TV! A TV NEEDED SO MUCH COURAGE...
I WAS ALL ALONE...
...UM... I WASN'T ACTUALLY ALONE, BUT I WAS...
...LIVING ALONE, AND THINGS WERE REALLY HARD!
...IT WAS REALLY DIFFI-CULT!
I REALLY...
...I'VE ALWAYS...
PLIP
PLIP
I...

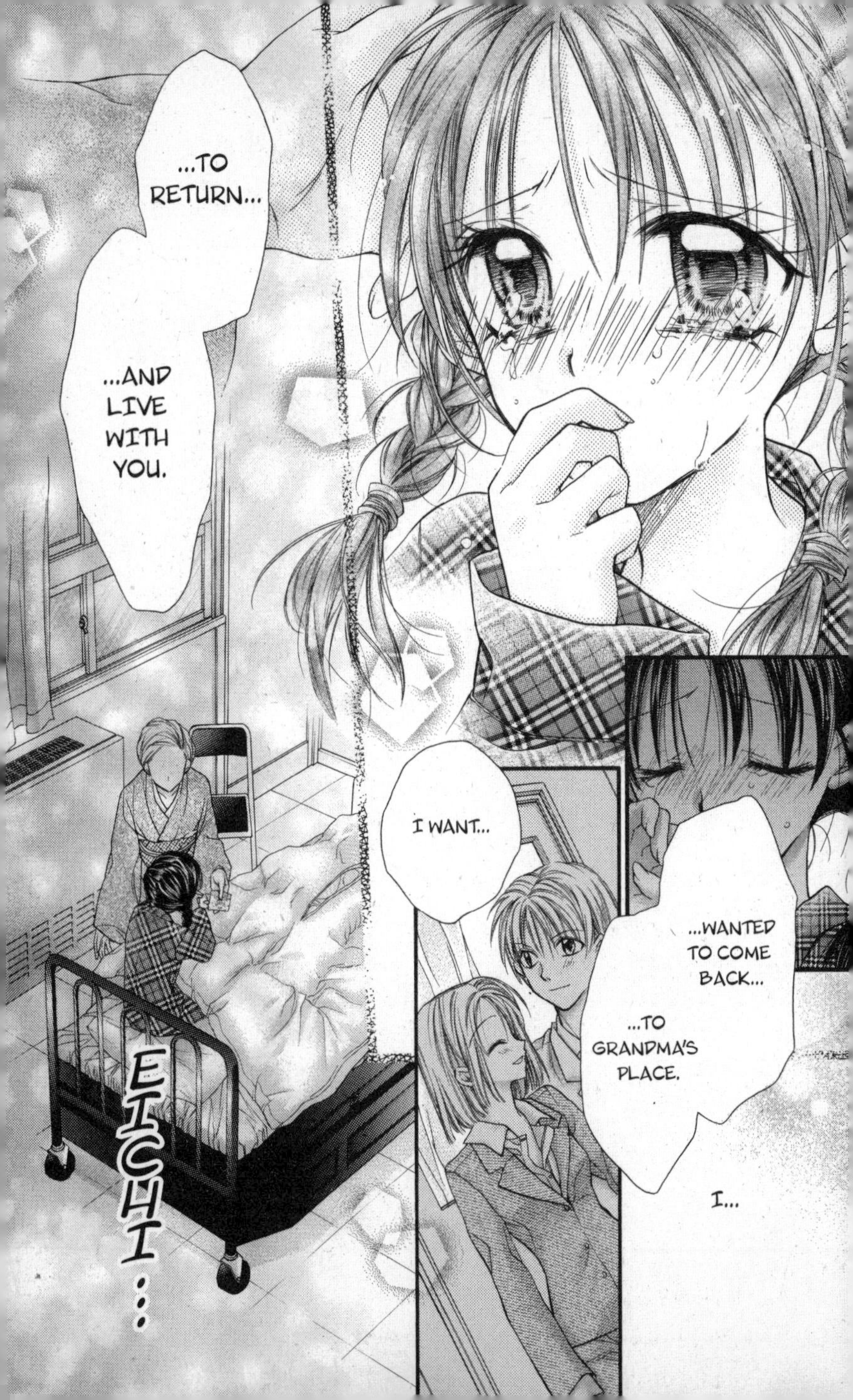
...WANTED TO COME BACK...
...TO GRANDMA'S PLACE.
I...
I WANT...
...TO RETURN...
...AND LIVE WITH YOU.
EICHI...

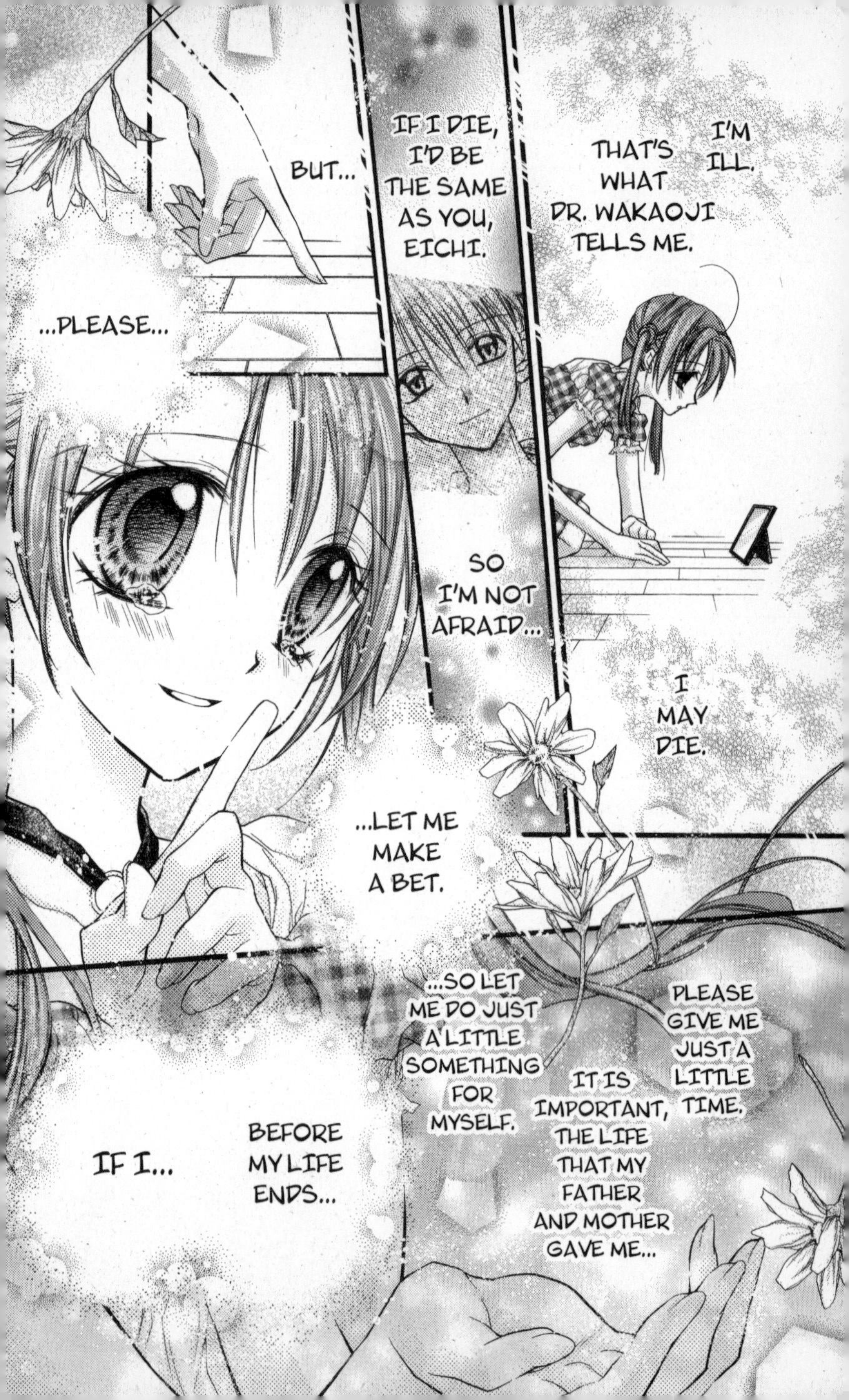
I'M ILL.
THAT'S WHAT DR. WAKAOJI TELLS ME.
I MAY DIE.
IF I DIE, I'D BE THE SAME AS YOU, EICHI.
SO I'M NOT AFRAID...
BUT...
...PLEASE...
...LET ME MAKE A BET.
PLEASE GIVE ME JUST A LITTLE TIME.
IT IS IMPORTANT, THE LIFE THAT MY FATHER AND MOTHER GAVE ME...
...SO LET ME DO JUST A LITTLE SOMETHING FOR MYSELF.
BEFORE MY LIFE ENDS...
IF I...

About the Letters I Receive 4

This is what my mother told me about the reasons for wanting to adopt.

♪I couldn't agree with her much in the beginning, but Tanemura-sensei's story and my mother's words convinced me to support her. Thank you for giving me the opportunity.

Ari I read this email very carefully, because the subject matter is so delicate.

You mother's decision is truly not an easy one to make—it is really a big decision. I'm already 26, so I can feel your mother's big tenderness in a real way. (To raise a child is a difficult task; ideals almost never work out.)

I also want to truly applaud your courage from my heart. But I'm a little worried that, how to say... whether there are unresolved feelings in your heart.

It is wonderful that you were able to agree with your mother's decision, but if there is anything you are worried about, you should tell your mother about it.

I believe your mother really cares about you, you who have grown up so wonderfully, so please believe your mother and talk to her.

Oh...I want kids too.
But if I have kids, I have to quit being a mangaka, so it may be impossible for me.
I want to be a mangaka for life.
My readers are my children?
Children of my heart! (smile)

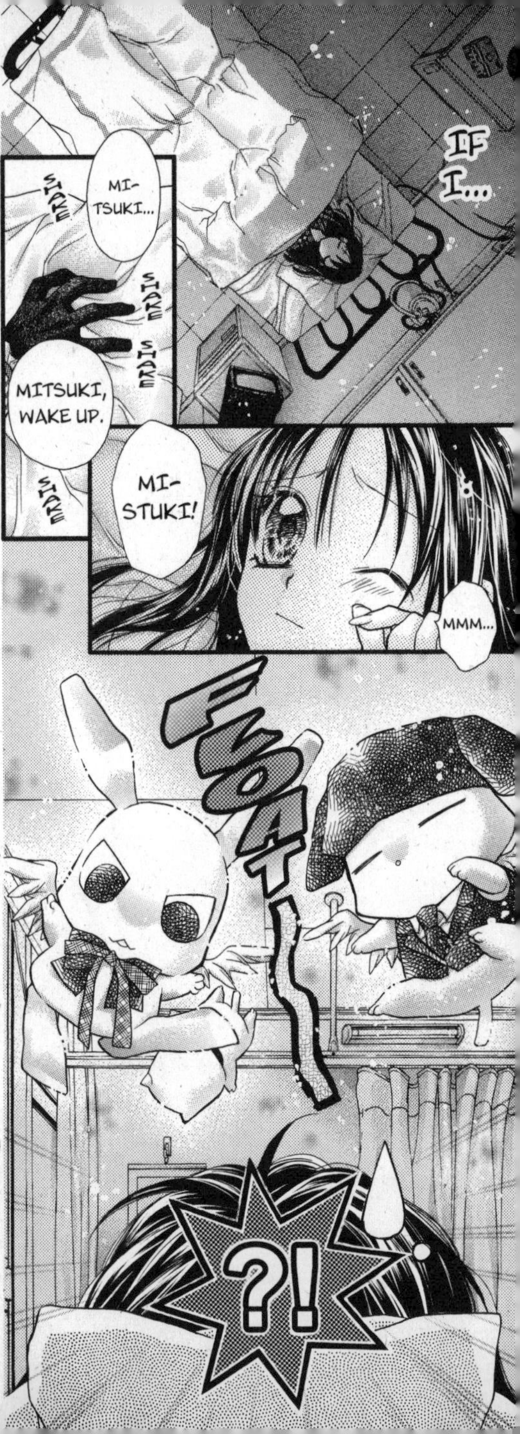
IF I...
MI-TSUKI...
SHAKE
SHAKE
SHAKE
MITSUKI, WAKE UP.
SHAKE
MI-STUKI!
MMM...
FLOAT!
?!

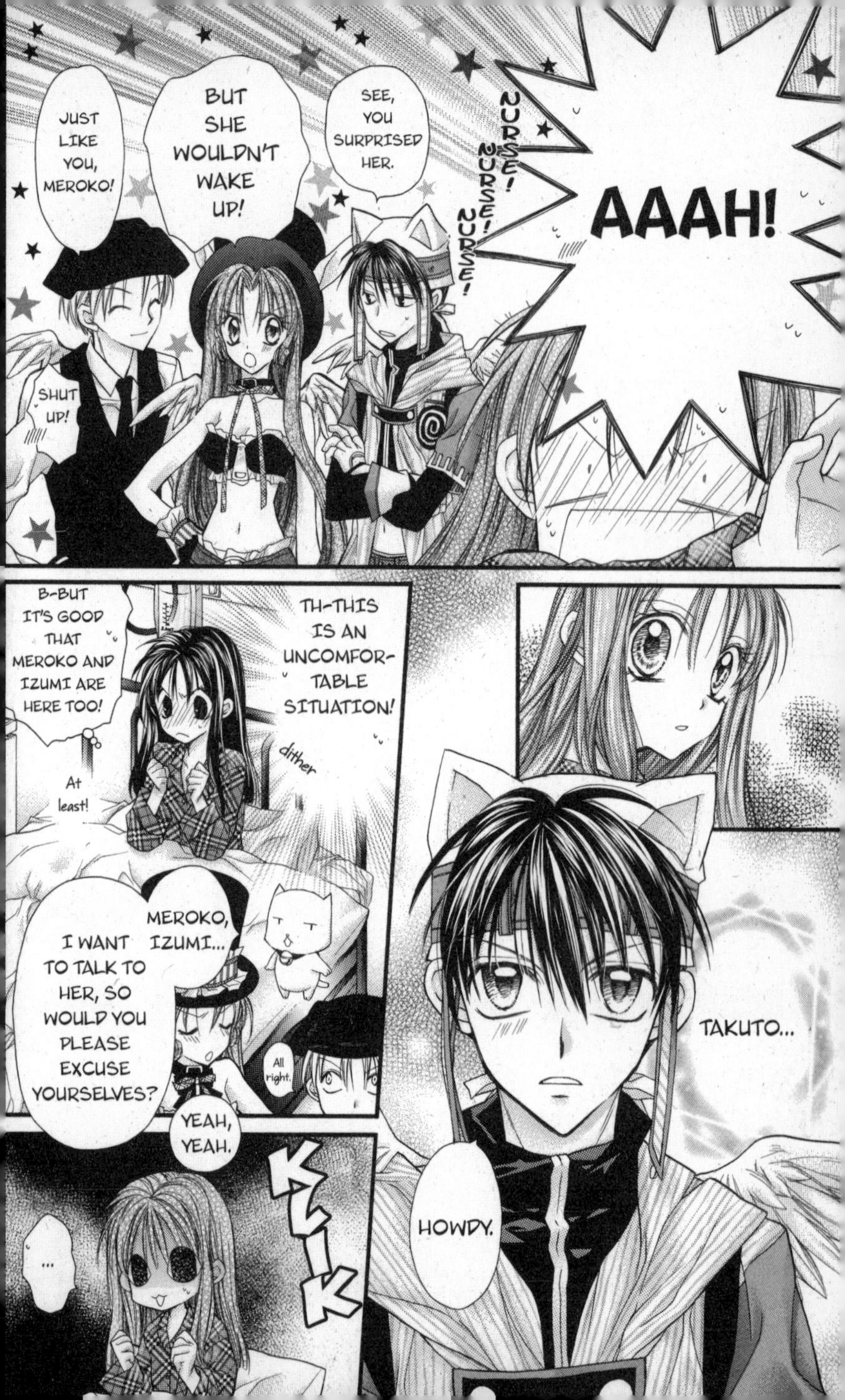
AAAH!
NURSE! NURSE! NURSE!
SEE, YOU SURPRISED HER.
BUT SHE WOULDN'T WAKE UP!
JUST LIKE YOU, MEROKO!
SHUT UP!
TH-THIS IS AN UNCOMFORTABLE SITUATION!
B-BUT IT'S GOOD THAT MEROKO AND IZUMI ARE HERE TOO!
dither
At least!
MEROKO, IZUMI...
I WANT TO TALK TO HER, SO WOULD YOU PLEASE EXCUSE YOURSELVES?
All right.
YEAH, YEAH.
KLIK
...
TAKUTO...
HOWDY.

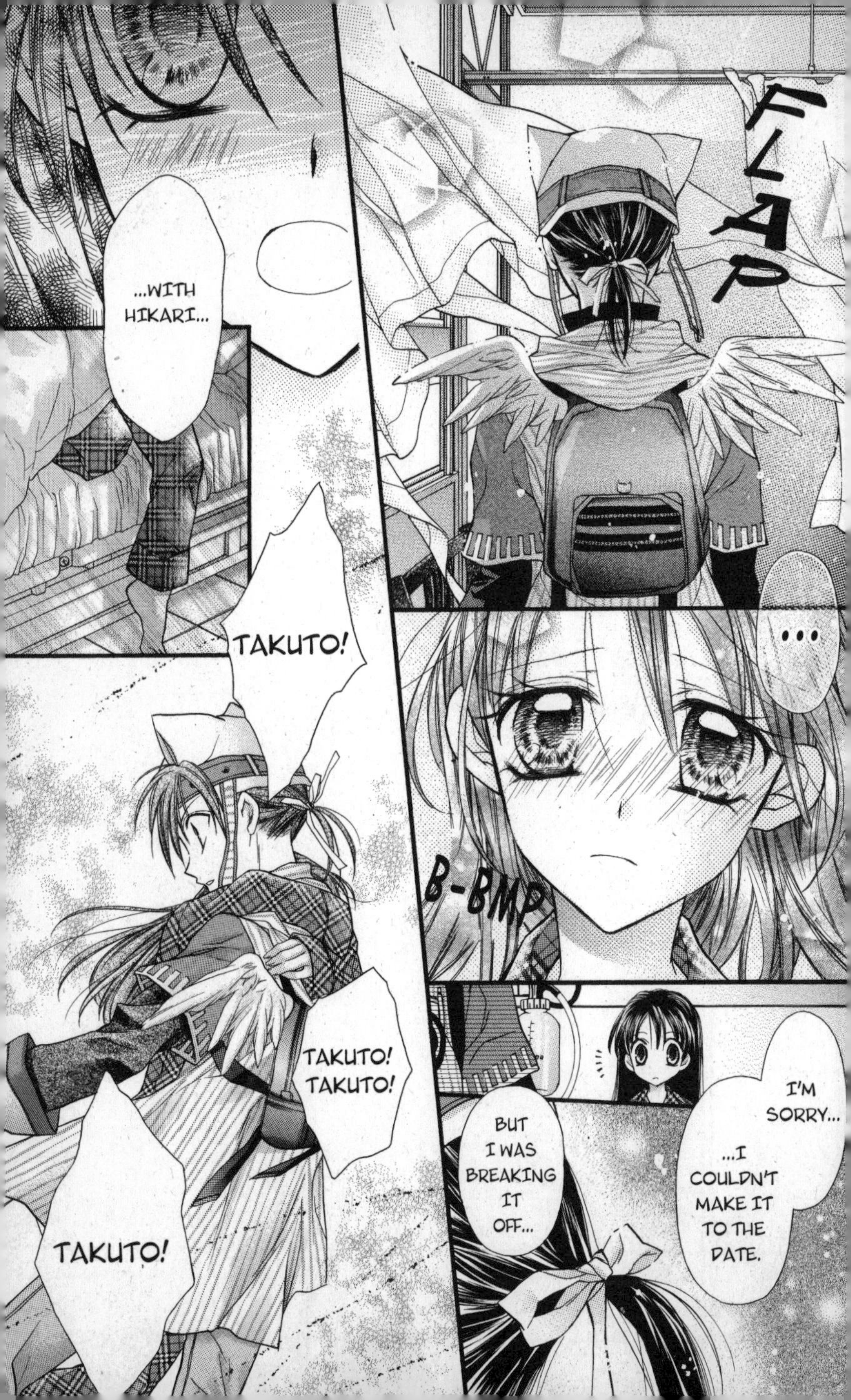
FLAP
...WITH HIKARI...
...
B-BMP
TAKUTO!
I'M SORRY...
...I COULDN'T MAKE IT TO THE DATE.
BUT I WAS BREAKING IT OFF...
TAKUTO! TAKUTO!
TAKUTO!

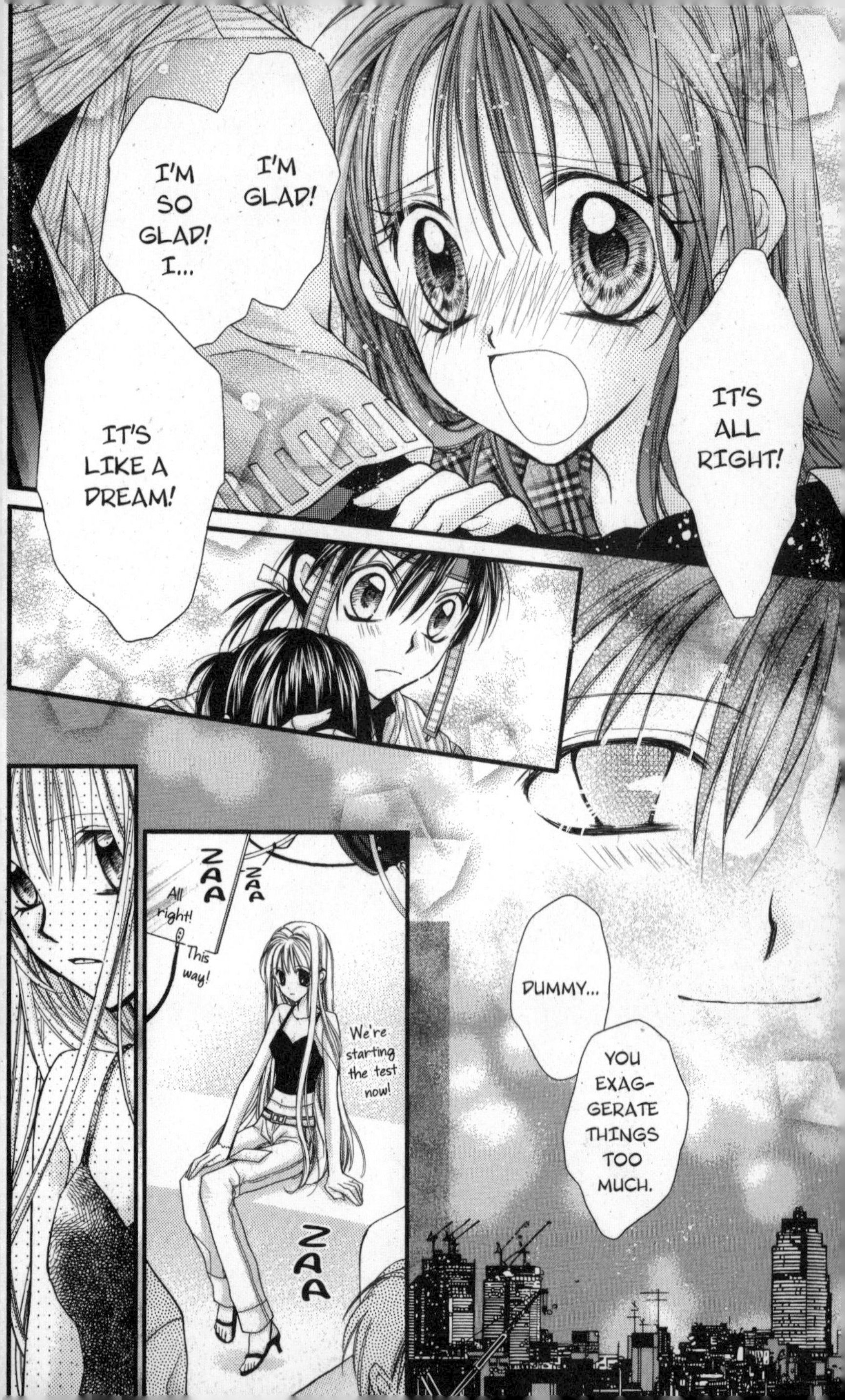
I'M GLAD!
I'M SO GLAD! I...
IT'S ALL RIGHT!
IT'S LIKE A DREAM!
DUMMY...
YOU EXAG-GERATE THINGS TOO MUCH.
ZAA ZAA
All right! This way!
We're starting the test now!
ZAA ZAA

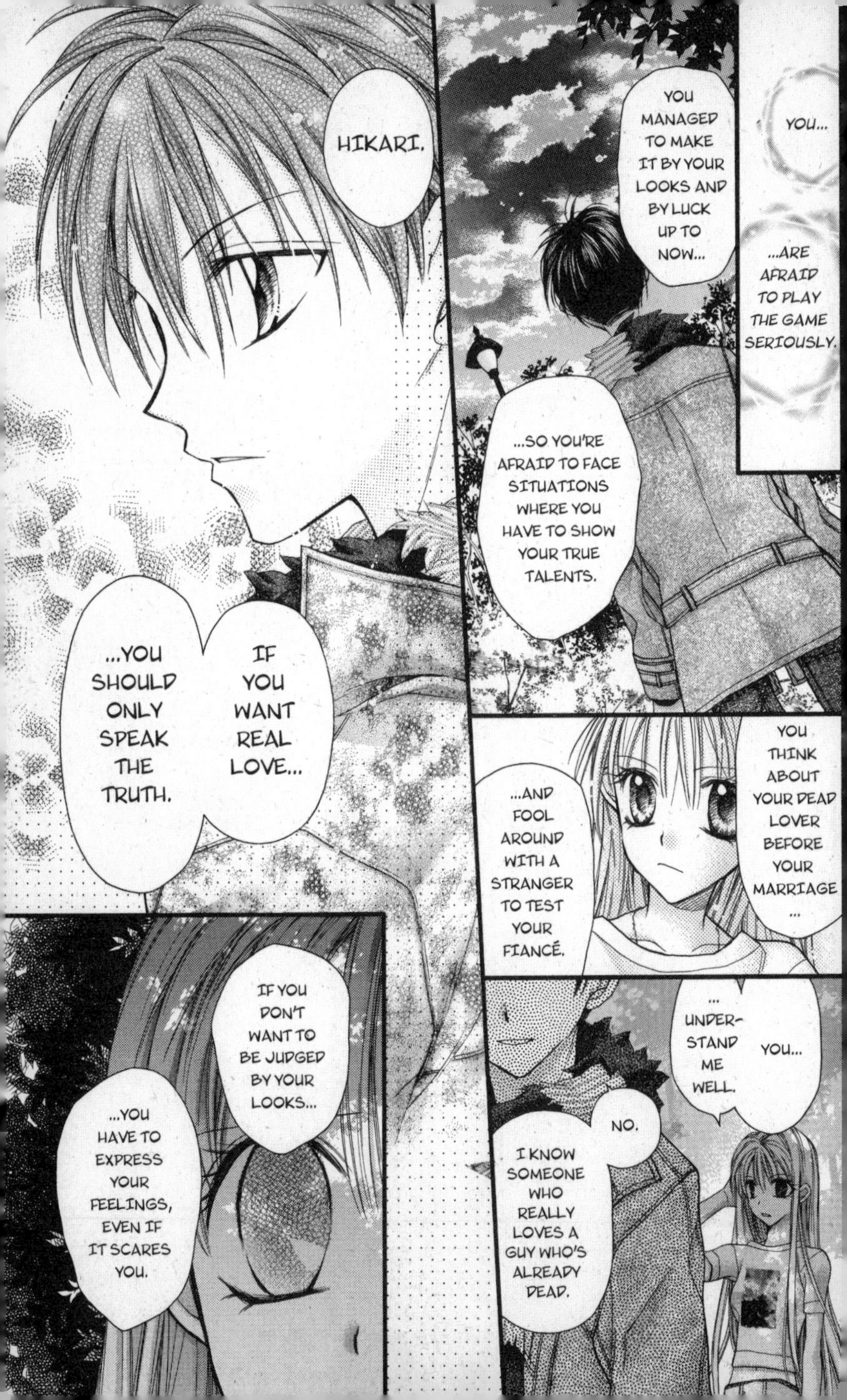
YOU...
...ARE AFRAID TO PLAY THE GAME SERIOUSLY.
YOU MANAGED TO MAKE IT BY YOUR LOOKS AND BY LUCK UP TO NOW...
...SO YOU'RE AFRAID TO FACE SITUATIONS WHERE YOU HAVE TO SHOW YOUR TRUE TALENTS.
YOU THINK ABOUT YOUR DEAD LOVER BEFORE YOUR MARRIAGE ...
...AND FOOL AROUND WITH A STRANGER TO TEST YOUR FIANCÉ.
HIKARI.
IF YOU WANT REAL LOVE...
...YOU SHOULD ONLY SPEAK THE TRUTH.
YOU...
... UNDER-STAND ME WELL.
NO.
I KNOW SOMEONE WHO REALLY LOVES A GUY WHO'S ALREADY DEAD.
IF YOU DON'T WANT TO BE JUDGED BY YOUR LOOKS...
...YOU HAVE TO EXPRESS YOUR FEELINGS, EVEN IF IT SCARES YOU.

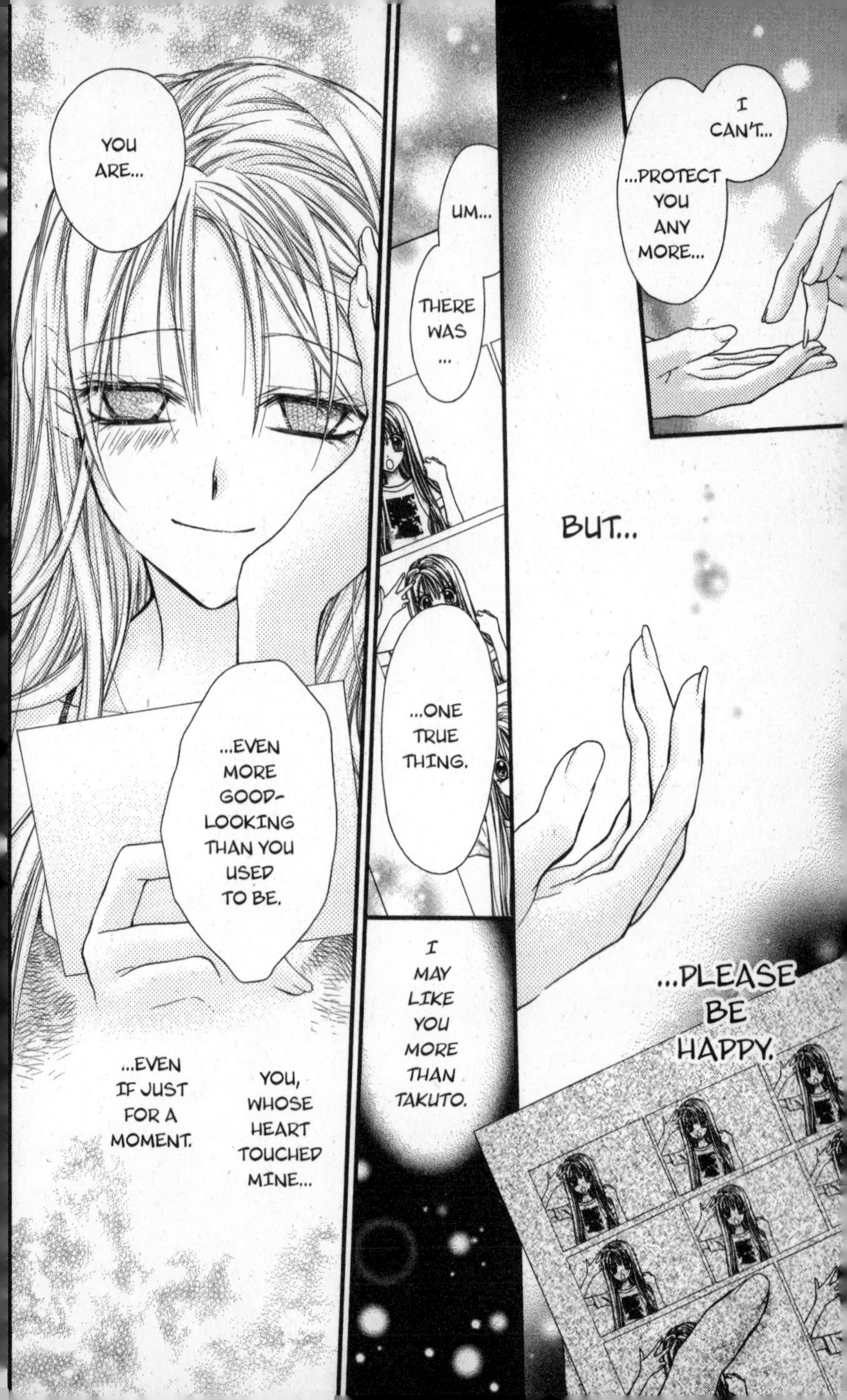
I CAN'T...
...PROTECT YOU ANY MORE...
BUT...
...PLEASE BE HAPPY.
UM...
THERE WAS...
...ONE TRUE THING.
I MAY LIKE YOU MORE THAN TAKUTO.
YOU ARE...
...EVEN MORE GOOD-LOOKING THAN YOU USED TO BE.
YOU, WHOSE HEART TOUCHED MINE...
...EVEN IF JUST FOR A MOMENT.

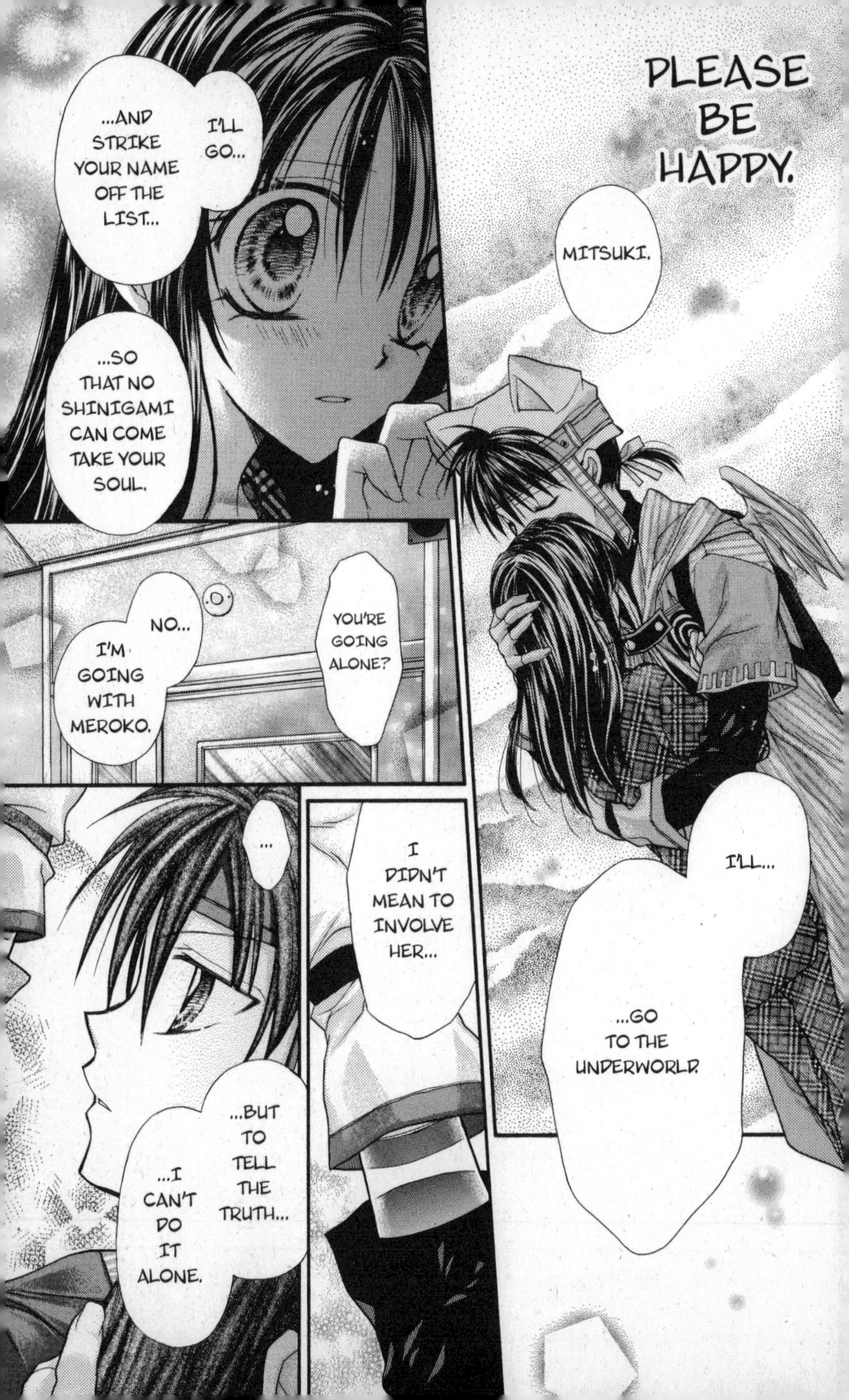
PLEASE BE HAPPY.
MITSUKI.
I'LL...
...GO TO THE UNDERWORLD.
I'LL GO...
...AND STRIKE YOUR NAME OFF THE LIST...
...SO THAT NO SHINIGAMI CAN COME TAKE YOUR SOUL.
YOU'RE GOING ALONE?
NO...
I'M GOING WITH MEROKO.
I DIDN'T MEAN TO INVOLVE HER...
...
...BUT TO TELL THE TRUTH...
...I CAN'T DO IT ALONE.

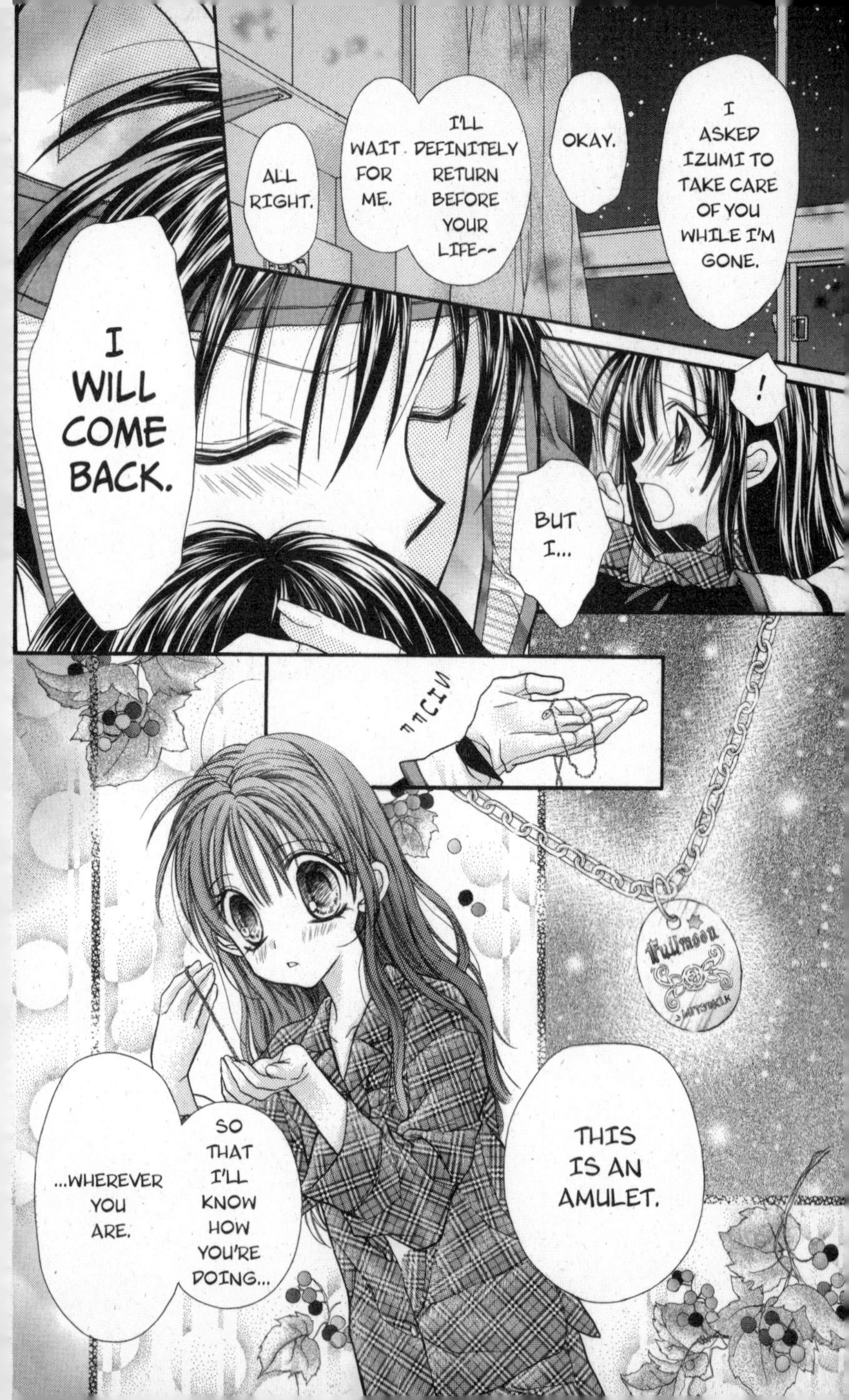
I ASKED IZUMI TO TAKE CARE OF YOU WHILE I'M GONE.
OKAY.
I'LL DEFINITELY RETURN BEFORE YOUR LIFE--
WAIT FOR ME.
ALL RIGHT.
!
BUT I...
I WILL COME BACK.
THIS IS AN AMULET.
SO THAT I'LL KNOW HOW YOU'RE DOING...
...WHEREVER YOU ARE.

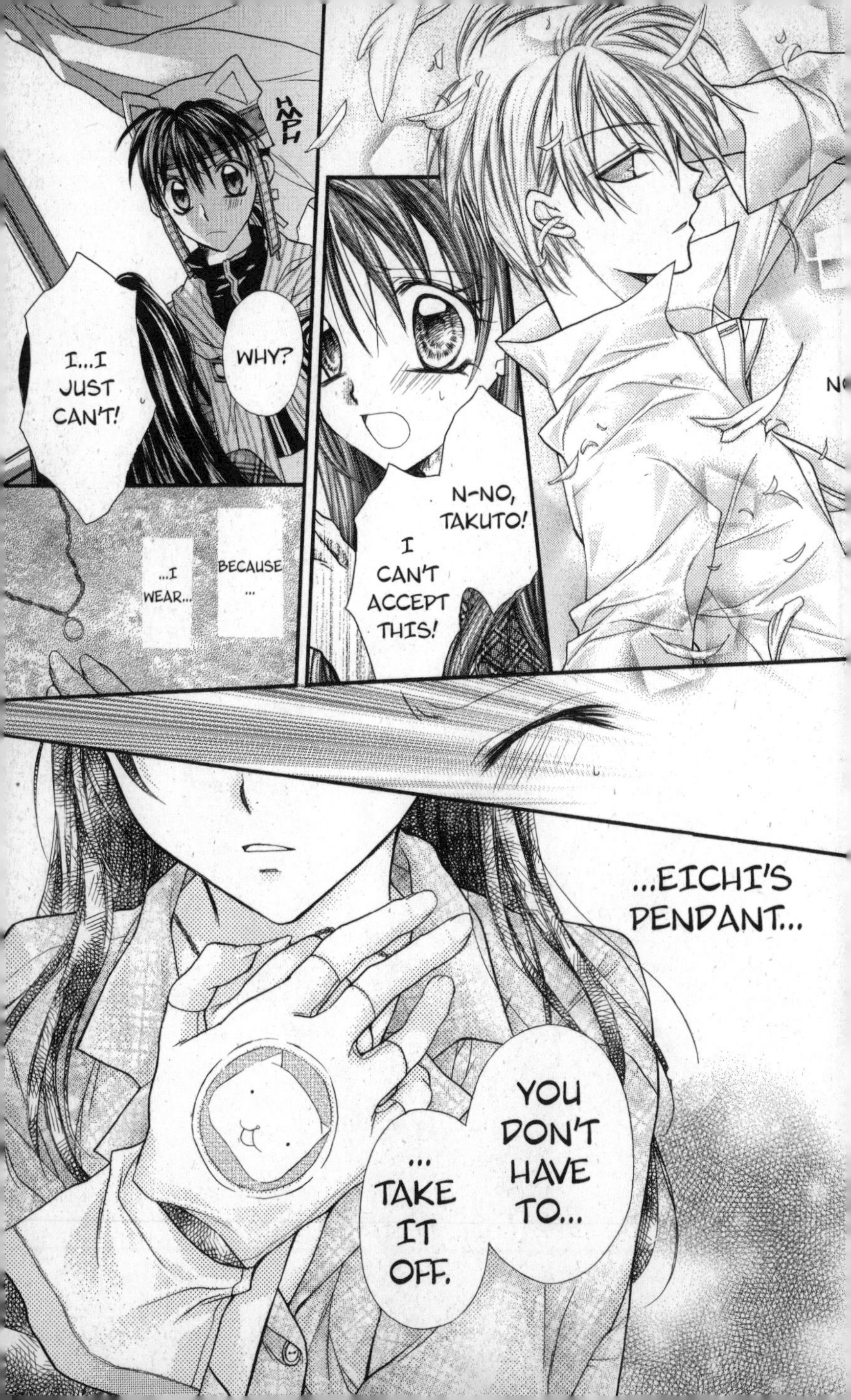
N-NO, TAKUTO!
I CAN'T ACCEPT THIS!
HMPH
WHY?
I...I JUST CAN'T!
BECAUSE ...
...I WEAR...
...EICHI'S PENDANT...
YOU DON'T HAVE TO...
... TAKE IT OFF.

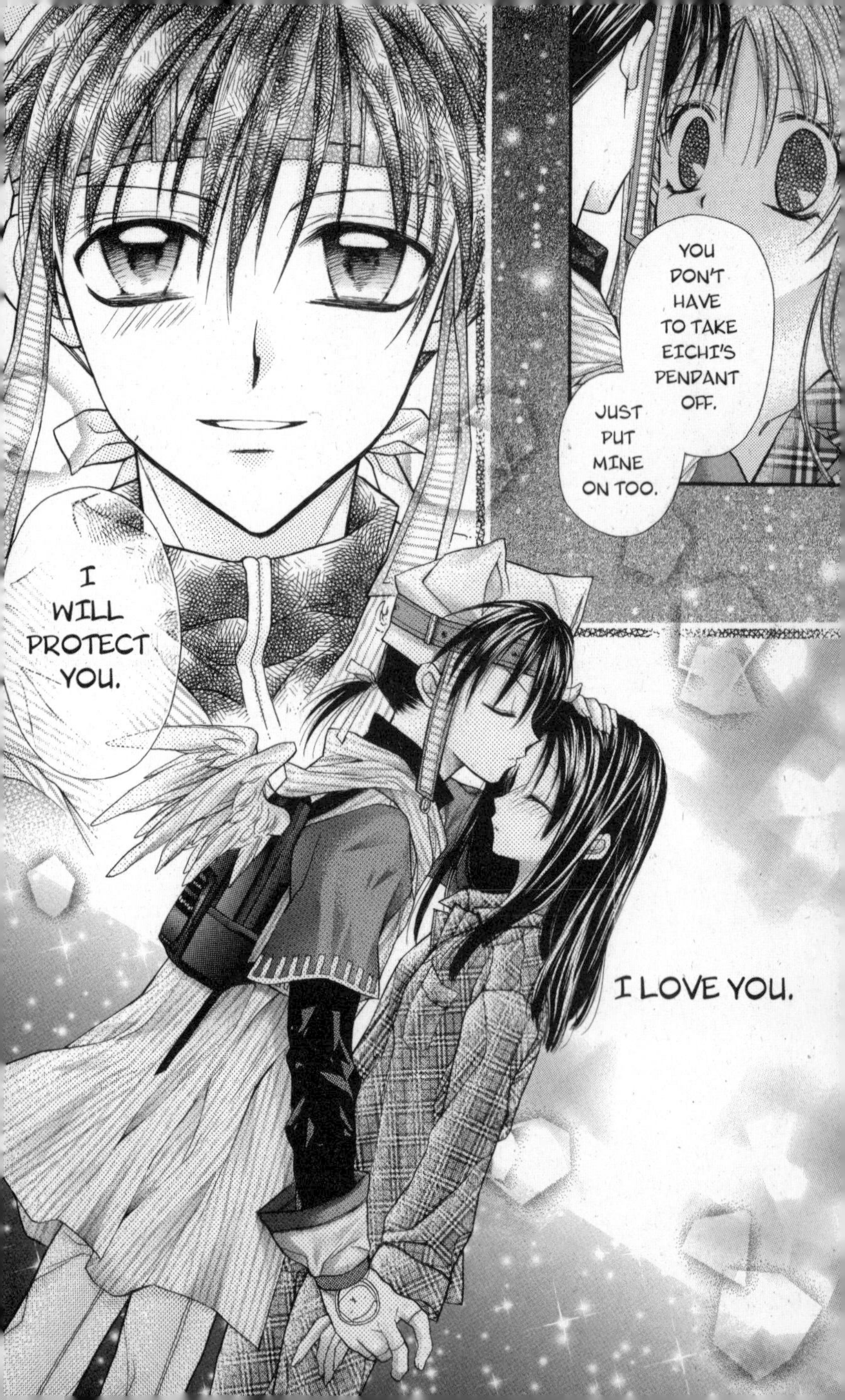
YOU DON'T HAVE TO TAKE EICHI'S PENDANT OFF.
JUST PUT MINE ON TOO.
I LOVE YOU.
I WILL PROTECT YOU.

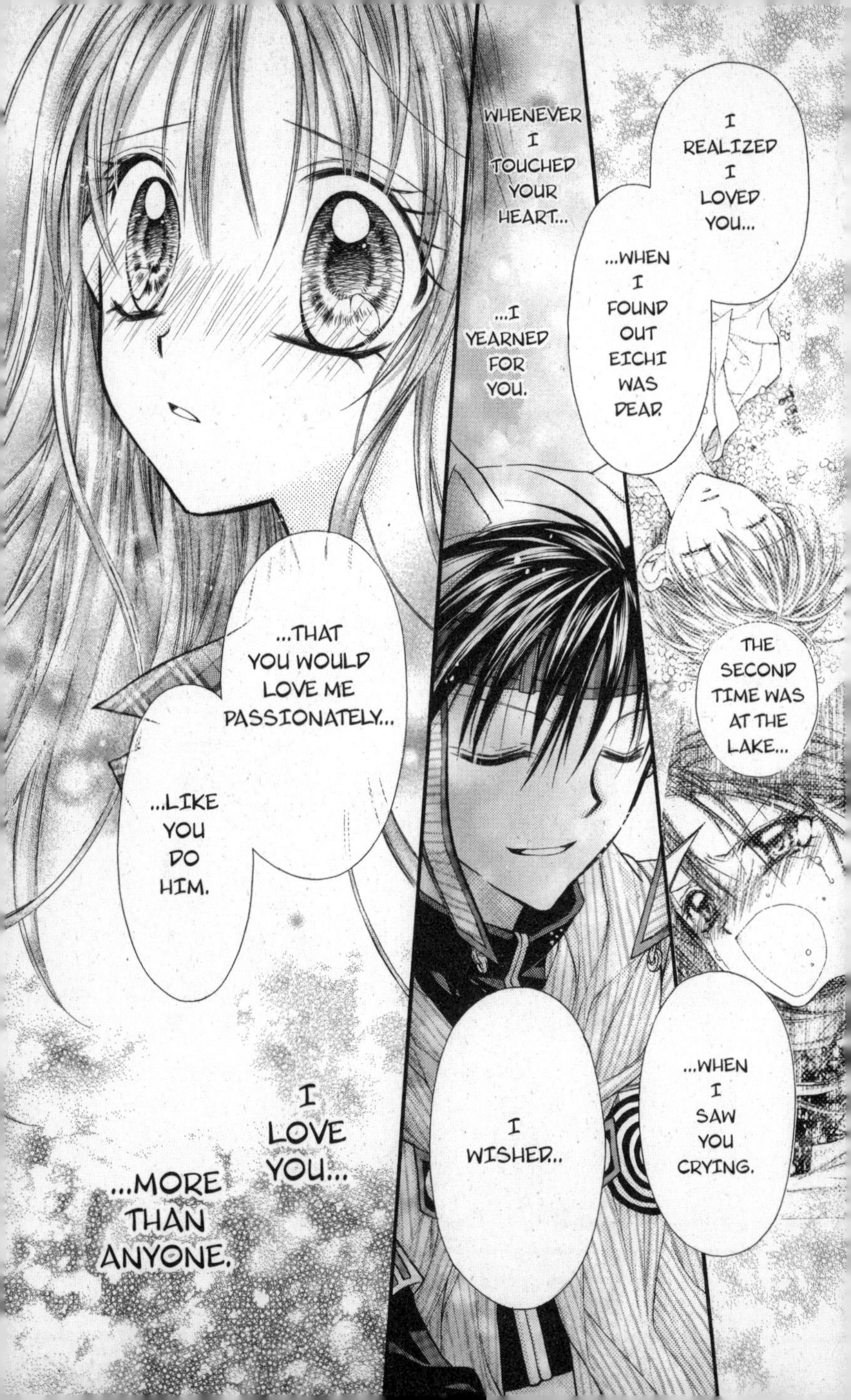
I REALIZED I LOVED YOU...
...WHEN I FOUND OUT EICHI WAS DEAD.
THE SECOND TIME WAS AT THE LAKE...
...WHEN I SAW YOU CRYING.
WHENEVER I TOUCHED YOUR HEART...
...I YEARNED FOR YOU.
I WISHED...
...THAT YOU WOULD LOVE ME PASSIONATELY...
...LIKE YOU DO HIM.
I LOVE YOU...
...MORE THAN ANYONE.

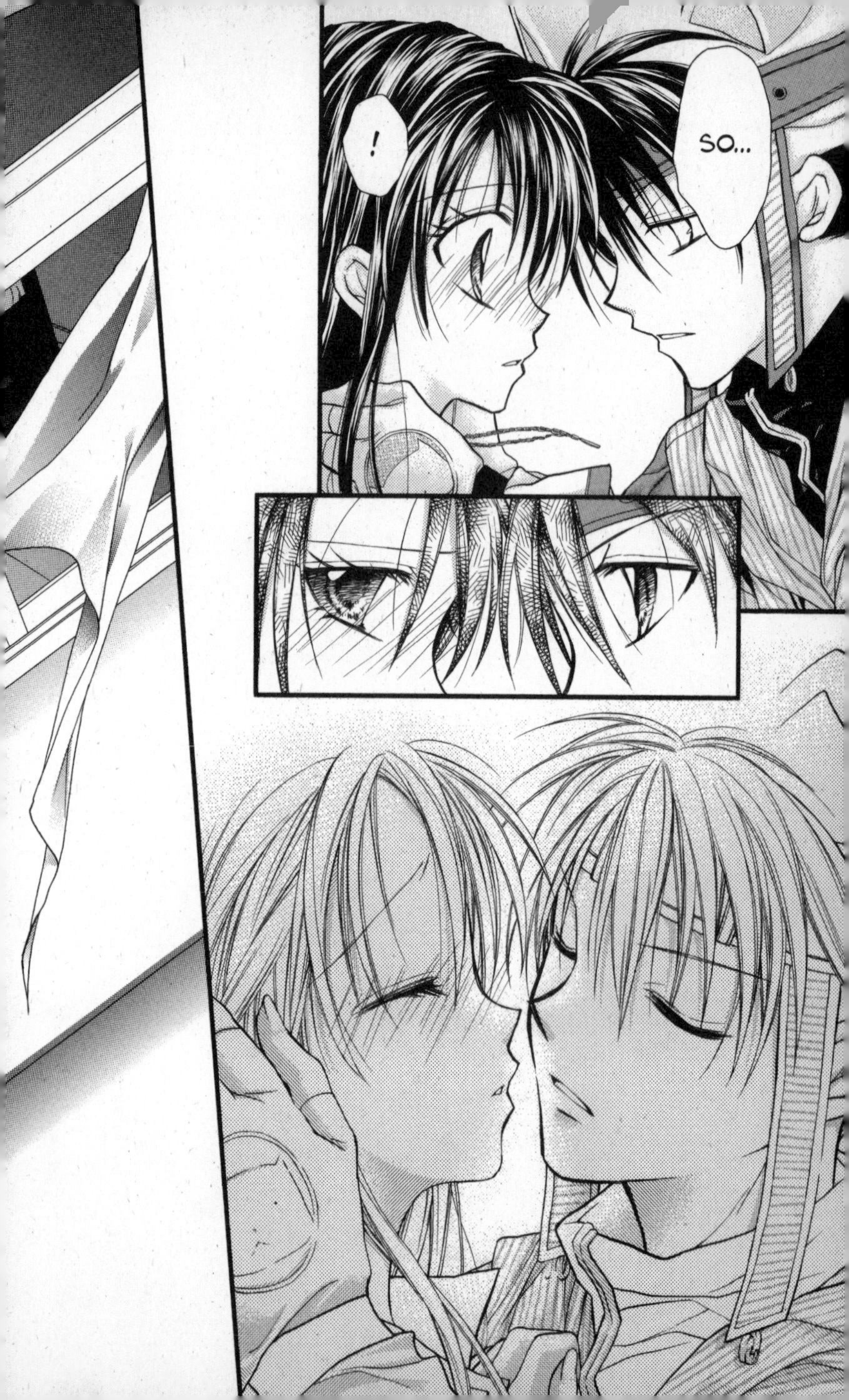
SO...
!

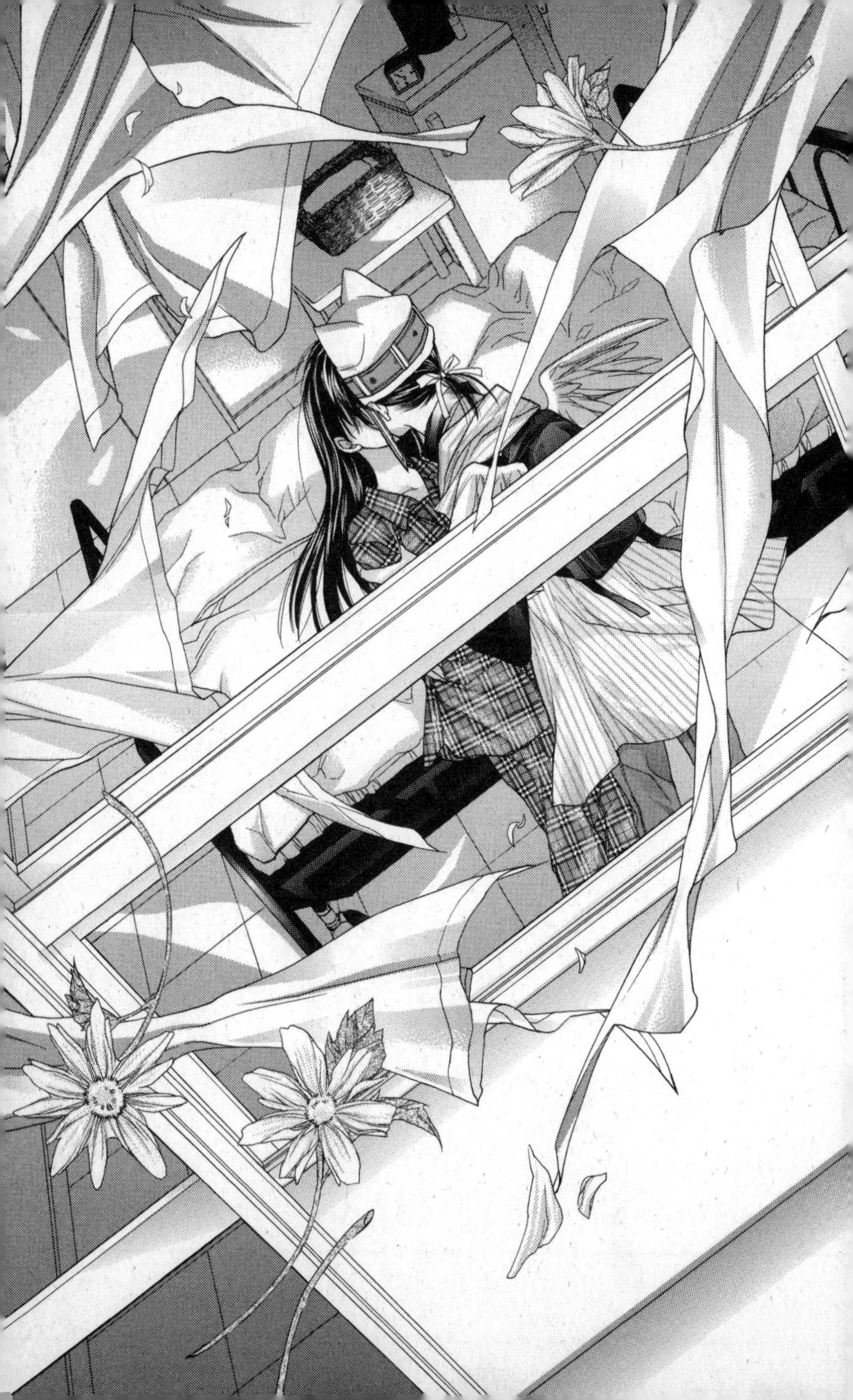

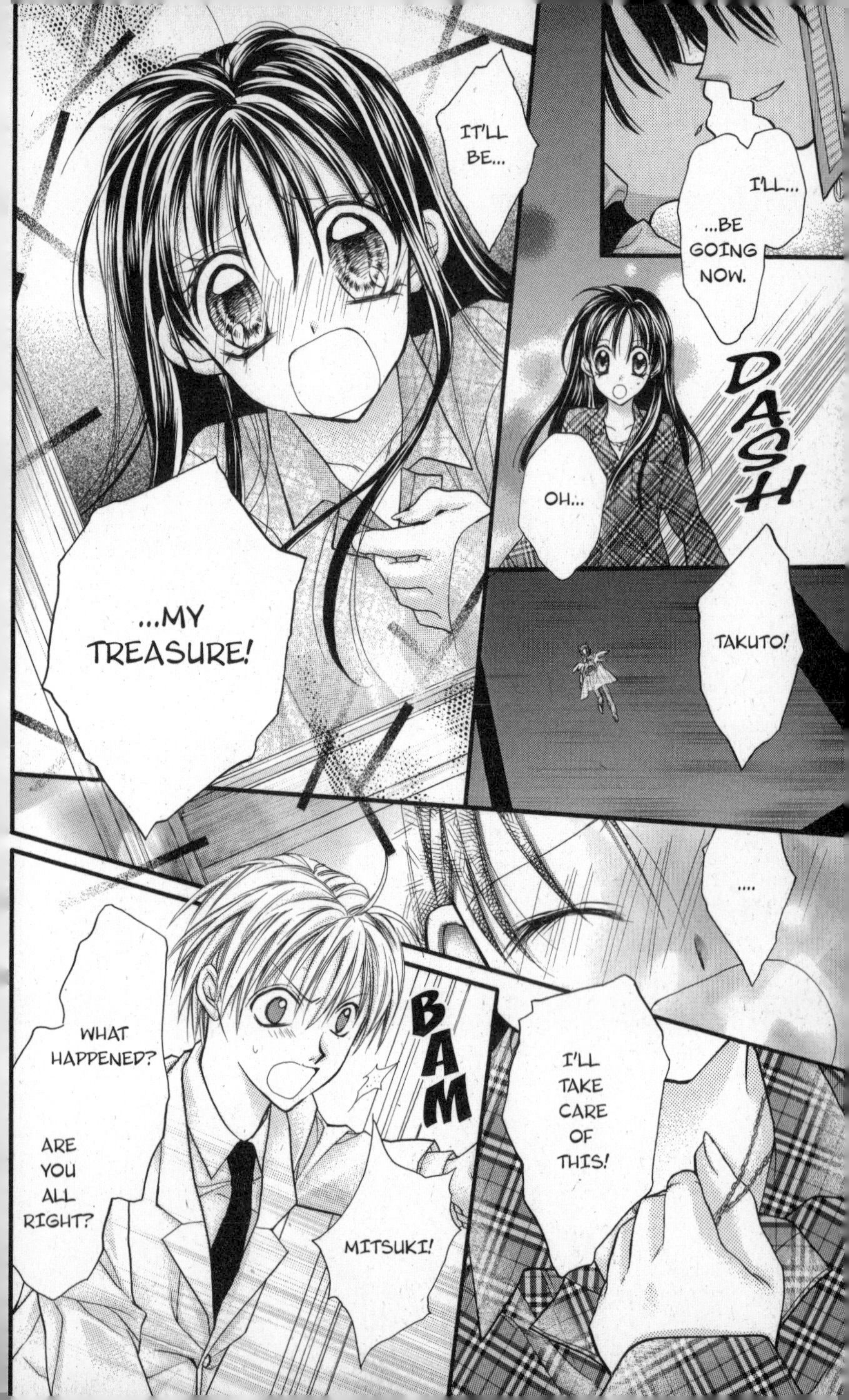
I'LL...
...BE GOING NOW.
DASH
OH...
TAKUTO!
IT'LL BE...
...MY TREASURE!
....
I'LL TAKE CARE OF THIS!
BAM
MITSUKI!
WHAT HAPPENED?
ARE YOU ALL RIGHT?

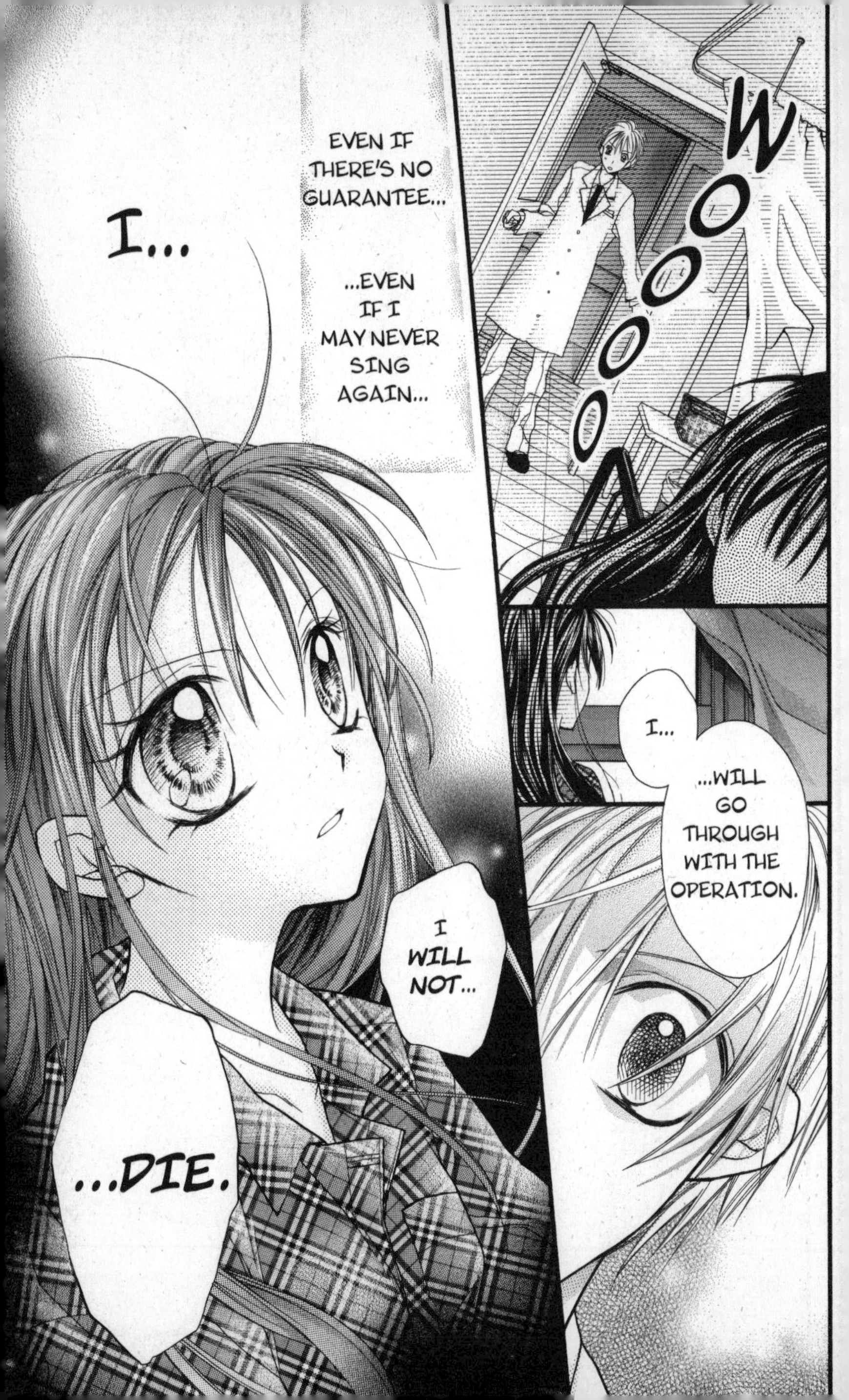

WOOOOOOO
I...
...WILL GO THROUGH WITH THE OPERATION.
EVEN IF THERE'S NO GUARANTEE...
...EVEN IF I MAY NEVER SING AGAIN...
I...
I WILL NOT...
...DIE.

READY, TAKUTO?

YEAH.

I WILL NOT.

...A FRIEND HELPED ME OUT.

It wasn't Fuzuki?

THEN WHO CAME TO SIGN THE CONTRACTS?

Interrogation of the good girl

YES...

UM...

OH...

I WON'T TELL THE COMPANY ABOUT YOUR ILLNESS. I'M PREPARED TO BE FIRED FOR THAT.

I'VE HEARD ENOUGH.

ALL RIGHT!

SO...

...YOU DYED YOUR HAIR AND BECAME A SINGER?

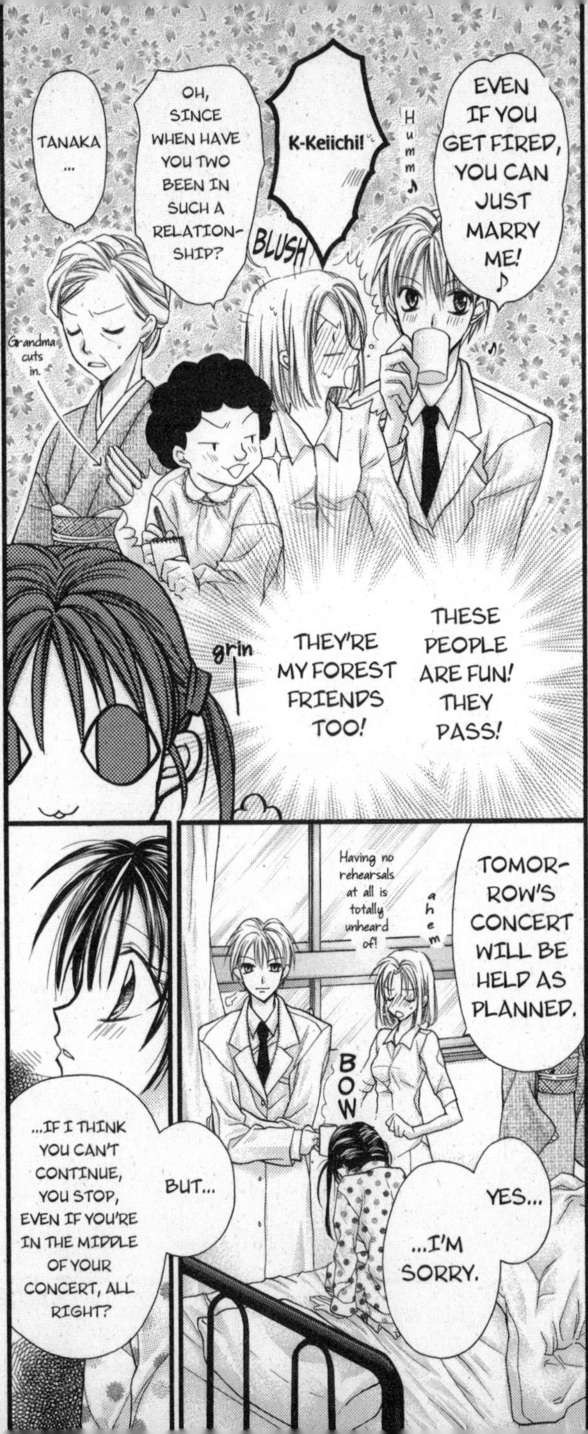
EVEN IF YOU GET FIRED, YOU CAN JUST MARRY ME! ♪
Humm ♪
K-Keiichi!
BLUSH
OH, SINCE WHEN HAVE YOU TWO BEEN IN SUCH A RELATIONSHIP?
TANAKA...
Grandma cuts in.
THESE PEOPLE ARE FUN! THEY PASS!
THEY'RE MY FOREST FRIENDS TOO!
grin
TOMORROW'S CONCERT WILL BE HELD AS PLANNED.
ahem
Having no rehearsals at all is totally unheard of!
BOW
YES...
...I'M SORRY.
BUT...
...IF I THINK YOU CAN'T CONTINUE, YOU STOP, EVEN IF YOU'RE IN THE MIDDLE OF YOUR CONCERT, ALL RIGHT?

Penshaki

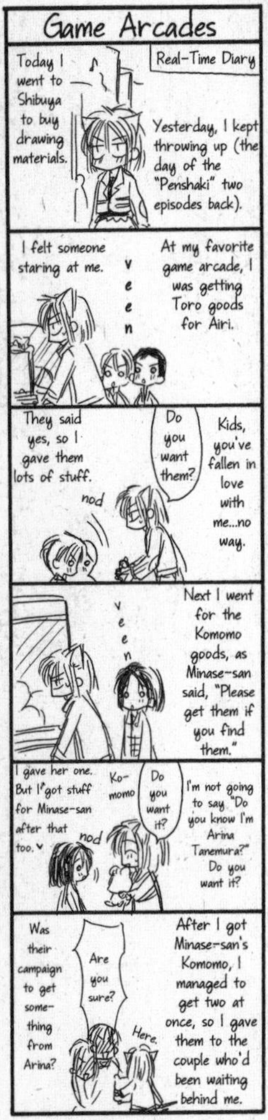
Game Arcades
Real-Time Diary
Today I went to Shibuya to buy drawing materials.
Yesterday, I kept throwing up (the day of the "Penshaki" two episodes back).
At my favorite game arcade, I was getting Toro goods for Airi.
I felt someone staring at me.
veen
They said yes, so I gave them lots of stuff.
Do you want them?
Kids, you've fallen in love with me...no way.
nod
Next I went for the Komomo goods, as Minase-san said, "Please get them if you find them."
veen
I'm not going to say "Do you know I'm Arina Tanemura?" Do you want it?
Do you want it?
Komomo
I gave her one. But I got stuff for Minase-san after that too.
nod
After I got Minase-san's Komomo, I managed to get two at once, so I gave them to the couple who'd been waiting behind me.
Are you sure?
Here.
Was their campaign to get something from Arina?

⋛ I got Airi's Toro too. Game arcades are fun. There's Purikura too.

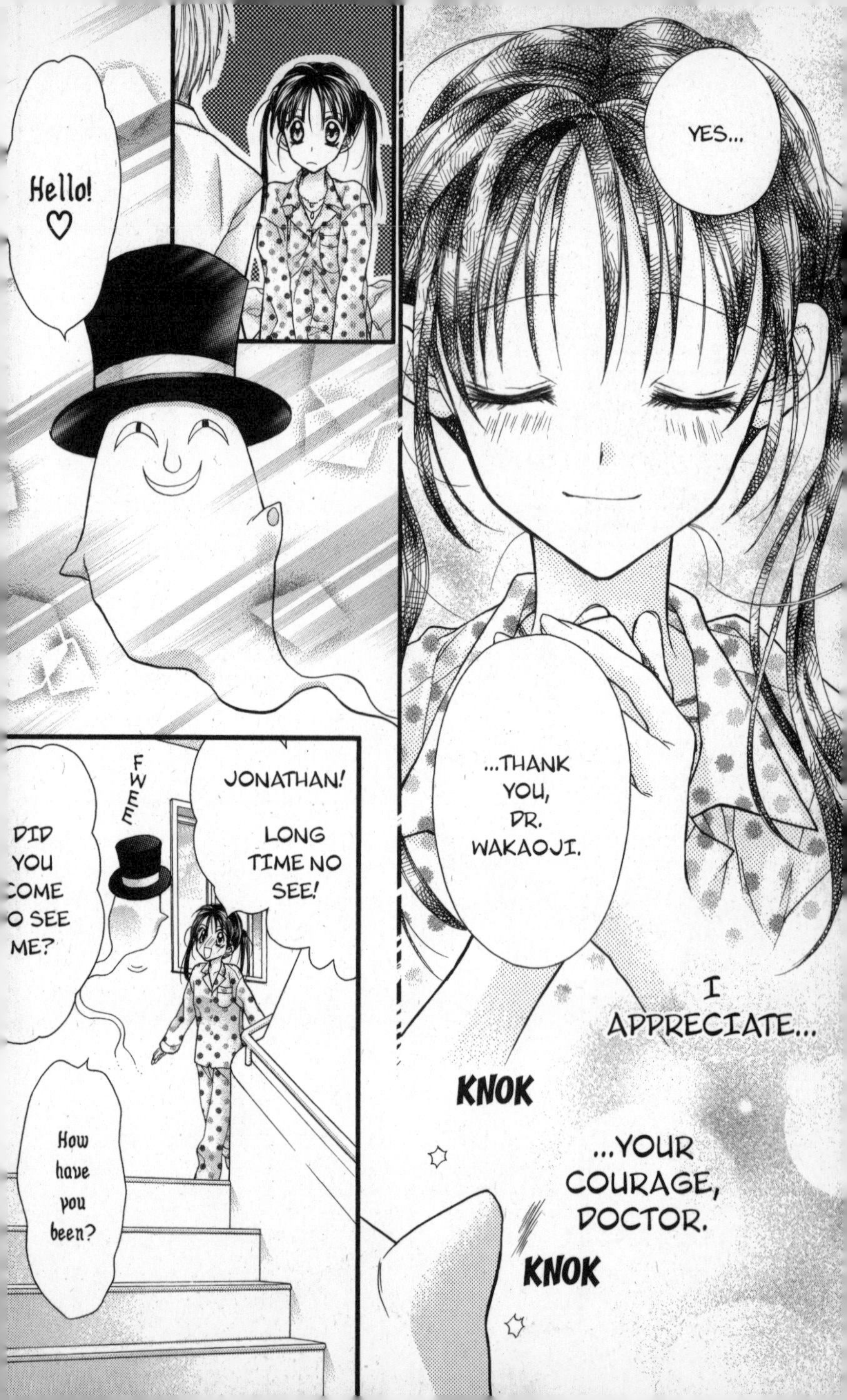
YES...
...THANK YOU, DR. WAKAOJI.
I APPRECIATE...
KNOK
...YOUR COURAGE, DOCTOR.
KNOK
Hello! ♡
JONATHAN! LONG TIME NO SEE!
FWEE
DID YOU COME O SEE ME?
How have you been?

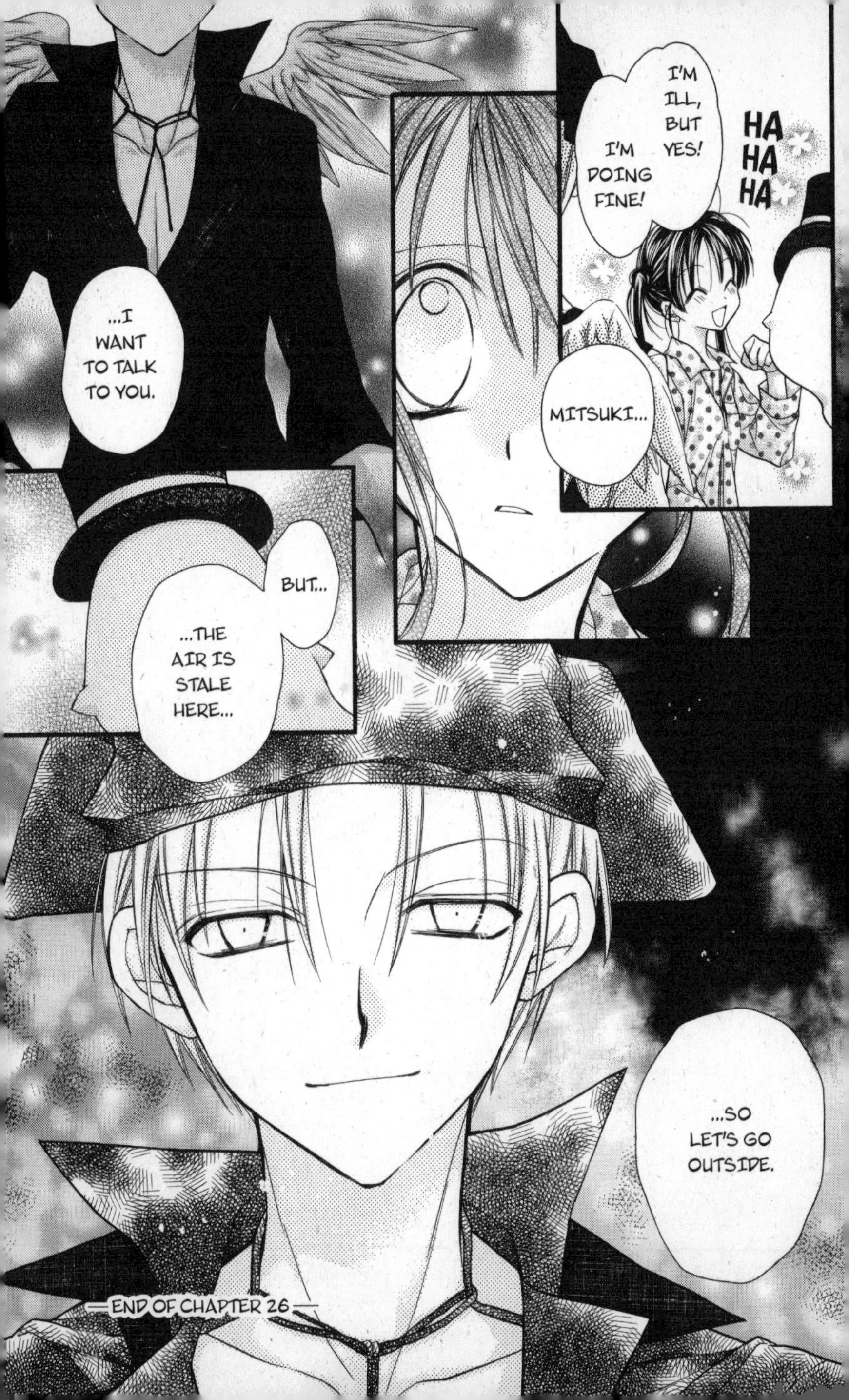

I'M ILL, BUT YES! I'M DOING FINE!
HA HA HA
MITSUKI...
...I WANT TO TALK TO YOU.
BUT...
...THE AIR IS STALE HERE...
...SO LET'S GO OUTSIDE.
—END OF CHAPTER 26—

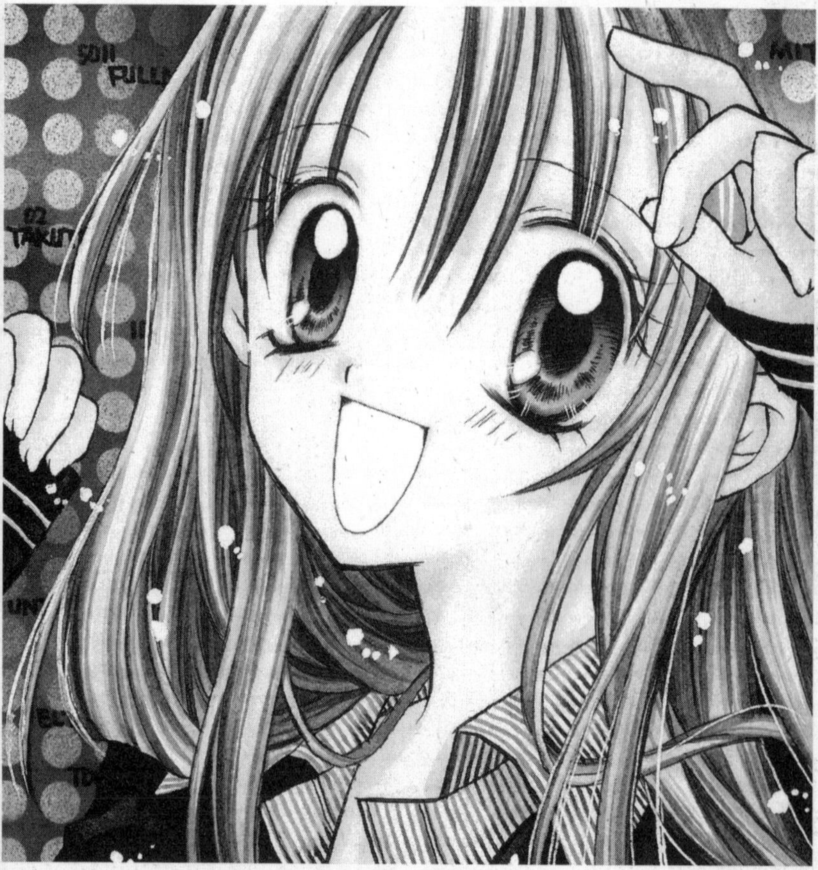

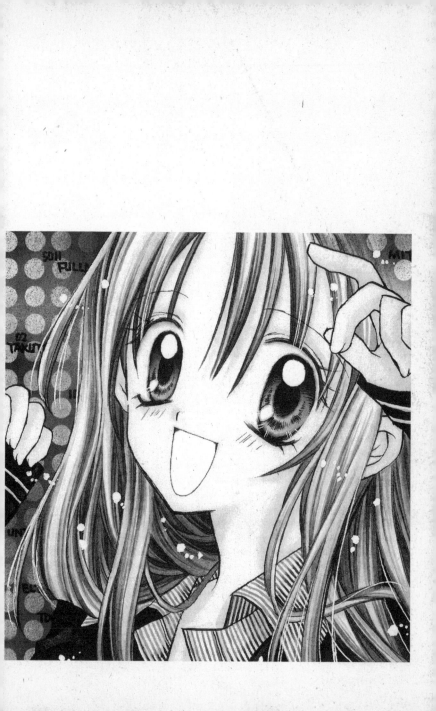

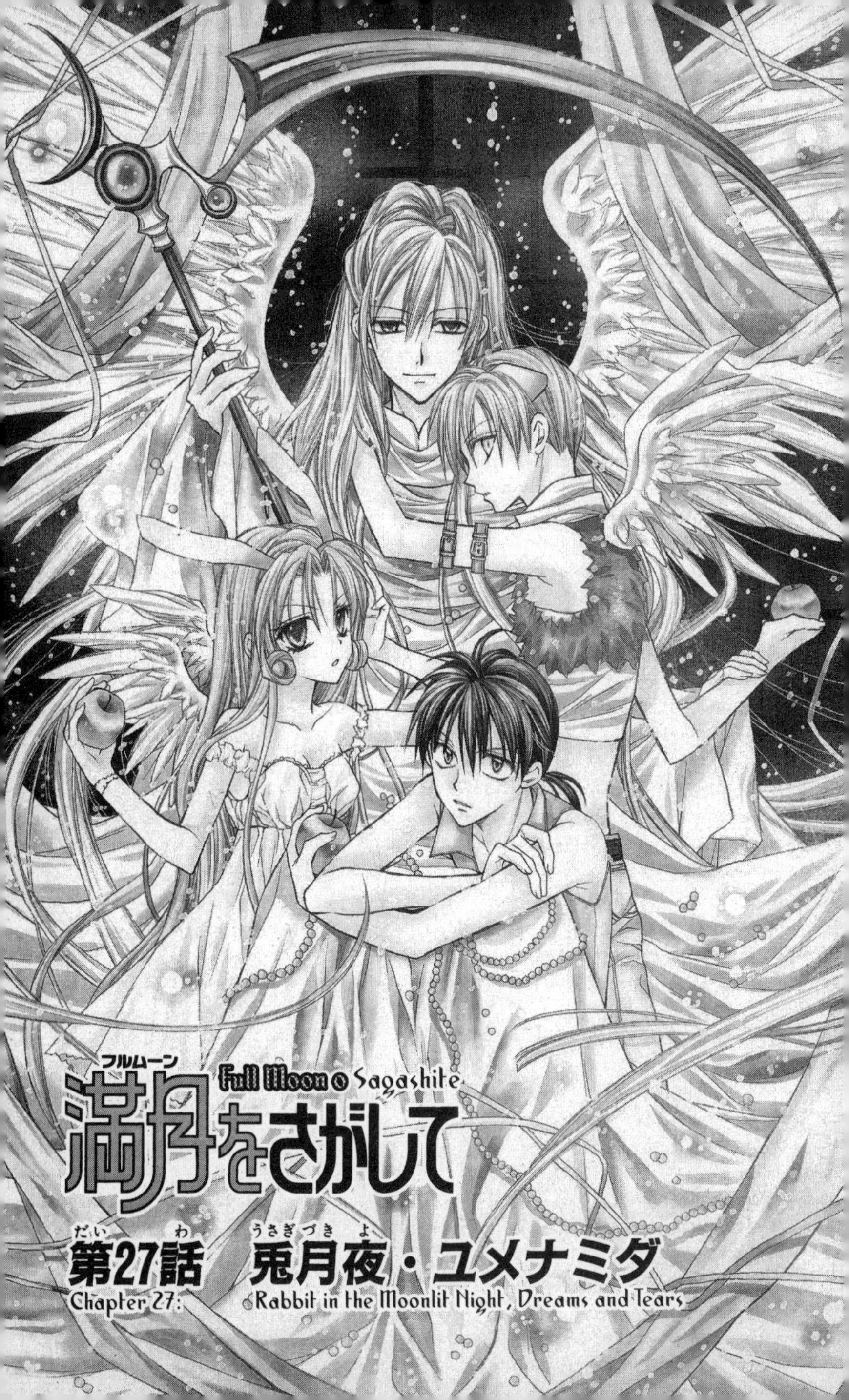
フルムーン
満月をさがして
Full Moon o Sagashite
第27話 兎月夜・ユメナミダ
Chapter 27: Rabbit in the Moonlit Night, Dreams and Tears

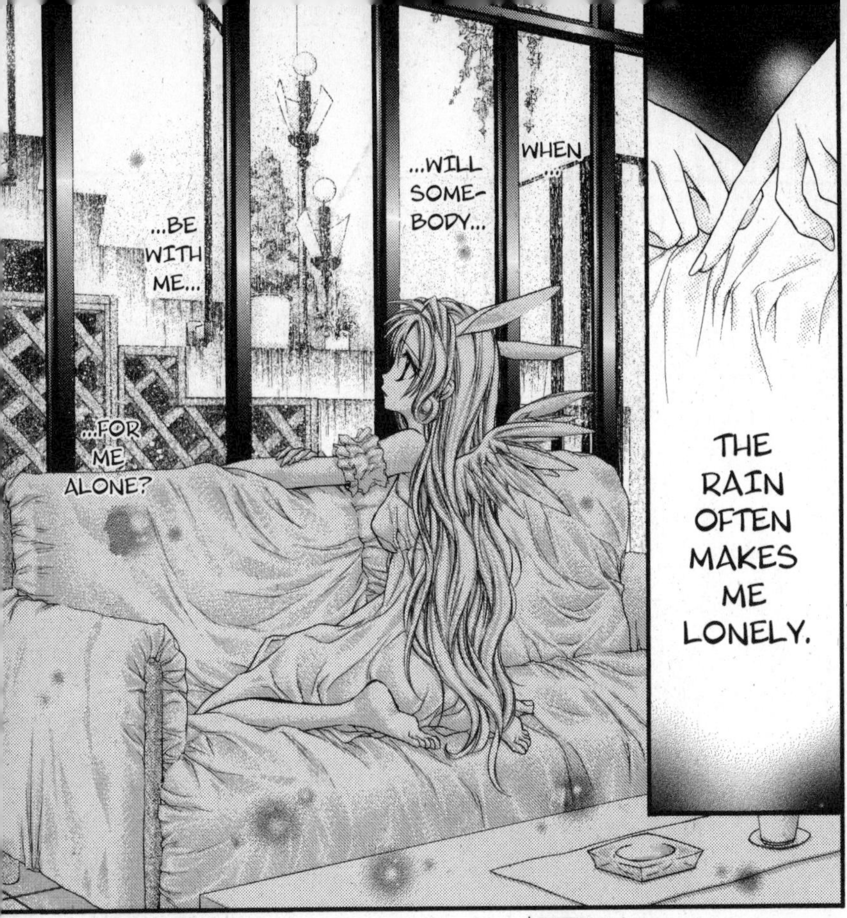
THE RAIN OFTEN MAKES ME LONELY.
WHEN...
...WILL SOME-BODY...
...BE WITH ME...
...FOR ME ALONE?

Chapter 27:
Rabbit in the Moonlit Night, Dreams and Tears
(spoilers follow)

Cover Copy Wouldn't you like to know the secrets of death when you are human?

This chapter is about Meechan. I like the first page very much. It's my image of rain. Like, the room is Meroko's heart... Who will come for her here, if he'll get wet in the rain? Meroko thinks, "The door is not locked, so why am I always alone?" It shows Meroko's selfishness well. She has to leave the room and go get that person at the door, or else he won't know she's here.

In the middle of the chapter there's a similar monologue. Meroko is moving forward slowly as well.

In the end, she loves Izumi. But she knows that she was seriously drawn to Takuto, who wouldn't accept her.

Among all the chapters, I think I did a particularly good job with this one.

Meechan, do your best. Only your heart knows where happiness lies.

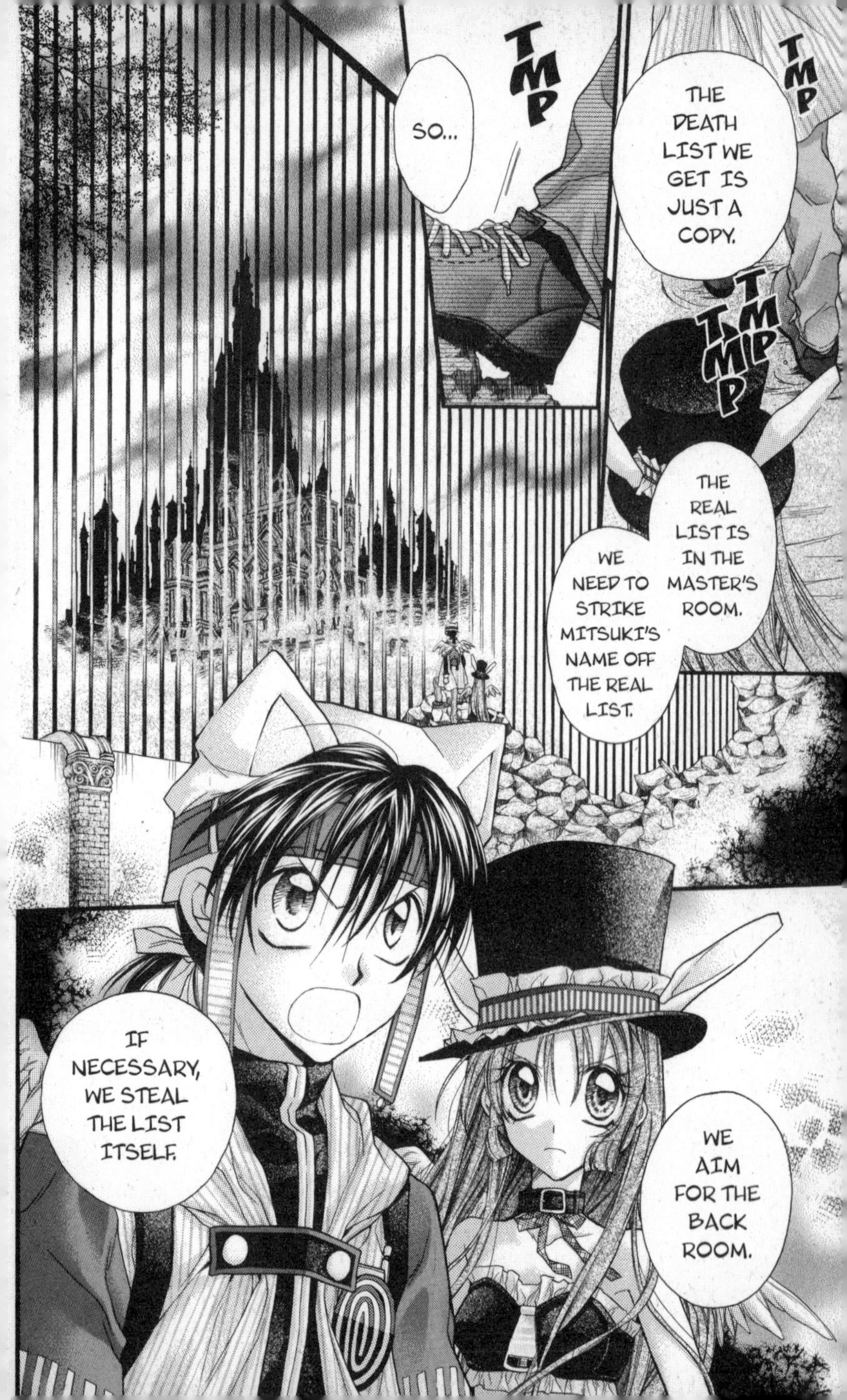
TMP
THE DEATH LIST WE GET IS JUST A COPY.
TMP TMP
TMP
SO...
THE REAL LIST IS IN THE MASTER'S ROOM.
WE NEED TO STRIKE MITSUKI'S NAME OFF THE REAL LIST.
WE AIM FOR THE BACK ROOM.
IF NECESSARY, WE STEAL THE LIST ITSELF.

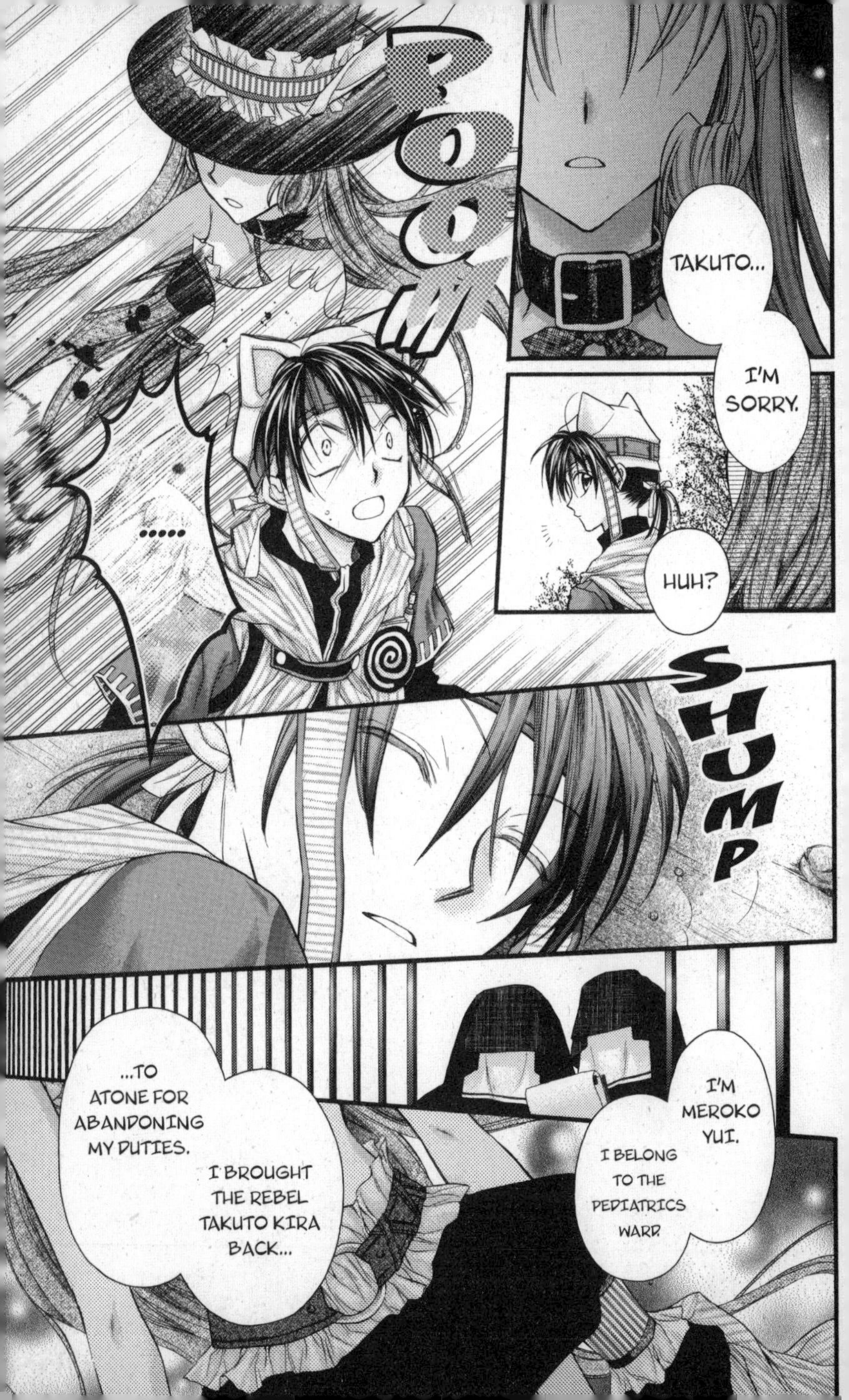
TAKUTO...
I'M SORRY.
HUH?
BOOM
.....
SHUMP
I'M MEROKO YUI.
I BELONG TO THE PEDIATRICS WARD.
I BROUGHT THE REBEL TAKUTO KIRA BACK...
...TO ATONE FOR ABANDONING MY DUTIES.

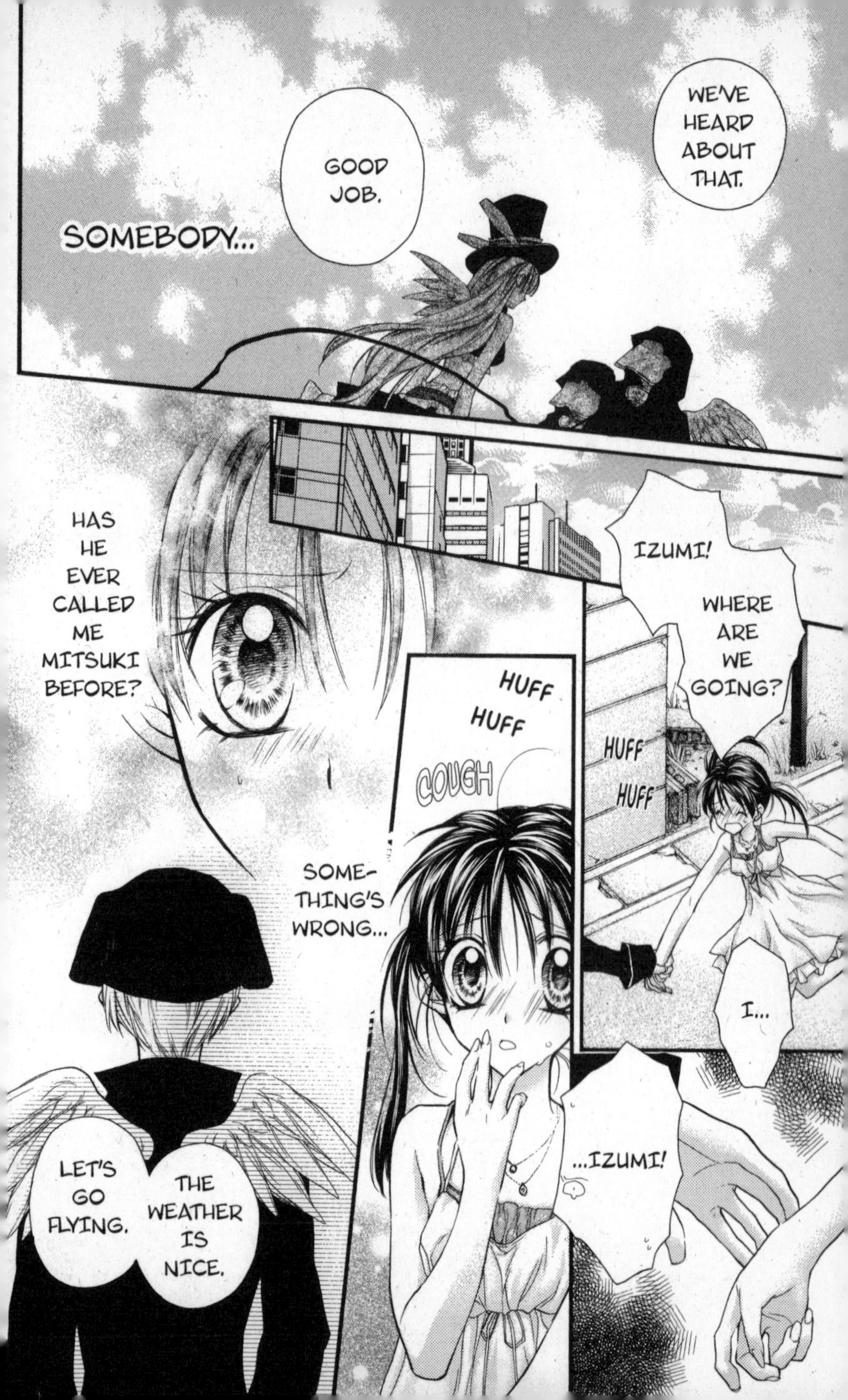
WE'VE HEARD ABOUT THAT.
GOOD JOB.
SOMEBODY...
IZUMI!
WHERE ARE WE GOING?
HUFF
HUFF
I...
HUFF
HUFF
COUGH
SOMETHING'S WRONG...
HAS HE EVER CALLED ME MITSUKI BEFORE?
...IZUMI!
THE WEATHER IS NICE.
LET'S GO FLYING.

About the Letters I Receive 5

The letters I've shown were mainly the ones I received through the *Ribon* website.

I put the rare ones in here. About 97% of them are always cute and bubbly and lively and have funny words of love. (There are also emails full of love too.)

"I really, really, really like you!" or
"I love you!!" or
"I'm looking forward to it!!"

I don't get angry much, unless people are rude to me (it's not true that I get angry easily or am weak), so it's okay.

It's okay not to use polite language in your email.

But when you meet someone in public, use polite language when you're talking to someone who's older than you. (No, you don't have to use it, but I like kids who have manners!)

Yes!!

What am I going to do...
One more, and then the sidebar is over. What about *Full Moon*?

I'll talk about it in the sidebars in Volume 7! (The Plan)

I've written a bit in the space at the beginning of each chapter.

Next is what I'm doing nowadays and "Special Thanks."

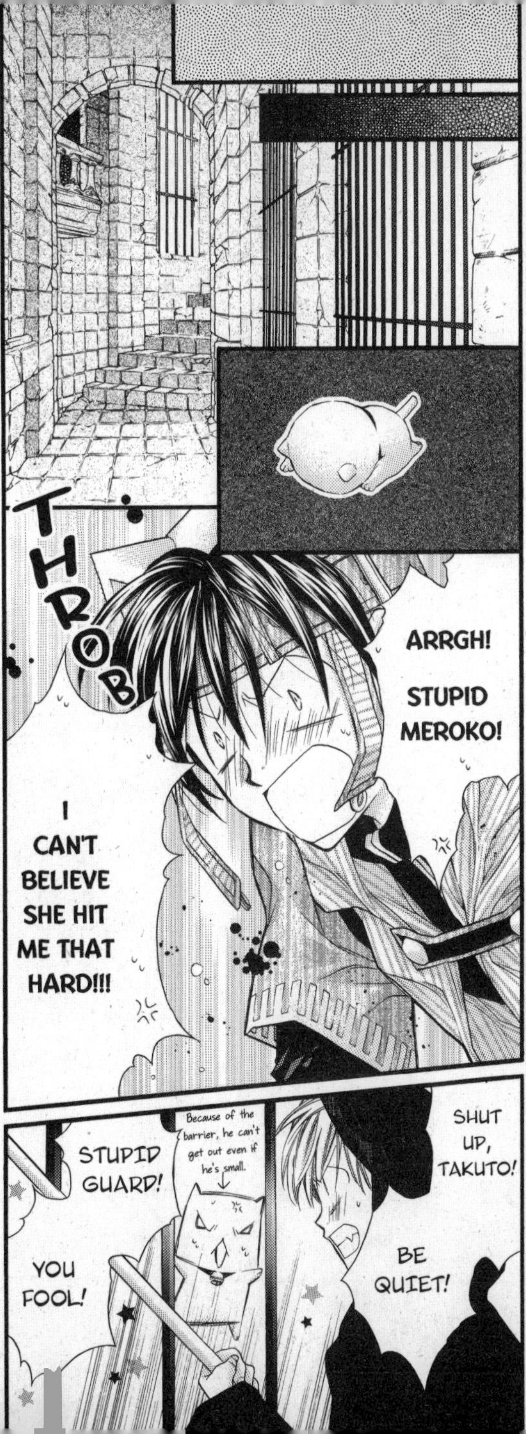
THROB
ARRGH!
STUPID MEROKO!
I CAN'T BELIEVE SHE HIT ME THAT HARD!!!
SHUT UP, TAKUTO!
BE QUIET!
Because of the barrier, he can't get out even if he's small.
STUPID GUARD!
YOU FOOL!

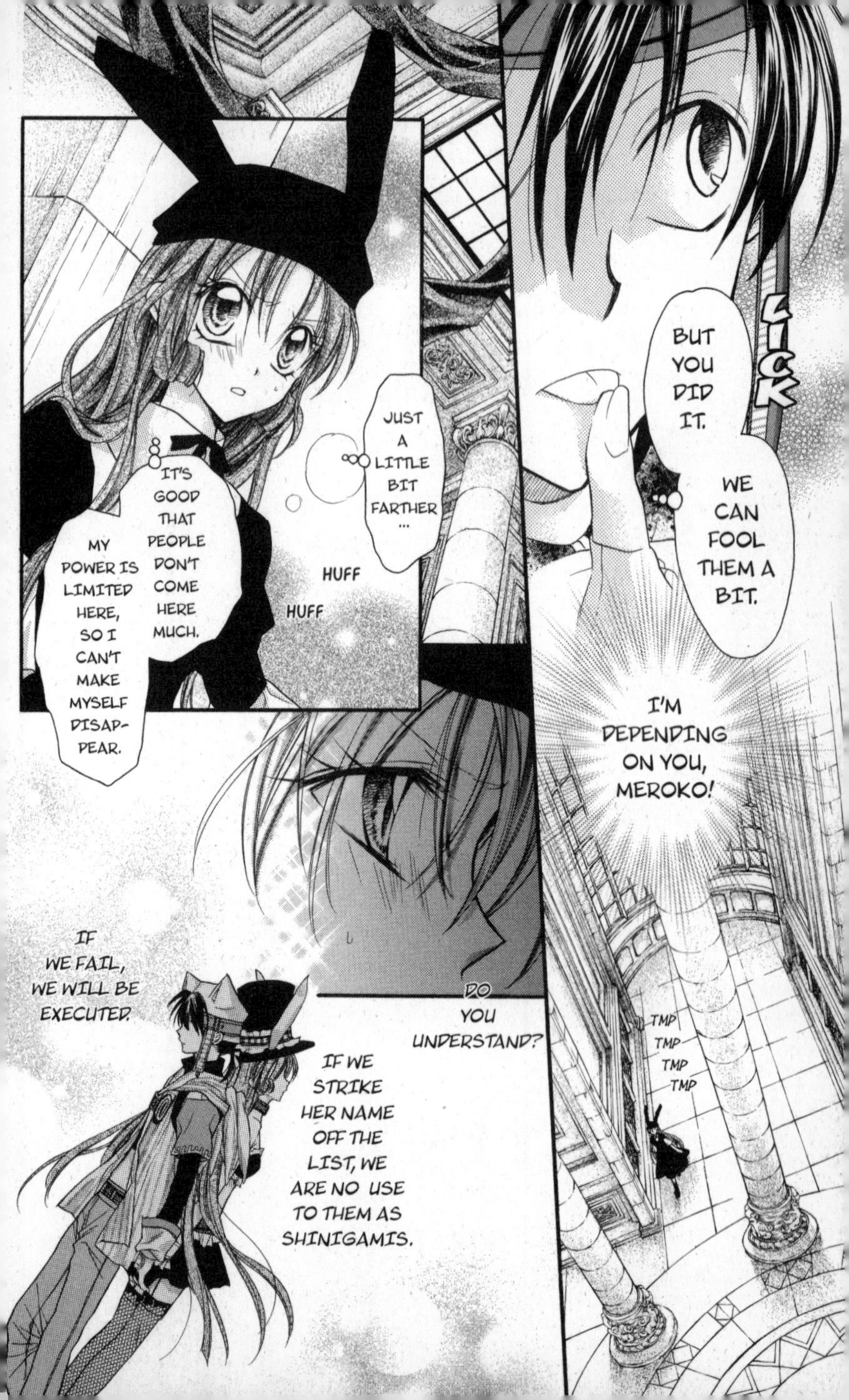
LICK
BUT YOU DID IT.
WE CAN FOOL THEM A BIT.
I'M DEPENDING ON YOU, MEROKO!
TMP TMP TMP TMP
JUST A LITTLE BIT FARTHER...
HUFF HUFF
IT'S GOOD THAT PEOPLE DON'T COME HERE MUCH.
MY POWER IS LIMITED HERE, SO I CAN'T MAKE MYSELF DISAP-PEAR.
DO YOU UNDERSTAND?
IF WE STRIKE HER NAME OFF THE LIST, WE ARE NO USE TO THEM AS SHINIGAMIS.
IF WE FAIL, WE WILL BE EXECUTED.

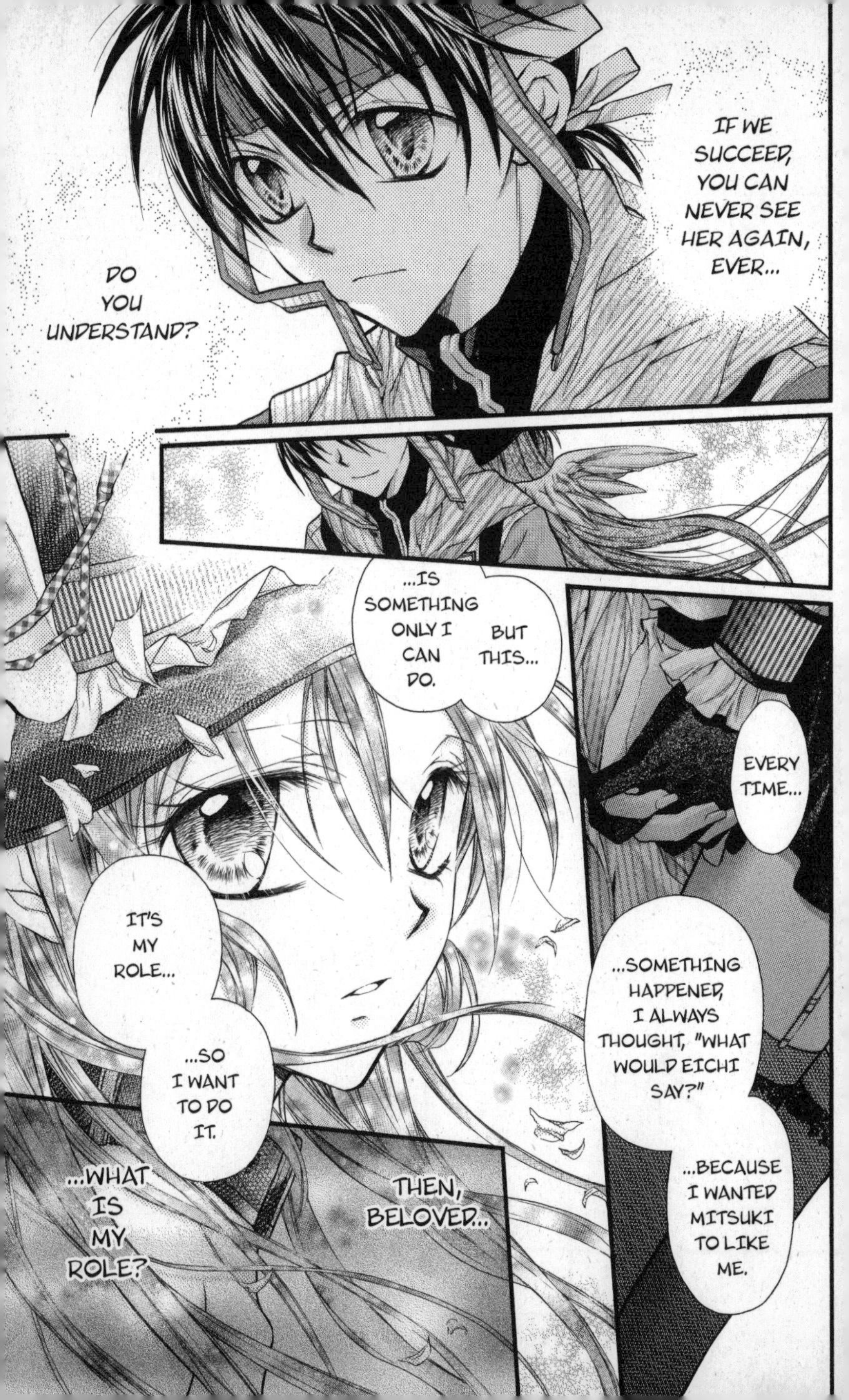
IF WE SUCCEED, YOU CAN NEVER SEE HER AGAIN, EVER...
DO YOU UNDERSTAND?
EVERY TIME...
...SOMETHING HAPPENED, I ALWAYS THOUGHT, "WHAT WOULD EICHI SAY?"
...BECAUSE I WANTED MITSUKI TO LIKE ME.
BUT THIS...
...IS SOMETHING ONLY I CAN DO.
IT'S MY ROLE...
...SO I WANT TO DO IT.
THEN, BELOVED...
...WHAT IS MY ROLE?

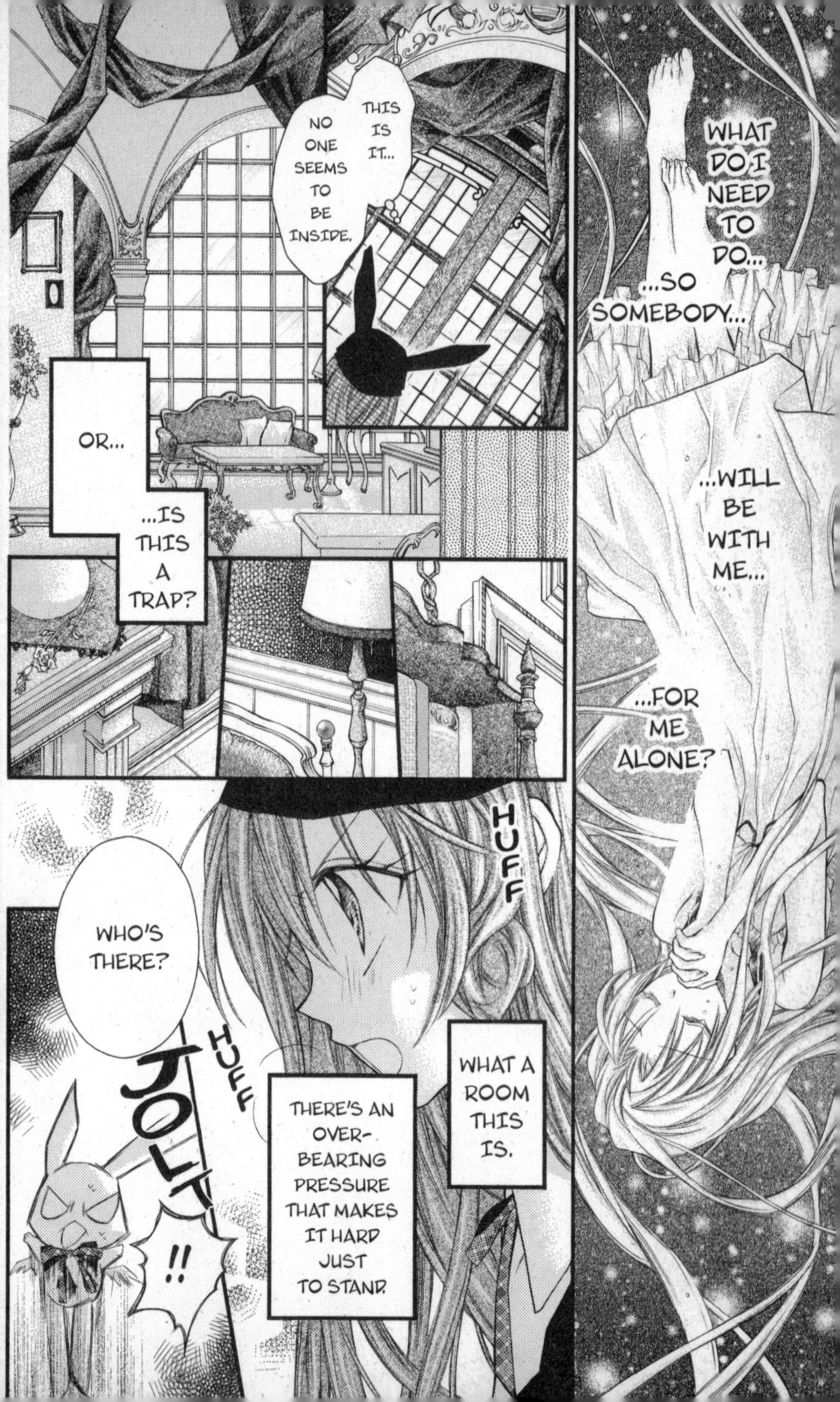
WHAT DO I NEED TO DO...
...SO SOMEBODY...
...WILL BE WITH ME...
...FOR ME ALONE?
THIS IS IT...
NO ONE SEEMS TO BE INSIDE.
OR...
...IS THIS A TRAP?
HUFF
HUFF
WHAT A ROOM THIS IS.
THERE'S AN OVER-BEARING PRESSURE THAT MAKES IT HARD JUST TO STAND.
WHO'S THERE?
JOLT
!!

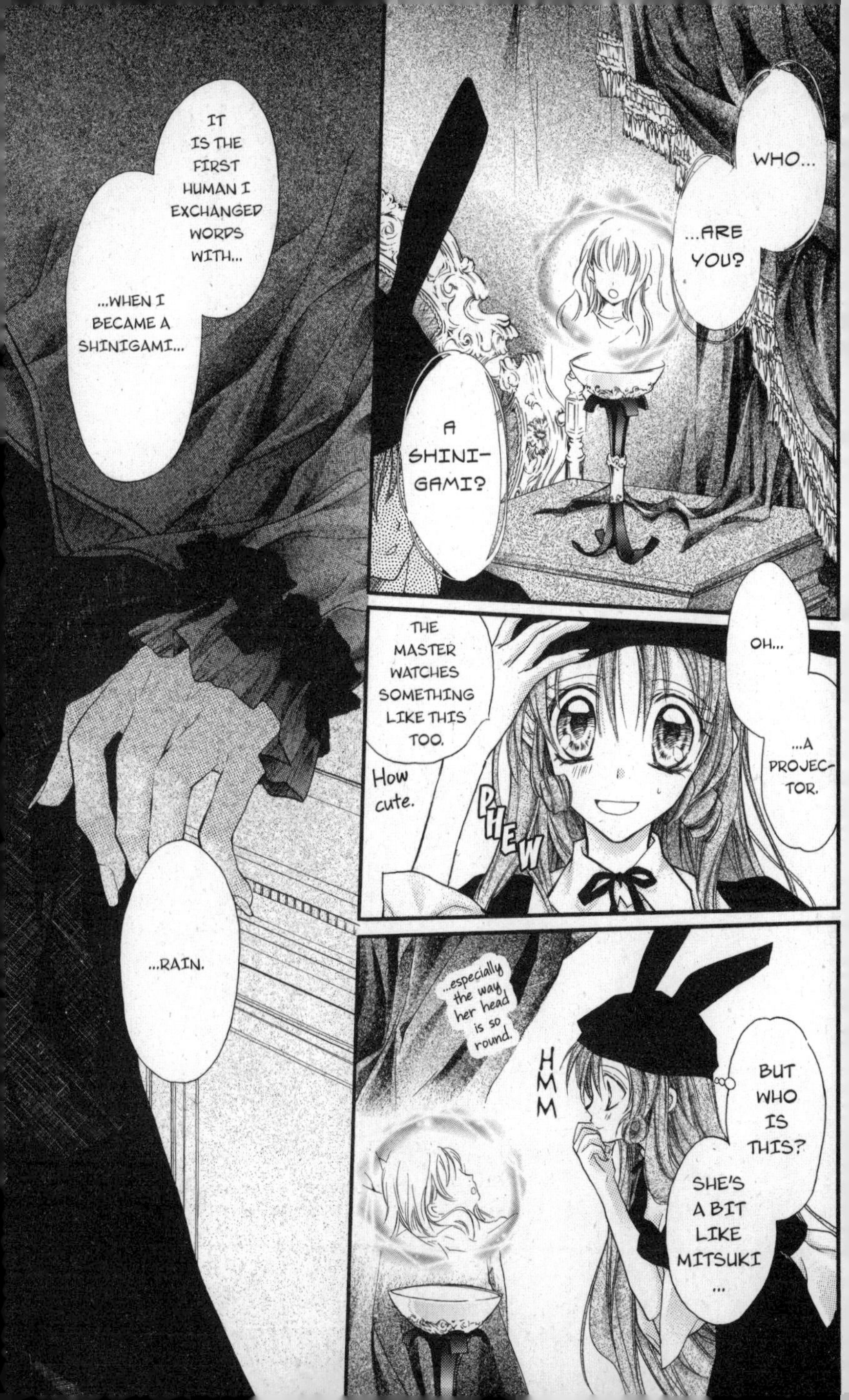
WHO...
...ARE YOU?
A SHINIGAMI?
OH...
...A PROJECTOR.
THE MASTER WATCHES SOMETHING LIKE THIS TOO.
How cute.
PHEW
BUT WHO IS THIS?
SHE'S A BIT LIKE MITSUKI...
HMM
...especially the way her head is so round.
IT IS THE FIRST HUMAN I EXCHANGED WORDS WITH...
...WHEN I BECAME A SHINIGAMI...
...RAIN.

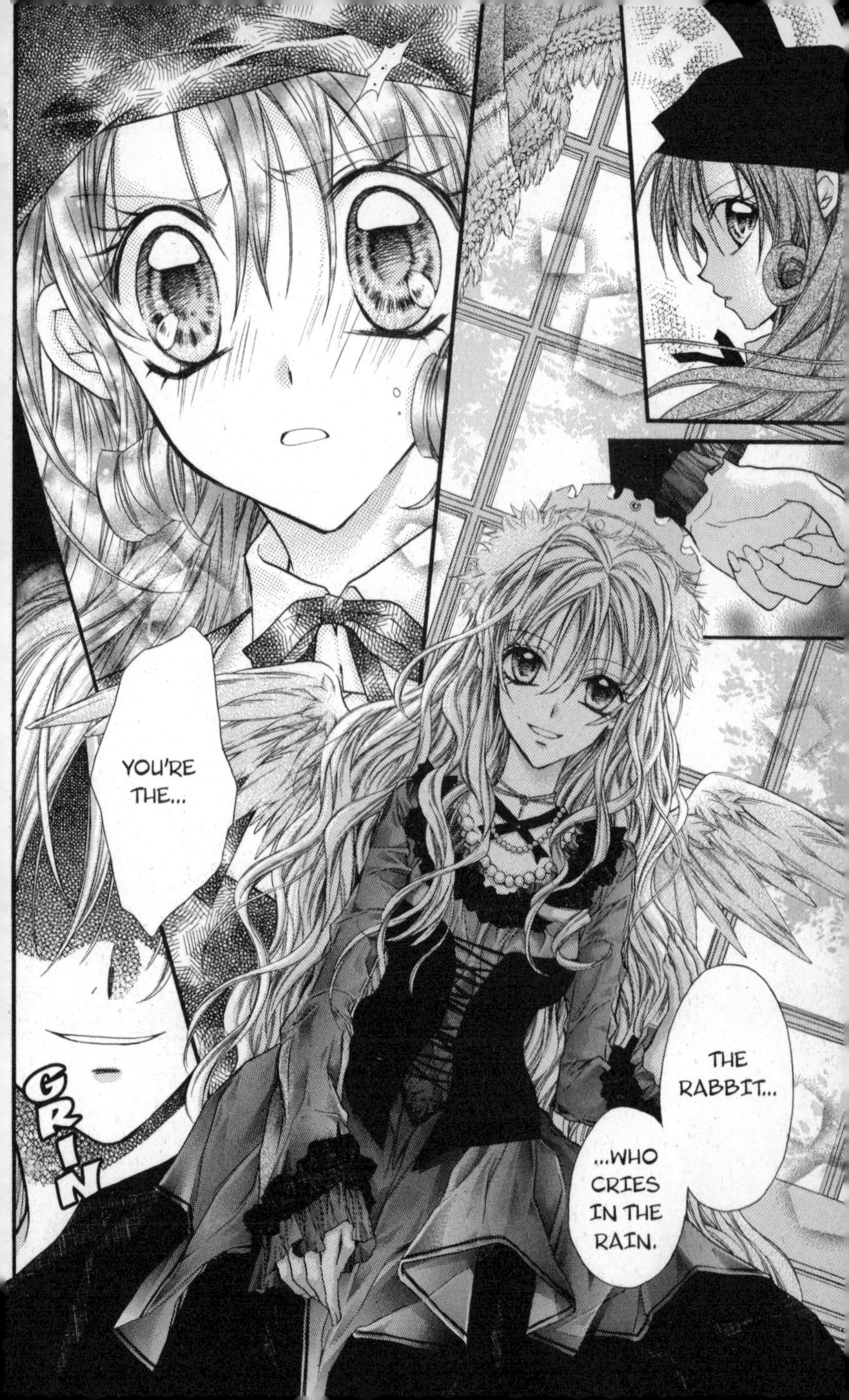
YOU'RE THE...
THE RABBIT...
...WHO CRIES IN THE RAIN.
GRIN

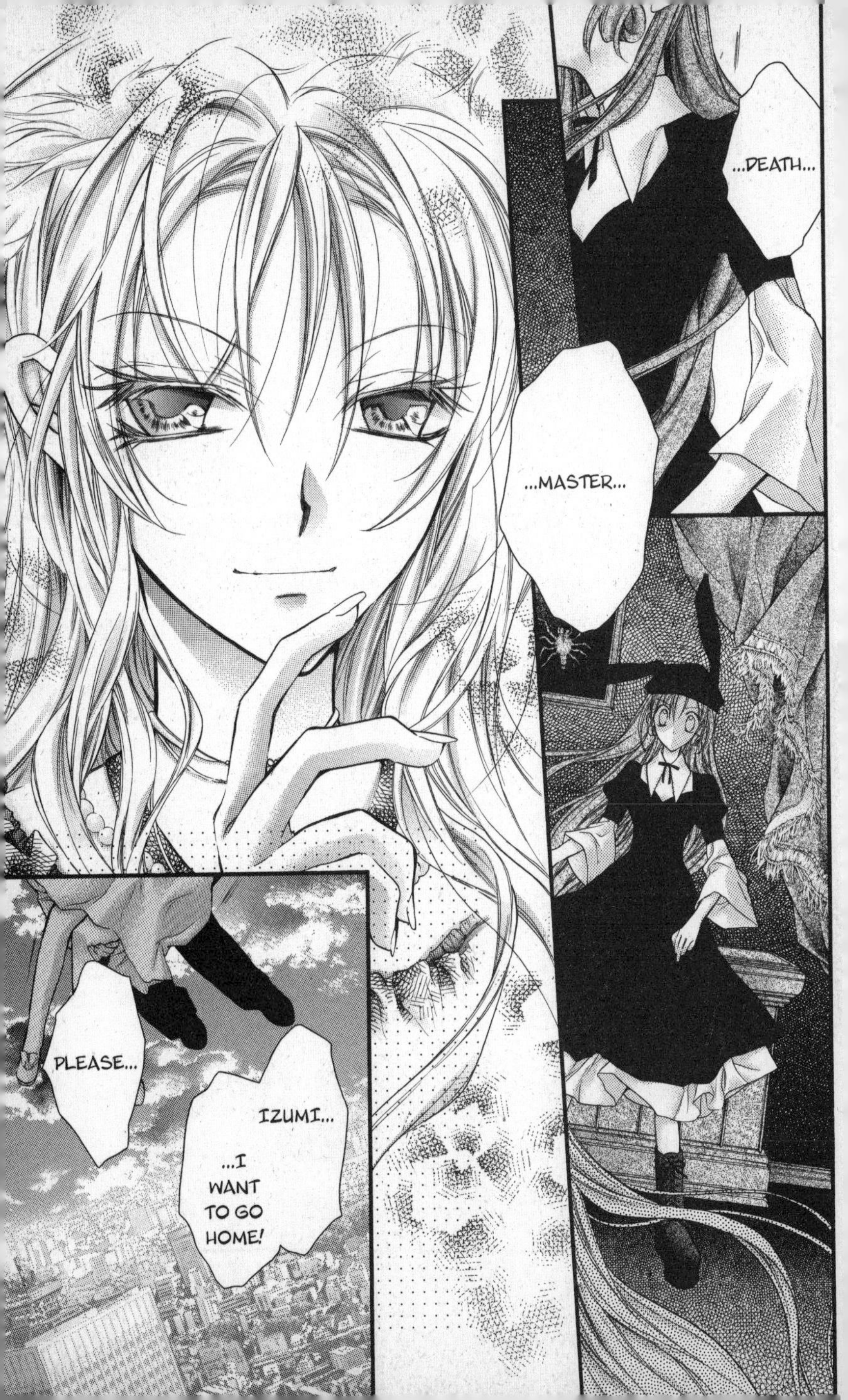
...DEATH...
...MASTER...
PLEASE...
IZUMI...
...I WANT TO GO HOME!

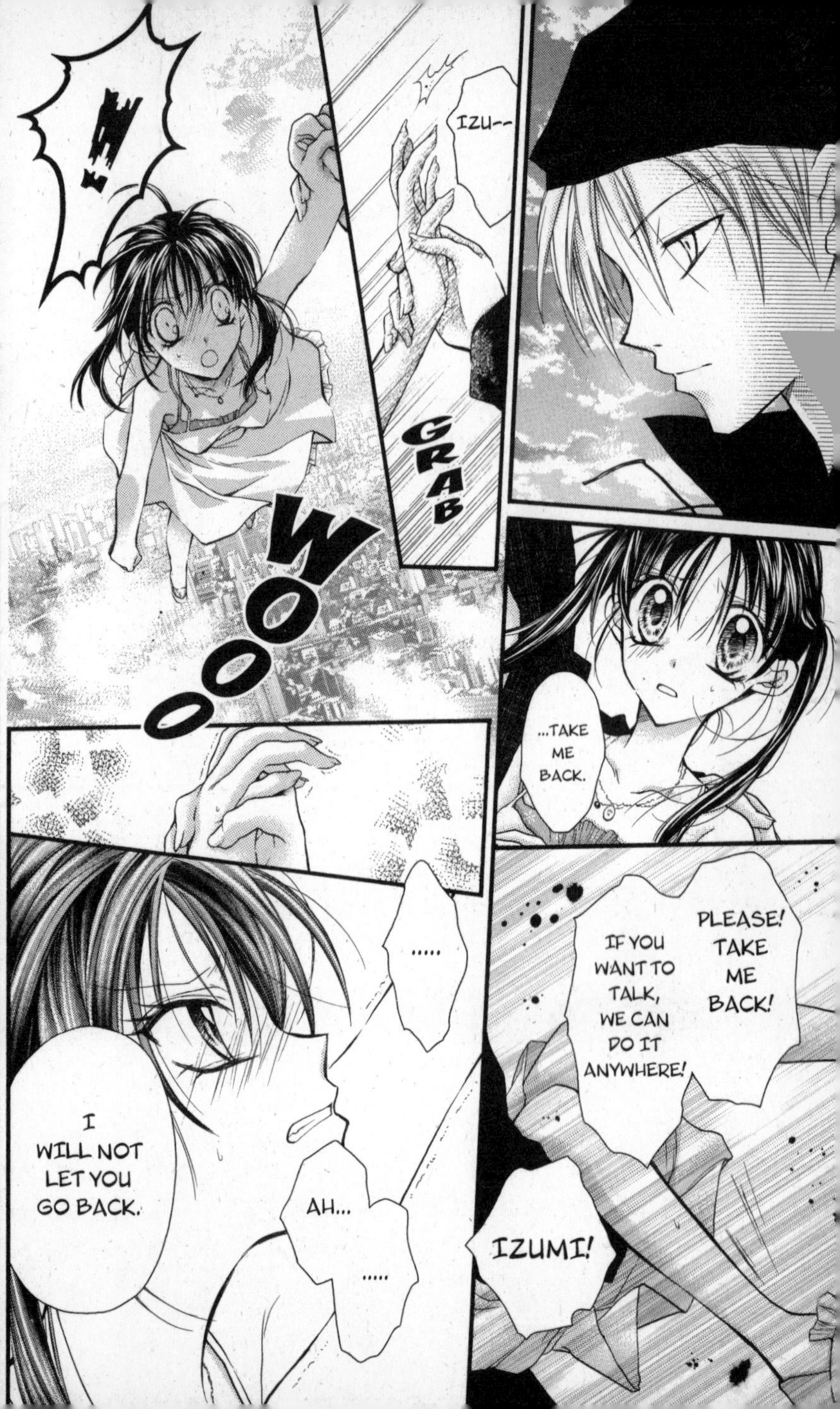
IZU--
GRAB
WOOOO
...TAKE ME BACK.
PLEASE! TAKE ME BACK!
IF YOU WANT TO TALK, WE CAN DO IT ANYWHERE!
IZUMI!
.....
I WILL NOT LET YOU GO BACK.
AH...
.....

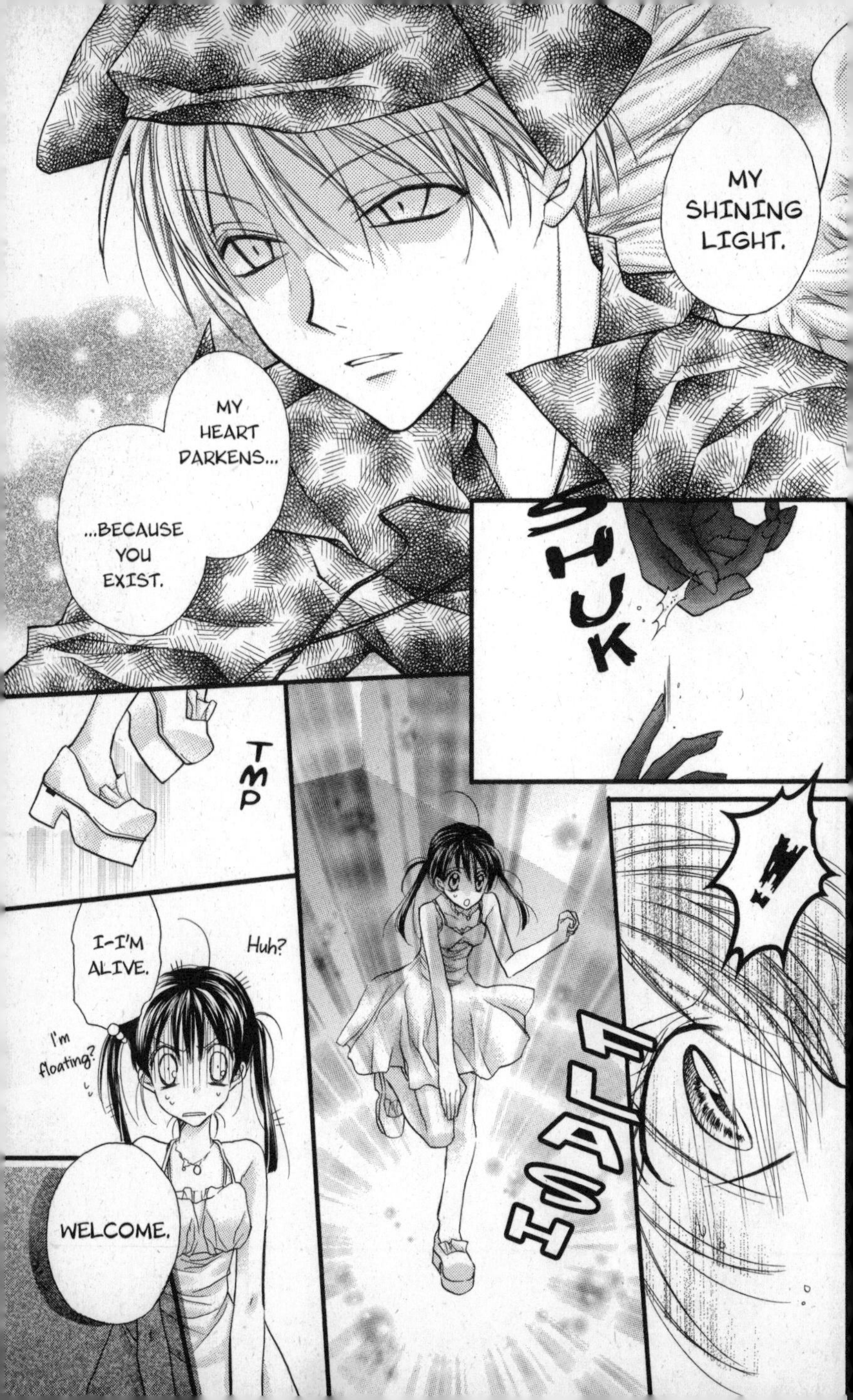
MY SHINING LIGHT.
MY HEART DARKENS...
...BECAUSE YOU EXIST.
SHUK
!!
FLASH
TMP
Huh?
I-I'M ALIVE.
I'm floating?
WELCOME.

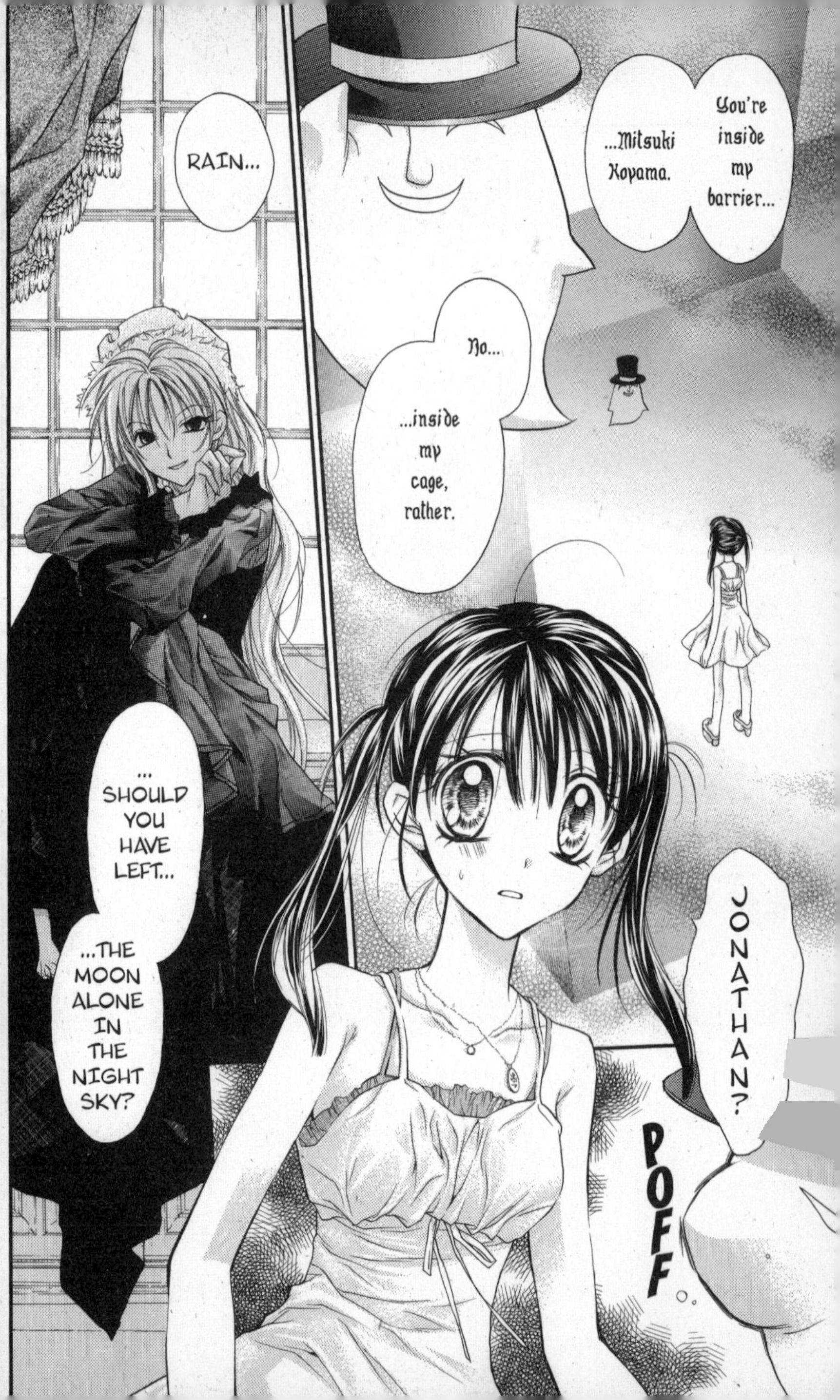
You're inside my barrier...
...Mitsuki Koyama.
No...
...inside my cage, rather.
JONATHAN?
POFF
RAIN...
...SHOULD YOU HAVE LEFT...
...THE MOON ALONE IN THE NIGHT SKY?

See You

Nowadays

The series just finished in *Ribon*, and my *Ribon* mangaka friends--Maekawa Ryo-kun, Tsuyama-san, Maki-san, Tomo-tomo--are going to do a "Party to Commemorate the Ending of the Series" for me. I'm looking forward to it! (Maki-san is in charge of it! //// Thank you Maki-san. I love you! ////

She's Maki Yoko-san of Aishiteruze ★★ Baby.

I appeared in Myco-chan's radio. I've been doing many things.

Special Thanks

Private Messages

- Kyakya Asano: (It's Kyakya. No, it's Kimiyo!)
- Ruka Kaduki: (The mountain is on fire!)
- Ai Minase: (Smeagol is a good one.)
- Airi Teito: (Was she like this?)
- Niki Seisou: (Joker...)
- Kanan Kiseki: (Thanks!!)
- Megumi Nakamura: (I'm Nakame!)
- Noriko Funaki: (Oh chiO chiO)
- Kayoru Asano: (Rebound, rebound)
- Konako: (I shall return to that store.)

Matsuda-san, Ribon Department

Nakahara-san, Ammonite

I'm going on a "Thanks for your work on *Full Moon Hokkaido Trip*" with my assistants, so I want to write a little about it in volume 7.

And my hospitalization--it was pretty funny so I'll draw that.

See you in the next volume!

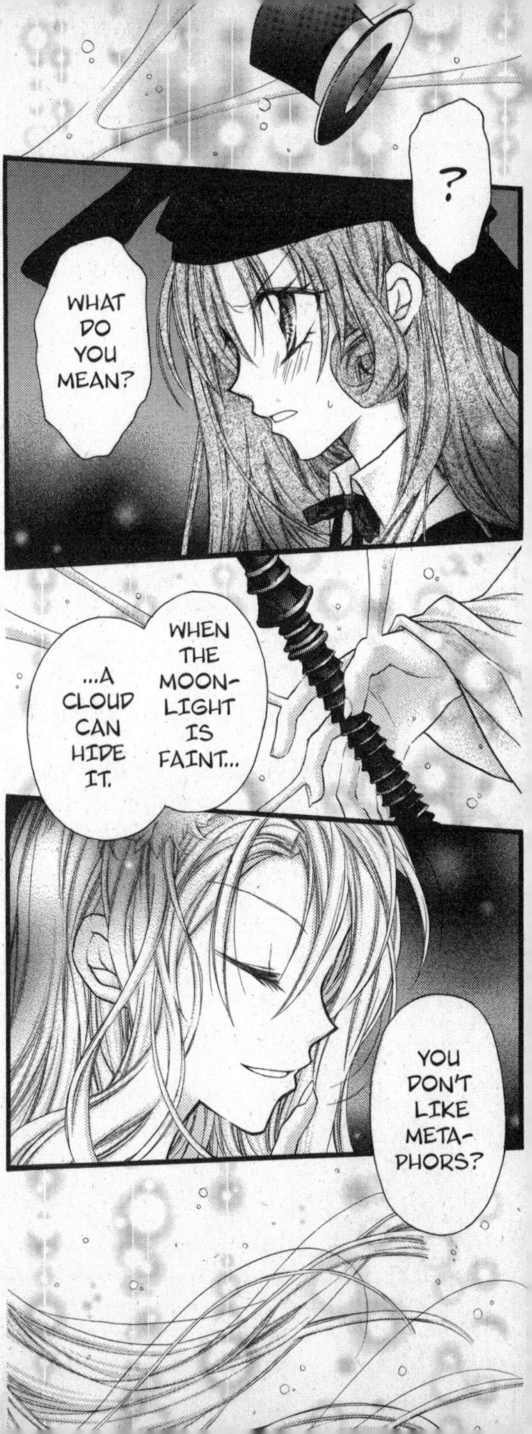
?
WHAT DO YOU MEAN?
WHEN THE MOONLIGHT IS FAINT...
...A CLOUD CAN HIDE IT.
YOU DON'T LIKE METAPHORS?

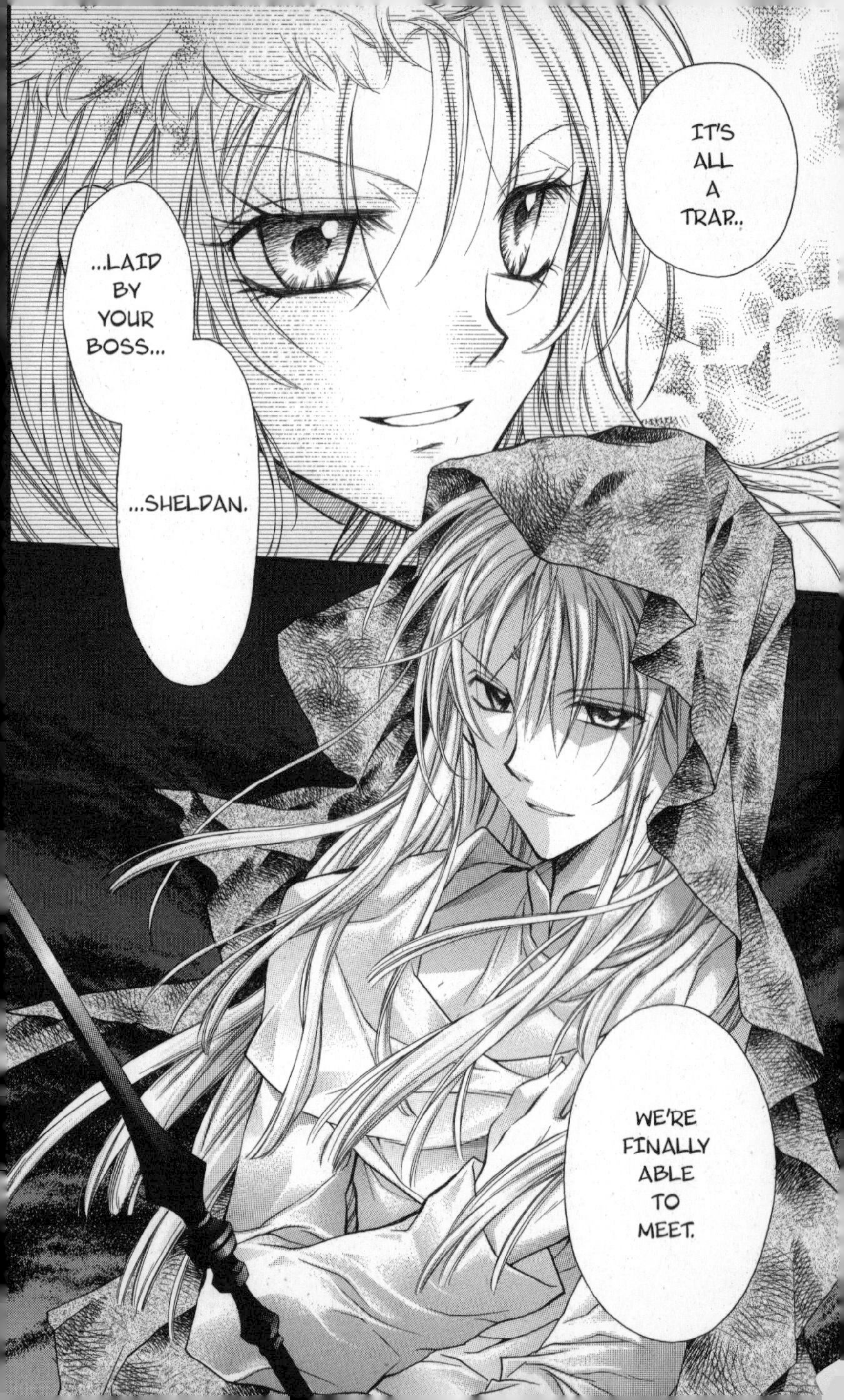
IT'S ALL A TRAP...
...LAID BY YOUR BOSS...
...SHELDAN.
WE'RE FINALLY ABLE TO MEET.

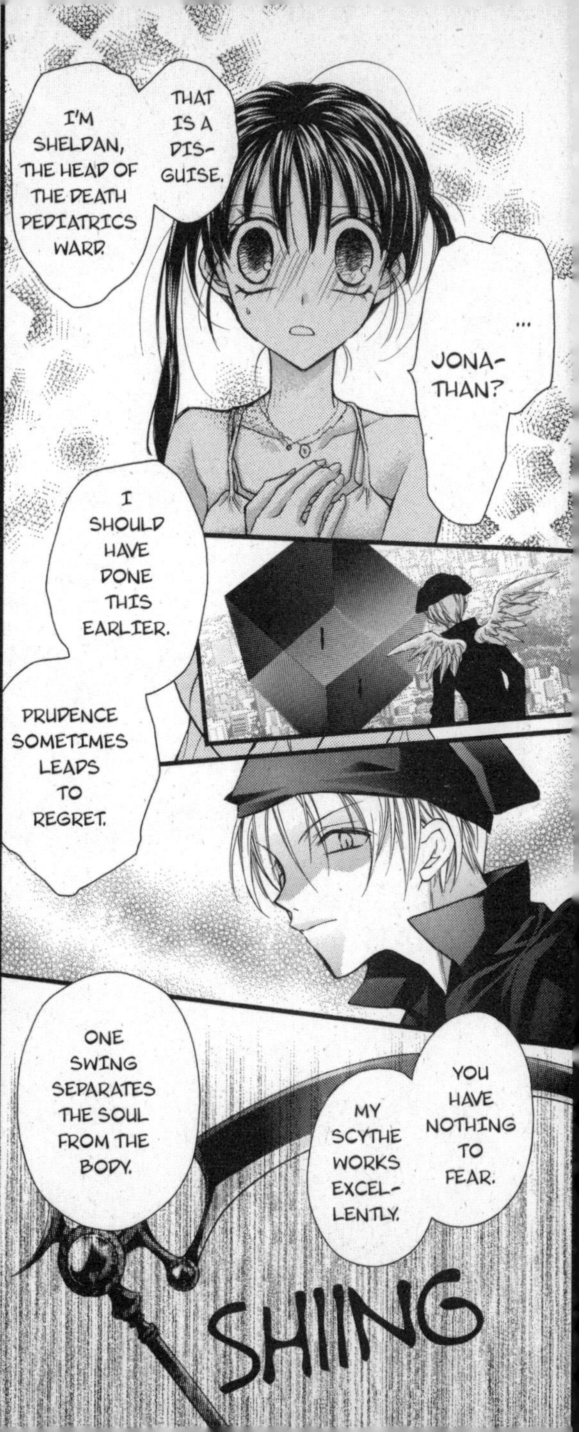
THAT IS A DIS-GUISE.
I'M SHELDAN, THE HEAD OF THE DEATH PEDIATRICS WARD.
... JONA-THAN?
I SHOULD HAVE DONE THIS EARLIER.
PRUDENCE SOMETIMES LEADS TO REGRET.
YOU HAVE NOTHING TO FEAR.
MY SCYTHE WORKS EXCEL-LENTLY.
ONE SWING SEPARATES THE SOUL FROM THE BODY.
SHING

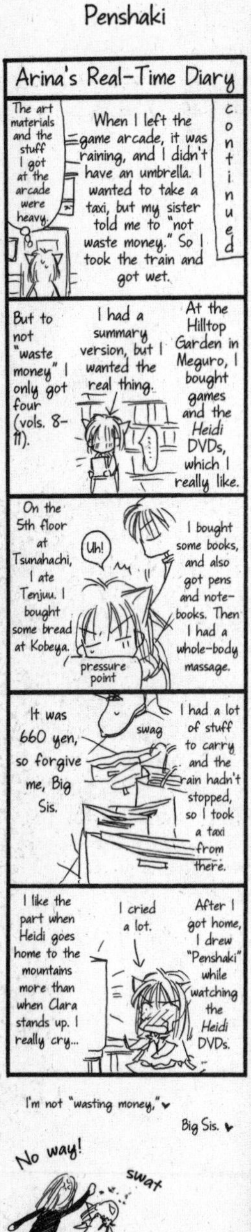
Penshaki
Arina's Real-Time Diary
continued
When I left the game arcade, it was raining, and I didn't have an umbrella. I wanted to take a taxi, but my sister told me to "not waste money." So I took the train and got wet.
The art materials and the stuff I got at the arcade were heavy.
At the Hilltop Garden in Meguro, I bought games and the Heidi DVDs, which I really like.
I had a summary version, but I wanted the real thing.
But to not "waste money" I only got four (vols. 8-11).
I bought some books, and also got pens and note-books. Then I had a whole-body massage.
Uh!
pressure point
On the 5th floor at Tsunahachi, I ate Tenjuu. I bought some bread at Kobeya.
I had a lot of stuff to carry and the rain hadn't stopped, so I took a taxi from there.
swag
It was 660 yen, so forgive me, Big Sis.
After I got home, I drew "Penshaki" while watching the Heidi DVDs.
I cried a lot.
I like the part when Heidi goes home to the mountains more than when Clara stands up. I really cry...
I'm not "wasting money,"
Big Sis.
No way!
swat

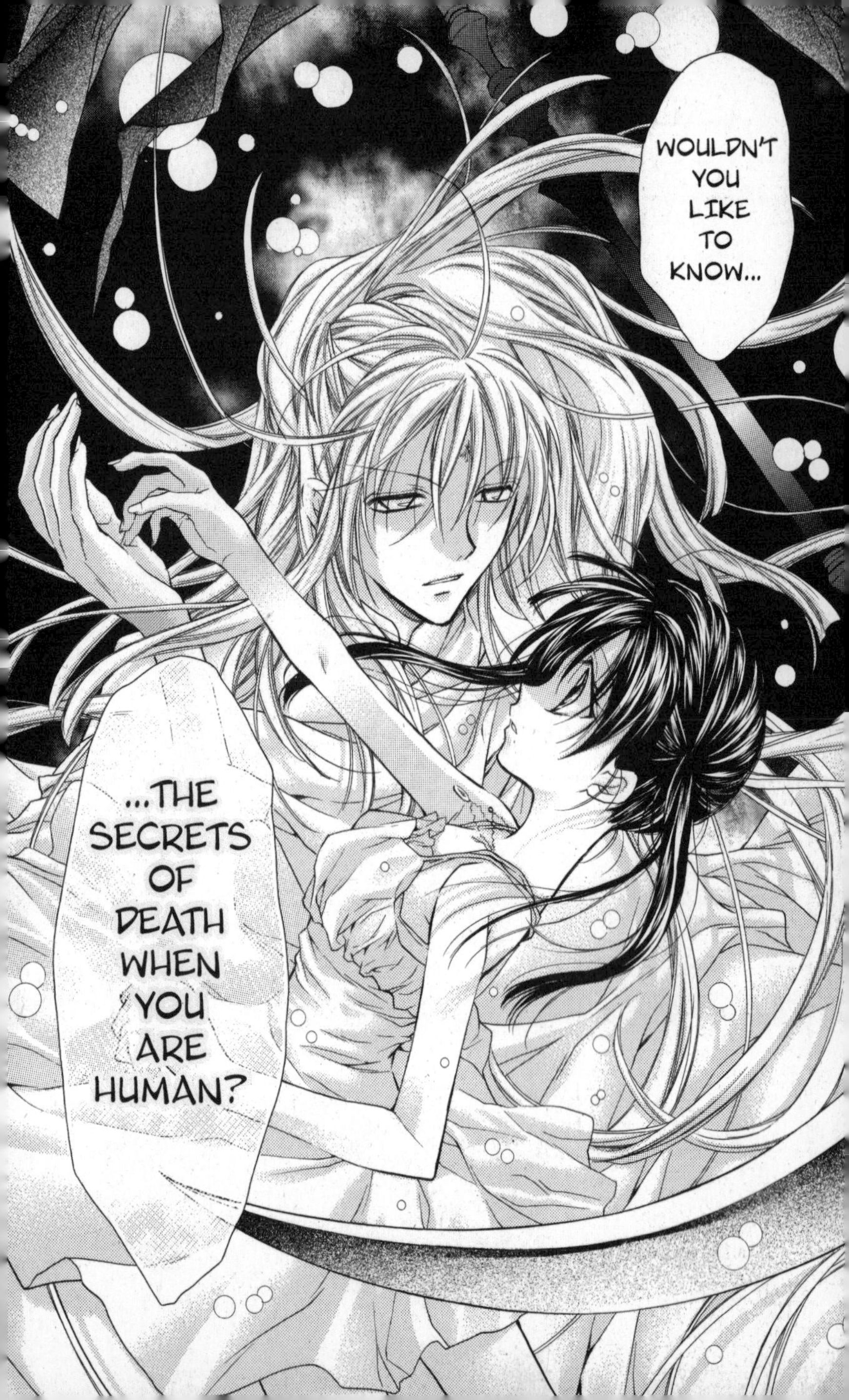
WOULDN'T YOU LIKE TO KNOW...
...THE SECRETS OF DEATH WHEN YOU ARE HUMAN?

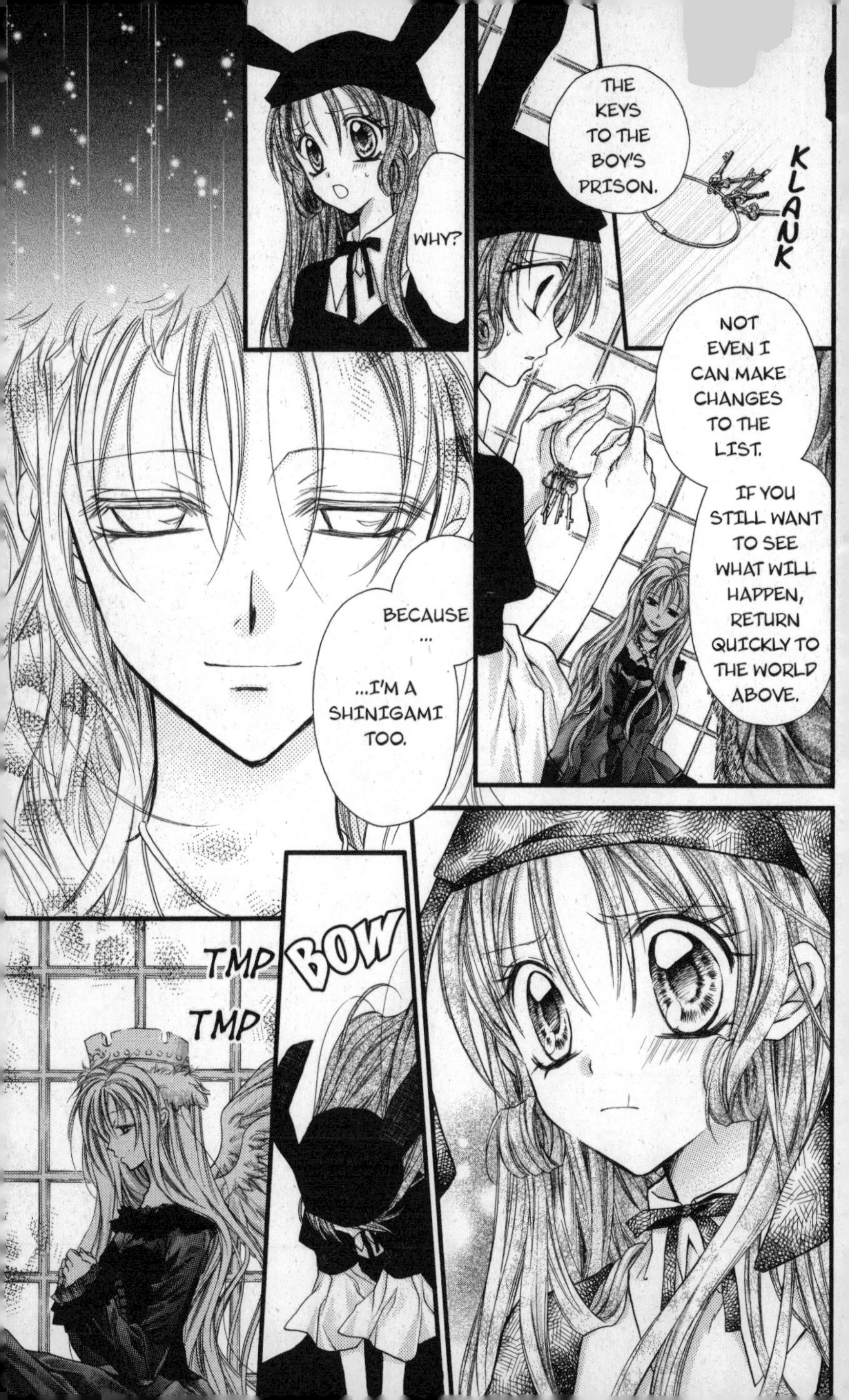
THE KEYS TO THE BOY'S PRISON.
KLANK
NOT EVEN I CAN MAKE CHANGES TO THE LIST.
IF YOU STILL WANT TO SEE WHAT WILL HAPPEN, RETURN QUICKLY TO THE WORLD ABOVE.
WHY?
BECAUSE ...
...I'M A SHINIGAMI TOO.
BOW
TMP
TMP

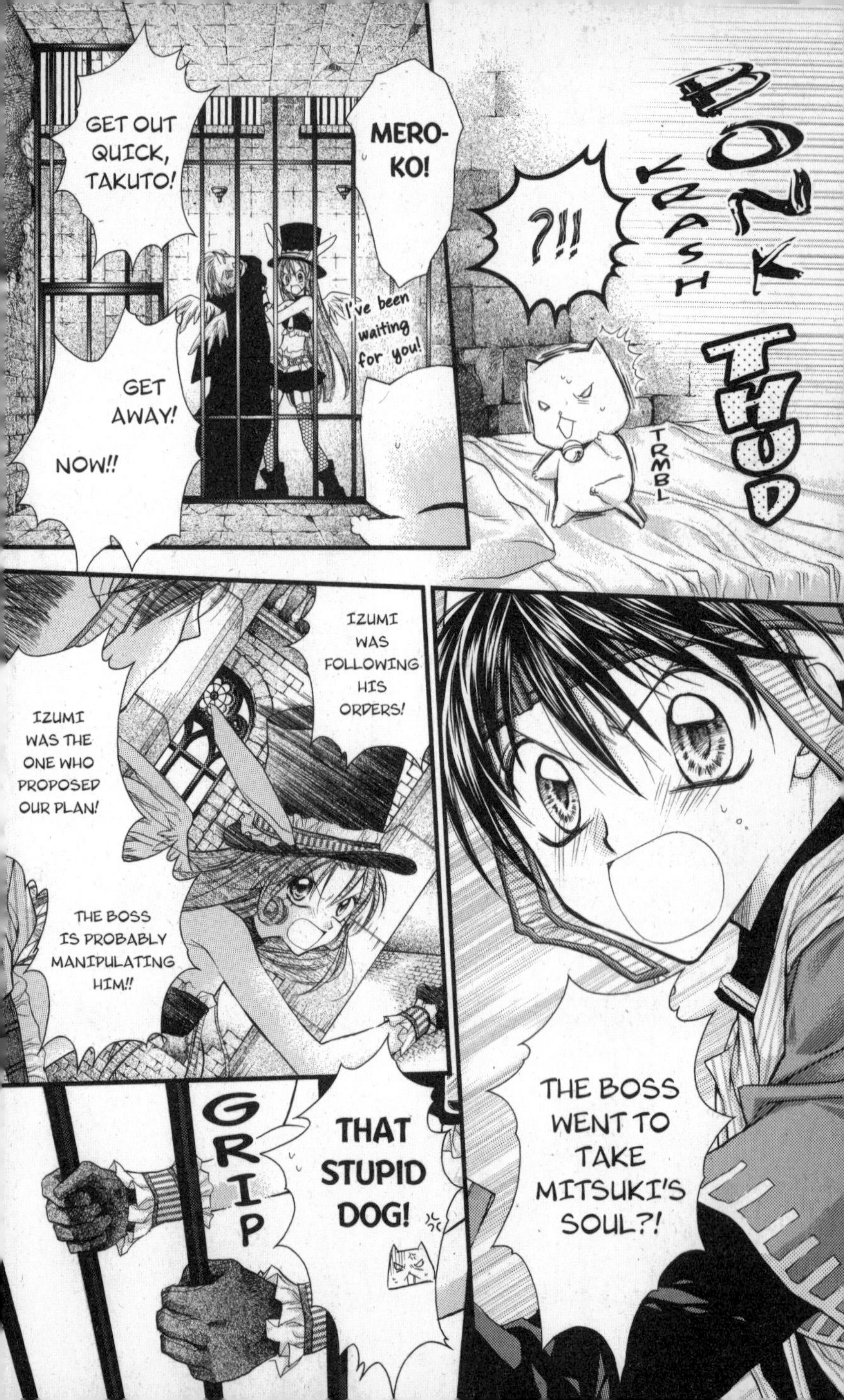
BONK
KRASH
?!!
THUD
TRMBL
MERO-KO!
I've been waiting for you!
GET OUT QUICK, TAKUTO!
GET AWAY!
NOW!!
THE BOSS WENT TO TAKE MITSUKI'S SOUL?!
IZUMI WAS FOLLOWING HIS ORDERS!
IZUMI WAS THE ONE WHO PROPOSED OUR PLAN!
THE BOSS IS PROBABLY MANIPULATING HIM!!
THAT STUPID DOG!
GRIP

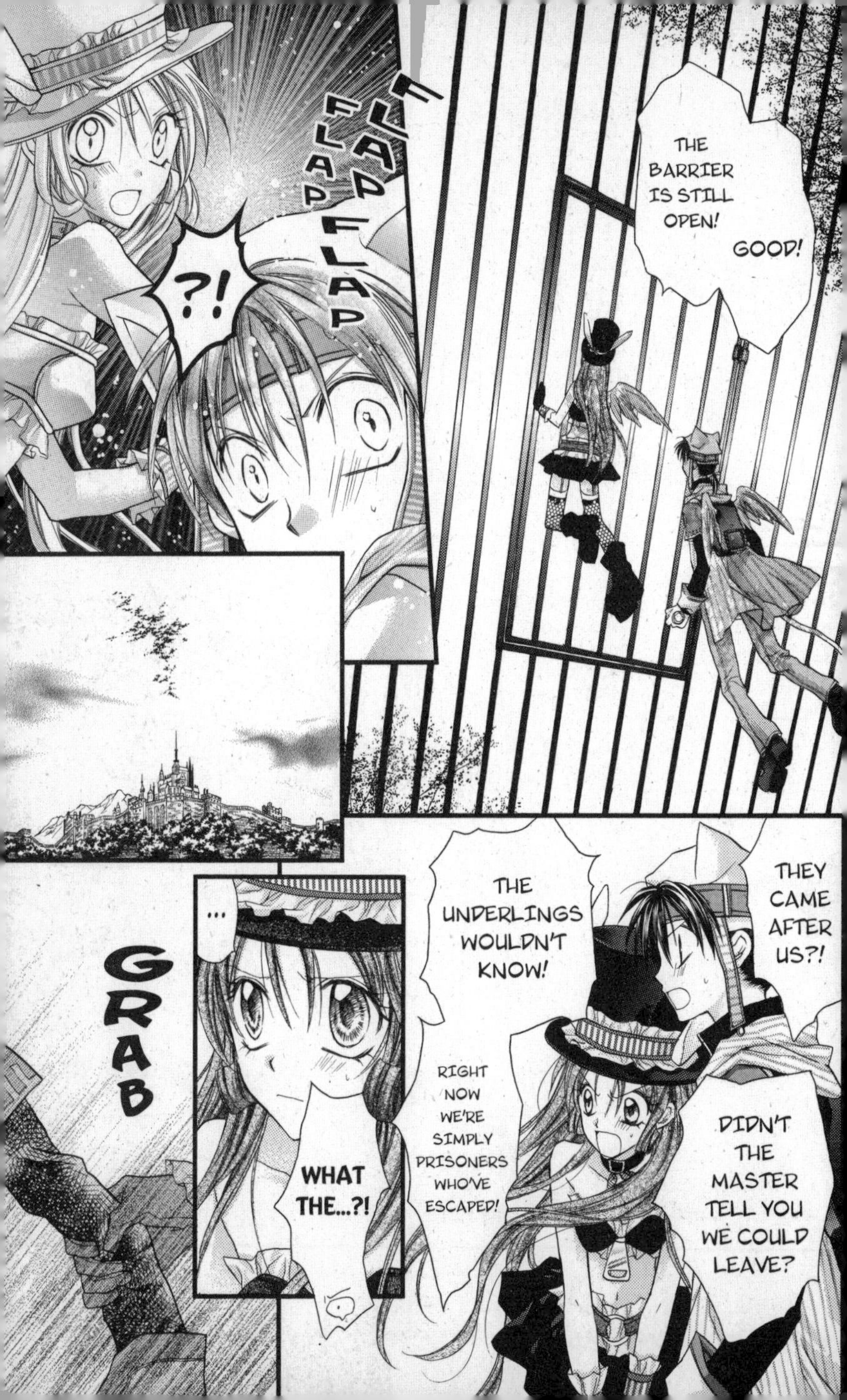

THE BARRIER IS STILL OPEN!
GOOD!
FLAP FLAP
FLAP FLAP
?!
THEY CAME AFTER US?!
THE UNDERLINGS WOULDN'T KNOW!
DIDN'T THE MASTER TELL YOU WE COULD LEAVE?
RIGHT NOW WE'RE SIMPLY PRISONERS WHO'VE ESCAPED!
...
WHAT THE...?!
GRAB

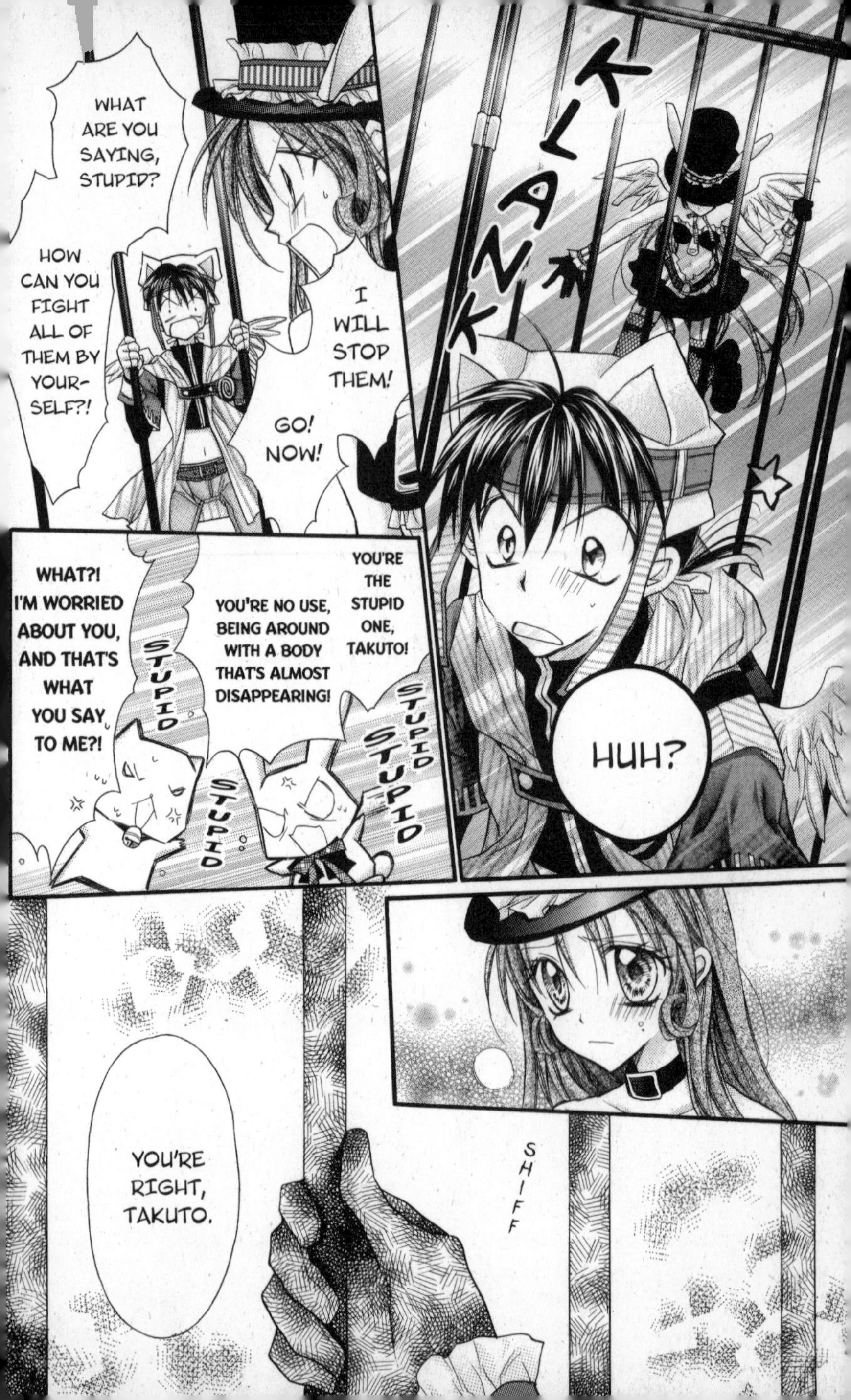
KLANK
HUH?
I WILL STOP THEM!
GO! NOW!
WHAT ARE YOU SAYING, STUPID?
HOW CAN YOU FIGHT ALL OF THEM BY YOURSELF?!
YOU'RE THE STUPID ONE, TAKUTO!
YOU'RE NO USE, BEING AROUND WITH A BODY THAT'S ALMOST DISAPPEARING!
STUPID STUPID
WHAT?! I'M WORRIED ABOUT YOU, AND THAT'S WHAT YOU SAY TO ME?!
STUPID
STUPID
SHIFF
YOU'RE RIGHT, TAKUTO.

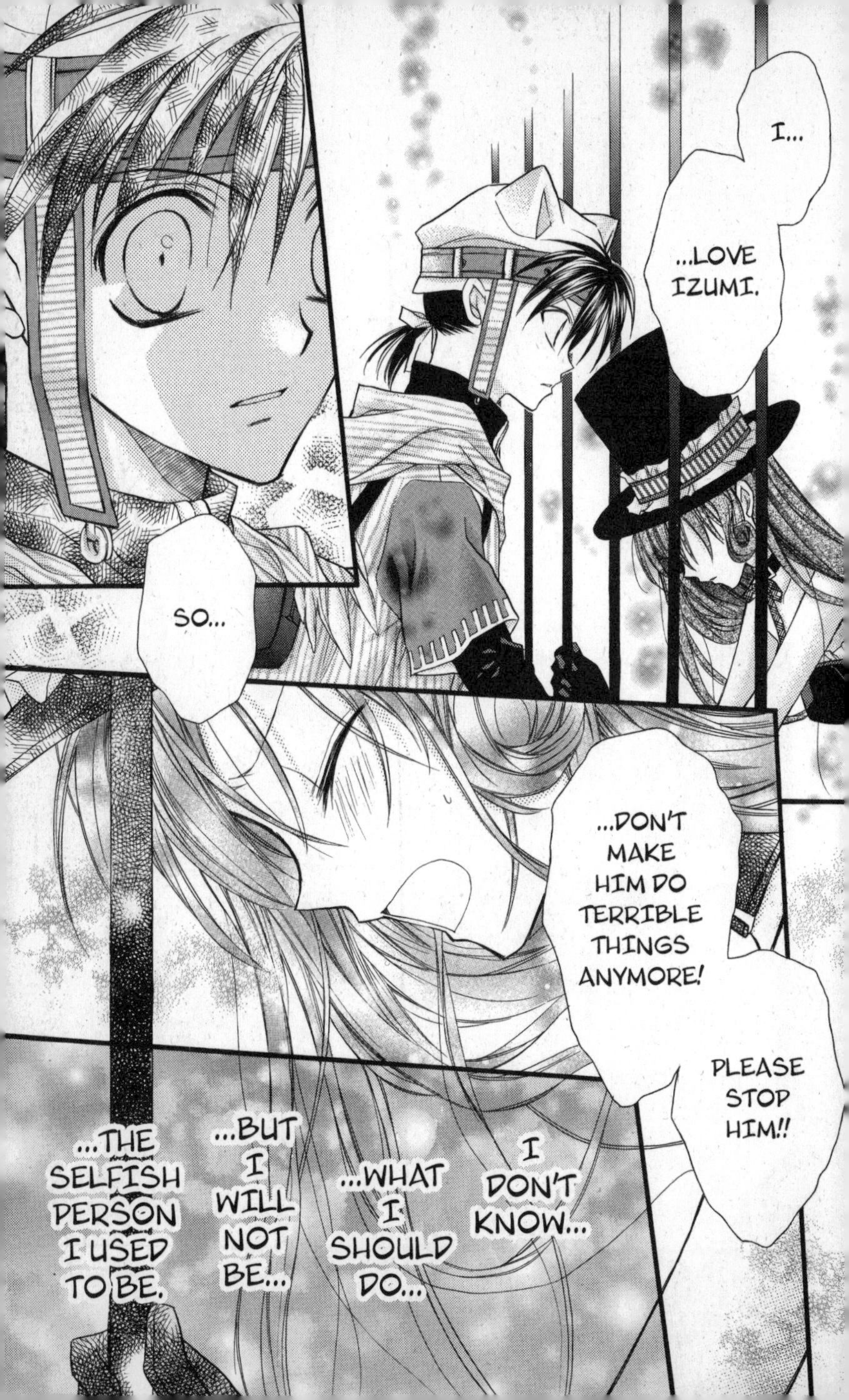
I...
...LOVE IZUMI.
SO...
...DON'T MAKE HIM DO TERRIBLE THINGS ANYMORE!
PLEASE STOP HIM!!
I DON'T KNOW...
...WHAT I SHOULD DO...
...BUT I WILL NOT BE...
...THE SELFISH PERSON I USED TO BE.

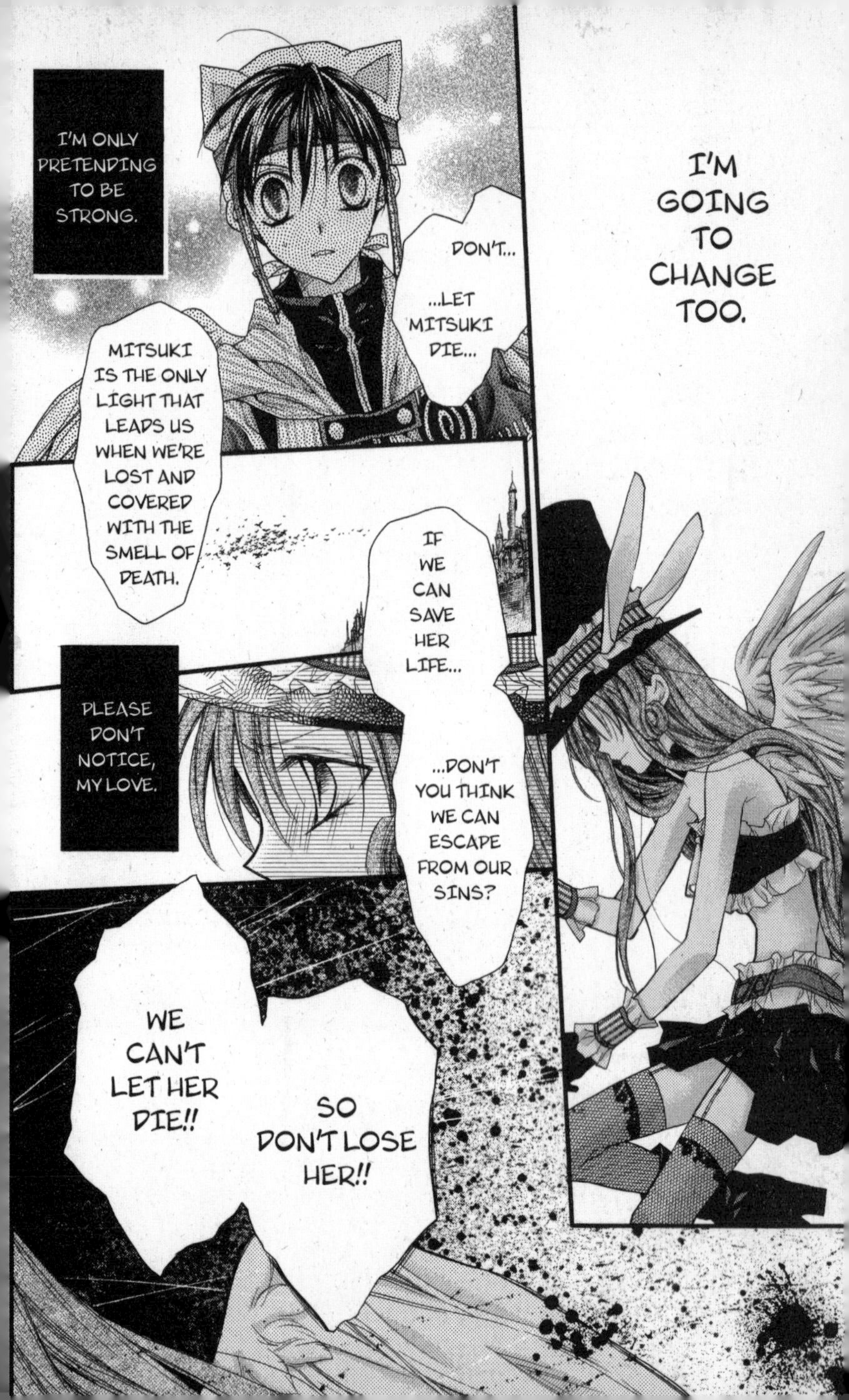
I'M GOING TO CHANGE TOO.
I'M ONLY PRETENDING TO BE STRONG.
DON'T...
...LET MITSUKI DIE...
MITSUKI IS THE ONLY LIGHT THAT LEADS US WHEN WE'RE LOST AND COVERED WITH THE SMELL OF DEATH.
IF WE CAN SAVE HER LIFE...
PLEASE DON'T NOTICE, MY LOVE.
...DON'T YOU THINK WE CAN ESCAPE FROM OUR SINS?
WE CAN'T LET HER DIE!!
SO DON'T LOSE HER!!

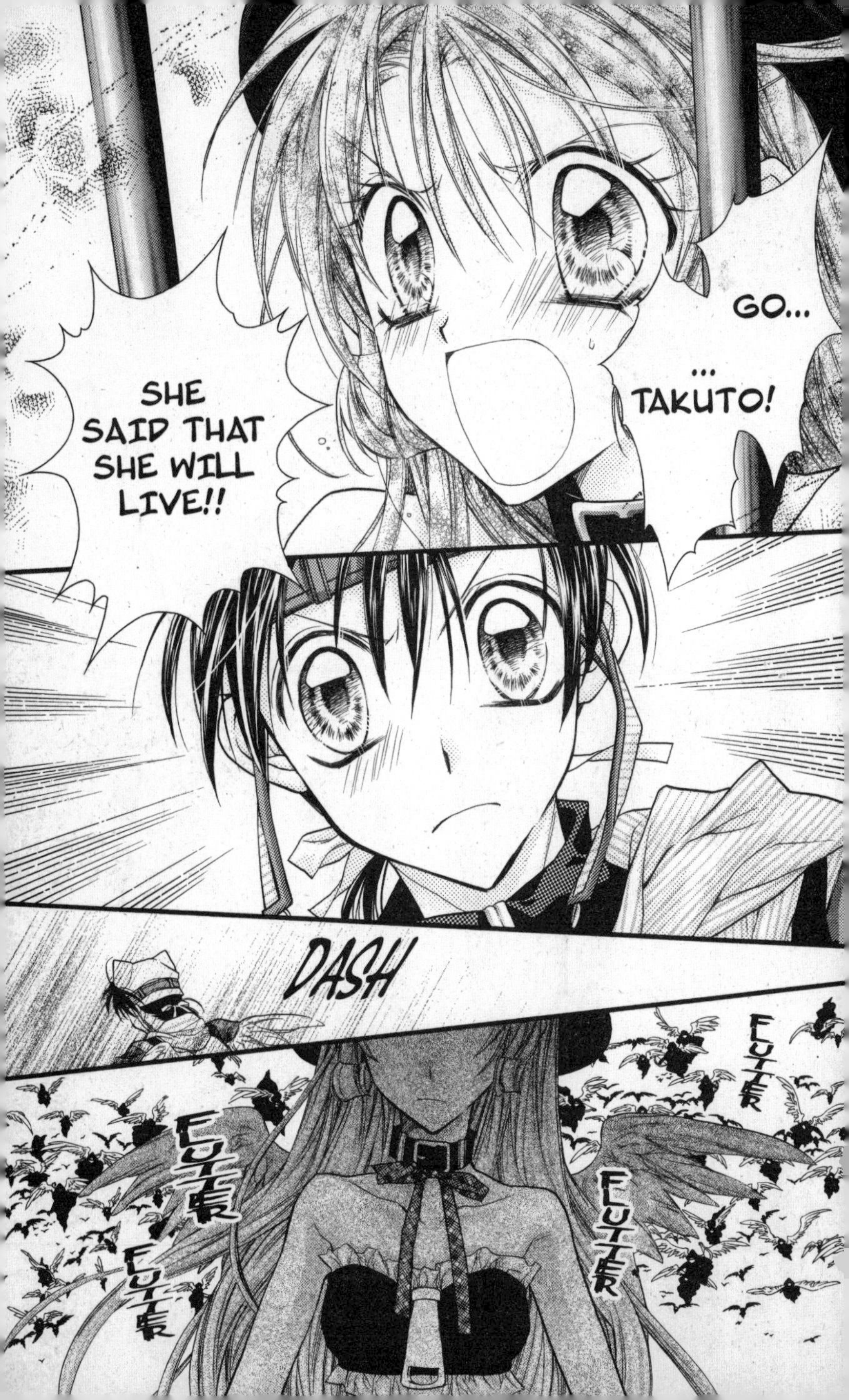
GO...
... TAKUTO!
SHE SAID THAT SHE WILL LIVE!!
DASH
FLUTTER
FLUTTER
FLUTTER
FLUTTER

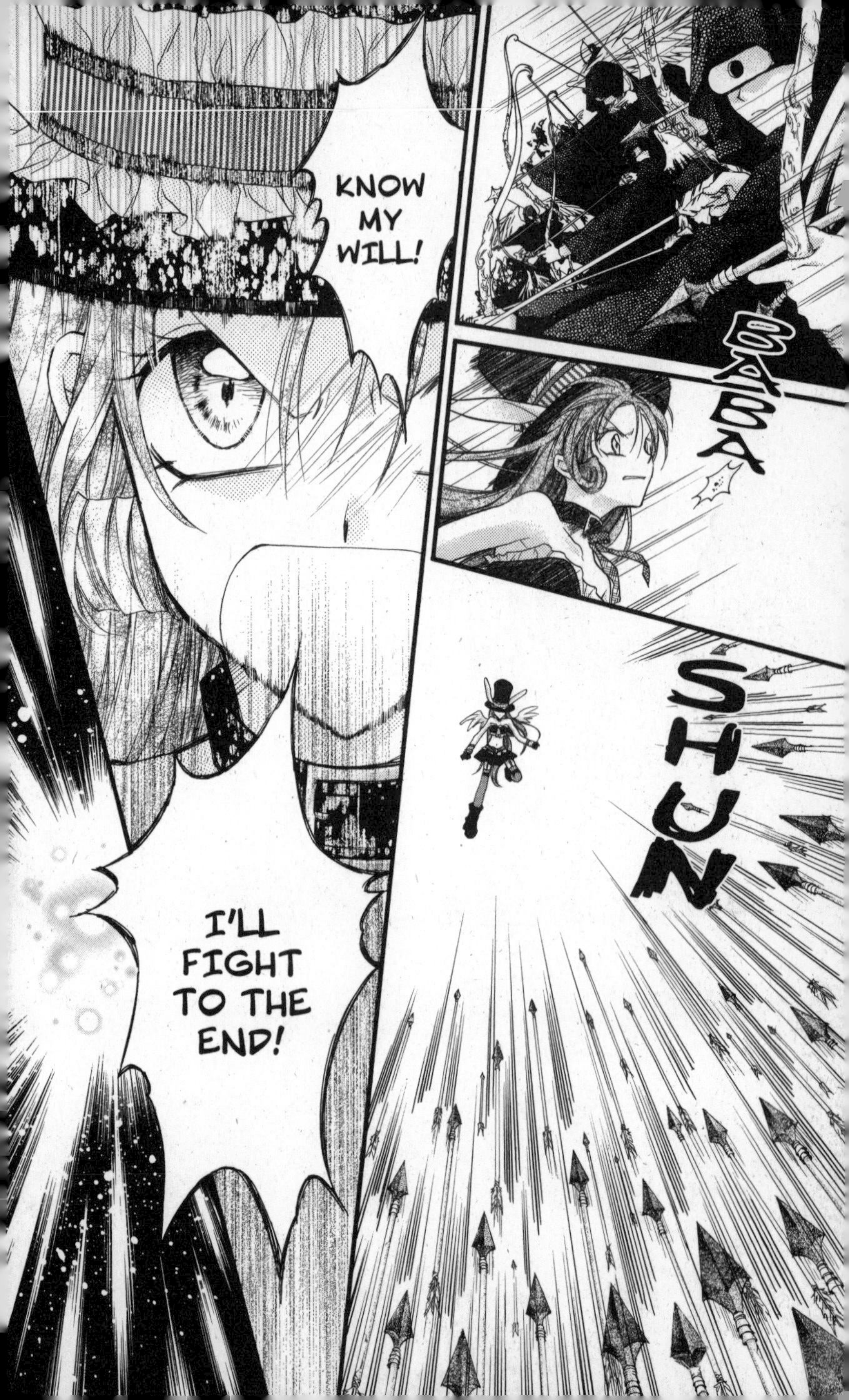
BABA
SHUN
KNOW MY WILL!
I'LL FIGHT TO THE END!

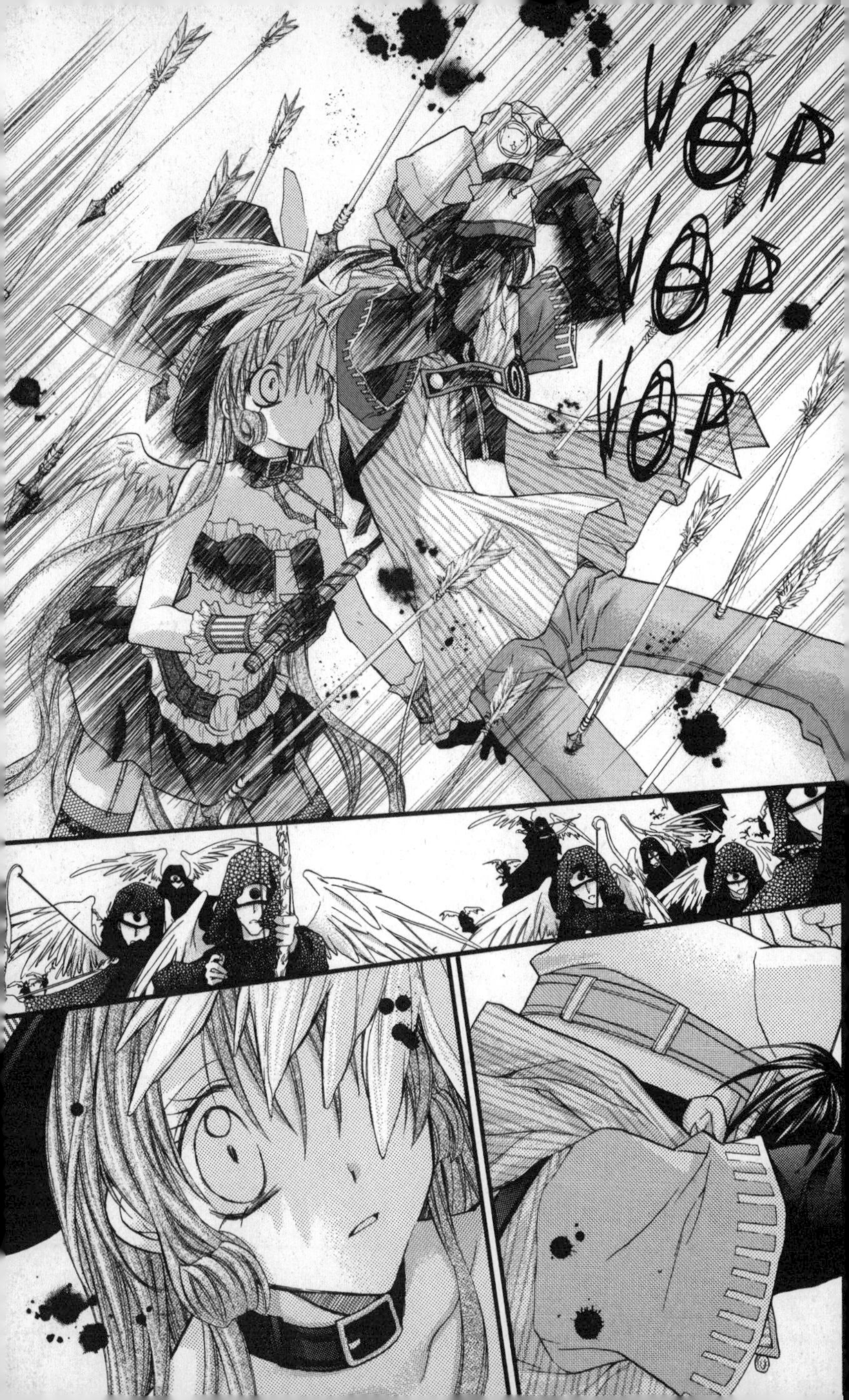
WOP
WOP
WOP

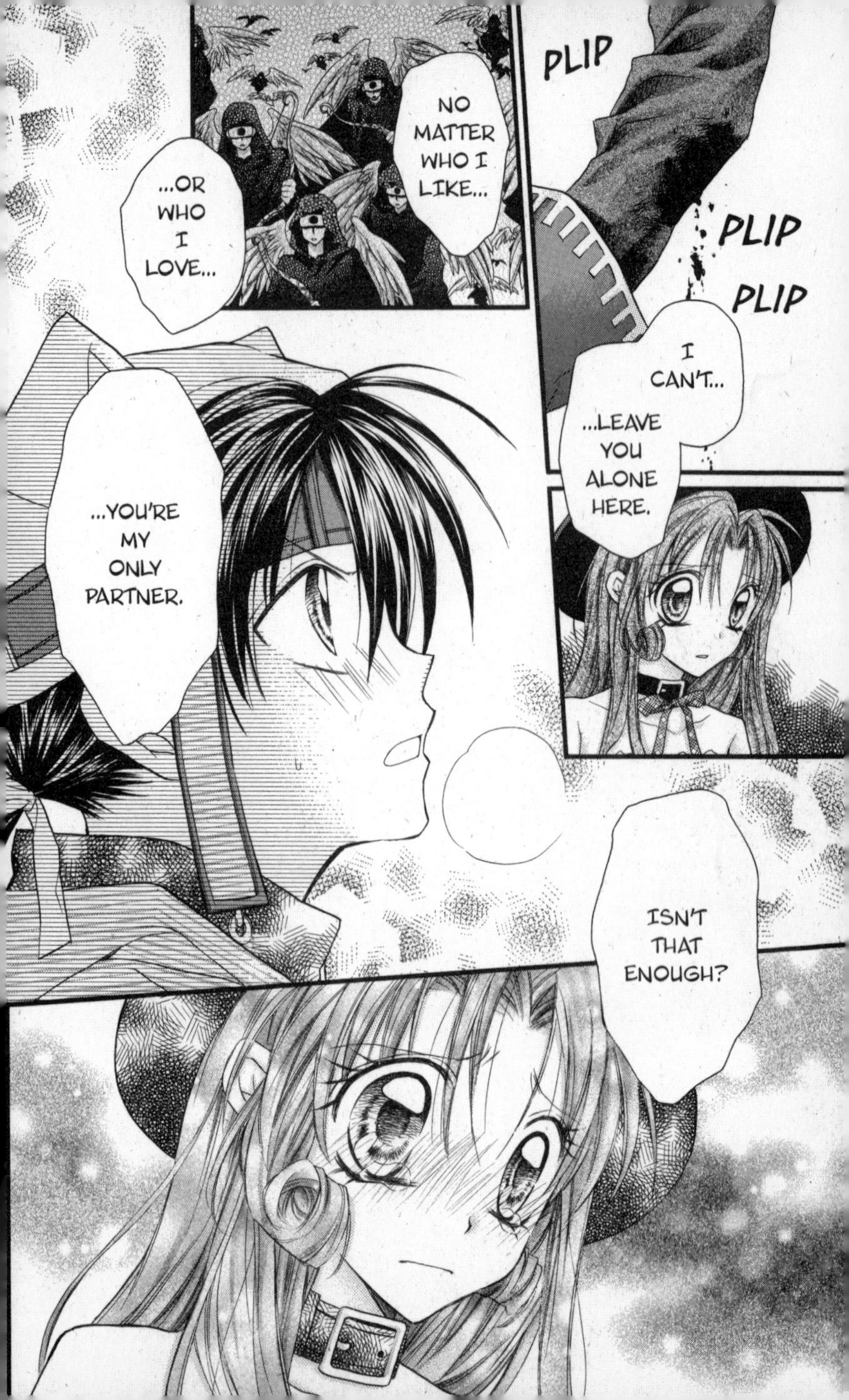
PLIP
PLIP
PLIP
I CAN'T...
...LEAVE YOU ALONE HERE.
NO MATTER WHO I LIKE...
...OR WHO I LOVE...
...YOU'RE MY ONLY PARTNER.
ISN'T THAT ENOUGH?

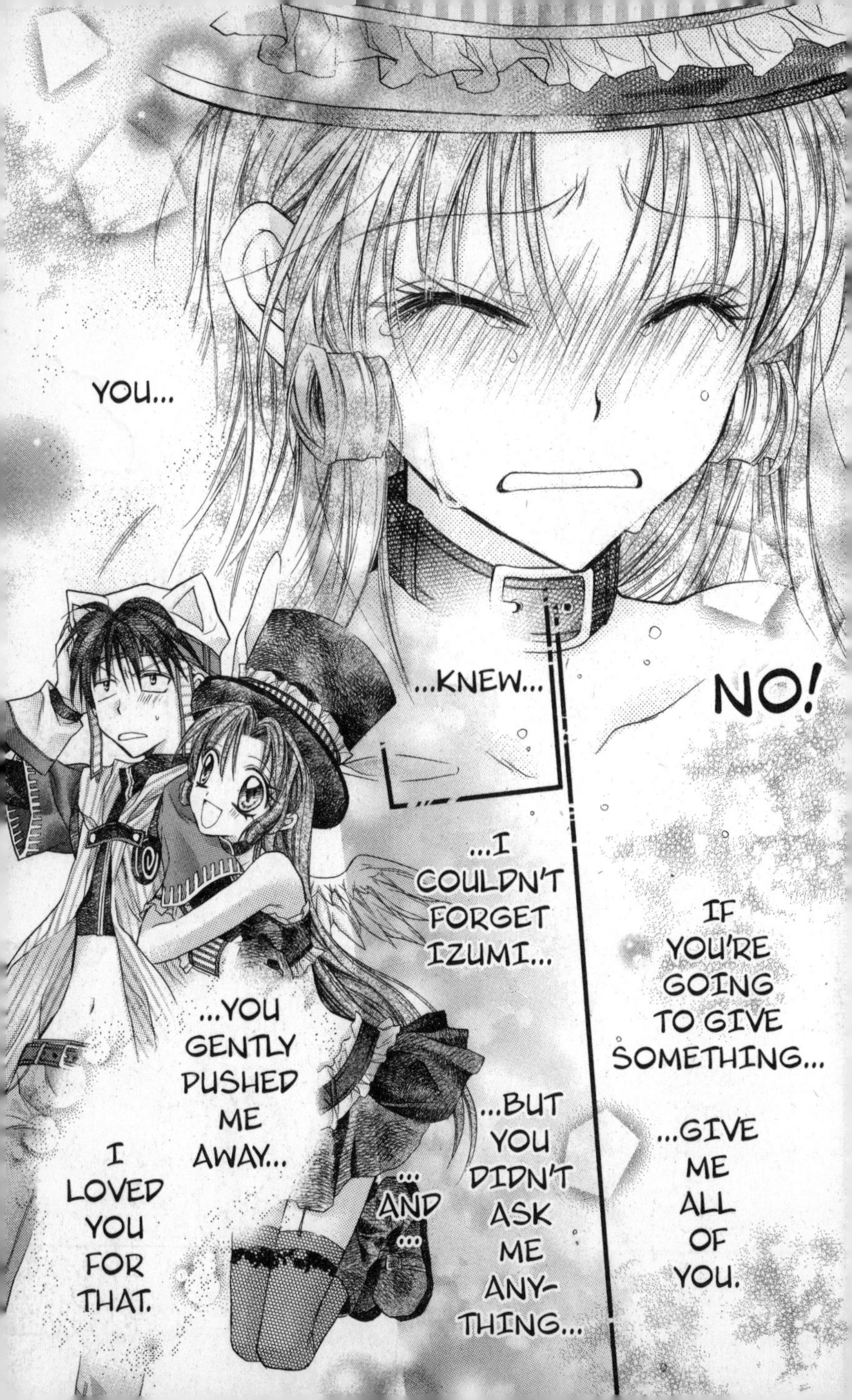
NO!
IF YOU'RE GOING TO GIVE SOMETHING...
...GIVE ME ALL OF YOU.
YOU...
...KNEW...
...I COULDN'T FORGET IZUMI...
...BUT YOU DIDN'T ASK ME ANYTHING...
...AND...
...YOU GENTLY PUSHED ME AWAY...
I LOVED YOU FOR THAT.

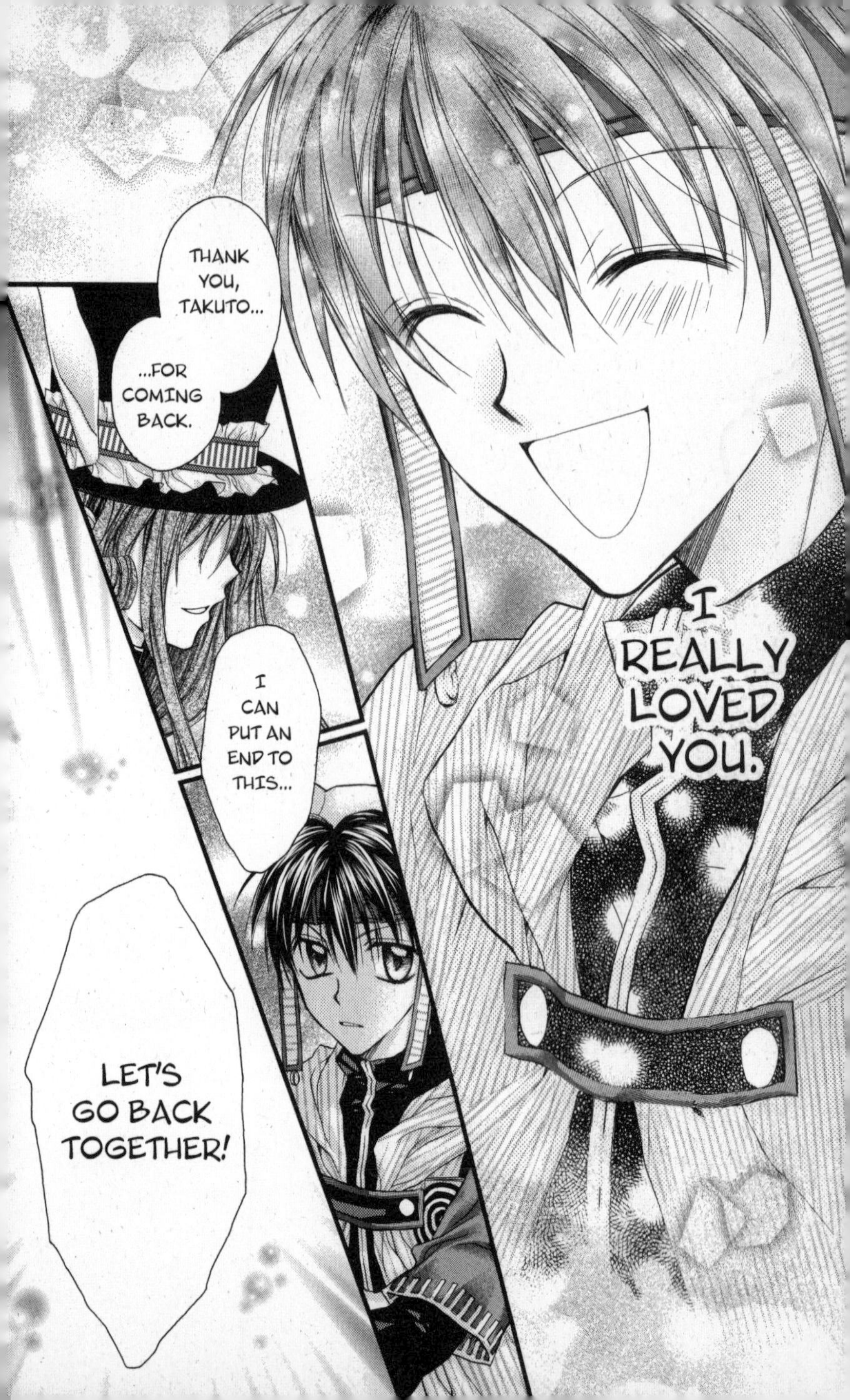
THANK YOU, TAKUTO...
...FOR COMING BACK.
I REALLY LOVED YOU.
I CAN PUT AN END TO THIS...
LET'S GO BACK TOGETHER!

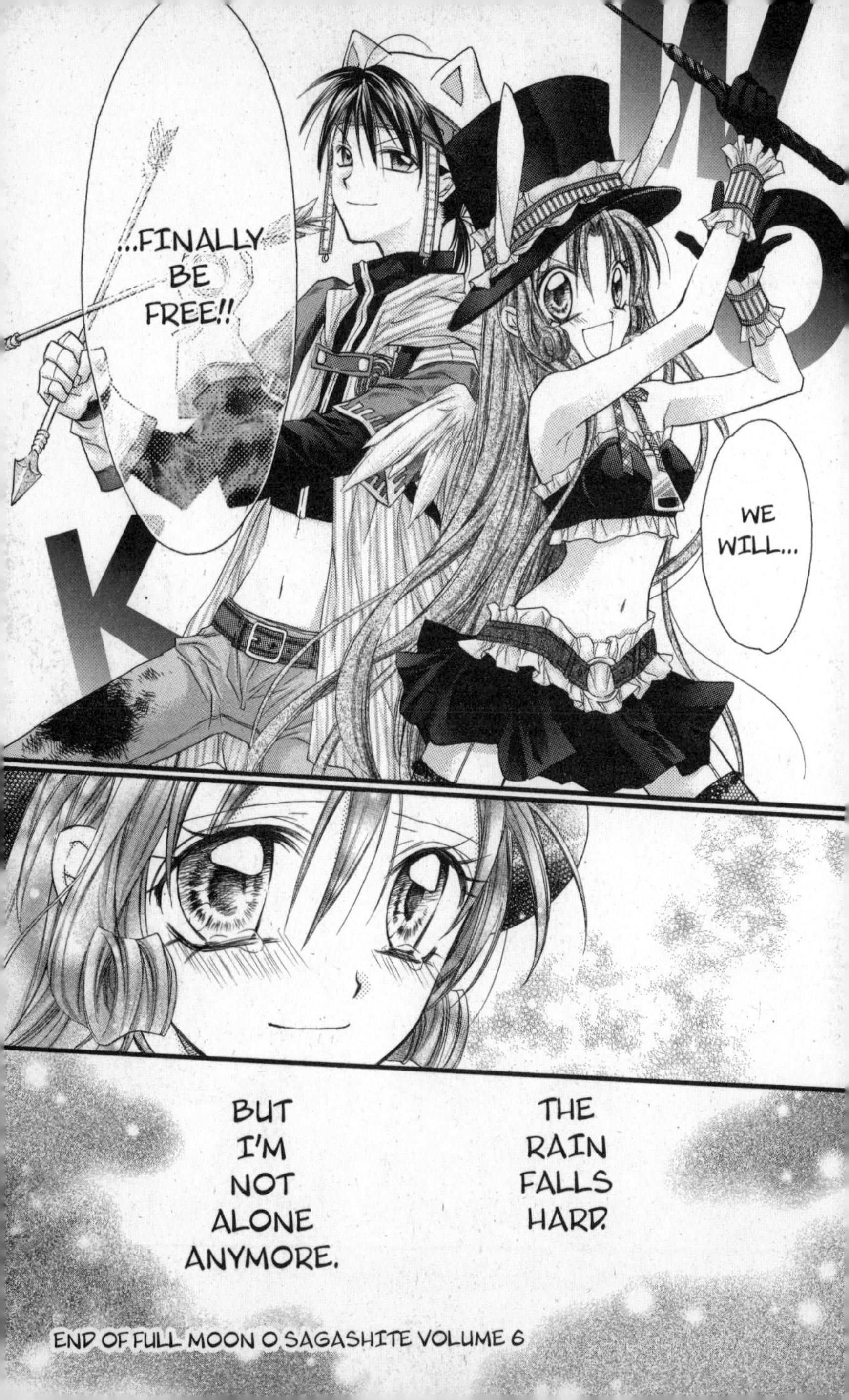
WE WILL...
...FINALLY BE FREE!!
THE RAIN FALLS HARD.
BUT I'M NOT ALONE ANYMORE.
END OF FULL MOON O SAGASHITE VOLUME 6

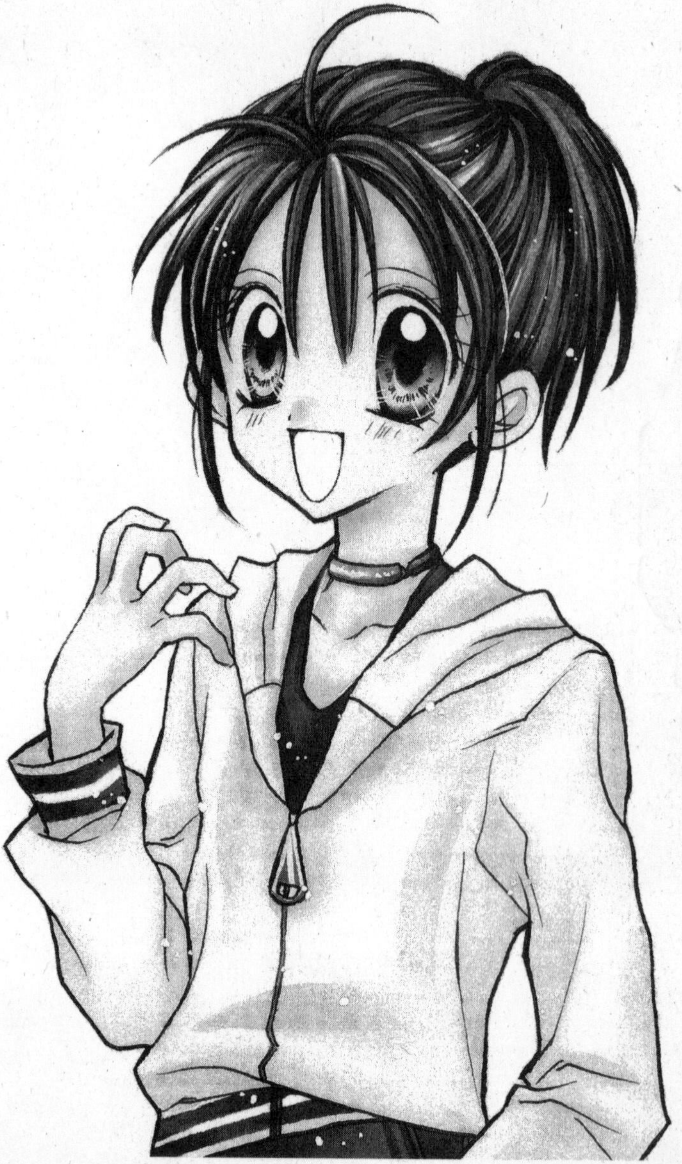

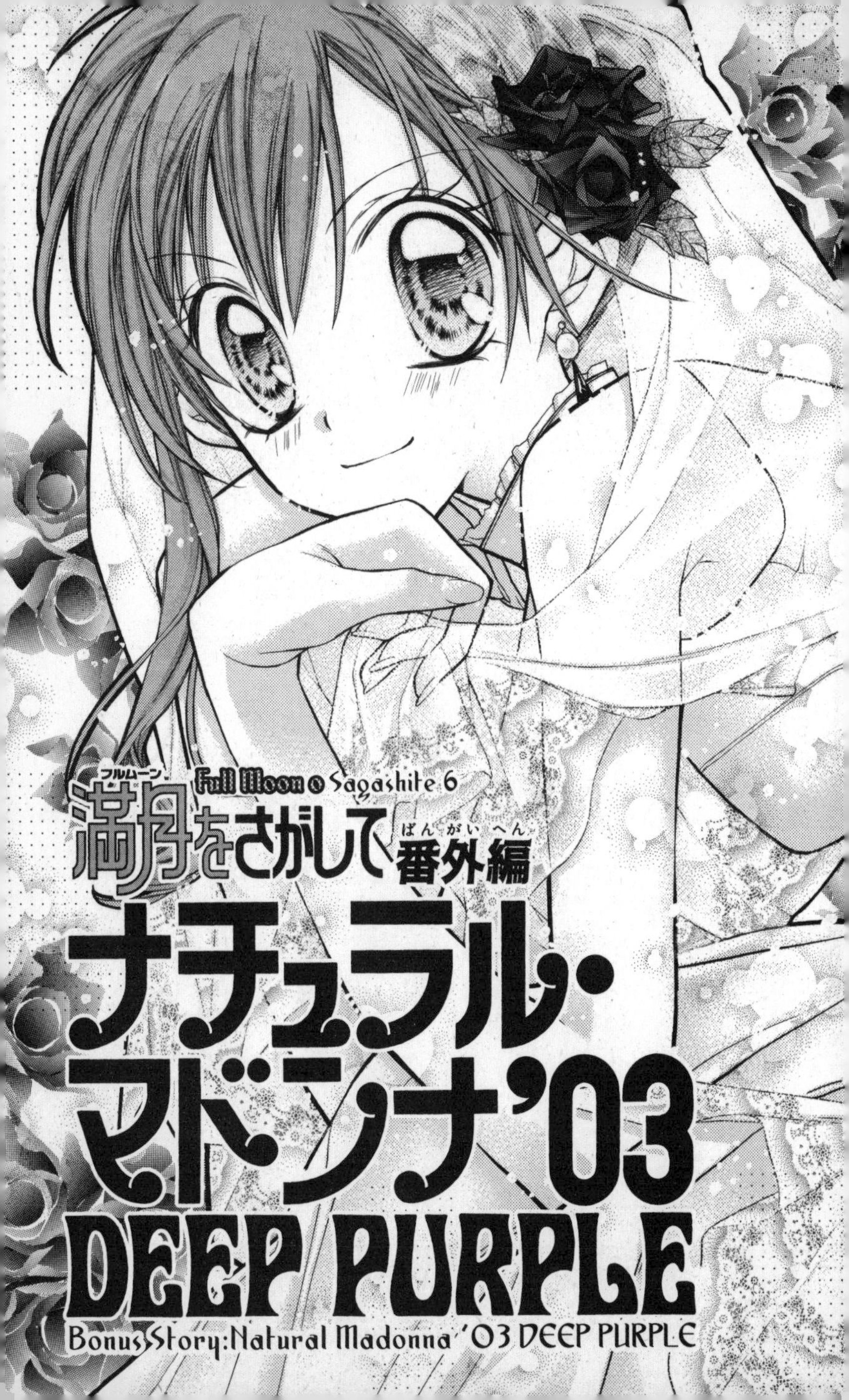
満月をさがして
Full Moon o Sagashite 6
番外編
ナチュラル・マドンナ'03
DEEP PURPLE
Bonus Story: Natural Madonna '03 DEEP PURPLE

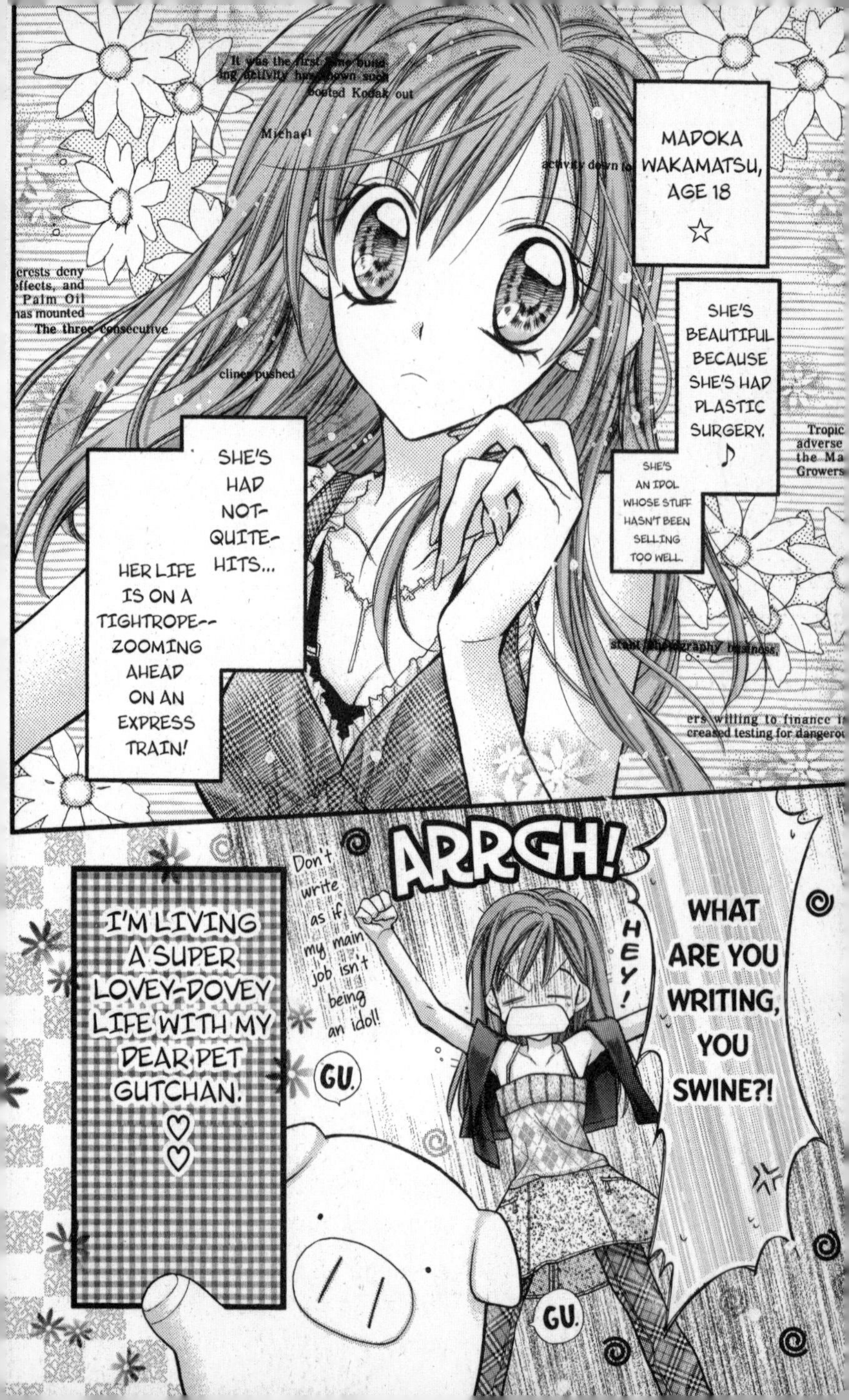
MADOKA WAKAMATSU, AGE 18 ☆
SHE'S BEAUTIFUL BECAUSE SHE'S HAD PLASTIC SURGERY. ♪
SHE'S AN IDOL WHOSE STUFF HASN'T BEEN SELLING TOO WELL.
SHE'S HAD NOT-QUITE-HITS...
HER LIFE IS ON A TIGHTROPE--ZOOMING AHEAD ON AN EXPRESS TRAIN!
ARRGH!
WHAT ARE YOU WRITING, YOU SWINE?!
HEY!
Don't write as if my main job isn't being an idol!
GU.
I'M LIVING A SUPER LOVEY-DOVEY LIFE WITH MY DEAR PET GUTCHAN. ♡ ♡
GU.

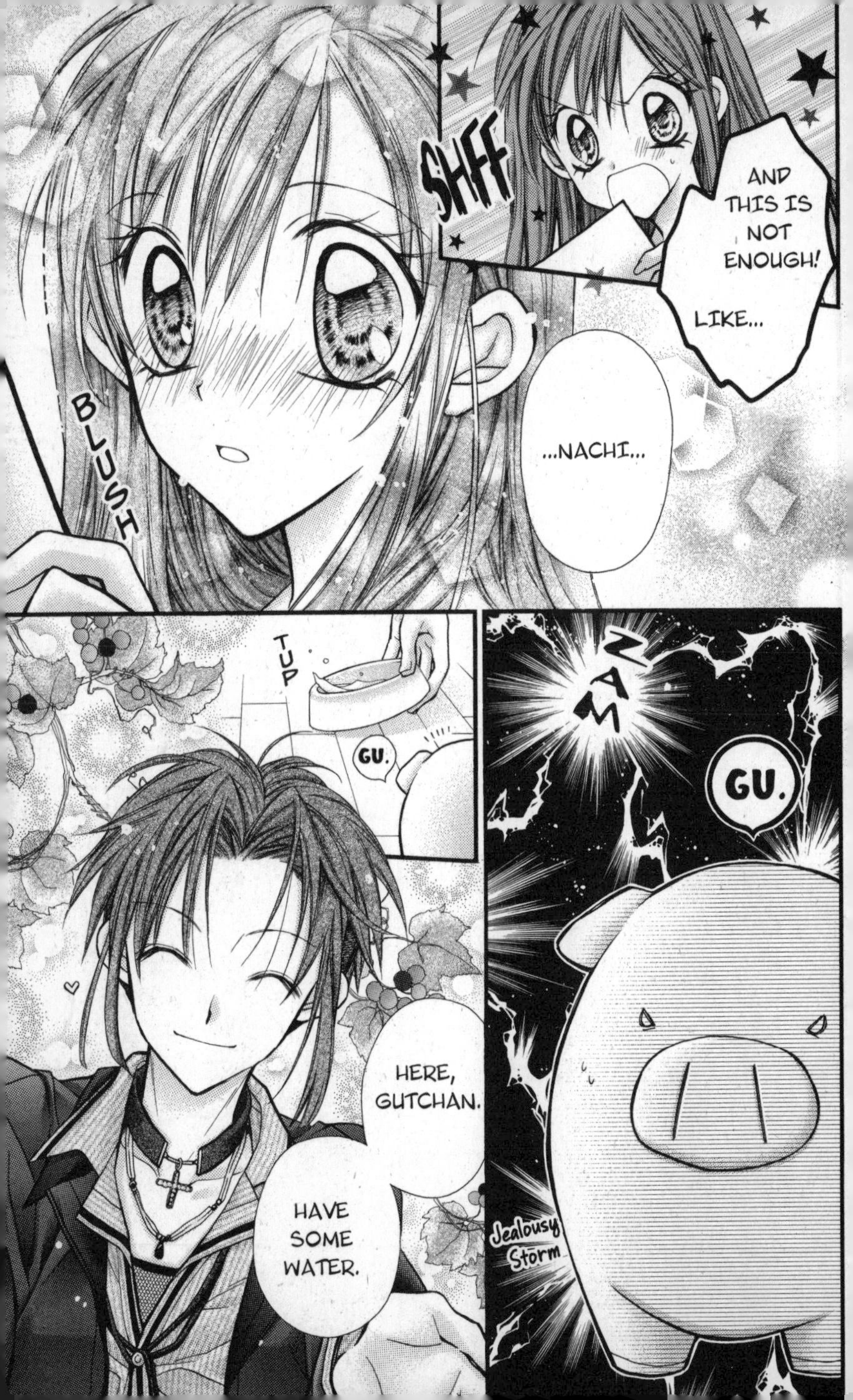
SHFF
AND THIS IS NOT ENOUGH!
LIKE...
...NACHI...
BLUSH
ZAM
GU.
Jealousy Storm
TUP
GU.
HERE, GUTCHAN.
HAVE SOME WATER.

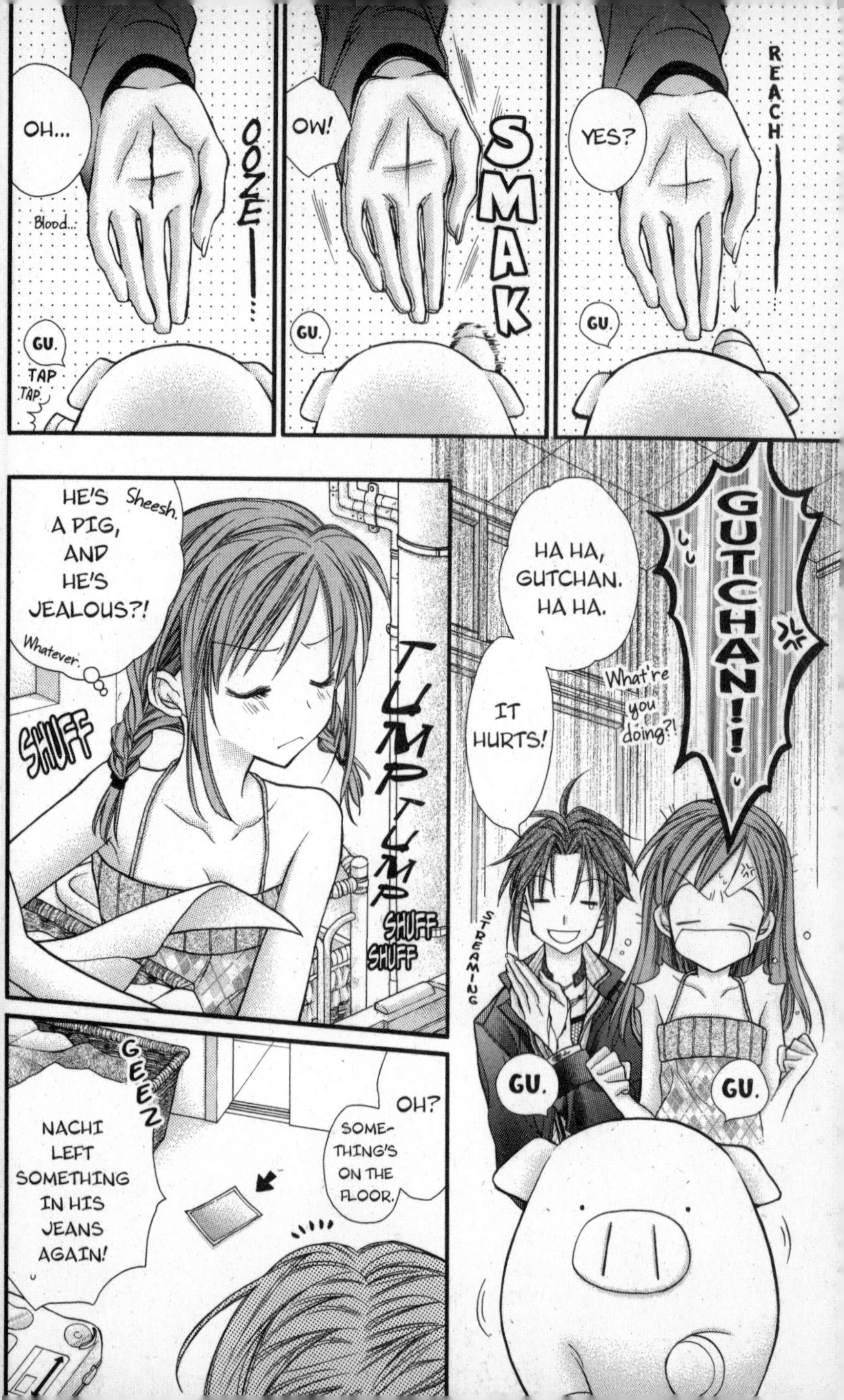
REACH
YES?
GU.
OW!
SMAK
GU.
OH...
Blood...
OOZE
GU.
TAP TAP
GUTCHAN!!
What're you doing?!
HA HA, GUTCHAN. HA HA.
IT HURTS!
STREAMING
GU.
GU.
HE'S A PIG, AND HE'S JEALOUS?!
Sheesh.
Whatever.
TUMP TUMP
SHUFF
SHUFF SHUFF
OH?
SOME-THING'S ON THE FLOOR.
GEEZ
NACHI LEFT SOMETHING IN HIS JEANS AGAIN!

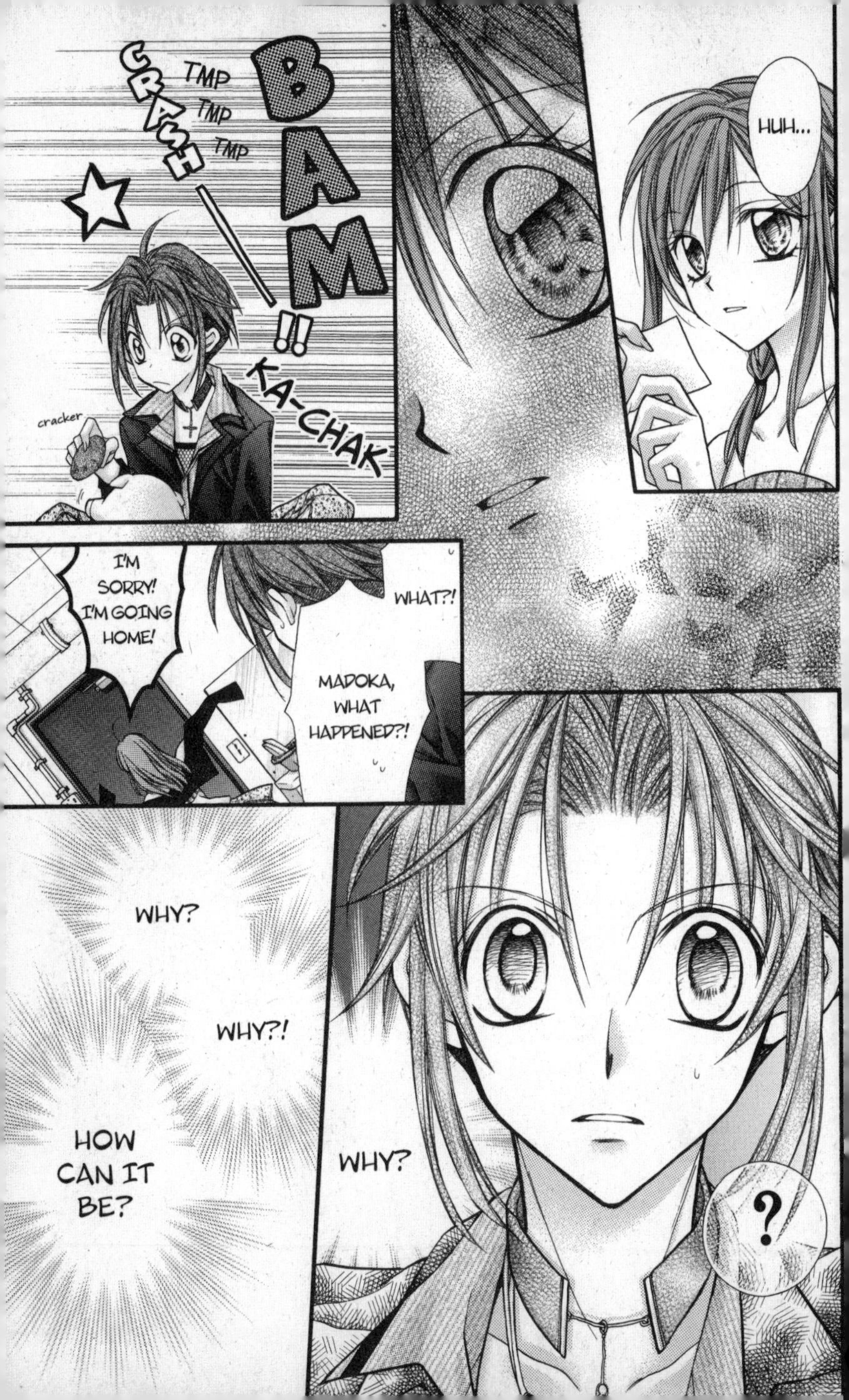
HUH...
BAM!!
CRASH
TMP
TMP
TMP
KA-CHAK
cracker
I'M SORRY! I'M GOING HOME!
WHAT?!
MADOKA, WHAT HAPPENED?!
?
WHY?
WHY?
WHY?!
HOW CAN IT BE?

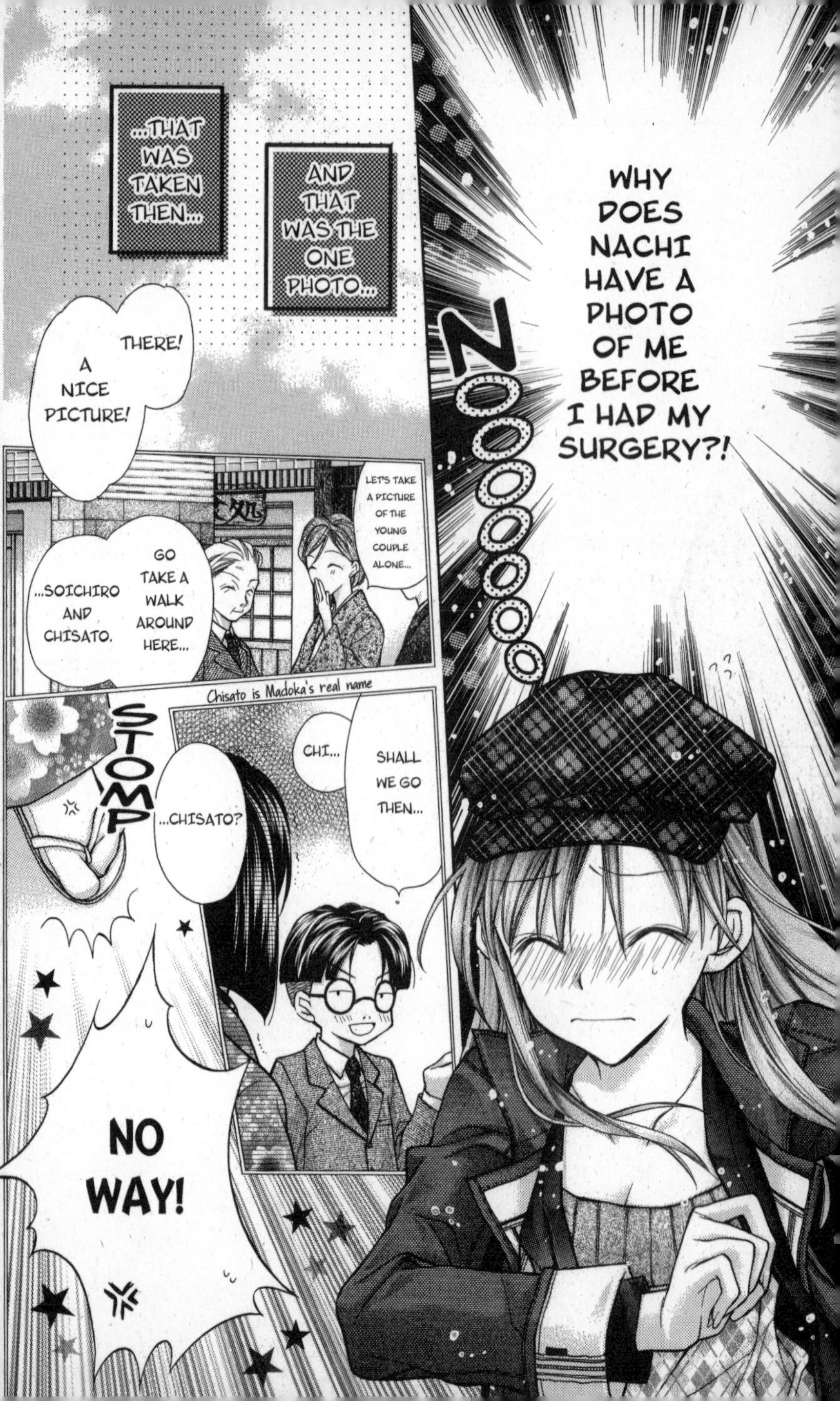
WHY DOES NACHI HAVE A PHOTO OF ME BEFORE I HAD MY SURGERY?!
NOOOOOOOO
AND THAT WAS THE ONE PHOTO...
...THAT WAS TAKEN THEN...
THERE! A NICE PICTURE!
LET'S TAKE A PICTURE OF THE YOUNG COUPLE ALONE...
GO TAKE A WALK AROUND HERE...
...SOICHIRO AND CHISATO.
Chisato is Madoka's real name
SHALL WE GO THEN...
CHI...
...CHISATO?
STOMP
NO WAY!

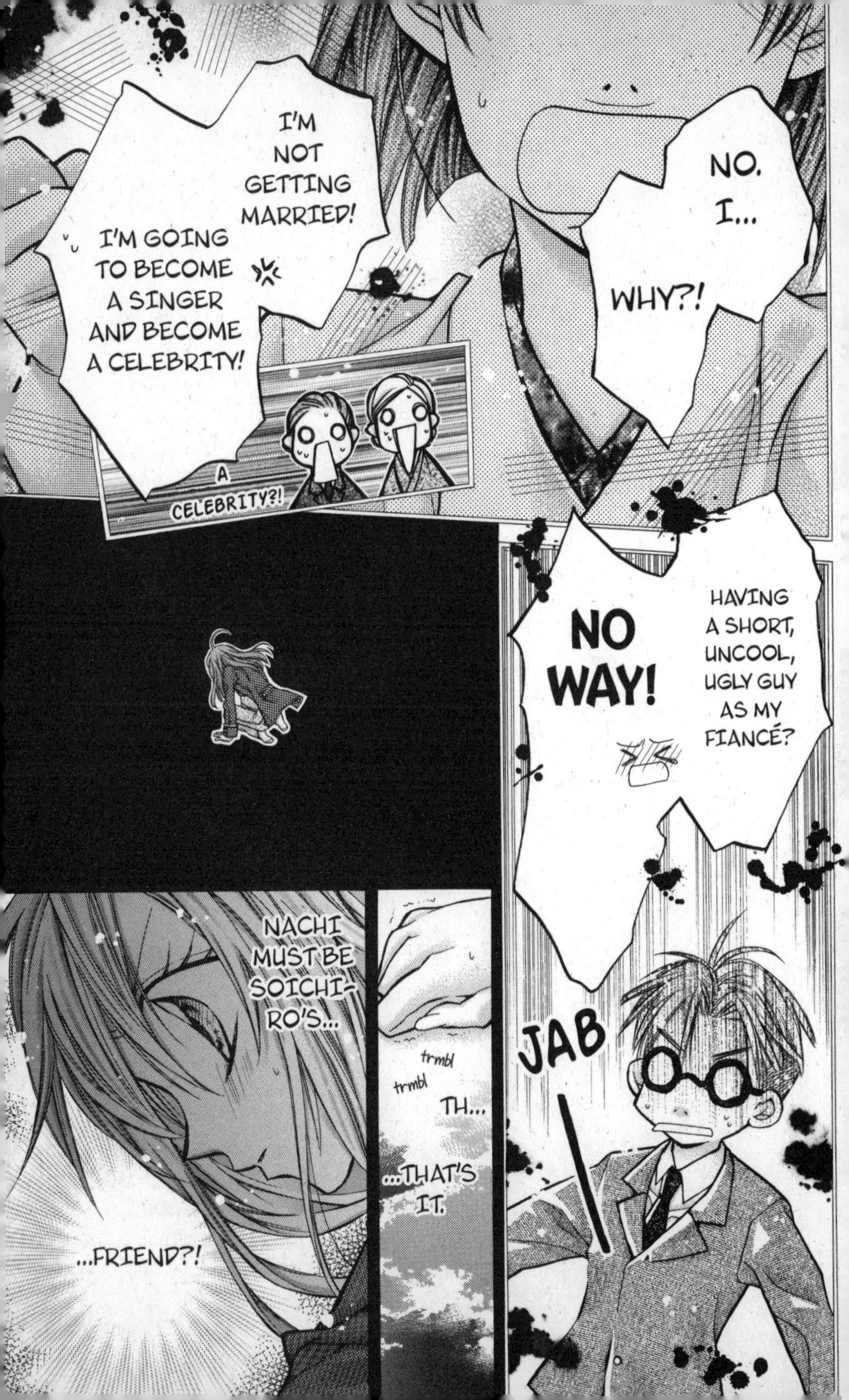
NO. I... WHY?!
I'M NOT GETTING MARRIED!
I'M GOING TO BECOME A SINGER AND BECOME A CELEBRITY!
A CELEBRITY?!
NO WAY!
HAVING A SHORT, UNCOOL, UGLY GUY AS MY FIANCÉ?
JAB
trmbl
trmbl
TH...
...THAT'S IT.
NACHI MUST BE SOICHI-RO'S...
...FRIEND?!

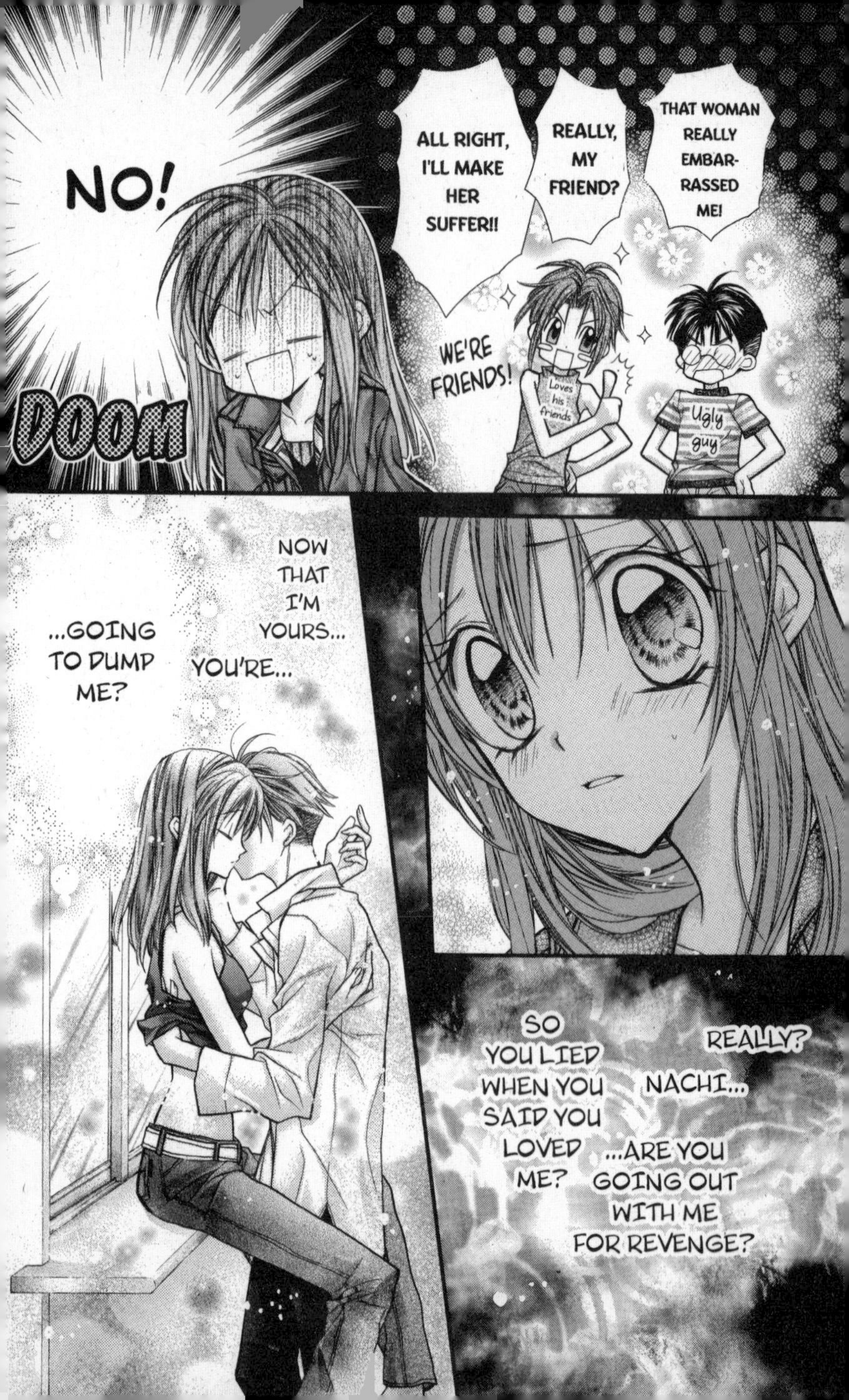
THAT WOMAN REALLY EMBARRASSED ME!
REALLY, MY FRIEND?
ALL RIGHT, I'LL MAKE HER SUFFER!!
WE'RE FRIENDS!
Loves his friends
Ugly guy
NO!
DOOM
REALLY?
NACHI...
...ARE YOU GOING OUT WITH ME FOR REVENGE?
SO YOU LIED WHEN YOU SAID YOU LOVED ME?
NOW THAT I'M YOURS...
YOU'RE...
...GOING TO DUMP ME?

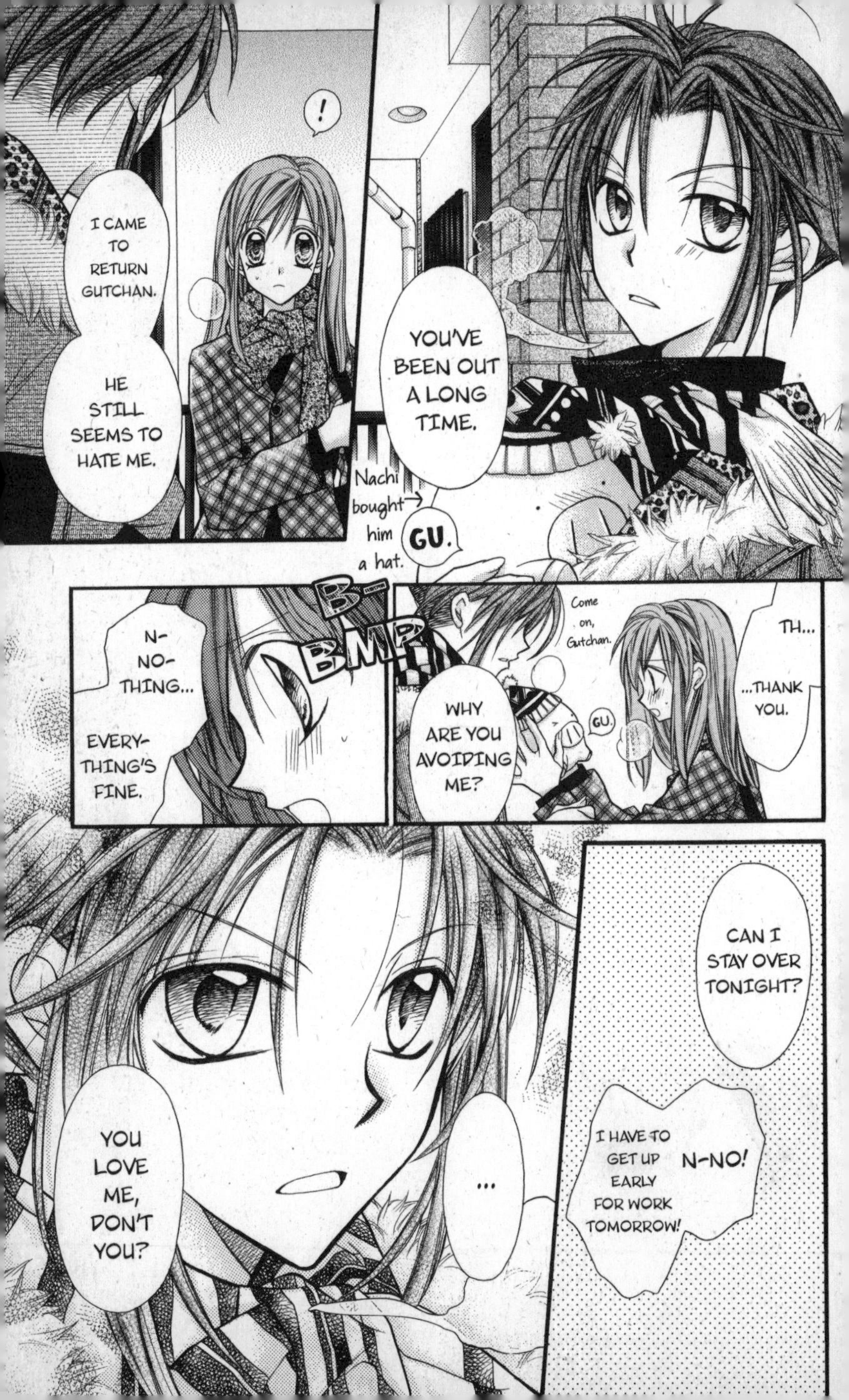
YOU'VE BEEN OUT A LONG TIME.
Nachi bought him a hat.
GU.
!
I CAME TO RETURN GUTCHAN.
HE STILL SEEMS TO HATE ME.
TH...
...THANK YOU.
Come on, Gutchan.
GU.
WHY ARE YOU AVOIDING ME?
B-BMP
N-NO-THING...
EVERY-THING'S FINE.
CAN I STAY OVER TONIGHT?
N-NO!
I HAVE TO GET UP EARLY FOR WORK TOMORROW!
...
YOU LOVE ME, DON'T YOU?

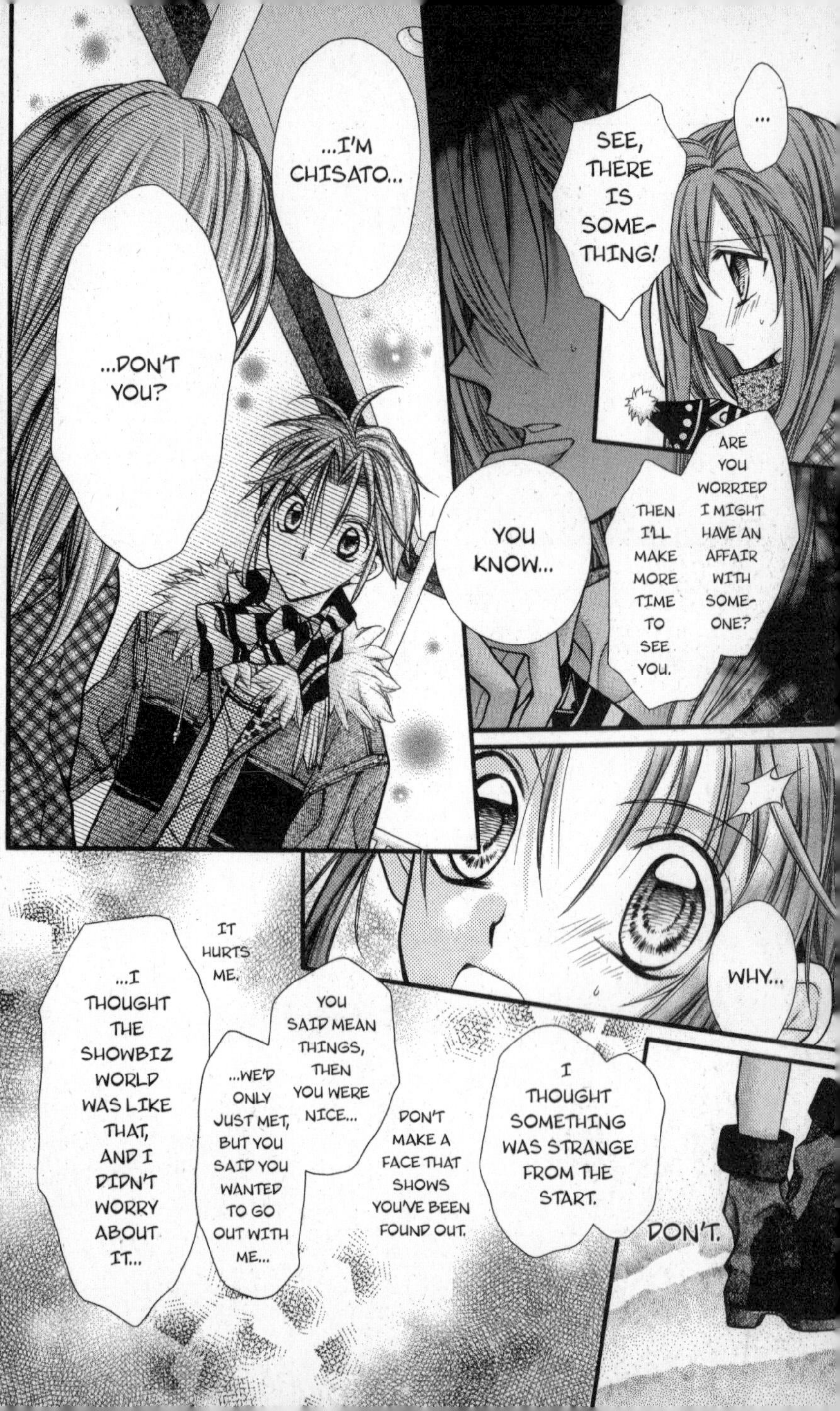
...
SEE, THERE IS SOMETHING!
ARE YOU WORRIED I MIGHT HAVE AN AFFAIR WITH SOME-ONE?
THEN I'LL MAKE MORE TIME TO SEE YOU.
YOU KNOW...
...I'M CHISATO...
...DON'T YOU?
WHY...
DON'T.
I THOUGHT SOMETHING WAS STRANGE FROM THE START.
DON'T MAKE A FACE THAT SHOWS YOU'VE BEEN FOUND OUT.
YOU SAID MEAN THINGS, THEN YOU WERE NICE...
...WE'D ONLY JUST MET, BUT YOU SAID YOU WANTED TO GO OUT WITH ME...
IT HURTS ME.
...I THOUGHT THE SHOWBIZ WORLD WAS LIKE THAT, AND I DIDN'T WORRY ABOUT IT...

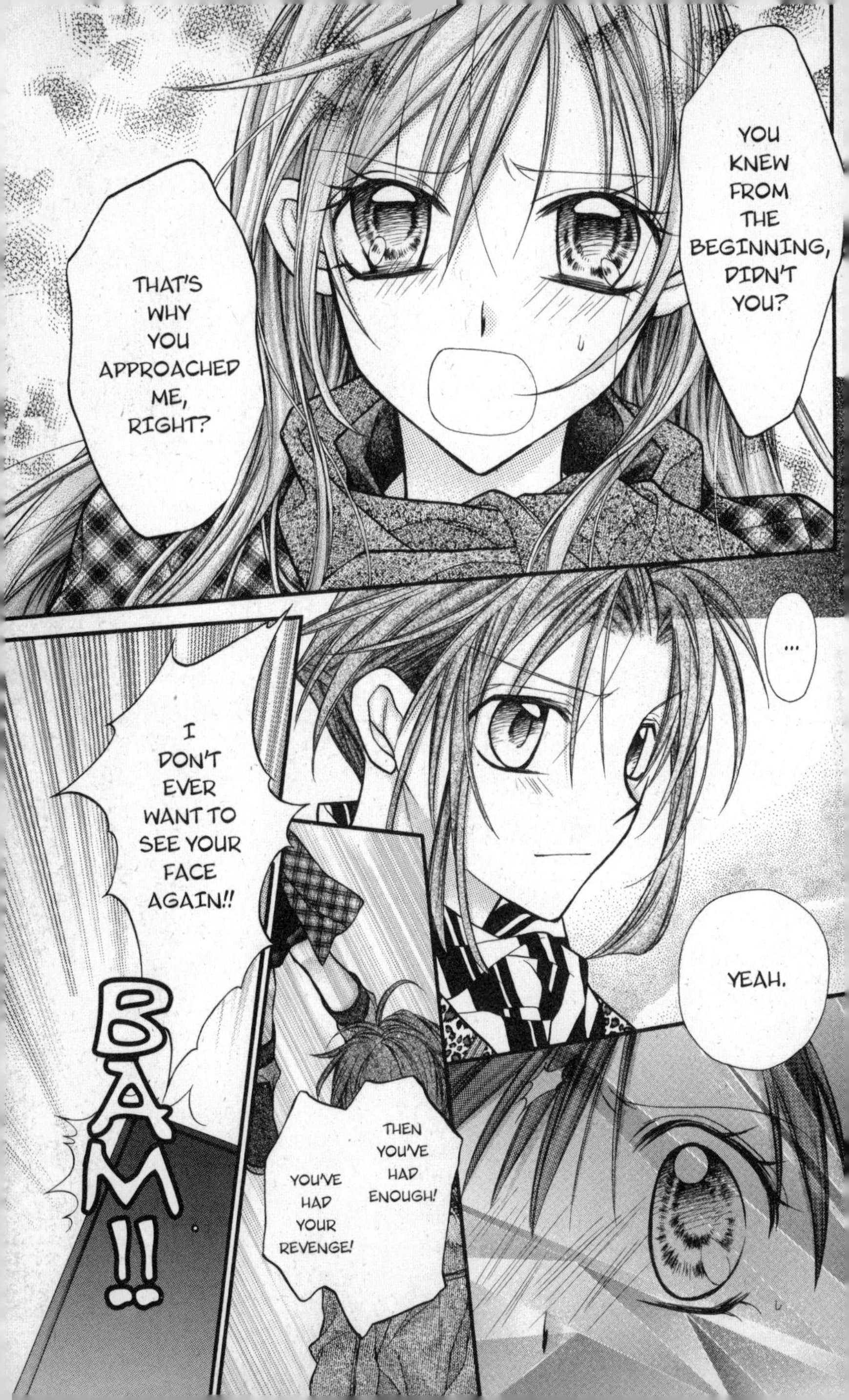
YOU KNEW FROM THE BEGINNING, DIDN'T YOU?
THAT'S WHY YOU APPROACHED ME, RIGHT?
...
YEAH.
THEN YOU'VE HAD ENOUGH!
YOU'VE HAD YOUR REVENGE!
I DON'T EVER WANT TO SEE YOUR FACE AGAIN!!
BAM!!

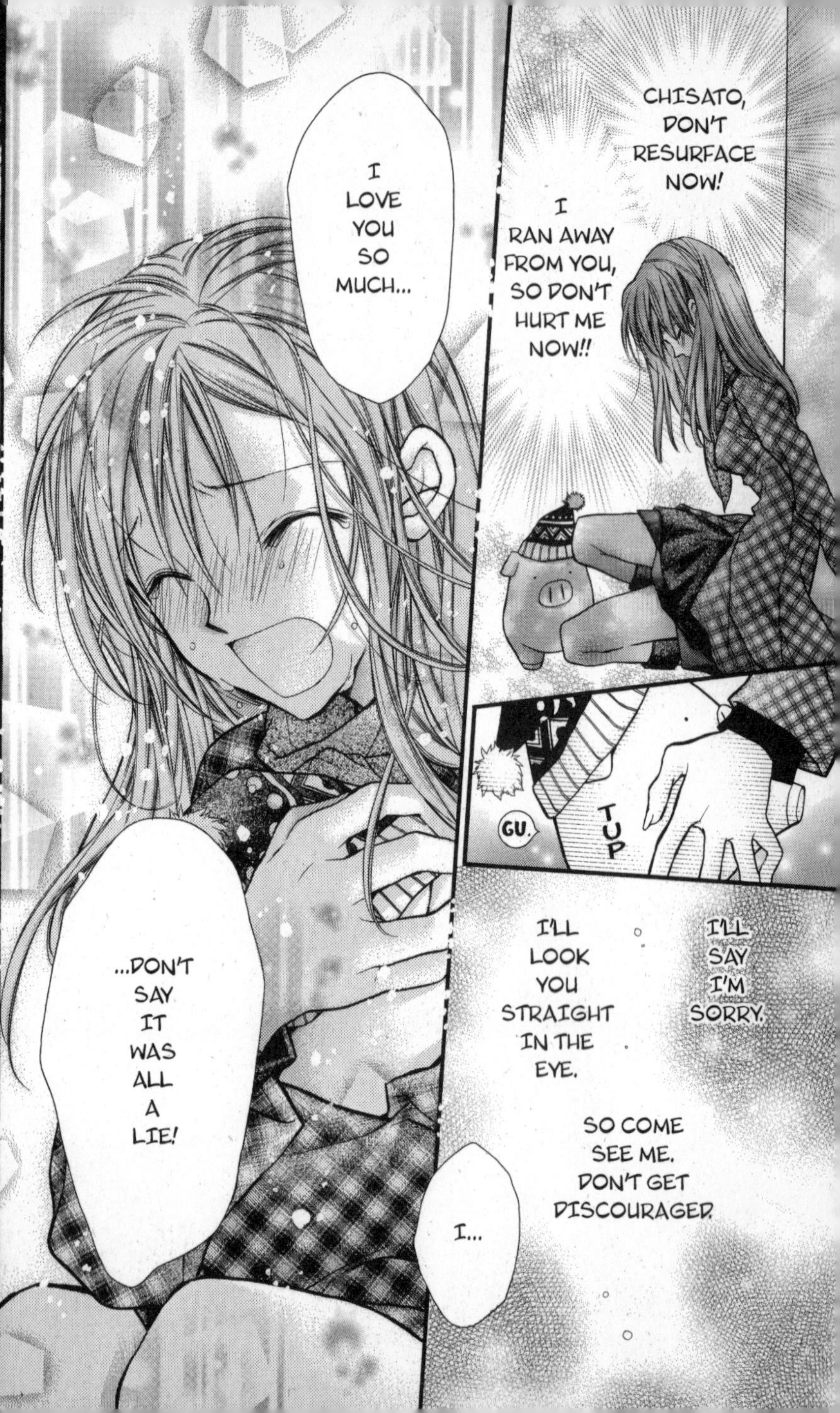

CHISATO, DON'T RESURFACE NOW!
I RAN AWAY FROM YOU, SO DON'T HURT ME NOW!!
TUP
GU.
I'LL SAY I'M SORRY.
I'LL LOOK YOU STRAIGHT IN THE EYE.
SO COME SEE ME. DON'T GET DISCOURAGED.
I LOVE YOU SO MUCH...
...DON'T SAY IT WAS ALL A LIE!
I...

NACHI...

NACHI...

GU.

SHIDO

.....

I'D HEARD THAT YOU HAD CHANGED YOUR FACE.

YOU'VE BECOME REALLY BEAUTIFUL...

THE ENGAGEMENT IS STILL VALID IF YOU WILL JUST SAY YES--

NO, NO, YOU DON'T HAVE TO APOLOGIZE.

... CHISATO.

I CAME TO APOLOGIZE TO YOUR SON...

...FOR WHAT HAPPENED DURING OUR MEETING FOR THE ARRANGED MARRIAGE.

I HAVE SOMEONE THAT I LOVE!

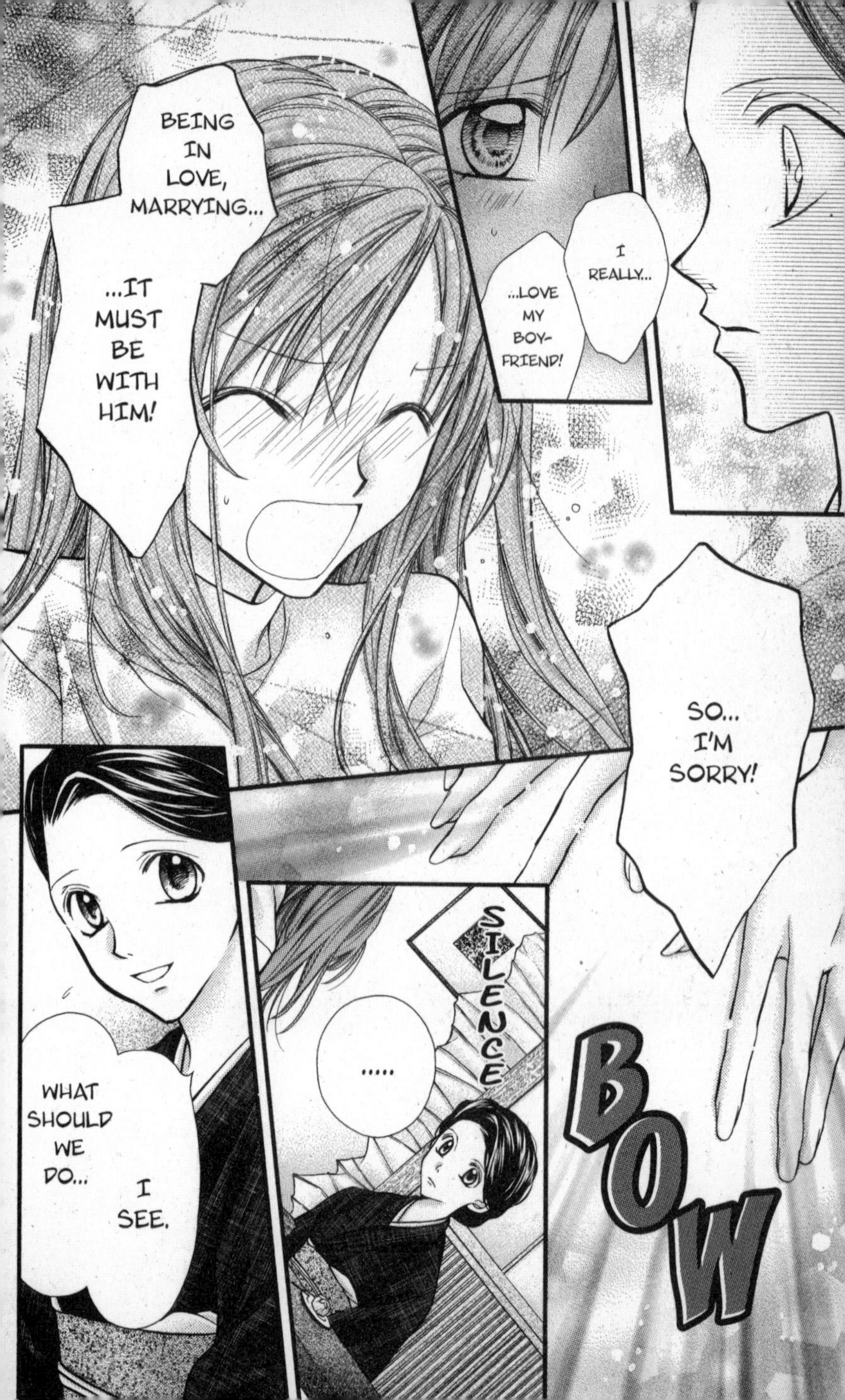
I REALLY...
...LOVE MY BOY-FRIEND!
BEING IN LOVE, MARRYING...
...IT MUST BE WITH HIM!
SO... I'M SORRY!
BOW
SILENCE
.....
WHAT SHOULD WE DO...
I SEE.

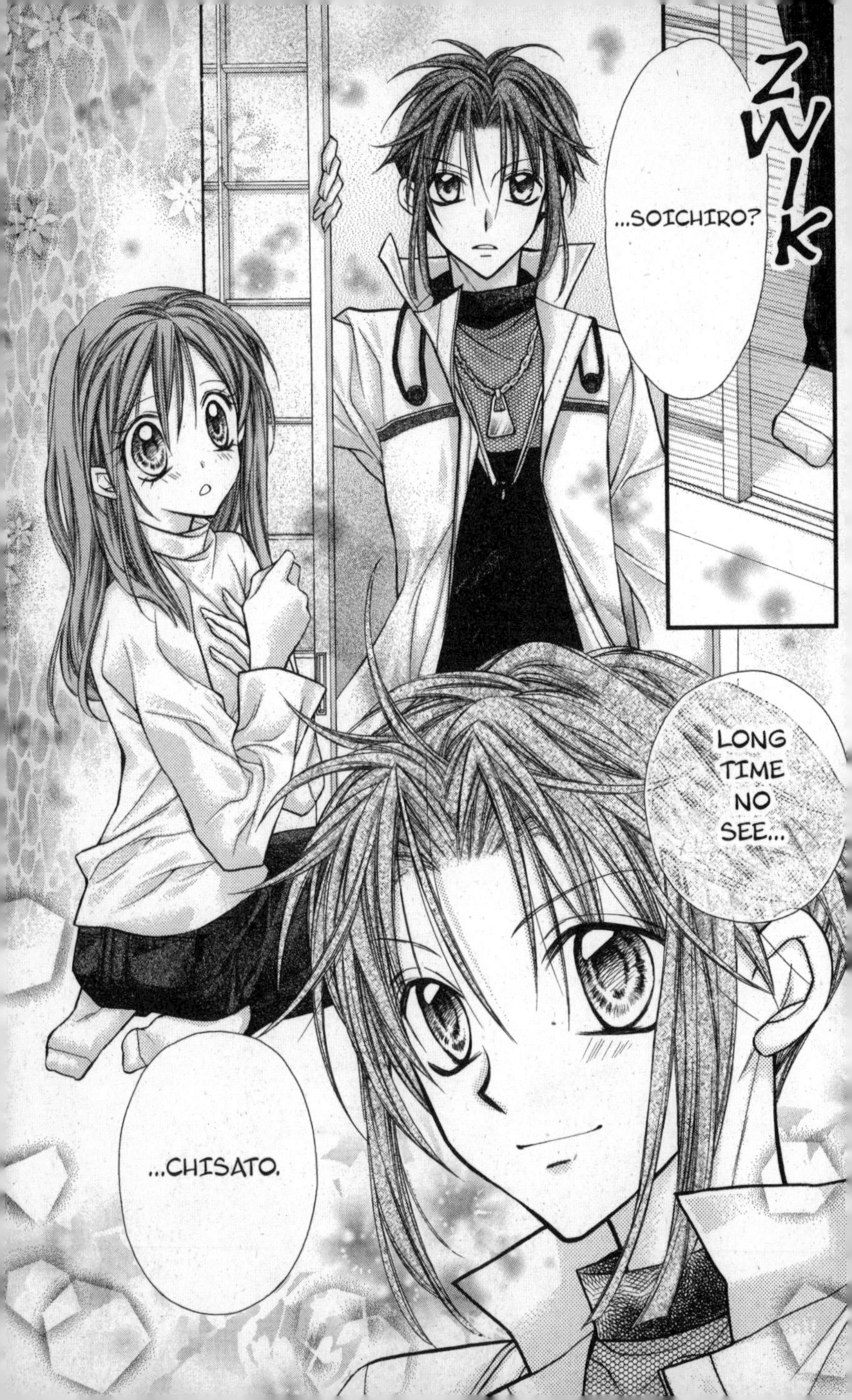
ZWIK
...SOICHIRO?
LONG TIME NO SEE...
...CHISATO.

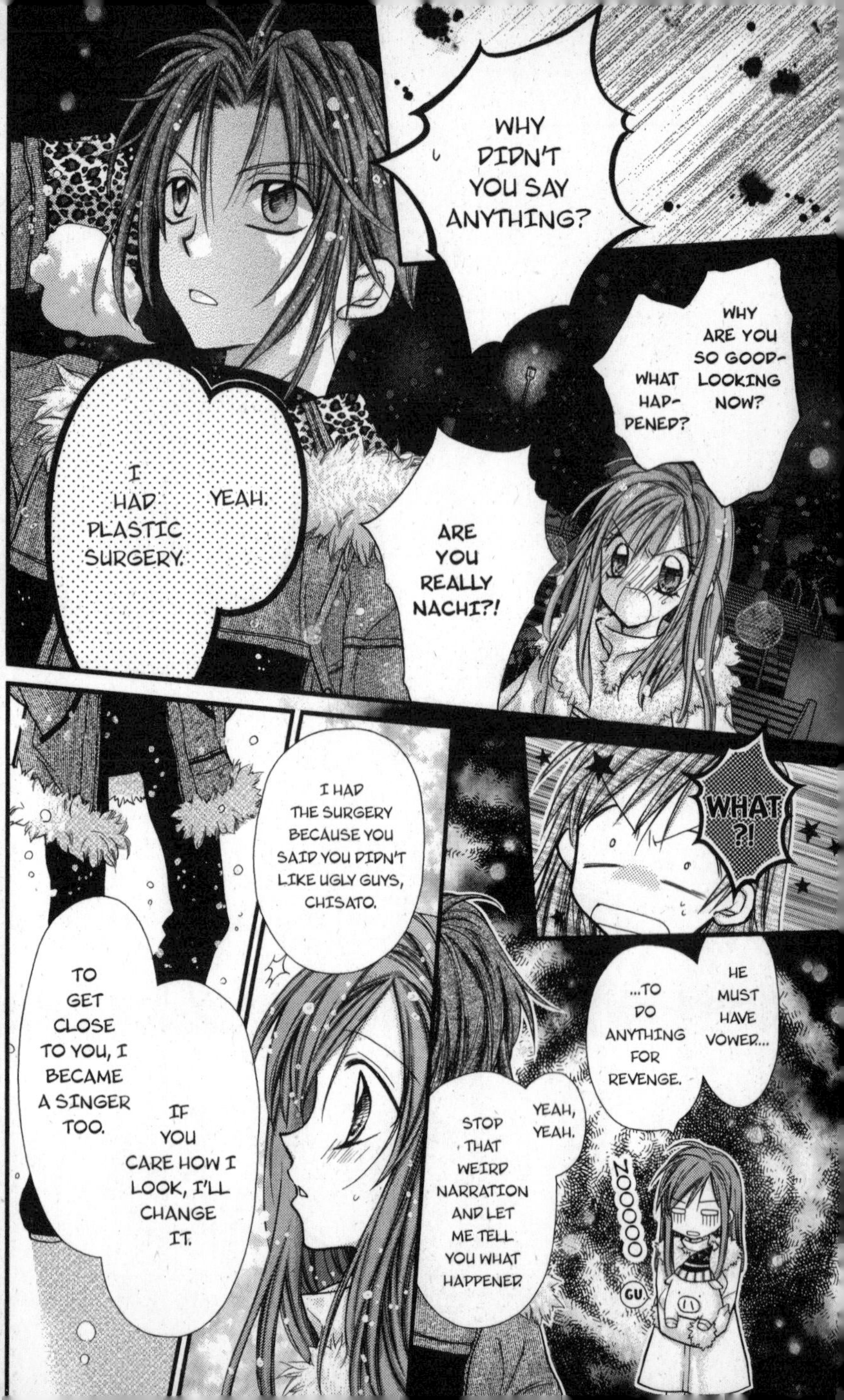
WHY DIDN'T YOU SAY ANYTHING?
WHY ARE YOU SO GOOD-LOOKING NOW?
WHAT HAPPENED?
ARE YOU REALLY NACHI?!
YEAH.
I HAD PLASTIC SURGERY.
WHAT?!
HE MUST HAVE VOWED...
...TO DO ANYTHING FOR REVENGE.
YEAH, YEAH.
STOP THAT WEIRD NARRATION AND LET ME TELL YOU WHAT HAPPENED.
NOOOOO
GU
I HAD THE SURGERY BECAUSE YOU SAID YOU DIDN'T LIKE UGLY GUYS, CHISATO.
TO GET CLOSE TO YOU, I BECAME A SINGER TOO.
IF YOU CARE HOW I LOOK, I'LL CHANGE IT.

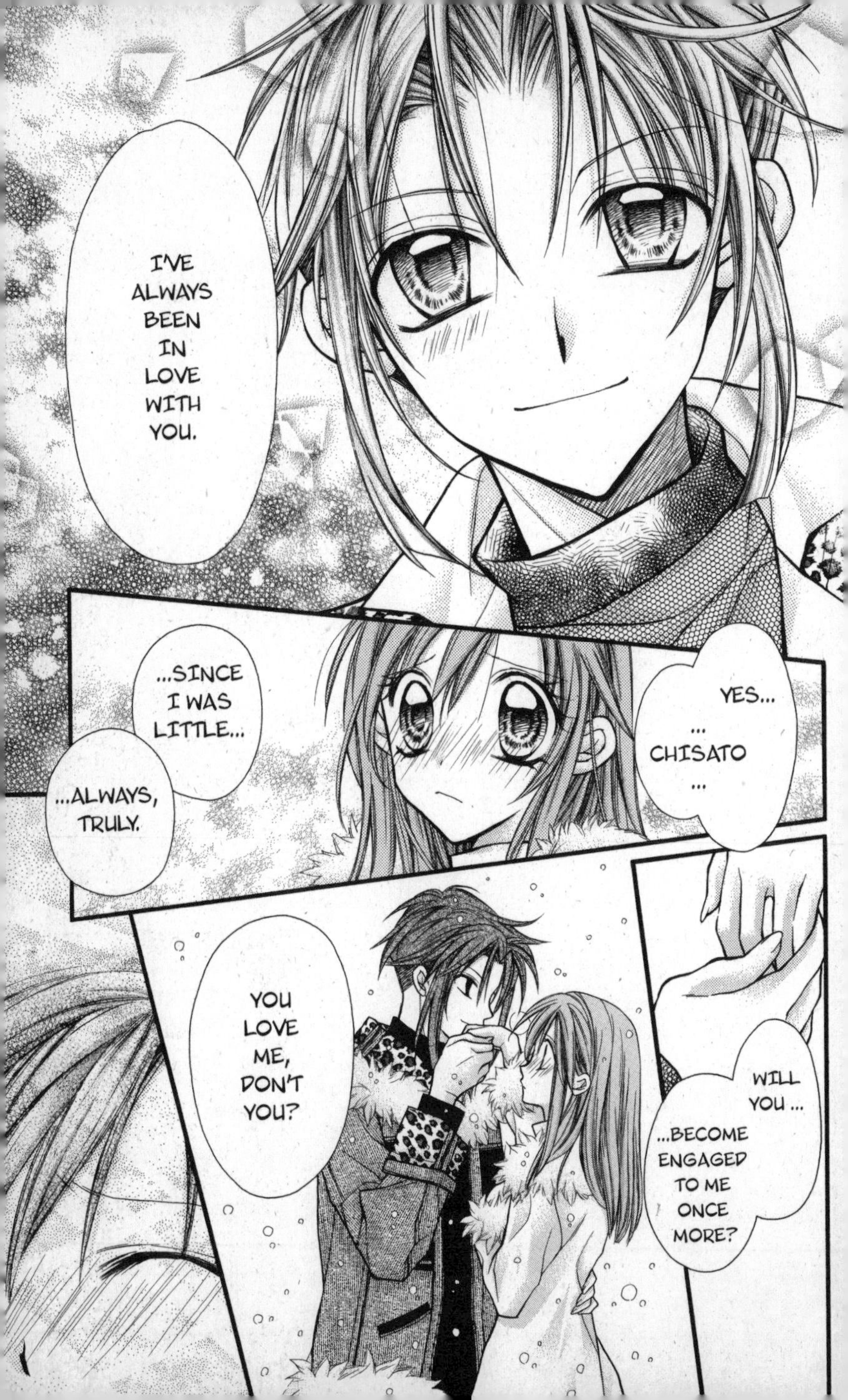
I'VE ALWAYS BEEN IN LOVE WITH YOU.
YES... ... CHISATO ...
...SINCE I WAS LITTLE...
...ALWAYS, TRULY.
WILL YOU ...
...BECOME ENGAGED TO ME ONCE MORE?
YOU LOVE ME, DON'T YOU?

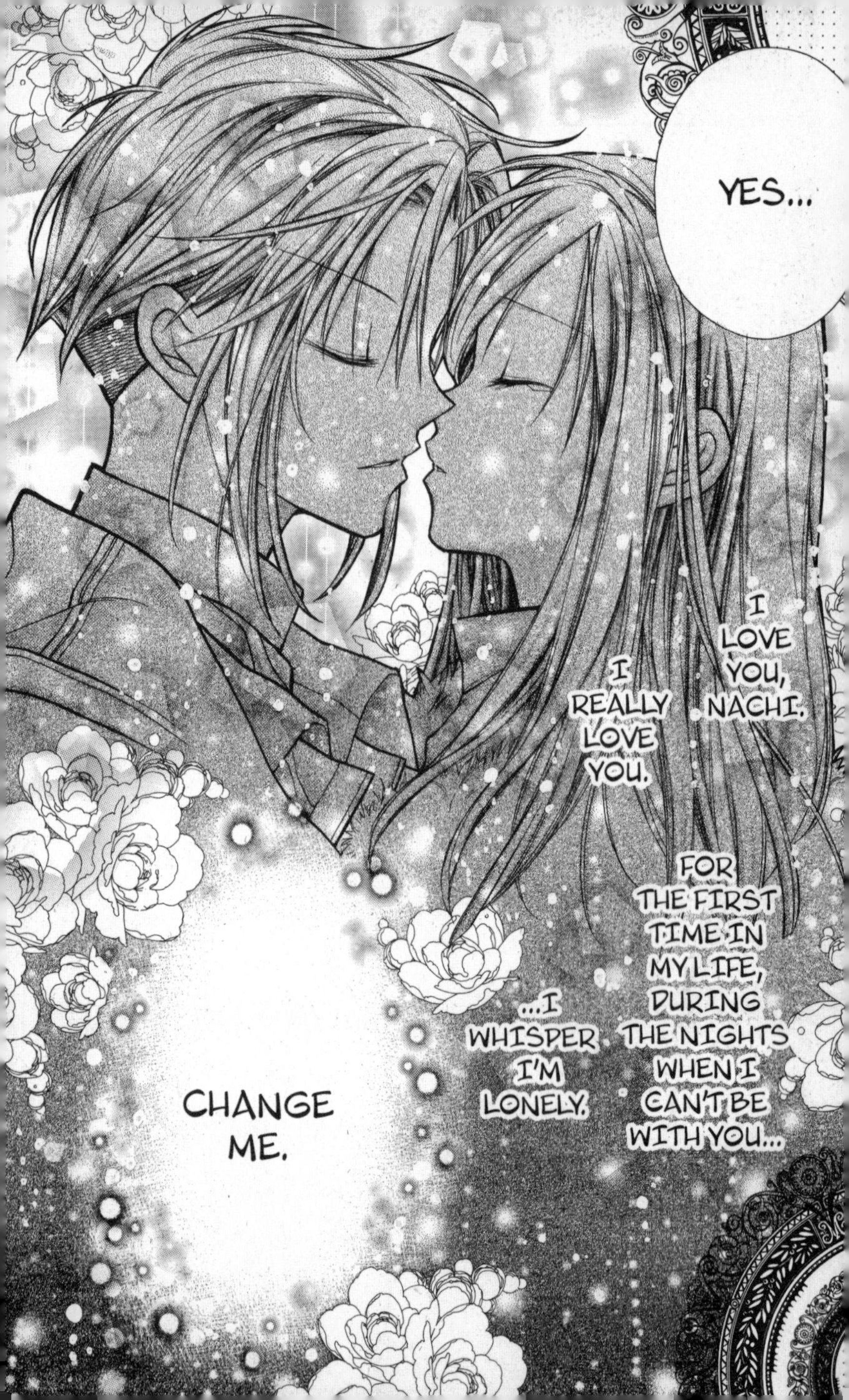
YES...
I LOVE YOU, NACHI.
I REALLY LOVE YOU.
FOR THE FIRST TIME IN MY LIFE, DURING THE NIGHTS WHEN I CAN'T BE WITH YOU...
...I WHISPER I'M LONELY.
CHANGE ME.

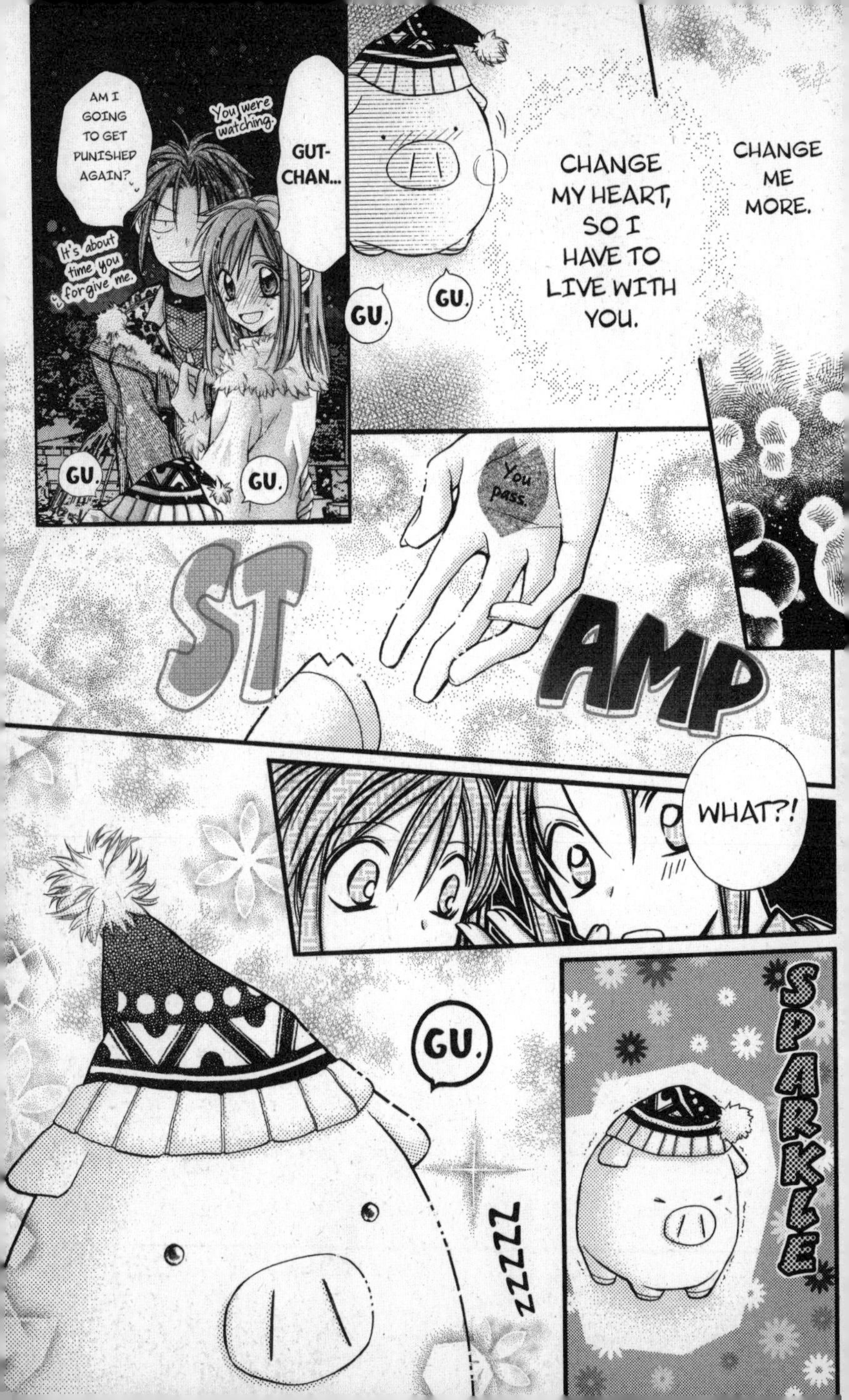
CHANGE ME MORE.
CHANGE MY HEART, SO I HAVE TO LIVE WITH YOU.
GU.
GU.
GUT-CHAN...
You were watching.
AM I GOING TO GET PUNISHED AGAIN?
It's about time you forgive me.
GU.
GU.
You pass.
ST
AMP
WHAT?!
SPARKLE
GU.
ZZZZZZ

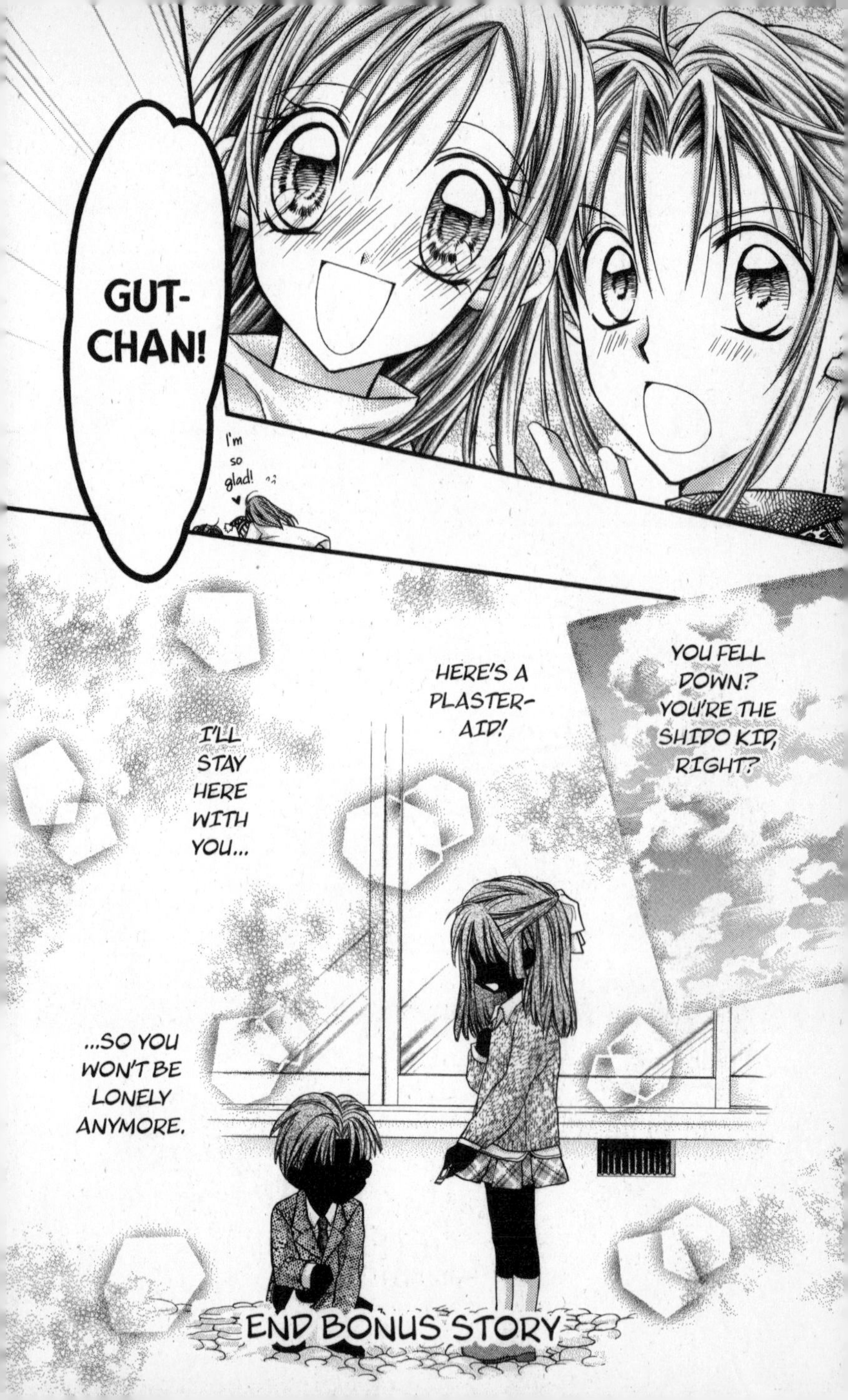
GUT-CHAN!
I'm so glad!
YOU FELL DOWN? YOU'RE THE SHIDO KID, RIGHT?
HERE'S A PLASTER-AID!
I'LL STAY HERE WITH YOU...
...SO YOU WON'T BE LONELY ANYMORE.
END BONUS STORY

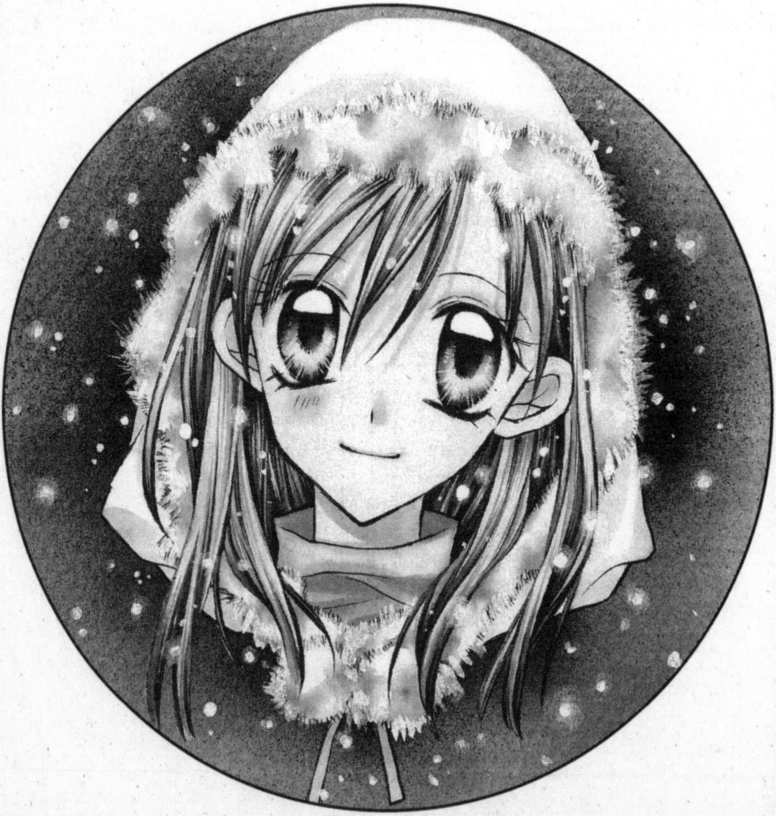

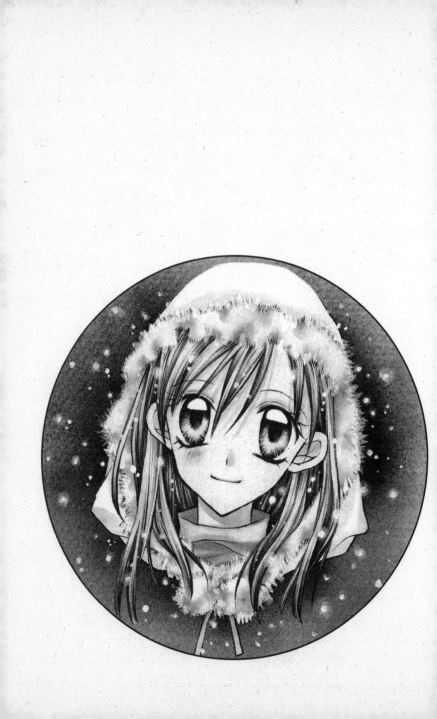

Full Moon o Sagashite

Totsugeki! Dokodoko☆ 4-Panel Manga

Zumiyan, Jonacchi

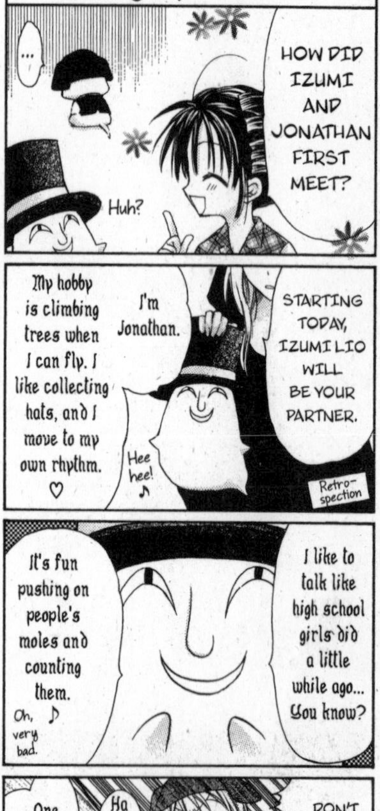
HOW DID IZUMI AND JONATHAN FIRST MEET?
...
Huh?
STARTING TODAY, IZUMI LIO WILL BE YOUR PARTNER.
Retro-spection
I'm Jonathan.
My hobby is climbing trees when I can fly. I like collecting hats, and I move to my own rhythm. ♡
Hee hee! ♪
I like to talk like high school girls did a little while ago... You know?
It's fun pushing on people's moles and counting them.
Oh, ♪ very bad.
DON'T PUSH ON MOLES AND COUNT THEM!!
THEY'LL INCREASE!!
Ha ha ha ha
One... ...two...
... three ...

Zumiyan, Jonacchi 2

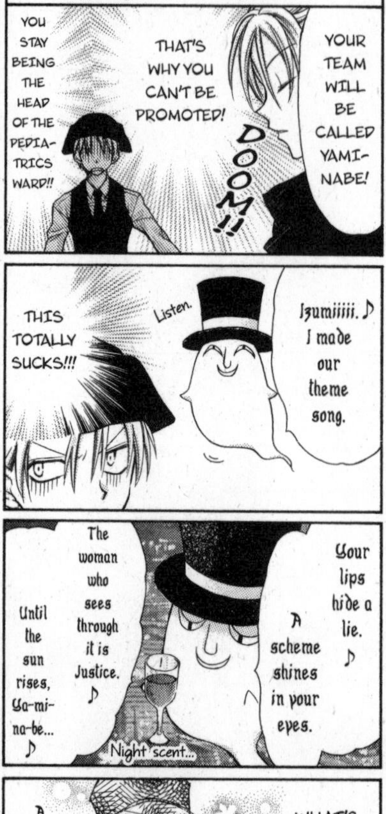
YOUR TEAM WILL BE CALLED YAMI-NABE!
DOOOM!!
THAT'S WHY YOU CAN'T BE PROMOTED!
YOU STAY BEING THE HEAD OF THE PEDIA-TRICS WARD!!
Izumiiiii. ♪ I made our theme song.
Listen.
THIS TOTALLY SUCKS!!!
Your lips hide a lie. ♪
A scheme shines in your eyes.
The woman who sees through it is Justice. ♪
Until the sun rises, Ya-mi-na-be... ♪
Night scent...
WHAT'S "JUSTICE," YOU GHOST? ♡
A goddess, you doggie! ☆

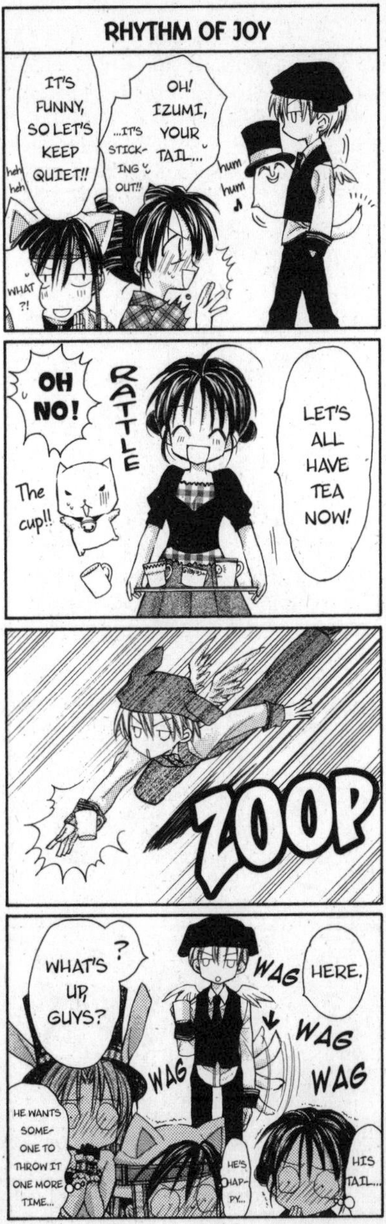
RHYTHM OF JOY
OH! IZUMI, YOUR TAIL...
...IT'S STICKING OUT!!
IT'S FUNNY, SO LET'S KEEP QUIET!!
hum hum ♪
heh heh
WHAT?!
LET'S ALL HAVE TEA NOW!
RATTLE
OH NO!
The cup!!
ZOOP
HERE.
WAG
WAG
WAG
WAG
WHAT'S UP, GUYS?
HIS TAIL...
HE'S HAPPY...
HE WANTS SOMEONE TO THROW IT ONE MORE TIME...

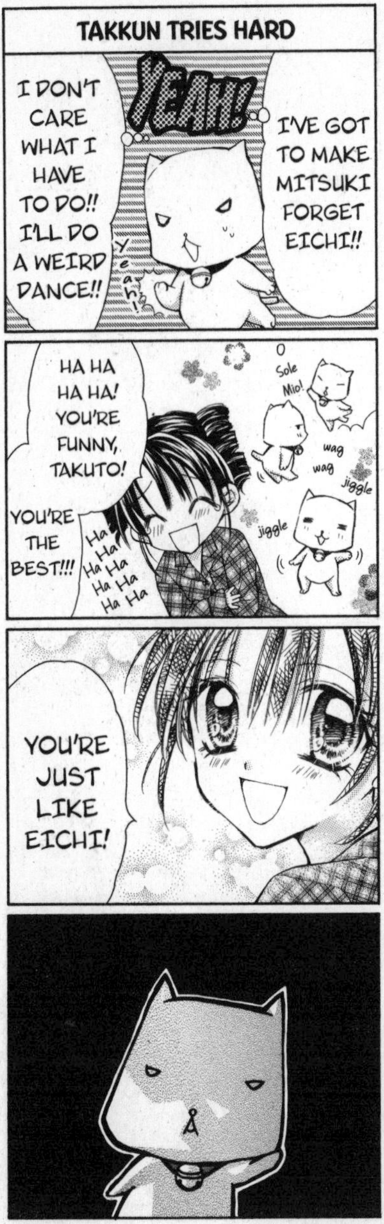
TAKKUN TRIES HARD
I'VE GOT TO MAKE MITSUKI FORGET EICHI!!
YEAH!
I DON'T CARE WHAT I HAVE TO DO!! I'LL DO A WEIRD DANCE!!
Yeah!
O Sole Mio!
wag wag
jiggle
jiggle
HA HA HA HA! YOU'RE FUNNY, TAKUTO!
YOU'RE THE BEST!!!
Ha Ha! Ha Ha Ha Ha Ha Ha
YOU'RE JUST LIKE EICHI!

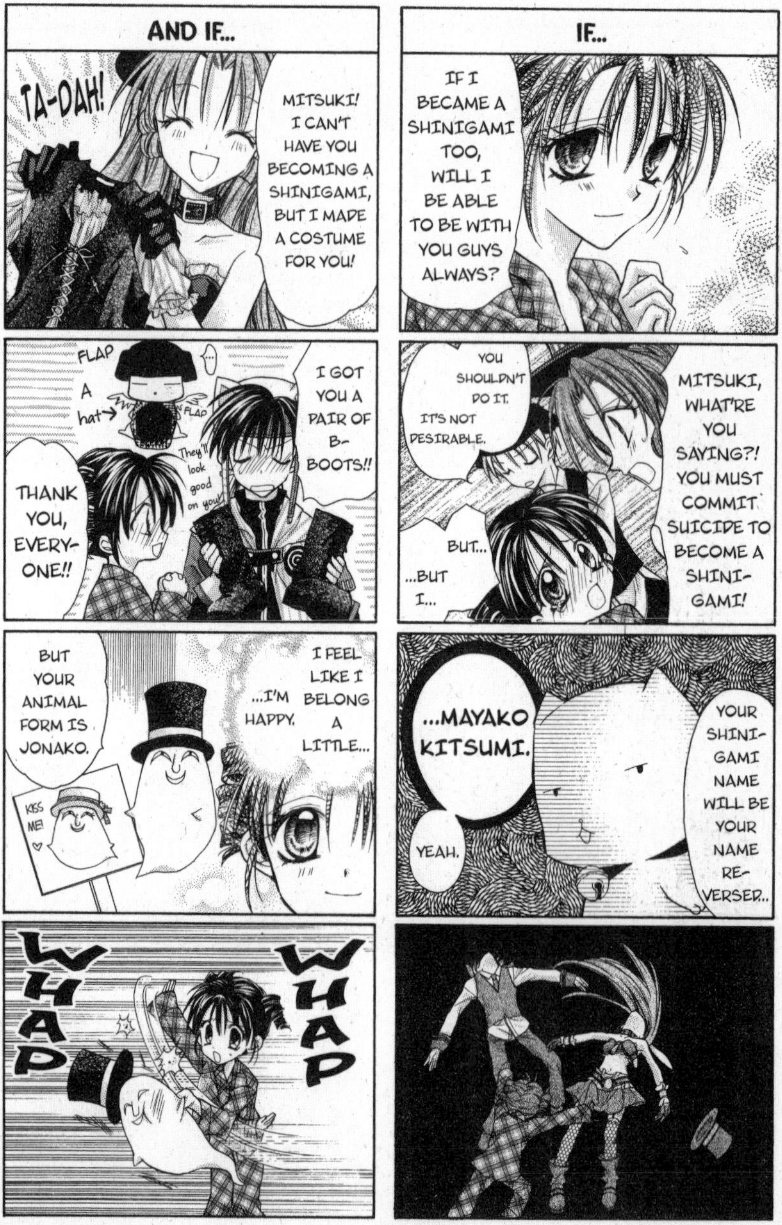
IF...
IF I BECAME A SHINIGAMI TOO, WILL I BE ABLE TO BE WITH YOU GUYS ALWAYS?
MITSUKI, WHAT'RE YOU SAYING?! YOU MUST COMMIT SUICIDE TO BECOME A SHINIGAMI!
YOU SHOULDN'T DO IT.
IT'S NOT DESIRABLE.
BUT...
...BUT I...
YOUR SHINIGAMI NAME WILL BE YOUR NAME REVERSED...
...MAYAKO KITSUMI.
YEAH.
AND IF...
MITSUKI! I CAN'T HAVE YOU BECOMING A SHINIGAMI, BUT I MADE A COSTUME FOR YOU!
TA-DAH!
I GOT YOU A PAIR OF B-BOOTS!!
They'll look good on you!
FLAP
...
FLAP
A hat→
THANK YOU, EVERYONE!!
I FEEL LIKE I BELONG A LITTLE...
...I'M HAPPY.
BUT YOUR ANIMAL FORM IS JONAKO.
KISS ME!
WHAP
WHAP

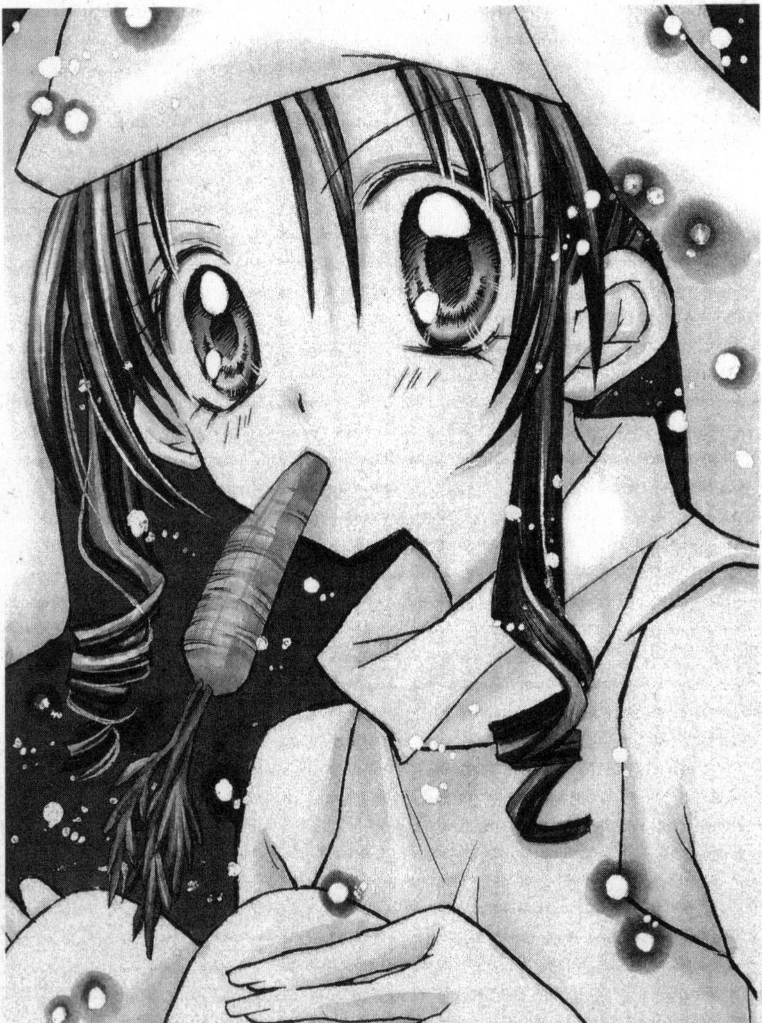

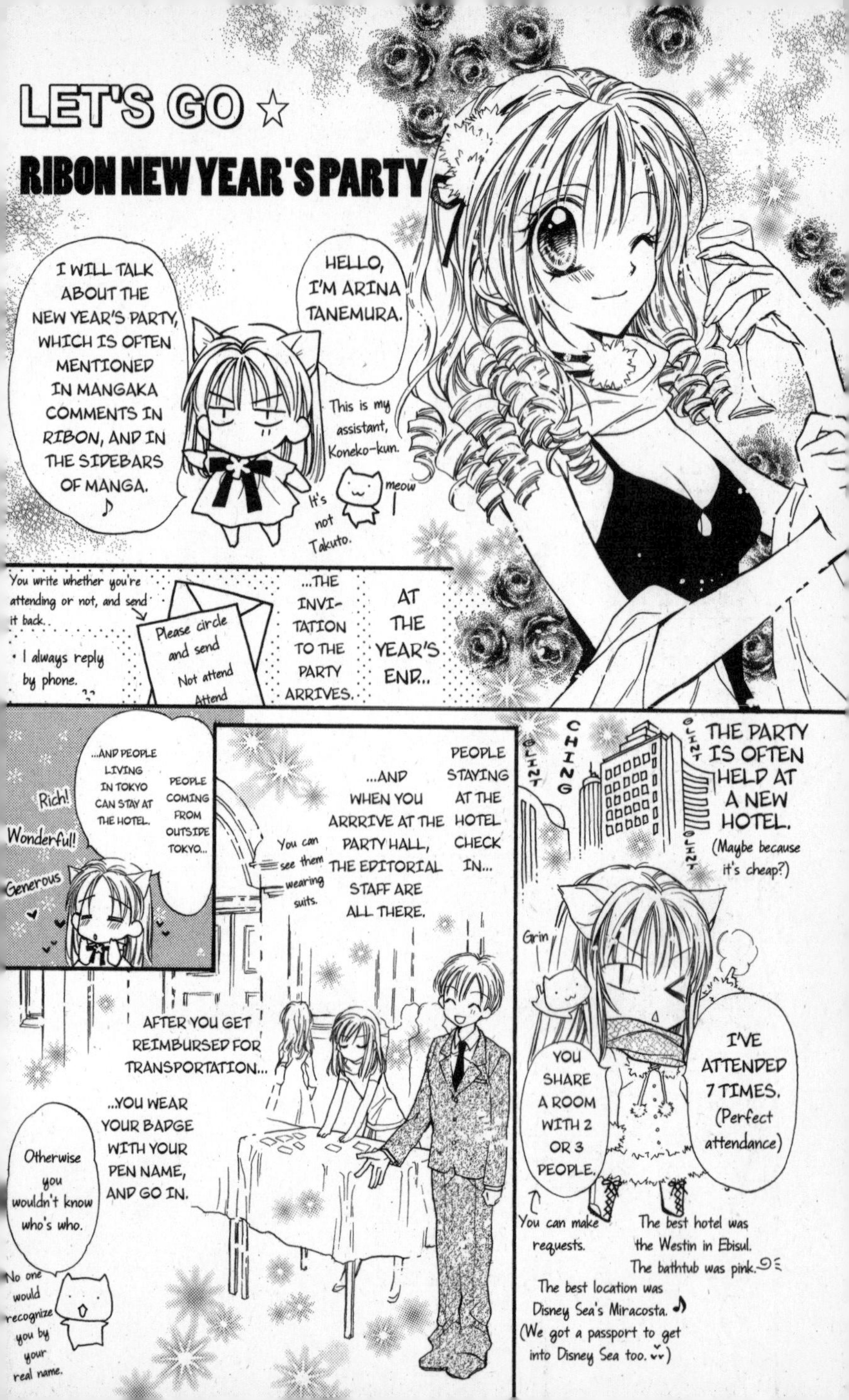
LET'S GO ☆
RIBON NEW YEAR'S PARTY
HELLO, I'M ARINA TANEMURA.
I WILL TALK ABOUT THE NEW YEAR'S PARTY, WHICH IS OFTEN MENTIONED IN MANGAKA COMMENTS IN RIBON, AND IN THE SIDEBARS OF MANGA. ♪
This is my assistant, Koneko-kun.
meow
It's not Takuto.
AT THE YEAR'S END...
...THE INVITATION TO THE PARTY ARRIVES.
You write whether you're attending or not, and send it back.
Please circle and send
Not attend
Attend
• I always reply by phone.
THE PARTY IS OFTEN HELD AT A NEW HOTEL.
(Maybe because it's cheap?)
CHING
GLINT
GLINT
GLINT
I'VE ATTENDED 7 TIMES. (Perfect attendance)
Grin
YOU SHARE A ROOM WITH 2 OR 3 PEOPLE.
You can make requests.
The best hotel was the Westin in Ebisu!. The bathtub was pink.
The best location was Disney Sea's Miracosta. ♪
(We got a passport to get into Disney Sea too.)
PEOPLE STAYING AT THE HOTEL CHECK IN...
...AND WHEN YOU ARRRIVE AT THE PARTY HALL, THE EDITORIAL STAFF ARE ALL THERE.
You can see them wearing suits.
PEOPLE COMING FROM OUTSIDE TOKYO...
...AND PEOPLE LIVING IN TOKYO CAN STAY AT THE HOTEL.
Rich!
Wonderful!
Generous
AFTER YOU GET REIMBURSED FOR TRANSPORTATION...
...YOU WEAR YOUR BADGE WITH YOUR PEN NAME, AND GO IN.
Otherwise you wouldn't know who's who.
No one would recognize you by your real name.

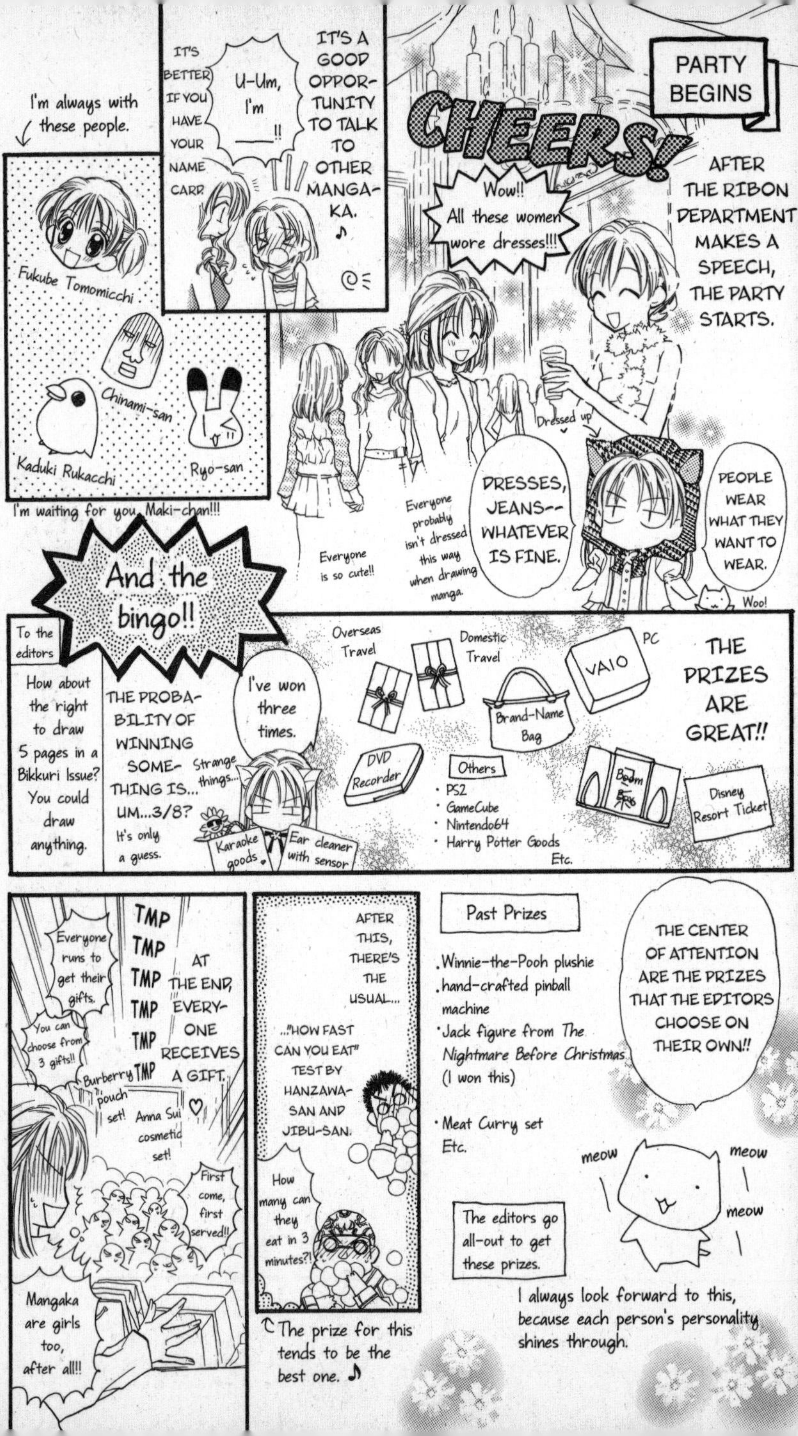
PARTY BEGINS
CHEERS!
AFTER THE RIBON DEPARTMENT MAKES A SPEECH, THE PARTY STARTS.
Wow!! All these women wore dresses!!!
Dressed up
PEOPLE WEAR WHAT THEY WANT TO WEAR.
Woo!
DRESSES, JEANS--WHATEVER IS FINE.
Everyone probably isn't dressed this way when drawing manga.
Everyone is so cute!!
IT'S A GOOD OPPORTUNITY TO TALK TO OTHER MANGAKA. ♪
U-Um, I'm ____!!
IT'S BETTER IF YOU HAVE YOUR NAME CARD
I'm always with these people.
Fukube Tomomicchi
Chinami-san
Ryo-san
Kaduki Rukacchi
I'm waiting for you, Maki-chan!!!
And the bingo!!
THE PRIZES ARE GREAT!!
PC
VAIO
Domestic Travel
Overseas Travel
Brand-Name Bag
Disney Resort Ticket
Boom Box
DVD Recorder
Others
· PS2
· GameCube
· Nintendo64
· Harry Potter Goods
Etc.
I've won three times.
Strange things...
Karaoke goods
Ear cleaner with sensor
THE PROBABILITY OF WINNING SOMETHING IS... UM...3/8?
It's only a guess.
To the editors
How about the right to draw 5 pages in a Bikkuri Issue? You could draw anything.
THE CENTER OF ATTENTION ARE THE PRIZES THAT THE EDITORS CHOOSE ON THEIR OWN!!
Past Prizes
.Winnie-the-Pooh plushie
.hand-crafted pinball machine
·Jack figure from The Nightmare Before Christmas (I won this)
·Meat Curry set
Etc.
meow
meow
meow
The editors go all-out to get these prizes.
I always look forward to this, because each person's personality shines through.
AFTER THIS, THERE'S THE USUAL...
..."HOW FAST CAN YOU EAT" TEST BY HANZAWA-SAN AND JIBU-SAN.
How many can they eat in 3 minutes?!
The prize for this tends to be the best one. ♪
TMP TMP TMP TMP TMP TMP
AT THE END, EVERYONE RECEIVES A GIFT.
Everyone runs to get their gifts.
You can choose from 3 gifts!!
Burberry pouch set!
Anna Sui cosmetic set!
First come, first served!!
Mangaka are girls too, after all!!

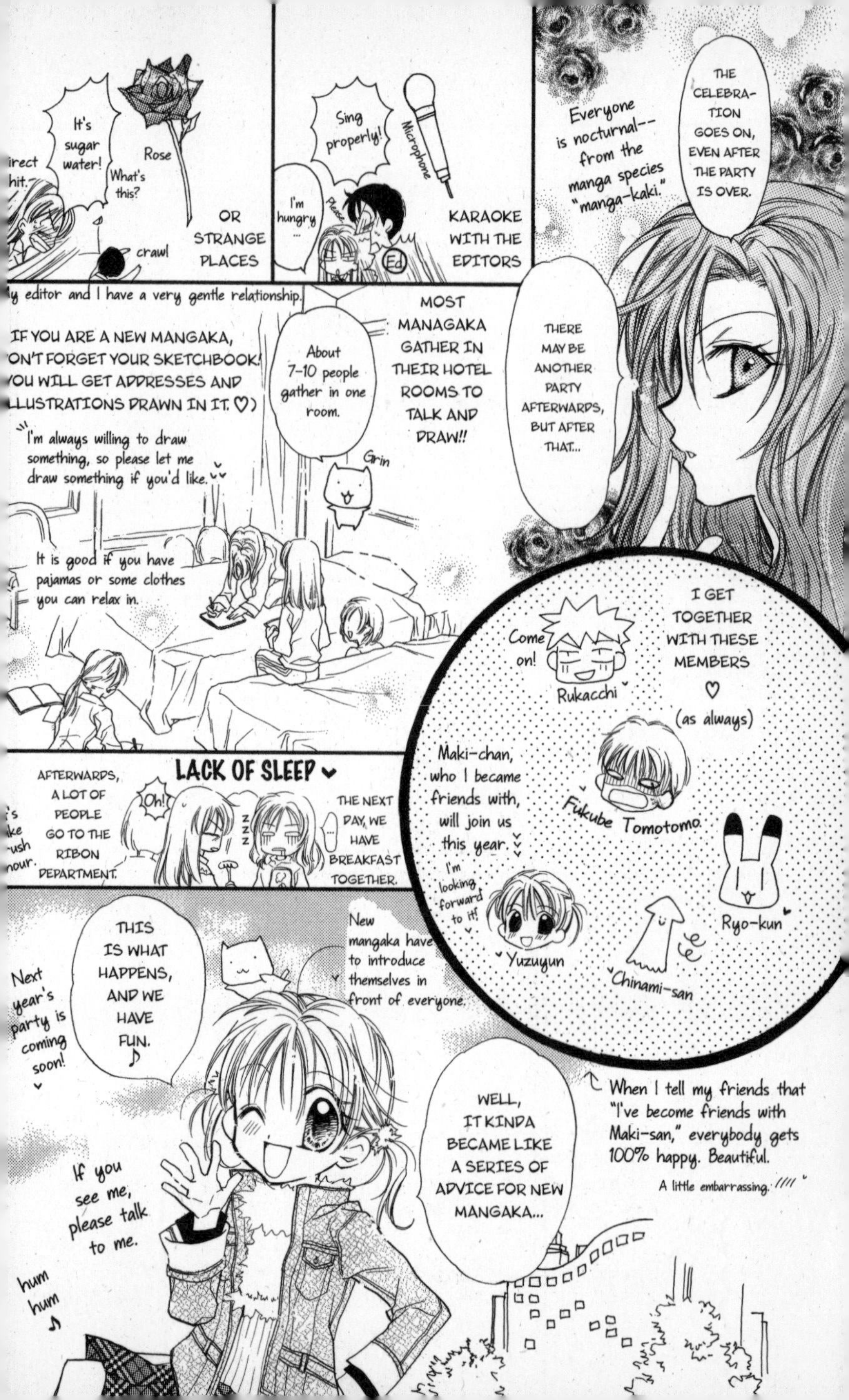
THE CELEBRATION GOES ON, EVEN AFTER THE PARTY IS OVER.
Everyone is nocturnal-- from the manga species "manga-kaki."
THERE MAY BE ANOTHER PARTY AFTERWARDS, BUT AFTER THAT...
KARAOKE WITH THE EDITORS
Microphone
Sing properly!
Please
I'm hungry ...
Ed
OR STRANGE PLACES
Rose
It's sugar water!
What's this?
irect hit.
crawl
MOST MANAGAKA GATHER IN THEIR HOTEL ROOMS TO TALK AND DRAW!!
About 7-10 people gather in one room.
ly editor and I have a very gentle relationship.
IF YOU ARE A NEW MANGAKA, ON'T FORGET YOUR SKETCHBOOK! YOU WILL GET ADDRESSES AND LLUSTRATIONS DRAWN IN IT. ♡)
I'm always willing to draw something, so please let me draw something if you'd like.
Grin
It is good if you have pajamas or some clothes you can relax in.
I GET TOGETHER WITH THESE MEMBERS ♡ (as always)
Come on!
Rukacchi
Fukube Tomotomo
Maki-chan, who I became friends with, will join us this year.
I'm looking forward to it!
Ryo-kun
Chinami-san
Yuzuyun
THE NEXT DAY, WE HAVE BREAKFAST TOGETHER.
...
LACK OF SLEEP
Oh!
z z z
AFTERWARDS, A LOT OF PEOPLE GO TO THE RIBON DEPARTMENT.
When I tell my friends that "I've become friends with Maki-san," everybody gets 100% happy. Beautiful.
A little embarrassing.
WELL, IT KINDA BECAME LIKE A SERIES OF ADVICE FOR NEW MANGAKA...
New mangaka have to introduce themselves in front of everyone.
THIS IS WHAT HAPPENS, AND WE HAVE FUN. ♪
Next year's party is coming soon!
If you see me, please talk to me.
hum hum ♪

Author Bio

Arina Tanemura was born in Aichi, Japan. She got her start in 1996, publishing *Nibanme no Koi no Katachi (*The Style of the Second Love*)* in *Ribon Original* magazine. Her early work includes a collection of short stories called *Kanshaku Dama no Yuutsu* (Short-Tempered Melancholic). Two of her titles, *Kamikaze Kaito Jeanne* and *Full Moon,* were made into popular TV series. Tanemura enjoys karaoke and is a huge *Lord of the Rings* fan.

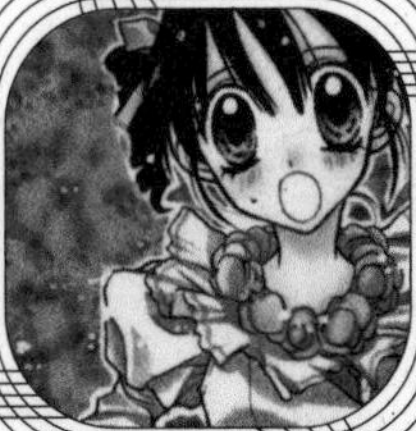

The next volume will be the final volume. I really had a difficult time drawing *Full Moon o Sagashite* in the beginning—I couldn't open my heart up and draw. But because it was difficult, I really, truly love this work now. The voices of my fans supported me. The series is ending soon, but please watch over how each character lives.

Full Moon o Sagashite

Vol. 6

The Shojo Beat Manga Edition

STORY & ART BY

ARINA TANEMURA

English Translation & Adaptation/Tomo Kimura
Touch-Up & Lettering/Elena Diaz
Graphics & Cover Design/Izumi Evers
Editor/Nancy Thistlethwaite

Printed in Canada

Published by VIZ Media, LLC
P.O. Box 77064
San Francisco, CA 94107

Shojo Beat Manga Edition
10 9 8 7 6 5 4
First printing, July 2006
Fourth printing, July 2011

www.shojobeat.com

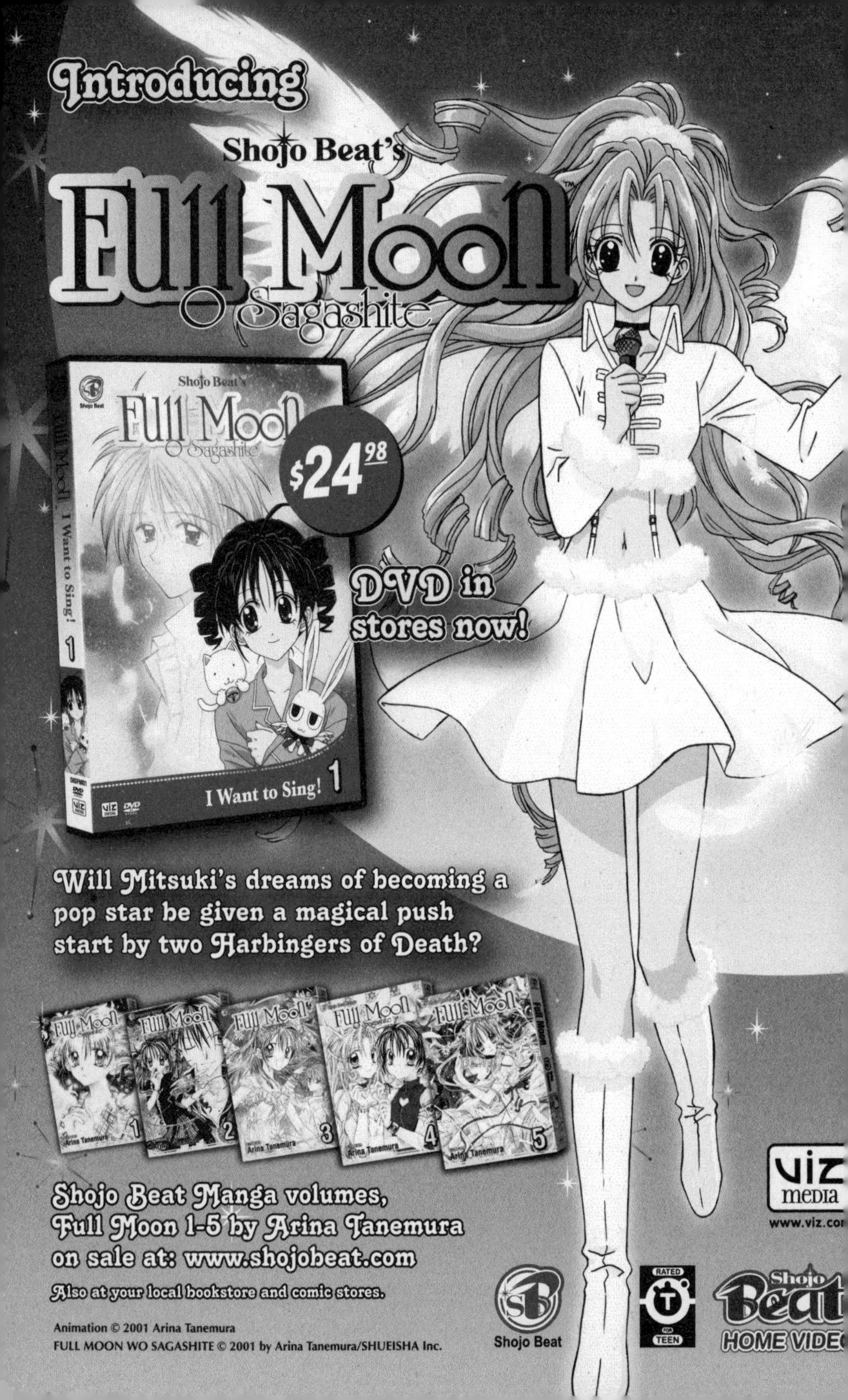
Introducing
Shojo Beat's
Full Moon™
O Sagashite
Shojo Beat's
Full Moon
O Sagashite
I Want to Sing! 1
$24.98
DVD in stores now!
Will Mitsuki's dreams of becoming a pop star be given a magical push start by two Harbingers of Death?
Full Moon
Arina Tanemura
viz media
www.viz.co
Shojo Beat Manga volumes, Full Moon 1-5 by Arina Tanemura on sale at: www.shojobeat.com
Also at your local bookstore and comic stores.
Animation © 2001 Arina Tanemura
FULL MOON WO SAGASHITE © 2001 by Arina Tanemura/SHUEISHA Inc.
Shojo Beat
RATED T FOR TEEN
Shojo Beat HOME VIDE

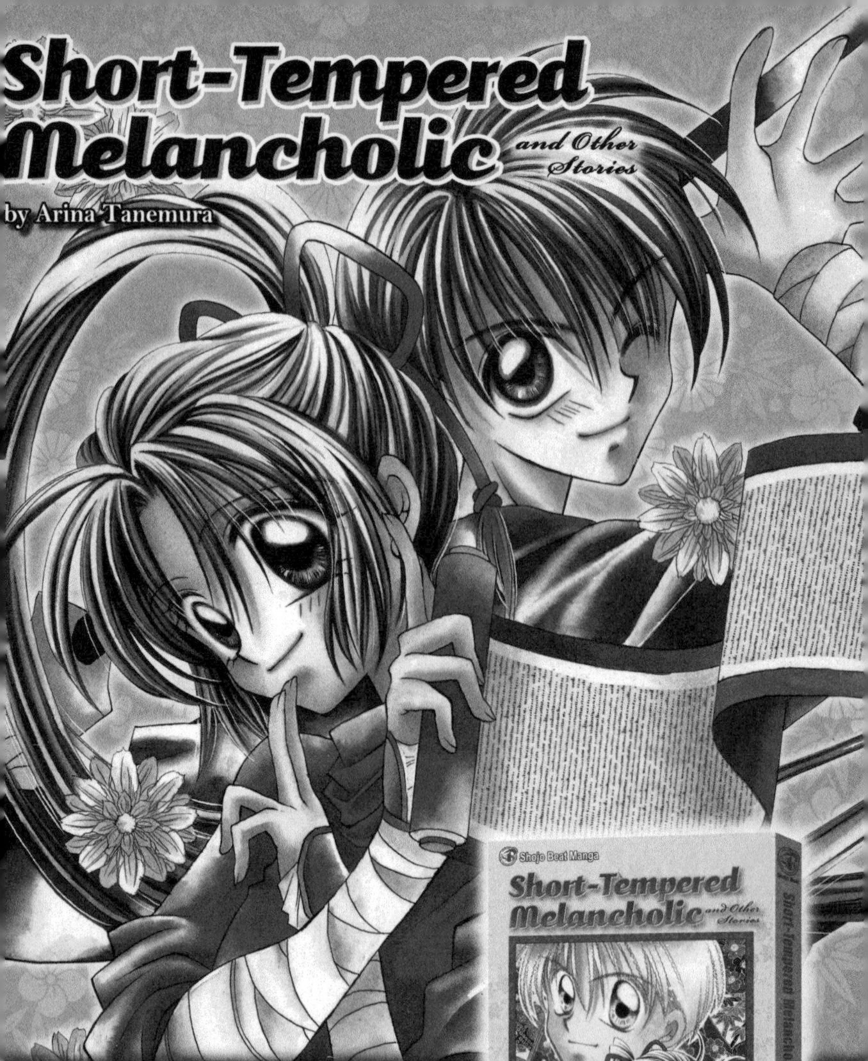
Short-Tempered Melancholic
and Other Stories
by Arina Tanemura
Shojo Beat Manga
Short-Tempered Melancholic and Other Stories
Story & Art by
Arina Tanemura

BY ARINA TANEMURA,
CREATOR OF *FULL MOON*
AND *THE GENTLEMEN'S
ALLIANCE* †

Ion Tsuburagi is a normal junior high girl with normal junior high problems. But when a mysterious substance grants her telekinetic powers, she finds herself struggling to keep everything together! Are her new abilities a blessing...or a curse?

Find out in *I•O•N*—manga on sale now!

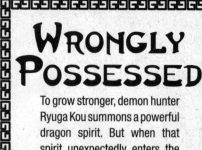

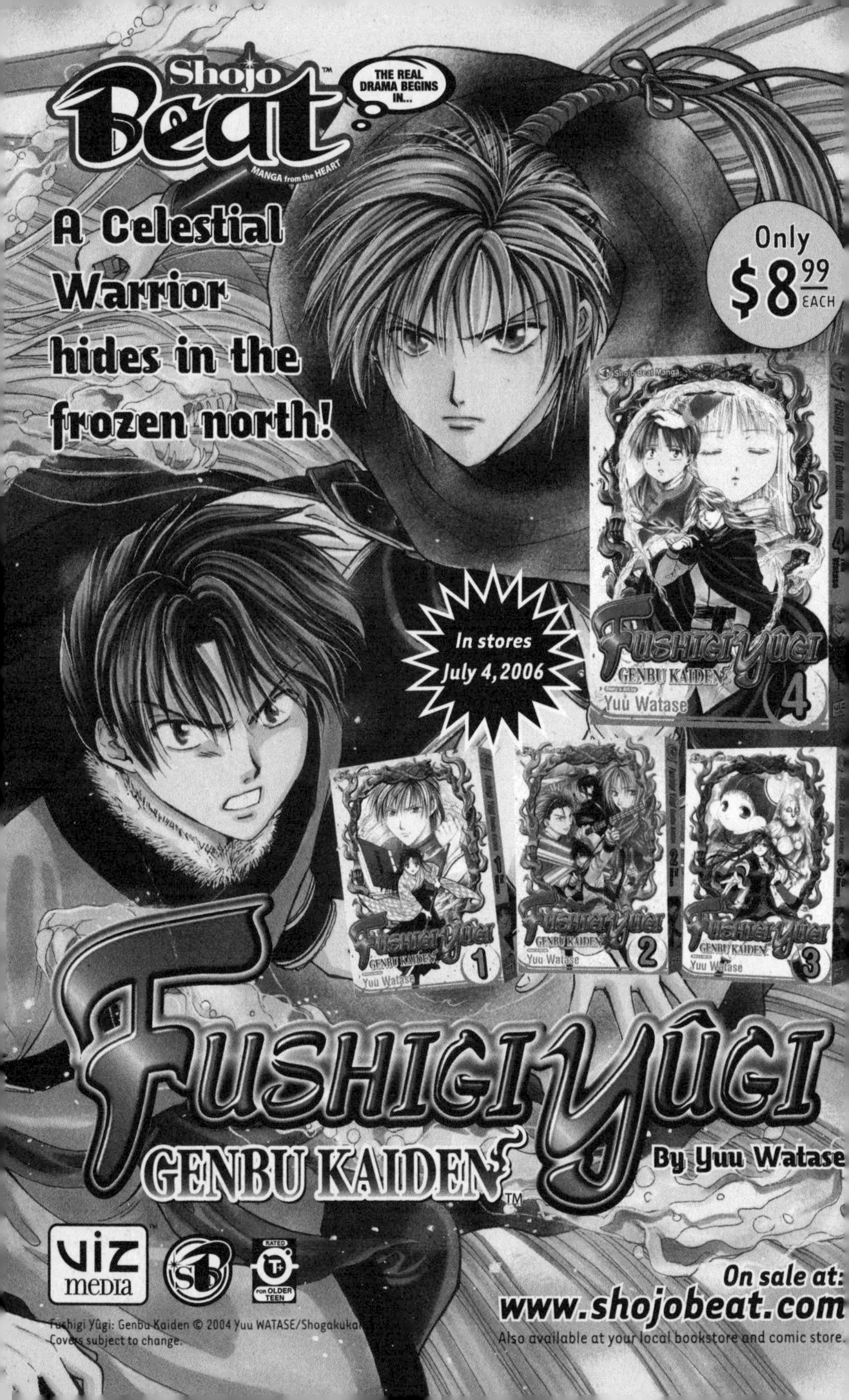
Shojo Beat™
THE REAL DRAMA BEGINS IN...
MANGA from the HEART
A Celestial Warrior hides in the frozen north!
Only $8.99 EACH
In stores July 4, 2006
FUSHIGI YÛGI GENBU KAIDEN™
By Yuu Watase
On sale at:
www.shojobeat.com
Also available at your local bookstore and comic store.
Fushigi Yûgi: Genbu Kaiden © 2004 Yuu WATASE/Shogakukan
Covers subject to change.

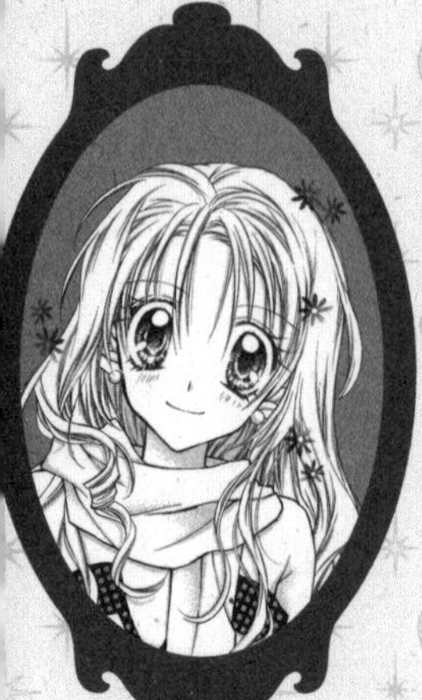

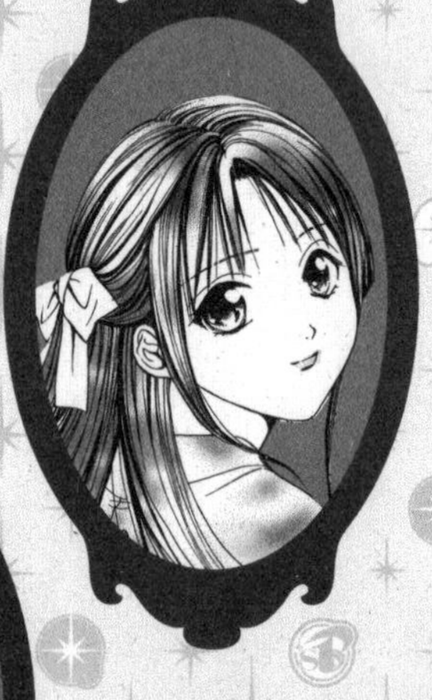

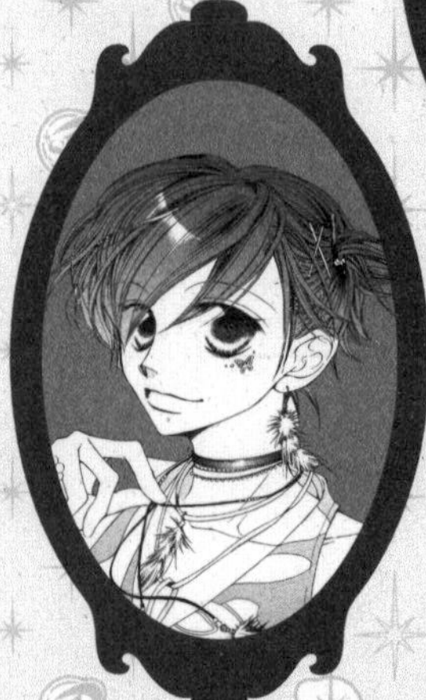